MW01033218

EVERYDAY LIFE IN THE
EARLY ENGLISH CARIBBEAN

EVERYDAY LIFE IN THE EARLY ENGLISH CARIBBEAN

Irish, Africans, and the Construction of Difference

JENNY SHAW

The University of Georgia Press

ATHENS AND LONDON

© 2013 by the University of Georgia Press
Athens, Georgia 30602
www.ugapress.org

The paper in this book meets the guidelines for permanence and durability of the Committee on Production Guidelines for Book Longevity of the Council on Library Resources.

Printed in the United States of America

17 16 15 14 13   P   5 4 3 2 1

LIBRARY OF CONGRESS CATALOGING-IN-PUBLICATION DATA

Shaw, Jenny, 1977–
  Everyday life in the early English Caribbean : Irish, Africans, and the construction of difference / Jenny Shaw.
     pages cm. — (Early American places)
  Includes bibliographical references and index.
  ISBN-13: 978-0-8203-4505-5 (hardcover : alk. paper)
  ISBN-10: 0-8203-4505-9 (hardcover : alk. paper)
  ISBN-13. 978-0-8203-4662-5 (paperback : alk. paper)
  ISBN-10: 0-8203-4662-4 (paperback: alk. paper)
  1. Irish—West Indies, British—History—17th century. 2. Irish—West Indies, British—Ethnic identity. 3. Catholics—West Indies British—History—17th century. 4. West Indies, British—History—17th century. 5. West Indies, British—Ethnic relations—History—17th century. 6. Slavery—West Indies, British—History—17th century. I. Title.
  F2131S427 2013
  972.9′03—dc23

                                        2013012009

British Library Cataloging-in-Publication Data available

For Mum and Dad with love and thanks

Contents

List of Illustrations		xi
Acknowledgments		xiii
Author's Note		xvii
	Introduction	1
1	"An Heathenishe, Brutish and an uncertaine, dangerous kind of People": Figuring Difference in the Early English Atlantic	15
2	"An exact account of the number of persons upon the Island": Enumeration, Improvement, and Control	44
3	"To live in perpetuall noise and hurry": Creating Communities on Caribbean Plantations	71
4	"Doing their prayers and worshipping God in their hearts": Ritual, Practice, and Keeping the Faith	101
5	"Endeavouring to raise mutinie and sedition": The Challenge to English Domination	129
6	"As quietly and happily as the English subjects": Property, Prosperity, and the Power of Emulation	156
	Epilogue	185
	Notes	193
	Bibliography	231
	Index	253

ILLUSTRATIONS

1   Title page of *Englands Slavery or Barbados Merchandize*   20

2   Detail from John Speed's *Theatre of the Empire
    of Great Britaine*   29

3   Cranford, *The Teares of Ireland*   32

4   Summary of the 1680 Barbados census   59

5   Summary of the 1678 Montserrat census   62

6   The Political Anatomy of Montserrat, St. George's District   68

7   Richard Ligon's drawing of a sugar "ingenio"   75

8   Bally Tree Hall Plantation in St. Joseph's Parish, Barbados   77

9   Cycle of sugar production on a Martinique plantation   80

10 Richard Ligon's estimation of costs for running a plantation   92

11 Akan funeral procession   106

12 Location of the Rice plantations in St. Philip's Parish,
    Barbados   116

13 Title page of *Great Newes from the Barbadoes*   133

14 Blake, *A Negro hung alive by the Ribs to a Gallows*   149

15 Cornelius Bryan's entry in the 1680 Barbados Census   160

16 Estate plan showing division of land in St. James Parish,
    Barbados   162

17 Blake's entry in the 1678 Montserrat Census   165

18 Coastal profile map of Montserrat   173

Acknowledgments

As I reflect back on the years over which this project has taken shape, I am overwhelmed by the sense that far from being a solitary endeavor, writing this book has in fact been a collective effort. At NYU I was fortunate to find myself under the expert tutelage of Karen Ordahl Kupperman. I cannot thank her enough for over a decade's worth of accumulated advice and encouragement. Karen's generosity and graciousness as a mentor and a scholar never cease to amaze me: she will always be my role model. The first iteration of this project also benefitted from the advice of faculty in the History Department at NYU, especially Thomas Bender, Lauren Benton, Martha Hodes, and Jennifer Morgan. I owe much to Alan Day at the University of Edinburgh for introducing me to the world of early America and for helping me to take my first step into the historical profession. At UA my colleagues in the history department have been consistently supportive; special thanks to my Chair, Kari Frederickson, for securing funds for image permissions.

Completing the research for this project would not have been possible were it not for the financial support of a number of libraries and institutions including the John Carter Brown Library, the Huntington Library, the John D. Rockefeller Library, the Lewis L. Glucksman Foundation, the Doris G. Quinn Foundation, the William H. McCracken Foundation, the Jean Downey Scholarship, the Center for Latin American and Caribbean Studies at NYU, and the Research Grants Council at UA. Thanks to the staff and archivists at the libraries listed above, and also those at the British Library, the National Archives, London, the John

Ryland Library, Manchester, the Barbados Department of Archives, the Bridgetown Public Library, the Barbados Museum and Historical Society, the National Archives, Ireland, the National Library of Ireland, and University College Cork for all of their expert advice. I would also like to recognize the dedicated librarians at the New York Public Library, the Elmer Holmes Bobst Library at NYU, and the Amelia Gayle Gorgas Library at UA. Some of the source material in chapter six appeared in "Subjects Without an Empire: The Irish in the Early Modern Caribbean," *Past and Present* vol. 210 (2011): 33-60. I thank Oxford University Press and my co-author Kristen Block for permission to reprint here.

A number of close friends and colleagues gave of their time and read all or most of this manuscript in one of its many forms for which I will be eternally grateful. Kristen Block, Sarah Cornell, Christian Crouch, Holly Grout, Karen Kupperman, and George Tomlinson offered their ideas, their critiques, and most of all their encouragement at every step. This book would not exist without their patience and generosity: it is much stronger for their intellectual engagement. I am enormously appreciative of everyone, named and unnamed, who offered comments, conversation, and help along the way in graduate school and beyond including: Margaret Abruzzo, Jennifer Anderson, William Armshaw, Nicolas Canny, Maggie Clinton, Frank Cogliano, Sasha Disko, Marcela Echeverri, Nicole Eustace, Marisa Fuentes, Noah Gelfand, Marc Goulding, Evan Haefeli, Sheryllynne Haggerty, Amy Holmes-Tagchungdarpa, Andrew Huebner, Heather Kopelson, Michael LaCombe, Priya Lal, Joseph Lee, Isabela Morales, Jennifer Morgan, Kate Mulry, Tracy Neumann, Simon Newman, Greg O'Malley, Elizabeth Manke, Renée Raphael, Sarah Rivett, Anelise Shrout, Anoush Terjanian, Susan Valentine, Jerusha Westbury, Natalie Zacek, and the fellows at the John Carter Brown Library and the Huntington Library. I have also benefitted from thoughtful and engaged feedback at a number of seminars and conferences: to everyone who commented on my work or who pointed me to scholarship or sources, thank you. I would like to offer special appreciation to the participants in the Atlantic World History Workshop at NYU, the Columbia Seminar in Early American History, the Harvard International Seminar on the History of the Atlantic World, and the American History Workshop at UA for their suggestions on specific chapters. I am also deeply grateful to the two anonymous readers for the press whose extremely generous feedback and suggestions for revision made this book better in myriad ways.

At UGA Press Derek Krissoff was an enthusiastic and supportive acquisitions editor. Mick Gusinde-Duffy picked up with similar energy where Derek left off, while Beth Snead did sterling work keeping everything rolling during the transition. Thanks also to Elizabeth Magnus for her thoughtful copyediting and to Tim Roberts, David Des Jardines, Jon Davies and everyone working on the Early American Places series for their expertise and assistance transforming this manuscript into a book.

In Tuscaloosa, the Sunday morning writing group at Edelweiss (Holly Grout, Jolene Hubbs, Sarah Moody, and Daniel Sweaney) has been an invaluable source of support, friendship, and good humor. A note of appreciation to the staff of Edelweiss and their simply stunning apple crumb cake which has fueled many a marathon writing session. My thanks also to the Pugilists for providing intellectual stimulation of a different kind. Jeannie and Rob Guthrie introduced me to the charms of the south; Lisa Davis, Andrew Huebner, and Matthew Orndorff have offered fun, friendship, and distraction in equal amounts. In New York City the members of GSOC-UAW Local 2110 taught me the importance of fighting for what is right and fair. At NYU Sarah Cornell and Christian Crouch helped me to navigate graduate school and they, along with Kristen Block and Holly Grout, continue to be the smartest, funniest, and most generous women I have the privilege of calling my friends. Across the pond Fay Ballard, Caroline Bates, Olwyn Ferguson, Hayley Rothwell, and Melanie Scott have sustained me with love, laughter, and support for more years than I can count.

I am grateful to the Rider and Tomlinson families for welcoming me with open arms and places to unwind in Wisconsin, California, and Vermont. Thank you to George, Ellen, Stanley, Mark, Erin, Thayer, Amit, (my nephew and main squeeze) Willow, Otto, Tom, Corrine, Annie, Rob, Mary, Stuart, and Jana, for your love and encouragement, and a special thanks to everyone at the Farm for providing the perfect summer writing haven. The Shaw, McCullagh, and McCall clans on the other side of the Atlantic Ocean family have been equally supportive, especially Roz, Colin, Richard, Isobel, Mervyn, Ray and Helen, who came to visit and who kept my cupboard stocked with good tea. Kevin deserves gratitude for unfailingly supporting his big sister over all these years; thanks also to his partner Maxine, and my superhero nephew, Leon. My grandmother has always been a wonderful storyteller; I hope she is proud of the stories Little Annie tells here. I have dedicated this book to my parents as a small token of my appreciation: Mum, Dad, I thank you from the bottom of my heart for all the years of home-cooked meals, sage advice, and unconditional support, but most of all for being my first and best teachers.

Author's Note

Dates have been modernized throughout, beginning the year on January 1, rather than on March 25, as was the case for England and its colonies under the Julian calendar until 1752. I have retained the original spelling and punctuation when quoting from sources, except when doing so would confuse the meaning of the quotation. I have also expanded archaic contractions and replaced *ye* with *the*.

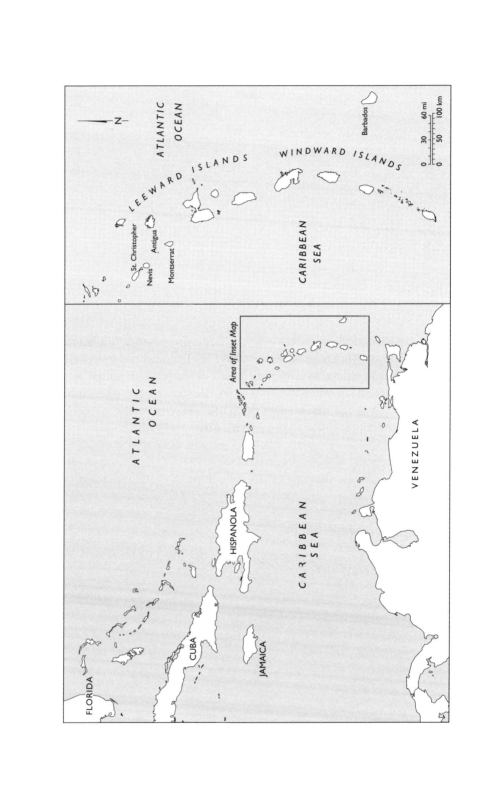

ATLANTIC OCEAN

LEEWARD ISLANDS

WINDWARD ISLANDS

Barbados

60 mi

30

100 km

50

0

St. Christopher

Nevis

Antigua

Montserrat

CARIBBEAN SEA

N

Area of Inset Map

ATLANTIC OCEAN

FLORIDA

CUBA

JAMAICA

HISPANOLA

CARIBBEAN SEA

VENEZUELA

Introduction

Irish laborer Cornelius Bryan began his Caribbean sojourn in the 1650s as the archetypical perfidious papist. Hauled in front of the Barbados Council, and accused of slandering English colonists by threatening to drink their blood, he was ordered to receive twenty-one lashes on his "bare back" at the Indian Bridge, a landmark that later gave one of the island's burgeoning ports its name—Bridgetown. Uncertain that the prescribed punishment would have the desired effect of subduing this particular Irish Catholic, English colonial officials ordered him to leave Barbados within the month. Yet thirty years later Cornelius died on the island, never having departed its tropical shores. The 1680 census recorded his rise to island planter and his acquisition of two servants and nine slaves to work his small estate in St. James' Parish. His will, proved seven years later, noted that Cornelius left behind a wife, Margaret, and six children (Cornelius, Alice, Katherine, James, Jeremiah, and Daniel) to whom he bequeathed his worldly goods. His property included a feather bed, a cedar chest, twenty-two acres of land, a black horse, and thirteen enslaved Africans (Betty, Grace, Tomy, Mingo, George, Anah, Old Pegg, Venus, Pegg, Nell, Jack, Young Tomy, and Cain), all of which were carefully parceled out among his progeny and his spouse. Cornelius Bryan, despite his precarious beginnings and his status as an Irish Catholic, ended his life resembling the very English elites he had maligned thirty years earlier: he was now a planter, albeit an Irish one.[1]

The seventeenth-century English Caribbean that Cornelius Bryan inhabited is most often depicted as a place of extremes: of unrelenting heat, of unspeakable brutality, of inescapable avarice; a region where the status of enslaved and free, and therefore the racial categories black and white, explained all in terms of hierarchy and difference. At first glance, Cornelius's story appears to fit into this framework. As a European, he was able to ascend the social ladder on Barbados, becoming a member of the planter elite. But on closer inspection his account reveals the malleable nature of social status in the early modern English Atlantic world. As a Catholic, Cornelius was held in suspicion by Protestant English authorities who believed him capable of acting against the empire from within. And his barbarous outburst, when combined with his ethnicity and his religious beliefs, marked him as uncivilized according to the standards of colonial elites. As such, Cornelius, and the thousands of other Irish Catholics who traversed the Atlantic Ocean in the seventeenth century, occupied an uneasy space in the hierarchy of the English colonies. They "were and were not white" in English eyes, their very genealogy rendering them suspect.[2]

Focusing on the indeterminate place of Irish Catholics, this book argues that defining difference in the English Caribbean was an attenuated process that cannot be explained through an analysis of race and slavery alone. Difference, in this context, encompasses the myriad cultural and ethnic markers that individuals used to understand what made themselves similar to, or distinct from, one another. Such distinctions were not value neutral: divisions between groups were employed to indicate social status and to create and enforce hierarchies of power. This process was not solely dictated by English elites. Ordinary women and men in the Caribbean—servants, slaves, laborers—shaped the categories through which hierarchy was understood and also created their own. But how did these marginal individuals manage to affect elite ideals or produce alternatives to prescribed imperial distinctions? More importantly, given archival sources created by and for island elites, how can historians hope to uncover the means by which they did so? The answers to these questions form the heart of this book.

To begin, it is important to trace the means by which someone like Cornelius Bryan made the remarkable transformation from treacherous Catholic to island planter despite living in a colony considered the jewel in Protestant England's burgeoning Atlantic empire. Marking his rise demonstrates how Irish Catholics influenced elite English ideas about difference. From the viewpoint of English officials, most Irish Catholics in the West Indies were suitable for little more than hard labor in the colonies' sugar fields. They worked alongside enslaved Africans, ate much of the same food and drink, and lived and slept with their enslaved counterparts. These women and men troubled any straightforward social and racial divisions of labor precisely because of bonds they forged with captives from Africa. As Hilary Beckles has shown, anxious English officials feared that at any moment antagonistic Irish servants and laborers might ally with enslaved Africans or Catholic European competitors on the island and in the region.[3] But Irish Catholics affected ideas about difference in other ways. Some, like Cornelius, made the shift from modest laborer to island planter, acquiring property in land and slaves, traversing a number of boundaries along the way. Other Irish (such as those in Donald Harman Akenson's study of Montserrat) arrived in the Caribbean with sufficient capital to purchase sugar estates. In the process they laid their own claims to a place among the planter elite, demonstrating that they were as likely to enslave Africans and behave in a capricious fashion as their English counterparts.[4] Irish interactions with English elites (both as troublemakers and as would-be equals) and with enslaved Africans (both as fellow laborers and as their masters) therefore resisted easy categorization by English imperial officials and forced the colonial leadership to reckon with the ambiguous status of Irish Catholics.

However, articulating the ways that Irish Catholics troubled the developing racial hierarchy in Barbados and the Leeward Islands simply inserts them into the framework of "becoming white," a construction that can be complicit with the overarching narrative of race as the central definition of difference in the early modern English Caribbean. To avoid such conclusions, it is necessary to explore how ordinary colonial subjects—indentured Irish servants and laborers and enslaved Africans—lived these disparities in the colonies. Tomy, Anah, Pegg, and Mingo, and the other enslaved women and men on Cornelius Bryan's plantation, worked to forge community with each other or to mark separations according to a whole host of factors that included language, ethnicity, sex, labor, age, and place of birth. And the hired and indentured servants who also worked the small St. James estate had other expectations about where solidarity might be found or where divisions should be enforced. All of these laborers had their own conceptions of difference when it came to laying down boundaries among and between each other and English colonists. Their markers and divisions were just as important to figuring difference in the West Indies as those categories proposed by English elites.

Accessing how ordinary Irish servants and enslaved Africans understood distinctions in the colonies is not easy—the thoughts and actions of prominent English colonists and imperial authorities dominate archival sources in the seventeenth century. So this book proposes a way of overcoming the inadequacies of the available source material by concentrating on the everyday life of ordinary colonial subjects to show how determining categories of difference was a mutually constitutive process. Such an approach is made possible by a focus on Barbados and the Leeward Islands because these jurisdictions held significant numbers of Irish Catholics whose interactions with other island inhabitants can be tracked, unlike Jamaica, which remained politically, demographically, and geographically isolated from the eastern Caribbean in this period.[5] It is also necessary to read the small fragments of sources that directly reference the lives of Irish Catholics or enslaved Africans as much for the silences they contain as for the information visibly present to reveal the perspectives of nonelites. After all, through their daily actions servants and slaves on the periphery of colonial archives shaped the sources contained therein. Through an investigation of the more voluminous records on the constituent parts of everyday life (for example, those that describe labor regimes on plantations), it becomes possible to glimpse the relationships between imperial subjects, despite an absence in such sources of references to specific individuals. Establishing hierarchy was not only the purview of colonial officials and prominent island planters; it also involved those who lived and labored at the heart of England's burgeoning Caribbean empire. Writing a history of how difference was constructed in the early English Atlantic thus requires a willingness to engage a problematic archive and pay attention to everyday people's lives.

* * *

Histories of the English Caribbean posit that the sugar booms of the mid-seventeenth century ensured both the plantation complex and England's fledgling empire and that the rise of slave societies and the development of racial slavery were therefore inevitable and practically instantaneous.[6] Indeed, the speed at which Barbadian planters transitioned to a sugar monoculture (effectively complete by the 1650s) appears to support such analysis. And when the Leeward Islands shifted to primarily sugar production by the late 1670s, these English "societies with slaves" became full-fledged "slave societies," the first to develop in English America, adding fuel to the argument of racial bifurcation.[7] Demography too seems to bear out this thesis. The labor-intensive nature of sugar production and high Caribbean mortality rates among both indigenous populations and new arrivals necessitated a continual influx of workers, so the numbers of enslaved Africans forcibly transported to English colonies skyrocketed in the second half of the seventeenth century. Simultaneously, the number of servants brought from England, Scotland, and Ireland declined precipitously as population growth in the British Isles stagnated and as wages for laborers at home improved.

The hierarchies that developed in the English West Indies were the result of the blending of these demographic and economic systems with ideological frameworks of difference that had long roots complicated by English imperial experiences. Connections between theology and ethnicity were intertwined in early modern elite English thinking. Holding to the relatively inclusive Mosaic understanding of history—namely that all the world's peoples had descended from Noah—English intellectuals believed that humanity held some essential similarities.[8] This belief, however, did not prevent them from identifying a range of ethnic, cultural, and religious distinctions between them and the peoples that they colonized as the key attributes that made the English superior to the rest of the people who inhabited their nascent empire.[9] On questions of gender roles, sexual behavior, land use, sartorial choices, and religious practices, English imperialists distinguished themselves from their colonial subjects, emphasizing their own civility against the barbarism of colonized peoples. Close to home, the Scots and especially the Irish were the first groups to be subsumed into these English ideologies, but they were followed quickly by Native Americans and Africans as England's Atlantic world expanded.[10] In this new world, the English defined a person of quality as one who was Christian rather than heathen; Protestant rather than Catholic; English rather than Irish or African or Indian; civilized rather than savage. There were more divisions among and between colonial subjects than simply black and white.

Increasingly, however, as sugar production became central to the success of the colonies, categories of labor took on special importance for English authorities trying to differentiate island society. Specifically, it was the distinctions between free and unfree laborers that came to the fore, with the latter category including both indentured servants and enslaved Africans. The strong institutional memory of feudal society continued to influence Europeans, so to English contemporaries African slavery and indentured servitude were the logical extensions of forms of bonded labor with which they were already familiar.[11] Enough indentured servants were kidnapped and shipped overseas that the place of their destination was turned into an active verb, "Barbadosed," but many had some choice in the manner and the destination of their arrival in the Americas, and even potential bargaining power in negotiating their terms of indenture. The vast majority of these servants were Irish Catholics, whose population in Barbados and the Leeward Islands reached the tens of thousands in the 1650s and continued to grow in the ensuing decades.[12] Crucially, after a period of years bound to a particular master or mistress, servants earned freedom and the chance (in theory at least) to become a property owner.[13] Enslaved Africans, on the other hand, were captured in their homelands and transported across the ocean against their will to plantations where they labored for life. Moreover, their status soon became inheritable, tying up race and reproduction in an unholy alliance that served to mark enslaved women as the centerpieces on which racial slavery was predicated, developed, and expanded.[14] This attention to unfree status began to ossify the racial categories of black and white that undergirded and enforced brutal plantation systems.

However, in a society still preoccupied with cultural markers of difference, bifurcation based solely on race was far from inevitable. For most of the early moderns who experienced life in the seventeenth-century Caribbean, religion was of paramount importance. In Europe, the Reformation pitted Catholics against Protestants in a series of bloody internecine wars that dominated both society at home and European expansion overseas. In West Africa, European incursions into the sub-Saharan zone added an extra element of tension as some rulers sought out Christianity or Islam, using monotheism as a way to consolidate political power and control in various regions.[15] And it was not only at the level of high politics that religion held power. Often enslaved Africans and Irish Catholics found themselves pushed into the Atlantic world as a result of religious conflict. Recent scholarship therefore pays attention to the craving for riches and wealth in the region within a framework that also emphasizes the importance of spiritual beliefs.[16] On Caribbean islands with horrifically high death rates, religious rituals and rites were central means of creating a sense of community and belonging in new settings, facilitating communion with ancestors, or returning home after death.[17] Although not static, and always evolving, religious practices provided a tangible connection between old worlds and new. These rituals infused daily life. Because English elites (concerned with their own spiritual well-being) left their laborers to their own devices on Sundays, non-Protestant workers took the opportunity on those days to further develop their own sacred spaces away from the prying eyes of masters and mistresses. Here, as elsewhere in the Caribbean, ordinary people engaged in everyday practices, religious and otherwise, as a way to understand and define their lives and their place in colonial society.

* * *

To understand nonelite ideas about difference, it is necessary to contemplate the hidden relationships in everyday life. Colonial authorities used a variety of strategies—the plantation complex, the threat and use of violence, the legal system, and the census—to create and enforce hierarchies based on social, economic, religious, sex, and racial distinctions. Servants and slaves fractured these attempts via a variety of tactics that subverted, rejected, and manipulated elite impositions of difference.[18] Their social, physical, and spiritual rituals of everyday life were more than the "obscure background of social activity"; they proved to be foundational moments for exposing difference in the early modern Caribbean. Nonelites' desires to transgress these official prescriptions on their lives and behavior "found expression *within and through* everyday practices and representations."[19] In other words, nonelites used their everyday experiences to build collective identities and to define their own ideas of belonging and separation, "invest[ing] their lives with extra-ordinary meaning" in the process. Thus the mundane acts of daily life took on new significance. Sometimes enslaved Africans and indentured servants found common cause with one another, making food together, sharing spiritual moments, even on occasion taking up weapons alongside one another against the colonial regime. At other moments servants and slaves mocked one another or distanced themselves from any comparisons that might be drawn between them, hoping to preserve their own deep feelings of difference. Though ordinary subjects had to live and work within existing elite structures of power in the Caribbean, the "less visible" moments of connection between them provide a critical opening for exploring nonelite ideas about difference.[20]

Identifying these less visible moments is an exercise in assembling fragments of archival source material in new ways. As Michel Rolph Trouillot has argued, the ability to write history is predicated on the arrangement of historical archives and the sources contained within. In his analysis of the power dynamics that shape archives, Trouillot demonstrates that some stories are more likely to be told than others, especially those that favor elites who decided what was worthy of recording in the past and who in the present continue to regulate what is worth preserving.[21] The colonial archive from which this study has drawn has unsurprisingly been constructed in such a way as to invite analyses of what English actors—especially those in the highest echelons of society—were thinking and doing. It is therefore imperative to reread colonial sources against the grain, and as much for what they do not say as for what they do, to work toward a better understanding of the subjectivities of those in the lower echelons of Caribbean societies. It is necessary, in other words, to focus on the "presence of absences" in the source material.[22]

Absences in this archive proliferate as silences. An English official's account of the interrogation of a slave named Ben following an alleged attempt at revolt on Barbados in the autumn of 1692 might exist, but the actual transcript of the questions and responses, much less a description of the kinds of violence enacted on Ben, does not. Even more perplexing is the almost complete lack of discussion by colonial officials, including an Irish governor, about Irish religious practices on Montserrat, despite the fact that the Irish were the majority European population on the island throughout the seventeenth century and though anxiety about their presence in England's Protestant empire remained high across this period. Women are scarce too—letters between family members could discuss the most intimate details of household arrangements without ever naming the women at their center. Will after will, and deed after deed, record the human property on plantations, often without assigning names to the subjects under consideration even as the men, women, and children attached to an estate were emphatic embodiments of the planter's wealth. And when the source material surrounds more elite figures, like the Irish Catholics who owned plantations, the record creates its own silences. One printed version of a set of letters between the Blake brothers from Galway includes their remembrances to Father Daniel, the family priest; the other omits his name and the religious reference altogether.

Paradoxically, an analysis of the everyday brings new potential to these seemingly oppressive silences and the politics of the particular archive that created them. Focusing on the everyday lives of lower-status colonials provides an avenue for imagining the possibilities of their experiences. It refuses the level of abstraction inherent in elite constructions of difference and attempts at classification. So it is possible to glimpse the unnamed female Irish indentured servant starching linens in a Bridgetown household while her master debates replacing her with an enslaved woman; to see the free couple of color and their children standing nervously at the baptismal font in a St. Michael church; to watch the group of nameless enslaved Africans send a loved one on a journey back to their homeland during a funeral ceremony on Colonel Drax's plantation; or to acknowledge the Irish laborer stripped to the waist, defiant despite his fear, as he waits for the hangman to lash his back twenty-one times at the Indian Bridge.[23]

An analysis of everyday life that draws on such "presence of absences" therefore necessitates the use of informed imagination. Natalie Zemon Davis discusses the importance of a judicious use of "invention . . . held tightly in check by the voices of the past" to write history from the perspectives of those on the margins of the archival record; surely this is always the starting point for a historian because writing history always invokes imagination.[24] Acknowledging the conjecture that necessarily accompanies an attempt to tell the lives of people of the past, whatever their social status, is one way to offset the inequities of the archive.[25] Indeed, not invoking speculation holds its own risks, shutting off various subjects, or subject matter, from scholarly consideration.[26] Careful archival work can uncover fragments of source material that when pieced together, or taken in the aggregate, begin to hint at the whole.[27] Drawing on years of research to create "educated reconstructions" is not the same as inventing wholesale what might have been.[28] Rather, it provides an opportunity to explore the possibilities open to people of the past and to expose new perspectives. This approach is one way to redress the imbalance in source material, even if the result provides only one imperfect alternative to the dominant narrative in place.

Despite a focus on reading sources creatively, this book utilizes quotations from English elites as part of each chapter title. The choice is deliberate: it serves as a reminder that these are the voices that shape our knowledge, the men whose words attempt to dictate the terms on which the past is understood. In a time and place where almost none of the protagonists get to speak for themselves, each chapter ends with an exploration of the lives of Cornelius Bryan (the Irish laborer who moved from the position of archetypal "perfidious papist" in the 1650s to small planter on Barbados in the 1680s) and two of the enslaved women he owned at the end of his life, Old Pegg and Pegg, most likely a mother and her daughter. Explicating their everyday lives through the process of informed imagination involves a close reading of the few sources that note their existence.[29] In the case of Cornelius, the sources are relatively plentiful: the minutes of the Barbados Assembly, a handful of deeds, the Barbados census of 1680, and his will. Old Pegg and Pegg appear by name only in Cornelius's will, their existence probably recorded numerically in the 1680 census. Although it is easier to piece together Cornelius's story—to whom he was married, how many children he had, where he lived, the amount of property he owned—his life is marked by some of the same silences that Old Pegg's and Pegg's suffer. Where their lives began, how precisely they found themselves in the Caribbean, how they all came to be on the same plantation: these questions remain largely unanswerable unless we expand their individual archives. Shading in the gaps, breathing life into the silences of the record, requires reading around their experiences. Knowing what individuals like them would have endured and how their lives were shaped provides context for an exploration of the lives of early modern people like Cornelius, Pegg, and Old Pegg.

* * *

This book begins with an investigation of early modern English ideas about difference. In both Ireland and the Caribbean, English elites used a variety of strategies—violence, the labor system, enumeration of populations, and legislation—to ensure that their colonization succeeded. Chapter 1 examines how elite conceptions of difference were worked out in Ireland and the Americas and engages two of the biggest legislative questions of the time—could Europeans be enslaved, and how would difference be codified in colonial settings? A major early modern characteristic of colonization was the drive to enumerate colonial populations, so chapter 2 explores the ideology behind demographic documentation in both Ireland and the colonies where the relationships of everyday life were quantified, an approach that provided the illusion of a set of homogeneous colonial populations that in reality were distinctly heterogeneous. This demonstration of imperial power masked the sorts of connections that authorities found threatening, such as those between Europeans and Africans, as well as the presence of religious dissidents. By a deconstruction of the census these absent categories come into view. At the same time this approach forces an examination of the everyday relationships that allowed these hidden classifications to develop.

The following two chapters move to examine some of these less visible categories and relationships through an analysis of the tactics that Irish indentures and laborers and enslaved Africans employed to create communities by forging their own ideas about difference. Chapter 3 focuses on daily plantation life—eating, drinking, sleeping, relaxing, and (of course) laboring—to overcome the inequities in the archive and to offset the imbalance in source materials, which are dominated by English accounts. Glimpses of the ways that servants and slaves thought about their relationships to one another and to the broader world outside the plantation are caught through a focus on the labor, the rituals, and the practices that they performed daily. The grim realities of their daily lives—the endless toil, the dangerous working conditions, and the ever-present threat and use of violence—also emerge. Chapter 4 keeps the focus on the everyday but concentrates on practices that marked religious beliefs. Making sense of the universe they inhabited meant that servants and slaves, just like other early modern Caribbean populations, were deeply attuned to the spiritual world and what it could teach them about life, death, and survival. In the signal moments of life—birth, marriage, and death—the kinds of practices that mattered deeply to island inhabitants come into view. This chapter explores the continuities and fractures between the kinds of religious practices that were common in West Central Africa and Ireland and those that flourished on Caribbean plantations to discuss how indentured servants, enslaved Africans, free people of color, and free laborers made religious connections, sometimes with one another, on occasion with English elites, all of which affected their understandings of solidarity and separation.

The final chapters examine the split between those Irish who continued to cleave to their own understandings of difference and those who chose to adopt the ideologies of English elites. The lower orders of Irish Catholics—indentured servants and free laborers—and enslaved Africans are the subject of chapter 5, which focuses on how these two groups built on the relationships they forged through everyday activity on plantations to actively challenge island hierarchies. The numerous sources that deal with servant and slave unrest on the islands are read creatively to explore how these unfree laborers grappled with forms of colonial discipline that were intended to regulate their behavior and used their responses to set forth their own visions for colonial rule. Chapter 6 turns to the lives of Irish Catholics who gained access to the upper echelons of island society by emulating English social and cultural norms and embracing English ideas about difference. Some of these Irish Catholics had arrived in the Caribbean with some capital, ready to buy plantations. Others began their lives as indentured servants or poor laborers but managed to acquire a small amount of property over decades of living in the colonies. Still others earned prestige by serving honorably in English military expeditions against Catholic enemies Spain and France. All, however, used their understanding of English conceptions of difference and the markers of elite status to advance. Their approach was twofold: first, emulating English ideas about gender and race; second, simultaneously finding ways to render their threat as Catholics in a Protestant empire unimportant, usually (like Cornelius Bryan) by continuing to practice their faith quietly.

* * *

Cornelius Bryan found a way to overcome his shaky beginnings on Barbados, ending up something of a modest success on the island, if success is measured according to the standards of the elites of this period. For Pegg, an enslaved woman who labored on his plantation, there was no such satisfaction, merely uncertainty. Bryan was the author of at least some of the sources that detail his life, even if the Barbados Council minutes, constructed by people so far removed from Bryan's status at the time, are the medium through which he first appears. Pegg's archival life begins and ends in a will inventory, so our knowledge of her is controlled, as she was, by her master. Attempting to write the lives of less visible historical actors, like Pegg, who exist on the margins of the archive, yet who were central to the functioning of colonial society, is an important historical contribution in and of itself: if the only histories that can be written are those of people who left plentiful records, then the majority of historical actors are condemned to an anonymity they already endure. In many of the moments that this book explores, the names of the people at their center have not survived or were not thought worthy of recording in the first place. For others, it is possible to chart experiences across several decades or to build up the apparatus surrounding their lives— the people who owned them, the plantation on which they labored, the circumstances under which they were freed, or the property they slowly acquired over time. Including their stories shifts perspective on the early Caribbean. It forces us to ask questions about relationships among and between groups that otherwise would remain obscured. By investigating the fragmented lives that have serendipitously found their way into the archive, and by reading sources alongside one another we can start to answer the question of what servants and slaves made of one another, despite their muted voices in the sources on this subject.

* * *

Cornelius Bryan arrived on Barbados as a laborer, having been ejected from Cromwell's Ireland and deposited in an unfamiliar English colony. Marking time on the island was difficult, as the seasons seemed to blend together in the tropics, but he knew he had been on Barbados for about one year. Christmas 1655 had just passed, and January was fast approaching. Cornelius was unhappy at his misfortune and unsure about where life in this new land might take him—so far he had found it difficult to make any headway in the colony. Laboring in the sugar fields was backbreaking work, but he hoped to make enough money soon to buy some sugar and eventually trade sufficient goods to buy a small piece of land. He worried about his immortal soul in a land of heretical Protestants, but he had heard that there were Catholic priests moving around the island in disguise. There were certainly enough of his fellow countrymen laboring in the colony, Cornelius reflected, to keep a good number of priests in business. He thought fondly of the religious leaders he had known in Ireland and the songs he had learned to keep the catechism straight in his head. It would be dangerous to play his pipes and sing in the tongue of his homeland, but perhaps that was a risk worth taking, especially if it upset some of the Protestants he worked alongside. Cornelius was becoming increasingly tired of the way English servants looked down on him, taunting him about his savageness. So far he had managed to hold his tongue, but he knew it was only a matter of time before he lost his temper. He had been talking with some other Irish laborers about causing trouble for the English. After all, none of them had asked to come to this land. Perhaps it was time to teach these Protestant dogs a lesson they would not easily forget.

On a hot and humid July day in 1681, Pegg stood at the edge of the sugarcane field, hunched over, blade in hand, ready to chop another of the six-foot stalks to the ground. Her back ached, and her hands stung as salty sweat poured over the hundreds of tiny cuts caused by handling the rough canes. Pegg longed to rest, even for a brief moment, so she could check on her mother, Old Pegg. Field work was harsh, but at least she was young and able to cut at a reasonable pace. Her mother found the constant bending and straightening much more taxing and with every harvest seemed to slow down another beat. But if Pegg stopped, she risked drawing the attention of their master, and his whip, something she wanted to avoid at all costs. She would have to pray that Old Pegg could avoid a "hurry-up" lash and that the midday break would provide enough respite for her mother to continue to labor through the afternoon. This season, Pegg had hoped that their master would assign her mother to a less physically exhausting task, but when the sugar crop was ripe it seemed that it was always a case of all hands on deck. Even Young Tomy, the youngest enslaved child on the plantation, had been given a job, snapping the sharp tops from the canes before they were bundled together. Later, Mingo and George would gather up the boiling-house-ready sugar and take it to the big plantation outside

Holetown because the twenty-two-acre estate owned by their master was too small to have its own sugar works. As she always did to make time in the fields pass more quickly, Pegg allowed her mind to drift. Born on Barbados, she had never known anything other than life in slavery on this island. But her mother told stories about a place far away across the sea, where she had had a happy childhood, and Pegg allowed her imagination to take her there.[30]

1 / "An Heathenishe, Brutish and an uncertaine, dangerous kind of People": Figuring Difference in the Early English Atlantic

On a September afternoon in 1661, Sir Henry Walrond placed his signature on the "Act for Better Ordering and Governing of Negroes." Following the upheaval of the interregnum, Walrond and the Barbados Assembly had put together the first comprehensive set of laws that would regulate slavery in their colony. Such action was necessary. Given that the "Laws of England" had offered "no Tract to guide us," the assembly members had instead collected the various orders approved over the preceding decades by island legislators into one document. Purporting to guard enslaved laborers "from the arbitrary Cruell and outrageous will of every evill disposed person," the laws instead codified Africans as chattel and provided more protections for their owners than for the subjects of the legislation. To ensure that there was no confusion about the differences between servitude and slavery, on the same day Walrond also placed his signature on the "Act for Good Governing of Servants, and Ordering the Rights between Masters and Servants." After all, just two years earlier the Protectorate government had been rocked by the suggestion that Englishmen were being treated as slaves. The recently restored government on Barbados wanted to avoid any such accusations, drawing a definitive line between those who would labor for life and those who would be contracted to work for a set number of years. The 1661 slave code identified the Africans who fell into the first category as "an Heathenishe, Brutish and an uncertaine, dangerous kind of People," underscoring the clear distinctions between the "negroes" of the act's title and both the civilized elite English who wrote the laws and those who fell into the second category, "servant," whose status in the legislation was often modified by the descriptor "Christian."[1] This conflation of religious and ethnic descriptions was a common practice among English officials across their Atlantic world.

The laws of 1661 are just one example of how England's colonial ventures forced English imperialists to find new ways to define difference. Ireland, the site of England's first imperial project, provided a fruitful "laboratory for empire," where English ideas about superiority and civilization were first worked out by those men charged with governance of the island.[2] While the Irish were not the only colonial population to shape these English theories, experiences in Ireland were nonetheless foundational to how the English read and understood distinctions elsewhere. Moreover, many of the lessons learned (and ignored) in Ireland informed English colonial policy in the Americas, including the ways that the English discussed non-English subjects.[3] Discourses about Irish inferiority certainly had their parallels in English descriptions of the poorer sorts of their own compatriots, but in a post-Reformation world it was the Catholicism of the Irish combined with their supposedly irregular customs that marked the island's population as fundamentally apart from English civilization. English observers, colonists, and commentators in Ireland used these ideas about inherent Irish difference to justify the poor treatment of the Irish Catholics they colonized and to lay claim to Ireland itself.

In the Caribbean English attempts to define difference took on new challenges. English colonists (like their compatriots throughout the Americas) did their best to replicate the England they had left behind. But for all that they tried to create a "little England" in the West Indies, authorities were forced to reckon with a set of circumstances very unlike those they encountered at home.[4] Cash crop production was so central to the financial success of the colonies that the issue of labor pushed its way to the top of the imperial agenda. Although at first the workforce on the islands was composed largely of English indentures, very quickly enslaved Africans and laborers from other parts of the Three Kingdoms of England, Scotland, and Ireland became the predominant sugar-producing forces on the islands, with the Irish making up the lion's share of non-African workers.[5] The presence of these populations significantly altered demography, making the Caribbean inescapably different from England. It also raised the question of the status of these laborers, particularly with respect to the growing institution of slavery. There was no

English common law to rely on when it came to questions of bondage, so colonial assemblies, like the one on Barbados, had to create legislation wholesale to deal with the system of slavery. The laws that assemblies produced reflected a tension in elite English concerns about how to order society. While their understandings of hierarchy come through in the sources, lawmakers were caught between emphasizing Christianity as a signifier of difference and accentuating distinctions based on a variety of other cultural and ethnic markers.

Arguments made by English elites in the 1650s that privileged Protestant Christianity as the arbiter of freedom were later displaced by reasoning that had a more racially motivated analysis at its heart. The shift took place in stages, and there was no strict progression from one position to the other. Part of the reason for the uneven transition lay with English lawmakers, who initially cleaved to ideas about difference determined on the basis of potentially malleable cultural practices rather than supposedly inherent and unchangeable biological realities. Cultural difference, they believed, could be overcome, so Irish Catholics might adopt the practices of Protestants, and heathen Africans might be able to imitate good Christians. Ultimately, however, English elites realized the dangers that such ideologies posed. To maintain their hierarchy of labor they needed an underclass who could be subjected to various degrees of bondage. Encouraging Irish Catholics and enslaved Africans to transform might cause them to challenge their subservient status or no longer render them suitable for servile labor. And in any case, such metamorphoses would always be suspect, exacerbating elite fears about trouble-causing populations in their midst. The English recognized another threat contained in these discourses about difference: if non-English subjects could be transformed, they reasoned, then perhaps the English could be too, and not necessarily for the better. Laws regulating sexual and religious norms and identifying disruptive behavior on the islands raised the potential for English colonists to be corrupted by other groups, recalling the degeneracy of the Old English in Ireland. These descendants of the Anglo-Norman invaders of the thirteenth and fourteenth centuries had risen to various positions of prominence on the island but were now accused of having "gone native" as a result of their exposure to the island's indigenous inhabitants.[6] So legislators moved to construct discrete categories and to legislate against the coming together of people from different religious or ethnic groups.

This chapter explores elite English struggles to fix categories of difference in the early modern Atlantic world through three sets of elite constructed sources that reflect their everyday experiences in Ireland and the Caribbean. It begins with the 1659 petition of two English gentlemen who argued that Englishmen in Barbados were being treated as slaves, and it follows the resulting parliamentary debate about whether Englishmen, even those who had taken up arms against the government, could be held in perpetual bondage. Next, the travel writing and observations of elite English in Ireland are investigated for what they reveal about classification on the site of England's first colonial venture. Discourses about differences in Ireland based on cultural practices—land use, sexual mores, clothing, and religion—paralleled English discussions about the people they encountered in the Americas and Africa during campaigns of colonization and exploration. These ideologies influenced the processes of defining difference in Caribbean settings, so the legal system that developed in Barbados and the Leeward Islands created hierarchies according to sex, labor, religion, and ethnicity. Although there are no extant transcripts of the debates that colonial assemblies engaged in as they wrote their legal statutes, the laws themselves provide context for the struggle that ensued, insofar as legislation responded to the vagaries of everyday life in the colonies.[7] Laws constructed by elites were therefore somewhat schizophrenic: some mirrored ideas about difference carried over from Europe; others reflected issues specific to life in the Caribbean; many combined elements of both.[8] Irish Catholics sat at the intersection of each of these discussions, whether they were in European or American settings. Paying attention to the space they occupied in between ideas separating African from English, heathen from Christian, and even black from white provides a window into the mechanisms through which the English figured difference in their early modern Atlantic world.

"By which you may discover whether English be Slaves or Freemen"

The radical demographic shifts of the 1650s that saw an increase in African captives and prisoners of war from England's civil conflagration entering into the Caribbean spurred a debate over the treatment of laborers in the English Caribbean that drew in participants from both the metropole and the colonies and that was grounded in the everyday experiences of the protagonists.[9] There was a larger context to these deliberations: for almost two decades the English had been embroiled in their own struggles at home as a sequence of bloody civil wars shook the country and its surrounding kingdoms to their core. At the heart of the conflict were questions of authority and tyranny, as the supporters of Parliament (Roundheads) challenged the supremacy of the monarchy and its royalist allies (Cavaliers). But even when parliamentary forces prevailed and beheaded Charles I in 1649, questions of control continued. Oliver Cromwell, hero of the New Model Army, was declared Lord Protector of England, Scotland, and Ireland by Parliament in 1653, taking on a role in the republic that closely mirrored that of a monarch. An uneasy relationship with Parliament followed, as some fervent Roundheads believed Cromwell to be too authoritarian. These troubles continued when his son, Richard Cromwell, took charge of the Protectorate upon Cromwell's death in 1658.[10] Within the year, debates in Parliament reflected the tensions raised by the Cromwellian regime as some in the republic attempted to distance themselves from what they saw as the tyranny of the previous decade. It was in this turbulent context that a petition from two English gentlemen was heard in the restored Rump Parliament.

In 1659 the English gentlemen Marcellus Rivers and Oxenbridge Foyle, who had been banished to Barbados for their part in a royalist uprising against the Protectorate, published a pamphlet entitled *Englands Slavery, or Barbados Merchandize* accusing the government of having "sold (uncondemned) into slavery" some "three score and ten more Free-born Englishmen."[11] Included along with the petition were four additional letters of appeal, all authored anonymously by royalists, and all decrying the experiences the writers had endured. The pamphlet stressed the innocence of the victims of transportation, detailed their harsh treatment in the Caribbean, and made direct comparisons between the fate of the men accused of taking part in the Salisbury Rising of 1655 and that of the enslaved Africans who labored on plantations by carefully charting the similarities of their everyday experiences. As Susan Dwyer Amussen has argued, Rivers and Foyle made their case on the basis of the illegality of all that had proceeded.[12] Even if their arrest and imprisonment could be understood as an oversight or a mistake in a time of civil war, the government had overreached, had condemned English men, and gentlemen at that, to service in Caribbean sugar fields: they had been "Barbadosed" like men from the lowest orders of society.[13]

Perhaps understanding that the question of whether fellow Christians could be enslaved was likely to be decided in their favor, Rivers and Foyle (and their anonymous co-correspondents) framed their petition as an affront to their status as Protestant Englishmen. On the front of their

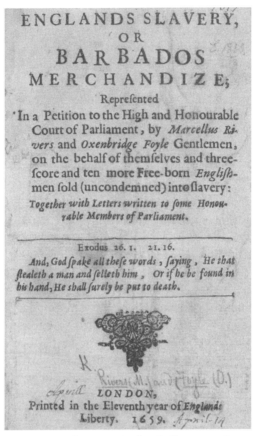

FIGURE 1. Title Page, *Englands Slavery or Barbados Merchandize*, 1659. General Reference Collection E. 1833. (3) © The British Library Board.

pamphlet they cited a biblical admonition against slavery: "And, God spake all these words, saying, He that stealeth a man and selleth him, Or if he be found in his hand, He shall surely be put to death."[14] The men also laid out the uncivilized treatment they received (being sold like livestock, being worked to the bone, suffering poor living conditions, being whipped "for their masters pleasure"), characterizing their handling as "beyond expression or Christian imagination."[15] These themes were emphasized by the anonymous co-petitioners, one of whom described Barbados as "the Protestants Purgatory" and drew on a popular Calvinist outcry—"Quousque domine quousque"—to emphasize his Protestant education and beliefs, and another who described the destinations of the prisoners as "heathenish."[16] And lest all these pleas to Parliament on the basis of shared religion go unnoticed, Rivers and Foyle ended their petition by unfavorably comparing the treatment they had suffered under the English with the actions of "cruell Turks" who despite their infidel status would not stoop so far as "to sell and enslave these of their own Countrey and Religion."[17] To them, the notion that one could place another person of the same Protestant faith in bondage was appallingly cruel. By drawing on religious arguments, the petitioners underscored their own Protestant Christianity: the unspoken counterpoint was the heathen Africans with whom they labored.

There can be no doubt that the choice by Rivers and Foyle to emphasize the similarity of their experiences to those of enslaved Africans was strategic, "a calculated attempt to shock" the parliamentarians who debated their fate.[18] Making the implicit case that they were being treated as heathens, the men stressed the similarity of their middle passage and experiences on Barbados to those endured by Africans.[19] Held captive against their will, the men were "snatcht out of their prisons . . . and driven through the streets of the City of Exon," much as African captives traveled in slave coffles through the streets of Whydah or Accra to the coast to board ships.[20] The anonymous author of the "fourth Letter" described how he had been "stifled up, for a whole year," before his transportation.[21] Being held prisoner before being taken to a ship recalled the kinds of scenes that occurred at slave forts like Elmina, where enslaved Africans could be held for months in dungeons before they moved through the Door of No Return to depart on vessels destined for the Americas.[22] And once they were on the ocean, the similarities continued: the men were "kept lockt under decks (and guards) amongst horses," in much the same manner as enslaved people.[23] Unlike servants who voluntarily headed to the Americas, or sailors aboard ships, the captives were not given hammocks to sleep in but (in the same way as captive Africans) were "forced to ly on the bare hard boards, they refusing to let us to have so much as mattes to ease our weary bones."[24]

Like Africans kidnapped or captured as the spoils of war, these English petitioners were also war captives, removed from their families and communities without notice, or warning, "none suffered to take leave of them." Indeed, after almost six weeks at sea, the men noted that they were now "four thousand and five hundred miles distant from their native countrey, wives, children, parents, friends, and all that is near and dear unto them." The men emphasized their feelings of loneliness and separation due to their complete dislocation from the life they had had before. One of the anonymous petitioners wrote at length about the "high agony of love, and grief, and fear, and danger" that one of the elderly captives felt at leaving his wife and children.[25] The same was true for Africans who were captured and separated from their families, although of course in Africa women and children were also kidnapped or seized as prisoners of war and sent to the Americas (the Salisbury petitioners were all men), and language barriers and cultural differences would have compounded their sense of dislocation.[26] Whatever lack of knowledge the English petitioners had about where they were going, or what they would do on arrival, they at least were able to comprehend the words of their captors. But while they did not fear that they would be cannibalized before they even set sail, there was a horror of a different kind posed by the circumstances of their capture: here were English treating their own countrymen with brutality and contempt.[27]

The men who petitioned Parliament asserted that their lot did not improve upon reaching Barbados. Once on the island, the petitioners charged, they had been bought by the "most inhumane and barbarous persons for 1550. pound weight of Sugar apiece." The author of the anonymous third letter noted the dehumanizing effects of being "sold in the publick market, as beasts," becoming in the eyes of those who purchased them "like those our fellow creatures that have no understanding," in other words, like enslaved Africans.[28] None were spared, neither the old, the religious, the officers, nor the gentlemen, in much the same way as slave ship captains endeavored to sell their entire cargos, young, old, men, women, and children alike.[29] According to the petitioners, all were "rendred . . . alike in this most insupportable Captivity," put to work "grinding at the Mills attending the Fornaces, or digging in this scorching Island." From the description, it is clear that the petitioners labored on sugar plantations, their experiences, again, mirroring those of slaves brought from Africa. And like their African counterparts, the English men were badly provided for in terms of food and shelter ("nothing to feed on but . . . Potatoe Roots," "sleep[ing] in styes worse then hogs in England"). Moreover, once they had settled on a plantation there was no guarantee that they would remain in that location. The author noted that they could be "bought and sold still from one Planter to another, or attached [to] horses and beasts for the debts of their masters," a similar fate to that suffered by enslaved Africans.[30]

Such descriptions may well have been utilized to shock English parliamentarians into recognizing the plight of the petitioners, but in their pamphlet Rivers and Foyle demonstrate how quickly some of the key traits that characterized slavery had become entrenched on Barbados. It is likely that many of the comparisons that the prisoners made came from observing the enslaved Africans they toiled alongside.[31] All would have seen the manner in which slave ships arrived in Barbados; some might have overheard discussions by ship captains or crew about what forms these voyages took. But it seems just as likely that the petitioners found ways to communicate with their fellow laborers in spite of the language barriers that had to be overcome, drawing on enslaved Africans' descriptions of their middle passages and their lives on plantations to make the comparison hit home. They would not have been the only English men to do so. Anabaptist Thomas Tryon, a fierce critic of slavery, spent time on Barbados in the 1660s. He composed an early antislavery treatise from the perspective of enslaved laborers, writing in the first person as though he had been brought over from Africa himself. He was able to write so vividly on the subject because his work as an urban tradesman put him in close contact with enslaved Africans, thus enhancing his understanding of their experiences.[32] The men sentenced to toil on Barbados plantations for their alleged part in the Salisbury Uprising may well have done the same.

However they gained knowledge of the Middle Passage, in their petition Rivers and Foyle unintentionally amplified the horrors that enslaved Africans experienced on plantations. There is no Olaudah Equiano or Mary Prince for this period, and while allowing elite English men to ventriloquize for African captives in their stead raises its own problems, the details articulated minutely in the pamphlet so perfectly reflect the labors endured by enslaved Africans that Rivers and Foyle did give voice to those whom they suffered alongside.[33] Of course neither man was an abolitionist. The juxtaposition with African experiences was supposed to underscore the horrors that the English men had lived through and to emphasize that their dehumanization was all the more appalling because the perpetrators were their countrymen. Many members of Parliament who heard the petition agreed with Rivers and Foyle that it was the association of selling English men that made transportation to the Americas so horrifying—the treatment of Africans did not factor into their calculations.[34] Edward Boscowan made the point most astutely, arguing that the petition needed to be heard because if it was not, "our lives will be as cheap as those negroes."[35] Sir John Lenthall, the MP for Gloucester, picked up the theme of commodification, stating that he hoped "it is not the effect of our war to make merchandize of men."[36] And when considering the appeal of another English man whose petition arrived at the same time as that of Rivers and Foyle, MP Thomas Gewen was clear: "I would not have men sold like bullocks and horses. The selling a man is an offence of a high nature."[37] None of these men so much as hinted that it was also improper to treat Africans in this manner.

"Our case is but your Touchstone, by which you may discover whether English, be Slaves or Freemen." This parenthetical challenge to Parliament was posed by the first of the anonymous petitioners included in Rivers and Foyle's pamphlet and summarizes the stakes for the debate that ensued.[38] In the political context of the 1650s, the question of the loyalty of the petitioners was raised frequently by MPs, but many parliamentarians believed the issue of slavery to be more important than divisions between the supporters of the Cromwellian regime and those who remained loyal to the monarchy. The prominent parliamentarian for Whitechurch Sir Henry Vane noted the significance of the case, arguing that the question of slavery was important to "the liberty of the free-born people of England."[39] Fellow Roundhead Major Robert Beake concurred, noting that "slavery is slavery, as well in a Commonwealth as under another form."[40] Emotions ran high as the petition circulated. Sir Arthur Haslerigge, whose staunch brand of republicanism often placed him in opposition even to supporters of the Cromwellian regime, claimed to have been moved to tears when he read Rivers and Foyle's appeal because "these men are now sold into slavery amongst beasts." While Haslerigge was probably referencing Africans when he used the term *beasts,* his comment may have been more metaphorical in intent. "Beasts" could just as easily have been an allusion to the English traders and planters on Barbados who subjected the petitioners to such harsh treatment. His commentary finished on a note of despair, lamenting that "if we have fought our sons into slavery, we are of all men most miserable."[41]

If the buying and selling of English bodies was too extreme a measure for many parliamentarians, the specific rights of English subjects remained an important topic of discussion when it came to decisions about who *was* suitable for enslavement. Another member of Parliament, Alexander Annesley, who had sympathy with the Cavaliers, was "sorry to hear Magna Charta moved against this House," arguing that if the petitioners were English men they should have the benefit of a proper trial, something the appellants stated they had not received. Claiming, "I know no law for banishment," Annesley couched his opposition to the forced removal of English to the Americas within a framework of the rights that all English should enjoy. Lenthall agreed, stating that he also viewed the Cavaliers "as Englishmen" and therefore as automatic beneficiaries of all that this status entailed. Moreover, he asserted, "I so much love my own liberty as to part with aught to redeem these people out of captivity." His ideas were based on his belief that the English were "the freest people in the world" and therefore could not be subjected to enslavement in the Caribbean or elsewhere.[42]

The deliberations of Parliament make clear that there were major concerns about the legality of placing English subjects in slavery, but this uneasiness did not necessarily extend to other subjects in the Three Kingdoms. The question of what would happen to Scots or Irish who were similarly transported to Barbados was not explicitly engaged, but the absence of such a conversation is important in and of itself. Only Major Knight, a member of Parliament from Scotland, suggested that taking the petition of Rivers and Foyle seriously might open the floodgates, resulting in a deluge of petitions from other transported prisoners of war. He asked "What will you do with the Scots taken at Dunbar, and at Durham and Worcester? Many of them were sent to Barbados. Will you hear all their petitions?"[43] Implicit in Knight's rhetorical questioning was his sense that Scottish prisoners of war would be worthy to be judged on the same basis as the English petitioners. Although he was opposed to officially hearing Rivers and Foyle's petition, Knight made no distinctions between the rights of English and Scots in his argument about why he was taking such a stance. In the colonies Scottish servants were considered to be almost as worthy as English indentures, and both were substantially preferred over Irish laborers. Whether they were Roundheads or supporters of the crown, Scots were overwhelmingly Protestant, making them much more similar to all English subjects than to Irish Catholics.[44] And unlike the Irish (or the Africans for that matter), the Scots did have at least one person in Parliament willing to voice the fact that a broad range of royalists could be taken as political prisoners and sold into bondage, not only those who claimed England as their home.

Parliament had nothing to say about Irish Catholics and where they fell in legal discussions of who could be free and who could be enslaved. The Protectorate was not inclined to think of Ireland in terms other than as a colony in need of subduing, with a population that required civilizing. And with such emphasis on the rights of English (specifically), Scots (implicitly), and Protestants (generally), the exclusion of Irish Catholics from this debate is a reminder of just how far removed they were considered to be from other subjects of the Three Kingdoms. Parliament, influenced by descriptions of horrific English suffering, and faced with making a decision about whether Englishmen could ever be considered to hold the same status as "negroes," would always err on the side of the rights of English. If Rivers and Foyle had proved that there were circumstances too terrible for Englishmen to endure, their petition made equally clear that some island inhabitants, like enslaved Africans, could be subjected to such repugnant practices. Closer to home, the English experience in Ireland taught colonizers that another group of transportees could be forced to labor under similarly harsh conditions: Irish Catholics, who were also "Barbadosed" during Cromwell's reign.

"In all thinges they intermix barbarous Customes"

English strategies of colonization were first worked out in Ireland. As part of the Elizabethan and Jacobean attempts at asserting dominance over the island and its inhabitants, a slew of elite English administrators, observers, and government officials worked to justify their ambitions by arguing that the Irish population was inferior and needed to be redeemed. As they encountered this group of people who were seemingly so distinct from themselves, English writers began to position themselves through discourses of barbarism and civilization. To be civilized was to conform to certain approved cultural practices: using resources productively, wearing the right clothes, engaging in legitimate relationships with women sanctioned by the church, and worshipping the correct God in an appropriate manner. Irish Catholics—the English had by this point conflated the Old English and native Irish into one group—failed on each count, their degradation and dissimilarity to English colonizers providing apparently indisputable evidence of their barbarous nature. English discussions about the inferiority of their Irish subjects became part of a much broader discourse about difference that would span the Atlantic world.

Of significant concern to English observers were the ways in which the indigenous population of Ireland did not make appropriate use of the island's resources, especially the land. English commentators frequently misinterpreted Irish practices of transhumance—moving livestock to different pastures in summer—as nomadism, which they took as evidence of an essential Irish incivility. Fynes Moryson (who traveled extensively in Europe and commented on a wide variety of cultures but who saved his greatest disapprobation for the Irish) commented that they "build no houses, but like *Nomades* living in Cabins, remove from one place to an other with their Cowes."[45] His contemporary, the English writer Edmund Spenser, concurred, noting that the Irish lived "the most part of the yeare in boolies, pasturing upon the mountaine, and waste wilde places," and "grow thereby the more barbarous, and live more licentiously than they could in townes."[46] Justifying the English presence in Ireland in 1612, John Davies, one time attorney general of the island, argued that the Irish could not be relied upon to "builde any houses of Bricke or stone . . . plant any Gardens or Orchards, Inclose or improve their Lands, live together in settled Villages or Townes." As a result, Ireland was left "so wast and desolate," its potential bounty untouched.[47] The connections between supposed land mismanagement and an unwillingness to live in more urban spaces where behavior could be observed and controlled confirmed for English commentators that the Irish were unsuitable stewards of their country and its resources.

Compounding this mismanagement of land was a practice of inheritance that rested more on who one's father was than on legitimacy. In Ireland, an individual's inclusion in a particular family was determined by paternity, not by whether one's parents had had their relationship solemnized by the church. Moryson suggested that "maryage was rare" among native Irish, at least according to how he recognized the institution. For Moryson, these loose and unsanctioned relationships caused problems in determining lineage. He described how a woman "on the point of death" would "name the true Father of each of her Children." Such antics, he contended, caused consternation, as children would leave the family where they had grown up to join that of their newly named father. But Moryson was also forced to acknowledge that the "stayne of Basterdy" mattered not in Irish society. To his disgust, it was "no shame to be or to beget a Bastard" in Ireland.[48] Thus the supposed trouble that Moryson presumed followed from the production of children in this manner had no social implications on the island. The lack of consequences, more than any other issue, seemed to trouble Moryson the most about such situations. This disregard for acknowledging the supremacy of legitimate births, as the English did, coupled with the casual Irish attitude toward land ownership, strongly countered English ideas about civility, status, and manhood that placed a premium on property ownership and primogeniture.[49] As such, they marked the incivility of the Irish.

Irish sartorial choices were also called into question by English observers, who, used to layers of clothing and the very specific hierarchy associated with elaborate costume, were confounded by what they assumed to be the Irish preference for comfort over prestige.[50] Spenser

suggested that the mantle (a blanketlike cloak) was an especially dangerous piece of attire. In his estimation the garment acted as "a fit house
for an out-law, a meet bed for a rebel, and an apt cloake for a thief."[51] But
it was not only the lowly or the lawless Irish who were associated with
mantles. In his 1612 engraving John Speed, an English cartographer, did
not differentiate between the elites and the "wilde" Irish when it came to
dress, attiring all six figures in variations of the same mantle. According
to the author of the account that accompanied Speed's image, Irish of all
social ranks wore "shagge rugge mantles . . . both sexes accounting idle-
ness their onely libertie, and ease their greatest riches."[52] Fynes Moryson
elaborated further, suggesting that "the very cheefe of the Irish, as well
men as women, goe naked in very Winter time, onely having their privy
parts covered with a ragge of linen, and their bodies with a loose man-
tell."[53] Mantles were a widespread clothing choice in Ireland, signifying
to English observers the extent of Irish barbarism, even in supposedly
elite quarters.

Perhaps the real English concern with the mantle was related to its
ability to conceal the sexual misconduct of Irish women, thus enabling
the garment to become an easily recognized symbol of the general
degeneracy of the Irish population. According to Spenser, the loose swirl
of fabric would allow an Irish woman "a coverlet for her lewde exercise,"
a reference to her alleged proclivity for sex with someone to whom she
was not married. Moreover "when she hath filled her vessell," she could
"hide both her burden, and her blame," under the material of the mantle,
and "when her bastard is borne, [the mantle] serves instead of swadling
clouts."[54] Spenser assumed that the soft woolen material and the relaxed
fit of the garment accounted for its popularity among Irish women. Like
Speed and Moryson, who noted that mantle wearing was widespread,
Spenser underscored the danger that the practice could extend to "good
women" who found the garment so comfortable that they would do no
work.[55] Moryson went further, connecting the loose covering to Irish
women's reluctance to corset themselves properly, resulting in "nasty"
bodies with breasts so large "as they give their Children sucke over their
shoulders."[56] These images of a tainted Irish womanhood that transgressed wealth, status, and birth were in stark contrast to the ideal of
the chaste elite English woman who attired herself properly and did not
behave in duplicitous or slatternly ways.

While land use, clothing, and alternative sexual practices and gender
norms all affected English perceptions of the Irish, Irish religious rituals
stood out as perhaps the greatest markers of difference between colonist

The Gentleman of Ireland
The Gentlewoman of Ireland
The Civill Irish Woman
The Civill Irish man
The Wilde Irish man
The Wilde Irish Woman

FIGURE 2. This detail from John Speed's *Theatre of the Empire of Great Britaine* (1616) shows that all Irish, regardless of rank, favored mantle-style coverings. By permission of the Folger Shakespeare Library.

and colonizer because they married two of the greatest (albeit contradictory) fears of English commentators: that the Irish were perfidious papists and that they were simultaneously barbarous heathens. At the turn of the seventeenth century many English observers questioned whether the Irish were Catholic at all. Spenser noted that they "be all Papists by their profession, but in the same so blindly and brutishly informed, (for the most part) that not one amongst a hundred knoweth any ground of religion, or any article of his faith, but can perhaps say his Pater noster, or his Ave Maria, without any knowledge or understanding what one word thereof meaneth."[57] Moryson offered a similar analysis: "They use generally the Rites of the Roman Church in which they persist with obstinacy," but with the caveat that "in all thinges they intermix barbarous Customes."[58] Although Irish Catholics would not have been the only followers of the faith to draw on traditional customs in their worship, the Protestant English who colonized the country in the late sixteenth and early seventeenth centuries saw so little of anything resembling Christian practice "that they branded the native Irish as pagan without question."[59] The particular ways they expressed their religious beliefs made the Irish seem especially deviant to English observers, even as the Irish themselves had no doubt that they were true adherents to the Catholic faith.[60]

Despite these negative assessments of Irish character, Spenser, Moryson, and Davies all believed that the Irish could be civilized if only they would allow the English to show them the way. Reformation was necessary in the areas of religion, politics, and culture, but the Irish were capable of throwing off their barbarism, provided that they remade themselves in an English image.[61] Indeed, the men driving English colonization believed fervently that by planting Ireland they were encouraging the redemption of the Irish people. As the seventeenth century progressed, however, ideas about the mutability of the Irish character gave way to notions of an inherently static and barbarous Irish population who were incapable of redemption in any of the ways that English colonists had previously hoped. The 1641 Irish uprising marked this watershed in English opinions of Irish Catholics.[62] In October of that year, Catholics in the northeast of the island rose up against Protestant colonists, killing thousands in Ulster. As a result, English ideas about Irish barbarity took a stronger hold, even as new stress was placed on the religious dimensions of the attack. News of the massacre of Protestant settlers by vicious Irish Catholics flooded the English pamphlet press.[63]

The Teares of Ireland, first published in 1642, set the tone of the commentary that followed by focusing on both the supposed religious savagery of Catholics and the attendant violence that resulted from such intransigent positions. The frontispiece promised "a List of the unheard off Cruelties and perfidious Treacheries of bloud-thirsty Jesuits and the Popish Faction." To help readers understand the depths of Irish Catholic depravity, the tract included eleven woodcuts to illustrate the barbarity of the 1641 attacks. One panel that depicted the treatment of an English man and his family described how "papists brake in and beate out his braines" before raping his wife and cutting her unborn child out of her body, tossing the remains onto a fire. Another image noted that after the Irish had "ravished Virgens & Wives" they bashed out the brains of English children in full sight of their parents, while a final wood-cut expounded on Irish sexual depravity, noting how one man had his "member cut of" by men who also "mangled" his body. Unlike Spenser and Davies, the author of this pamphlet rejected any possibility of Irish improvement. The images included in *The Teares of Ireland* made it eas-ier for English readers to view Irish Catholics as beyond redemption, inscribing their savagery through visual expressions of violence.

In *The Irish Rebellion,* published first in 1646, Sir John Temple, Mas-ter of the Rolls in Ireland, put forth what would become the authorita-tive English account of the uprising. Like *The Teares of Ireland*, Temple's tract argued that the 1641 massacre proved the Irish to be incapable of progressing to civility. Temple used the depositions of Protestant survivors of the attack to prove his case, focusing on the depredations of the Irish, who (he alleged) attacked the very old and the very young among the Protestant population, sexually molested dead bodies, and devoured other English corporeal remains. His account of unnatural terror included the actions of Irish woman and children who killed English Protestants of their own sex and age.[64] In his testimony, Eng-lish colonist Peter Hill supported Temple's claims of Irish cannibal-ism, noting that it was "a very comon and ordinary thing for the Irish to murther and devoure and eate the persons of such English as they could light upon" and going on to describe two separate instances when "divers barbarous Irish women" ate English men or Irish chil-dren.[65] Uniting an antipathy toward Catholicism with the barbarism of the Irish, Temple's popular tract fixed Irish Catholics as ethnically and religiously deviant. In Temple's eyes, the Irish were not simply degen-erate as a result of their Catholicism: the Catholicism itself had been corrupted, placing the Irish beyond Christianity altogether. *The Irish Rebellion* set the tone for English perceptions about Irish inferiority at midcentury.[66]

FIGURE 3. Woodcuts from James Cranford, *The Teares of Ireland* (1642). By permission of the Folger Shakespeare Library.

English ideas about Irish difference were especially important because they had profound repercussions in the Caribbean. The events of 1641 prompted a desire to dominate Ireland once and for all, sending Oliver Cromwell and his armies into the country as they attempted to bring England's civil war to the neighboring island. Cromwell's decision to run the Irish off their lands and into the western (and most infertile) province of Connaught precipitated the process of transplantation overseas. What began as an internal movement of recalcitrant Irish Catholics ended with Cromwell's forced migration of large numbers of the Irish population to Barbados and the Leeward Islands. These women, men, and children were thrust into another Protestant English colonial setting where questions of hierarchy and difference took on new forms. In the West Indies, living alongside Protestant Scottish and English prisoners of war, thousands of African captives, and some few, but present, Native Americans, they encountered a demographic situation very different from that in Ireland. The memories of 1641 were fresh in the minds of English administrators, who feared potential uprisings among the Irish population and the brutal violence that might accompany such rebellion, including that performed by women and children. Moreover, the threat of war with Catholic Spain was ever present. All Irish who suffered the misfortune of being "Barbadosed" were therefore viewed with mistrust and anxiety.

With the expansion of English exploration and colonization, many populations besides the Irish found themselves targets for English critiques and suspicions. English colonizers justified their claim to indigenous lands in North America by asserting that Indians did not manage the land properly, drawing on many of the same observations and arguments they used against the Irish in Ireland.[67] They spilled much ink on the cultural practices of Indians, West Africans, and Scottish Highlanders, remarking on their different dress, religious rituals, and gender relations to underscore their lack of civility, even if they sometimes were forced to acknowledge that elements of these cultures were not so different from their own.[68] The mantle reappeared in an expanded Atlantic world, noted as a dangerous form of dress in African and American contexts.[69] And indigenous Americans and Africans were as likely to be accused of cannibalism as the Irish.[70] Moreover, the seeming ability of Irish, African, and Indian women to experience childbirth without pain marked all of these groups outside a Mosaic conception of humanity, emphasizing again each group's lack of civility.[71] To the English, Africans and Indians were heathens, a fact that some English believed marked them closer to redemption than the Irish, or at least excused them from apostasy. After all, individuals could not be blamed for their lack of Christianity if they had never been introduced to the faith in the first place. The Irish, on the other hand, had failed miserably in this regard. Rather than embrace the true Protestant faith, they continued to cleave to Catholicism: they could not claim ignorance as a justification for their plight. The uncertainties raised by these diverse colonial populations— on questions of ethnic, religious, and cultural difference—manifested themselves in a variety of ways in Barbados and the Leeward Islands, but most especially through legal statutes produced in the colonies.

The Scandal of Christianity

In the Caribbean, English elites found that daily interactions between colonial subjects necessitated a range of measures to regulate and control behavior and to enforce categories of difference. Imperial officials were especially concerned about the ability of certain island populations to masquerade as something they were not. Irish Catholics might appear to be loyal but could expose their true perfidious nature when the right circumstances presented them with an opportunity to ally with other Catholic powers. Christian servants might be induced to engage in "unchristian" practices if they associated too closely with enslaved Africans. But the ability to change could have positive associations too. Those same Irish could be persuaded to swear their loyalty and become faithful subjects. Enslaved Africans who demonstrated their fealty to the crown might become good Christians or at least behave in a godly fashion with the right inducements. And indigenous inhabitants of the islands might also prove capable of conversion. All the Leeward Islands had small but significant Carib Indian populations, despite attempts by both the French and the English to banish indigenous inhabitants to Dominica in the 1620s.[72] Even Barbados, an island virtually uninhabited when the English first ventured onto its shores, had a small Native American population because of the Indian slave trade from New England in the wake of the Pequot War of 1637.[73] But for all that they held out the possibility that these populations could change, English elites ultimately feared such transformations, especially when they threatened the entire colonial project. The Caribbean legislation of the seventeenth century demonstrates the numerous ways that English lawmakers attempted to create distinct categories of difference, at first promoting religious boundaries between Christians and heathens but slowly embracing a discourse that privileged apparently biological distinctions over all others. The seeds for that transition were sown in some of the

Caribbean's earliest acts, well before Rivers and Foyle raised the problem of English slaves in 1659.[74]

Written in 1644, Antigua's Act "Against Carnall Coppullation between Christian and Heathen" demonstrates that from the very beginning of their Atlantic incursions the English experienced tensions in their ideologies about difference. Centered on religious categories (as the labels "Christian" and "heathen" in the Act's title suggest), the language of the law also included ethnic references, such as "white," "negro," and "Indian." Without ever directly conflating "Christian" with the former category, or "heathen" with the latter two, the language of the act nonetheless effectively created a universe in which only "white" people could be Christian, leaving the category "heathen" for "negroes" and "Indians." This shift in language laid bare a continuing problem for English authorities who were struggling with a worldview formerly dominated by their ideas about religious difference but increasingly becoming inflected with theories about more biologically based distinctions among and between groups.[75]

The 1644 Act raised the specter of the corrupting nature of non-English sexuality.[76] Although Irish Catholics were not mentioned in the legislation, its parameters were reminiscent of the fears of Spenser, Davies, and Moryson. Those English commentators had been convinced that the demise of the Old English in Ireland was directly connected to their propensity to engage in sexual congress with indigenous Irish women, who then raised their children according to Gaelic customs, religion, and language. The Antigua Act developed this theme, stressing that any English who participated in sex with "heathens" were "defiling" themselves and violating the sacredness of the Christian body. The use of the language of defilement is particularly important, for prohibitions on fornication turned to it only when non-English were involved, indicating that there was something especially distasteful about engaging in sex with individuals outside one's own religious realm.[77] The language suggested that it was the Christian who was transformed by the encounter, not the other way around, raising worries for authorities that even the most trusted of island populations could be vulnerable to degradation and might even become heathen themselves.

It was, however, the problem posed by the existence of children—living, breathing evidence that sex between Christians and heathens had taken place—that caused the greatest consternation for authorities, particularly those birthed to Christian women who did not have the protection of a husband.[78] These children were not only evidence that English men did not have mastery over their female counterparts (as any civilized man should) but also visible reminders that such sexual congress had taken place.[79] After all, it was possible for a white woman to give birth to a non-white child, a fact noted by the authors of the act.[80] Officials decreed that the offspring of these unions would be examined for signs of the child's paternity; the infant's appearance would, the act implied, be visible proof of her mother's transgression. In a move that marked the punishment for Christian women as harsher than that for Christian men, the Antigua Assembly proposed to banish offending women and their offspring from the island, in addition to the fines and whippings and extensions of service that were meted out to all Christians who violated the law, male and female alike.[81] The presence of children who would not be considered English but who were nonetheless born to English mothers was seriously troubling for island administrators. Rather than deal with this blot on their attempts to make clean and simple categories of difference, legislators opted to remove the problematic evidence of mixing from Antigua's jurisdiction altogether.[82] Christian women, then, were viewed as being especially corrupted by their encounter with a heathen: it was they who were being colonized by heathens, not the other way around, a trend that had potentially serious implications for England's colonial project.

Banishing English (or European) women and their nonwhite children did not solve the problem of what to do with the children born of sexual liaisons between Christian men and heathen women, most of who were enslaved Africans. Women of color giving birth to children who would also not be considered white was less dangerous to societal hierarchies than the results of white women's transgressions: although the assembly noted that ascertaining paternity in these cases would be fraught, they understood that determining whether a Christian man was the father would be extremely difficult because appearances alone could not prove conclusive.[83] Though African and Indian women faced serious punishment in the form of whipping and branding, neither they nor their children were sent off the island. Instead, the legislators chose to force religious conformity on the children.[84] According to the law, as soon as the child of the union was old enough to be "able to give A Reason of their faith," he or she would "Be Baptized." Moreover, these children would not be enslaved for life. Boys would be freed at the age of twenty-one, girls at eighteen, and in either instance they would receive "foure hundred pounds of good tobacco in Role" from their master at the moment of emancipation.[85] By freeing these children and ensuring their Christianity, colonial elites were guaranteeing that at least the categories that linked Christianity and freedom would not be complicated. Of course most planters ignored these provisions and allowed the children born to slave women to be absorbed into the enslaved population of Antigua.

Differentiating between Christians and heathens continued with the Barbados slave code of 1661. Not only did the preamble of the act refer to Africans as "heathens," but later parts of the legislation developed the idea that Christians and slaves were distinct categories, ordering an ever-increasing array of punishments—severe whipping, nose cutting, face burning—for any "Negro either Man or Woman" offering "any violence to any Christian as by striking or the like."[86] This clause effectively ignored the possibility that an African could also be a Christian, making the two categories mutually exclusive. But the very next section of the 1661 act introduced some complexity to these supposedly most separate of categories. Africans who aided their masters by deterring slave unrest or preventing enslaved Africans from absconding could at least take on the veneer of Christianity. Masters identified loyal enslaved Africans with "a Badge of a Red Crosse on the Right Arme whereby [the slave] may bee knowne and cherished by all good People for his good service to the Country."[87] The choice of a red cross as a sign of fidelity was no coincidence: not only was the emblem the mark of Christianity, but it was also the flag of English patron Saint George.[88] It signified the continued importance of connecting Christianity with the notion of a good colonial subject. On the one hand, enslaved Africans could be brutish heathens; on the other, some might imitate good Christians even if they had not been baptized into the faith themselves. Conflating "Negro" with "heathen," and "European" with "Christian" was not absolute so long as there were Africans in the colonies who were faithful to Protestant rule and who might be "Negro" and "Christian" at the same time.[89]

A 1675 Nevis law suggested that this ability to imitate certain categories might be the purview not only of Africans but also of Christians deviating from their faith. The act, entitled "White Men Not to Keep Company with Negroes," appeared to be an attempt to fix the identities of Africans and English once and for all by reserving the category of Christian for "white" people alone. But in the description that followed, lawmakers indicated that the main cause for concern was associations or interactions between European settlers and enslaved Africans that would lead to the potential degeneration of whites. The act declared that such connections were "unchristian," the implication being that it was Europeans who were lessened by fraternization with Africans. Explaining their rationale, the legislators noted the "many mischiefs" that arose between whites and Africans, particularly when they were "drinking together in common upon the Sabbath dayes when they should be at better exercises." Such behavior "dishonnour[ed]" God and was "the scandal of Christianity." The English belief that it was the white participant who was changed for the worse by "playing, or conversing with Negroes" was demonstrated by the fact that only Europeans were punished for this crime.[90] Clearly the suggestion that laborers might interact or even enjoy each other's company was deeply disturbing for English officials. Breaking the Sabbath was certainly a problem in and of itself. But here, as with the Antigua Act, it was the notion that white subjects could be transformed into "unchristian" island inhabitants that caused the most consternation for authorities.

Slaves potentially becoming Christians and indeed whites abandoning their civilized ways were not the only imitations that concerned island authorities. The presence of Irish Catholics who claimed to be Christian, but whom English Protestants perceived as following a false faith, troubled the waters further, especially at times of war, when the Irish were suspected of making allegiances with Catholics from rival empires. In the mid-1650s Oliver Cromwell, convinced by his advisors that England's imperial success lay in the Caribbean, organized his ill-fated Western Design. Fusing providentialism with his religious beliefs, Cromwell hoped that his holy quest to secure a puritan empire in the Atlantic would succeed.[91] He intended to push Catholic Spain out of the Caribbean altogether and claim the riches pouring out of the South American continent for England's coffers. Unfortunately for Cromwell and his supporters, the enterprise ended in almost complete failure. During English attempts to take Hispaniola from the Spanish in 1655, Irish Catholics engaged in the ultimate subterfuge, leading Protestant English forces into a trap by pretending to be loyal to the English troops until the very last moment.[92] Only Jamaica, a buccaneer and pirate paradise, fell to the English attack, and even here the costs of England's victory were great.[93]

War with Spain also allowed Irish Catholics to take advantage of imperial distractions elsewhere in the Caribbean to rise up alongside enslaved Africans in English jurisdictions. On Barbados in the winter of 1655 the Irish challenged English officials to consider their servile status when they were accused of being "out in Rebellion in the Thicketts & thereabouts" with enslaved Africans.[94] Steps were taken in the short term to disrupt such interactions, with the militia ordered to round up the malcontents, but authorities still remained worried about Irish disloyalty. They were rewarded two months later when Irish men Anthony Clarke, Daniel Halsee, and Cornelius Bryan answered charges about their own misbehavior in front of Governor Daniel Searle and the island's council and were punished accordingly. Eventually the Barbados Assembly felt compelled to put forth a set of laws that would minimize Irish opportunities for transgressing boundaries, specifically because in this "time of wars betwixt the Commonwealth of England & Spain both in Europe & here in America," the "Excess of the Irish" proved too great a threat.[95] The 1657 prohibitions on Irish behavior restricted "the considerable number of Irish freemen and servants" from "wander[ing] up and down from Plantation to Plantation." Worried about the ability of these free-spirited Irish to encourage other Irish servants "to the same kind of Ille & wicked courses" by "their example & persuasions," the Barbados Council ordered that any Irish person, man or woman, who arrived on a plantation "& cannot give a ready & good accompt of the reason of their coming" should be "severely punished."[96] In addition, no Irish were permitted to "have any arms or ammunition with their Houses or Custody," and anyone found with weapons would be "forthwith disarmed." Recent Irish perfidy in the Caribbean undergirded these regulations, but memories of Irish treachery in Ireland in 1641 also informed English attitudes.

In the 1660s, English authorities continued to worry about the propensity for Irish subterfuge during times of war. With Charles II back on the throne, the Irish (in theory at least) should have been mollified—their chief tormentor, Cromwell, was dead, and a monarchy that appeared to be sympathetic to their religious needs was restored. But English authorities in the Caribbean held out little hope that the Irish in their jurisdictions had changed. In 1666 the enemy was France, but the concerns about Irish collaborations with co-religionists took much the same form as they had in the 1650s when England had challenged Spain for its Caribbean colonies. The proximity of French islands in the region accentuated English fears. Of particular concern was the island of St. Christopher, whose territory had been split into English and French jurisdictions since its settlement by both sets of Europeans in 1624. And perhaps the English had good reason to be suspicious. Not only did the Irish on Montserrat freely side with the French in 1666 when they laid claim to the island, but English officers also accused them of aiding the enemy on St. Christopher the following year.[97] On both islands the behavior of Irish Catholics was argued to have been suspect at best and outright rebellious at worst.

In an attempt to neutralize the Catholic threat and force the Irish to at least outwardly proclaim their loyalty to England, imperial officials in the metropole ordered new declarations of faithfulness to the Protestant religion. The new oaths of loyalty to Charles II included specific anti-Catholic language and ideology among their provisions: in addition to swearing allegiance to the crown, officials had to avow that they "believe[d] that there is not any Transubstantiation in the Sacrament of the Lord's Supper." The insistence on the rejection of a key tenet of the Catholic faith reflected concerns about the spread of Catholicism in England and abroad. Over the course of his reign, Charles II became increasingly relaxed in his attitude toward Catholics, issuing the Declaration of Indulgence in 1672, which granted tolerance for religious dissidents. Rumors also persisted about a promise he made to Louis XIV of France that he would officially convert to Catholicism; his deathbed conversion provided proof for many Protestants that he had been a Catholic all along. In the Caribbean, where the proximity of France and Spain heightened tensions, officials continued to be reminded about the need for vigilance against the Irish in their midst.[98] So the oaths required Irish Catholics with colonial aspirations to outwardly endorse the Protestant regime, whatever their inward desires might have been.[99] Toward the end of the seventeenth century the Irish were encouraged to transform, to transgress a boundary, but only if they were willing to swear fealty and remain on its right side, together with Protestant English officials and colonists. In this way they were similar to those Africans who were gauged to be loyal by English observers and were rewarded with a physical emblem of their faithfulness in the form of a red cross to be worn on their sleeve. But unlike enslaved Africans, who needed a visible marker to confirm that they were among the trustworthy on the islands, Irish settlers who adopted Protestant practices could blend seamlessly into the European fold.

* * *

When Marcellus Rivers and Oxenbridge Foyle claimed that their capture, transportation, and treatment on Barbados mimicked that of enslaved Africans, they were arguing against the abomination (as they saw it) of forcing English gentlemen to imitate the debased, degraded lives of slave laborers, not against slavery itself. The debate that ensued in Parliament certainly followed along these lines. Martin Noell, one of the merchants involved in shipping prisoners of war to Barbados, and accused of selling Rivers and Foyle and their fellow petitioners, suggested that the men had mischaracterized the nature of their service when he defended his actions in Parliament. He claimed that these prisoners of war, like all servants, "serve most commonly five years, and then have the yearly salary of the island." Juxtaposing labor on Barbados with that in England, Noell argued that husbandmen at home had it worse than servants abroad. Indeed, he continued, "The work is mostly carried on by the negroes," and he contended that therefore life as a laborer on Barbados was "not so odious as is represented."[100] By claiming that servants of all kinds were treated well, Noell was implicitly arguing that demeaning treatment was reserved for workers from Africa alone.[101] But of course in the Caribbean these distinctions were not so simply made. English men (and women) were not the only servants forced to work on island plantations. Even if they did receive better treatment than Africans, it was less clear whether Scots or Irish, who also occupied servant status, would be accorded the same courtesies.

Coming to a decision about these other non-English servants kept questions of religion and ethnicity at the forefront of English conversations about difference. The forced mimicry of Rivers and Foyle had no direct corollary in island legislation, but here laws raised the possibility of the permeability of categories that separated colonial subjects. On occasion, as with loyal Africans wearing a symbol of Christianity, or Irish Catholics swearing their fealty to the Protestant English crown, English lawmakers believed that such flexibility was a positive force. But when the subjects being altered were Christian and English, the malleability of categories was viewed as dangerous corruption. By the end of the seventeenth century, colonial administrators had worked to create distinct and immutable categories of difference that could not be crossed. In 1681 the Barbados Assembly declared unequivocally that "negroes" were incapable of becoming Christians thanks to their "savage Brutishness."[102] And in the second comprehensive slave code of the island, collated in 1688, the status of enslaved Africans was not left open to interpretation. The Barbados Assembly noted the "Disorder, Rapines, and Inhumanities" to which slaves were allegedly "naturally prone" and declared that the "barbarous, wild, and savage Natures" of African laborers rendered them "wholly unqualified to be governed by the Laws, Customs, and Practices of our Nations," thus removing them completely from consideration as an incorporated part of English colonial society.[103]

If the position of Africans was cemented by the end of the seventeenth century, the place of Irish Catholics continued to be less well defined. Although the events of 1641 in Ireland had marked the Irish as ethnically (not just religiously) distinct from English subjects, in the West Indies they continued to move between categories, sometimes included in the category "Christian" and sometimes not. The Scots (although far fewer) also posed an interesting conundrum. The parliamentary debate had implied that they should be treated as English servants in the Caribbean, but the language that referred to their status was hardly definitive. During the second half of the seventeenth century, colonial administrators and elites continued to debate the place of Irish and Scots. These discussions moved beyond the realm of legislation and into the exciting new philosophy of political arithmetic, which promised fresh avenues for the regulation of people within colonial jurisdictions. For there was more than one way to define island populations, or indeed to develop the means to control them. The obsession with enumerating the populations who inhabited their colonies occurred simultaneously in Ireland and the Americas.

* * *

Old Pegg remembered her trip across the ocean, although she wished she could not. When she thought back to the moment she had last seen her homeland, last heard someone call her by her real name, it almost felt like a dream, as though she had not lived a life before this one of captivity and toil. She remembered the circumstances under which she had been taken, snatched as she played with her younger brother, knowing almost instantly that she would probably never see him again. Then came the long walk to the coast, where she finally saw the vast ocean and the looming fort at the water's edge. She had been jostled among other people, shuffling in shackles, but there was no one close by who spoke words she could understand. It was only later, in the dark, damp, foul-smelling room in the base of the castle, that she found someone from her land, someone with whom she could talk, someone who told her that she would be sent away, across that vast expanse of water, never to return. Sure enough, she found herself taken out of the dungeon and marched onto a ship, where she was again chained and locked below decks as the vessel lingered on the coast, a handful of people added every day to the cargo as the captain attempted to fill the ship to maximum capacity. After what seemed like an interminable wait, the hold was finally deemed to be full. The ship departed, and when the coast was out of sight she was allowed on deck with the other women and girls. Although she had been relieved to breathe clean air, being up above had its own share of horrors. Old Pegg recalled her terror at being in such proximity to the ugly, pale, sailors who threw overboard dead bodies from below with such cavalier abandon. She remembered too the woman who had thrown herself into the churning ocean below rather than suffer another moment on board the vessel, hoping for a return to her country in death that she could not expect in life. Finally, there was land again, and terrors of a different kind, as she was thrust into the world of plantation slavery on Barbados.

Old Pegg did not know it, could not have conceived of it, but the man who had prodded and poked her to decide whether she would make a good investment for his fledgling plantation had undergone a middle passage of his own. Cornelius Bryan was from the southwest of Ireland. As Cromwell's armies swept across his country, he had attempted to keep out of their way. A musician valued for his quick wit and his way with words, Cornelius was unwilling to submit to English laws and conventions, so he, along with thousands of others, was rounded up by English soldiers and forced to remove to the province of Connaught. But when he reached Galway City he discovered that worse was to come—marked as a particularly troublesome Irish man, Cornelius was sentenced to transportation to the Caribbean. Hustled under armed guard onto a ship departing "beyond the seas," Cornelius was not sure where he was going or what he could expect to find upon his arrival. He spent much of that journey locked below decks as the nervous English sailors above worried about the potential for an Irish uprising. They were right to be concerned. Although there was no trouble on the voyage across the Atlantic, Cornelius and his fellow prisoners of war vowed to challenge English authority every chance they got once they arrived at their destination. There was hope that they might be able to flee to Spanish or French jurisdictions, or perhaps find a way to make the English they were working among uneasy. Cornelius was sure of one thing: he was going to make his captors sorry that they had ever thought him worthy of being "Barbadosed."

2 / "An exact account of the number of persons upon the Island": Enumeration, Improvement, and Control

On a June morning in 1678 William Stapleton, the Irish governor of the Leeward Islands, sat at his desk melting some vermillion sealing wax into a spoon. Collected before him were the returns from the census he had ordered taken across Antigua, Montserrat, Nevis, and St. Christopher.[1] In neat rows and columns the heads of households had been recorded on vellum by his teams of administrators, the black ink standing out against the crisp cream pages. His men had also counted the enslaved property laboring on the islands. But their names were not recorded for posterity. They appeared as Arabic numerals, their disembodiment encapsulated by an enumeration that stripped away their humanity. Stapleton's men had included a variety of identifiers for landowners, including "Irish" and "English," the numbers of the former proving on paper how important his fellow countrymen were to the success of England's Leeward Island chain. The French and Dutch on St. Christopher had been identified by the administrator on that island so the Lords of Trade and Plantations could better understand the problems the island faced at times of interimperial war. Unwilling to delegate the task of preparing the package for dispatch to London to his secretary, Stapleton carefully folded the important papers and dripped the melted wax over the seam before pressing his seal into the blood-red pool. Once it dried he sent it out to the ship, which was waiting to take the precious document back to London and the imperial officials who so anxiously awaited its arrival. Counting colonial subjects was not, on immediate inspection, the most important venture of a man who had succeeded in keeping the turbulent Leeward Islands calm and peaceful for almost a decade. But for the Lords of Trade and Plantations who were so keen to master colonial subjects, Stapleton's actions could not have been more timely.

When he created the Leeward Islands' census, Stapleton was employing a key tool of English imperial governance: calculations based on population appeared in Ireland, North America, and the Caribbean with increasing frequency and accuracy as the seventeenth century progressed. There was no state system in place to assist with the counting, so colonial governors and travel writers usually sent estimated figures back to the capital, secure in the knowledge that no one would be able to prove their assessments false.[2] In the 1650s in Ireland, counting became more precise with the "Down Survey," which delineated the location and numbers of Irish Catholics and English Protestants on the island. Two decades later, the Lords of Trade and Plantations requested that more detailed census returns also be collated in Barbados and the Leeward Islands. By this time the numbers were no longer wholly fabricated or estimated; rather, they were collected by churchwardens in each parish on Barbados and by militia commanders in the Leeward Islands. The seemingly endless lines of information contained in the census appeared to be comprehensive, giving the impression of accuracy to the men who interpreted their meaning. This sense of precision allowed colonial officials to feel confident about the lessons they drew from enumeration.

Scholars have used the voluminous information contained in the statistics produced by colonial officials in Ireland and the Americas to explore both the social and cultural ramifications of quantification. Social historians have broken down the numbers to calculate the distribution of Irish Catholics in Ireland, the numbers of enslaved and servant laborers living on Barbados, or the percentage of the Leeward Islands' population that was Irish.[3] These records reveal how the colonies were divided (into parishes or militia regiments), who claimed ownership of the land, and how much property in acres and slaves each planter declared. Scholars interested in the ideological frameworks that shaped enumeration in the seventeenth-century English Atlantic have analyzed how questions of authority and control became connected to population evaluations and how these assessments, in turn, affected colonial policies across the English empire.[4] Both approaches are relevant for investigating the connections between quantification and control.

Colonial counting was also an important strategy employed by English colonial officials to demonstrate imperial power.[5] Notations on the page served to remind London that island governors were good colonial administrators, the neat rows and columns demonstrating the wealth of the islands in land and laborers laid out for the Lords of Trade and Plantations to admire. By quantifying the relationships of everyday life, the census generated seemingly homogeneous categories into which imperial subjects could be placed. These categories obscured the presence of populations who made elites uncomfortable: free people of color, for example, or the children produced by sexual liaisons across the color line. As such, then, demographic accounting provides an excellent guide to elite English ideas and aspirations about difference. Although idiosyncratic, and in many ways a work in progress, the census data from the Caribbean in the latter part of the seventeenth century shows how officials attempted to created categories that were distinct and immutable. By tracing the development of enumeration across the Atlantic, and by exploring the discourse surrounding questions of improvement in both Ireland and the Caribbean, the categories of the late seventeenth-century censuses can be understood as indicative of English ideas about difference, rather than solely as statistical descriptions of island populations. Authorities imposed this artificial order on colonial life as a demonstration of their mastery of island populations, of nature, of the land, and of production itself.

Enumeration in the English Atlantic therefore centered on creating the illusion of imperial control. If potentially disruptive populations were identified and counted, policies to confine them, to improve them, or to disappear them altogether could be deployed.[6] Quantifying colonial populations and mapping their locations allowed English officials to develop policies to manage threats. On the one hand, they envisioned scenarios in which certain unruly populations (like the Scots, and perhaps the Irish) could be transformed into good colonial subjects (by relocation, intermarriage, or land ownership). On the other hand, they accepted that some groups (usually Africans) could never be sufficiently improved. The beauty of these policies was that the first group of redeemed malcontents could be employed in the disciplining and controlling of the second. This "government by demographic manipulation" became a hallmark of seventeenth-century English colonial policy.[7] In Ireland, questions about the potential for Irish Catholics to be transformed into productive and loyal subjects and therefore rendered neutral drove quantification. In the English Caribbean, the outpouring of "calculating" officials was spurred by the need to control an ever-increasing enslaved population and a discontented (and often outright hostile) number of Irish servants and laborers.[8] The artificial nature of colonial counting meant that the numbers collected and returned to London were much more reflections of English ambitions and desires for their colonial project than accurate statistics.

Analyzing the methods of quantification also opens up the question of what was not included in the census data. Erasing the relationships of everyday life through quantification simplified the processes of governance for English officials, who could justify requests to London for more indentured servants from a particular location or address the militia needs of the colonies on the basis of numbers that were inaccurate, yet seemed precise. By reducing human bodies to mere numbers on a page, colonial officials made the conceptual move of erasing the humanity of the populations under observation.[9] Stemming from this enumeration of humans was a desire to mark people as belonging to one category only: the headings at the top of census columns were specific, and an individual could not be placed in more than one category, or indeed between columns. Quantification shattered kin and familial connections, focusing instead on the ways in which people were connected to one another through their labor power—or rather, the ways they were divided between those who provided the labor and those who owned the laborers. Reading the Colonial Office record books that include the voluminous census material from the Caribbean in the late 1670s is therefore an exercise in uncovering the lives that are obscured by abstract statistics.[10] So it becomes just as important to pay attention to what is omitted, to what the power of enumeration obscures—the living, breathing people who were the subjects of colonial counting.

Improving the "Body Politick" in Ireland

Colonial counting was not born in Ireland, but it was here that the English most specifically articulated ideologies connecting numeracy with management of the body politic as imperial officials struggled to gain control over the Irish Catholic population. Englishman William Petty, educated in France, and a former professor of anatomy at Brasenose College, Oxford, drew on his experiences on the island in the middle of the seventeenth century to write *The Political Anatomy of Ireland* in 1672; the tract was finally published in 1691. Only twenty-nine years old when he first arrived in Ireland in 1652 as a physician general in Cromwell's army, Petty moved from county to county and from barony to barony, carefully enumerating the populations he encountered in what would become known as the "Down Survey."[11] Beyond distinguishing between "profitable" and "unprofitable" lands, Petty used the Down Survey to map the population of the country according to political and religious factions, noting the number of English, Scots, and Irish present in each county and barony.[12] This mapping allowed him to see quickly where the largest number of Irish Catholics resided (and thus where danger for the English might lurk) but also to identify Protestant strongholds as places of likely productivity. Recording family names provided an additional element of certainty to the statistics that Petty was creating, his specificity producing a facade of precision.[13]

William Petty grounded his theory of political arithmetic in assumptions about the inherent connection between numeracy and objectivity. Building on the work of John Graunt, one of the first practitioners of demography in England, Petty was drawn to quantification by its illusion of impartiality.[14] He made his case by stressing that "Arguments of Sense" and mathematical calculations undergirded his assessment of Ireland.[15] In *Political Anatomy* he argued that to preserve the "Health and Strength" of the "Body Politick" one needed to know its "Symmetry, Fabrick, and Proportion."[16] He went on to assert "the Observations or Positions expressed by *Number*, *Weight*, and *Measure*, upon which I bottom the ensuing Discourses, are either true, or not apparently false." Most interestingly, Petty seemed to believe that if the crown endorsed his figures the power of the state would render uncertainty moot, transforming suspect numbers into accurate ones: "If they are not already true, certain, and evident, [they] yet may be made so by the Sovereign Power."[17] Here Petty suggested that government policy and numerical evaluations should be intertwined (up until this point they had been considered separate realms) and, more importantly, that this connection rendered the assessments of the state more perfect, objective, and grounded in fact, rather than based on the whims of politicians' particular passions or biases.[18] Petty's idea that numbers, especially those sanctioned by the crown, held an essential truth shaped his solutions to the Irish problem.

Petty (who was also inspired by the work of philosophers and scientists Francis Bacon, Thomas Hobbes, and Robert Boyle) believed that coming to terms with the composition of Ireland's population would lead to more than mere financial and proprietary gain for the English imperial project. In *Political Anatomy*, he explicitly connected a functioning body politic with the quantity of productive human bodies that could be deployed in service of the colonial project. Ireland held few persons whom Petty considered to be of the right quality, so the improvement of the island's population became one of his core goals. Petty's survey underscored the lack of "symmetry" in the makeup of the Irish population, suggesting that the constitution of the country was imbalanced. His comprehension of the composition and distribution of Irish inhabitants was therefore a necessary first step to improving both the island and those who lived and labored on it and to diagnosing why Ireland (and therefore the Irish) had not reached their full potential. Petty was not invoking the human body solely as a metaphor for the body politic. He identified a literal connection between the two entities: one could not separate the island's population from its governance, and Ireland's populace was sickly because of its religious and political affiliations. Improving the physical bodies of Irish subjects would necessarily improve the metaphorical political body.[19] The two were inextricably linked.

While Petty took care to note the names of Irish Catholics in the Down Survey, in *Political Anatomy* he preferred to articulate his ideas about the Irish population and its improvement through categories that stressed economic associations.[20] Petty identified what he viewed as the most essential categories: those that connected to labor and to land and ordered the Irish accordingly. His divisions included those "as live upon the King's Pay," those who were "Owners of Land and Freeholds," "tenants and lessees to the land of others," and finally "workmen and labourers."[21] Containing the largest numbers of Irish people, this final category was of central importance to Petty. Harnessing the labor power of these "workmen and labourers" became necessary to turn Ireland into a productive colonial enterprise. Older English ideas about Irish misuse of land and the inherent laziness of Irish men (articulated by Spenser, Davies, and Moryson) influenced Petty's assumptions about the worth of the Irish labor force. His statistical assessment of the island and its people centered the problem on categories of labor and allowed state officials to see the potential for Irish productivity, if only the workers' energies could be harnessed to the greatest advantage.

Petty's concentration on labor was no mere exercise in semantics. To persuade skeptical English officials that the Irish were capable of becoming improved laborers, he worked to eliminate the threat posed by Irish religious beliefs, which many commentators believed to be a crucial bar to Irish civility. Estimating the numbers of Irish Catholics at around eight hundred thousand, Petty suggested that if "they must have priests" the number should be reduced from between two and three thousand to one thousand.[22] Crucially, the priests were to be English—Petty was evidently of the opinion that English Catholics would be less likely than Irish priests to incite rebellion among the Irish population, noting that the "Priests, who govern the Conscience," would restrain Irish men from taking up arms against the English.[23] While he hoped these policies would reduce problems caused by Irish ethnicity and religious beliefs, in the rest of his writing Petty concentrated on the language of labor and land when he discussed Irish Catholics. Unlike religion and ethnicity, these categories did not have overtly political connotations and could certainly be seen as disinterested. But the use of these alternative forms of organization had at their heart an intensely political goal.[24]

To transform the Irish into useful colonial subjects, Petty argued for a further "transmutation," specifically the intermarriage of Irish and English women and men. English prejudices about Irish barbarism were rooted in their disdain for Irish sexual practices as much as they were in alleged Irish land mismanagement. By marrying and procreating with English women, Petty believed, the Irish would be made anew. Moreover, he asserted, forcibly transporting Irish men to England would speed up the conversion, as if being in a different place would magically alter their behavior.[25] For Petty, as for other theorists of political arithmetic, the alchemy was clear: location and reproduction would ensure the alteration. Two hundred thousand Irish were to be sent into England, and the same number of English would arrive in Ireland. Next "unmarried marriageable Women" from Ireland (of whom Petty estimated there must be only about twenty thousand) would be shipped to England over a two-year period. A similar number of English women would be "brought back and married to the Irish." Petty reasoned that English women, "who influence other powerful appetites," would calm the violent passions of Irish men.[26] Ultimately, "when the Language of the Children shall be English, and the whole Oeconomy [sic] of the Family English, viz. Diet, Apparel, &c., the Transmutation will be very easy and quick." Petty estimated the Irish population could be completely transformed within five years.[27]

At the heart of Petty's discussion of the transmutation were his assumptions about the social roles of women.[28] If Irish men were marrying English women, who would be responsible for the child's early education, then they would create families where children would be reared as good English subjects. As those who were primarily responsible for religious education, English mothers would also slowly convert their families to the Protestant religion. Finally, the intimacy of sharing a home and a bed with an English woman would, Petty hoped, allow Irish men to see the English in Ireland in a more favorable light. Hanging his analysis on these particularly female abilities to secure the transformation paralleled earlier assumptions by Spenser about the role of women. Spenser's analysis blamed Irish women for the corruption of Old English men, and therefore the demise of Old English civilization in Ireland.[29] In Petty's hands, this idea became especially powerful: according to his understanding, the key to Irish redemption in Ireland lay in the civilization of the male population at the hands of English women.[30]

Arguing vociferously for the impartiality of numbers, Petty engaged in the dangerous political game of abstraction.[31] In his analysis, the reduction of the Irish to categories of labor rendered them knowable and thus controllable. But the process of abstraction erased the violence committed by the imperial regime when human beings were reduced to mere statistics. It allowed the agents of government (in this case, Petty), to forget or ignore the individuals whose lives were subjected to colonial policies precisely because their existence was reduced to a financial calculation. In one of the most revealing passages in *Political Anatomy*, Petty discussed the comparative worth of Irish and English laborers, using the categories of "slaves and Negroes" as his benchmark. Petty's specific comparison was no accident: the shorthand was effective because he knew his readers would understand his choice. After all, counting all colonial populations (including enslaved Africans) had become an important part of imperial policy. In England, "the value of people, Men, Women, and Children" was said to be on average £70 "per head." The Irish, on the other hand, were to be accounted at only £15, "as slaves and Negroes are usually rated," with "Men being sold for £25, and Children £5 each."[32] He did not mention what Irish women were worth, perhaps because he thought they had no role to play in Irish improvement.[33] But the message was clear—Irish bodies were equivalent in the financial sense to those of "slaves and negroes."

In this move, Petty substituted the religious and political valences that he saw as the root cause of centuries of bloodshed for a nascent racial ideology that would prove no less bloody in the centuries to come.[34] By doing so, Petty made the case for forced transportation and breeding without ever having to contemplate how individuals caught up in such policies would be affected. For all his allusions to the importance of improved bodies for the successful functioning of the body politic, Petty showed remarkable disregard for the lives of real flesh-and-blood people. But of course, in choosing whom to count, how to count, and what categories to assign the various people he enumerated, Petty made judgments of his own. His version of political arithmetic was all the more dangerous for its appearance of neutrality: the insidious creep of racist ideologies and the connection between land and labor held within Petty's analysis of Ireland would be magnified when transferred to American settings. Indeed, Petty's ideas about the transmutable nature of the Irish—that they could be turned into good English subjects by intermarriage and transportation—was part of a larger conversation about the improvement of populations that spanned the Atlantic. And the way in which he disguised outright violence as benevolent control and improvement also had its corollary in the Caribbean.

"People are the foundacon and Improvement of all Plantacons"

At the same time as William Petty enumerated Ireland's inhabitants and formulated his ideas about political arithmetic, officials in London were growing increasingly concerned with similar questions about population control in Barbados and the Leeward Islands. From the mid-seventeenth century onwards, usually at the behest of imperial officials in the metropole, reports from the colonies discussed the sorts of people who inhabited Caribbean settlements. Most of these accounts included some estimate of the islands' populations, as well as an assessment of the relative productivity of each identified group. The figures returned to London often exaggerated the size of colonial populations to underscore the progress being made by the good governance of diligent imperial administrators, all the while stressing their accuracy, usually putting the word *true* somewhere in the title.[35] Charts recording the importation of goods and laborers and exports of staple crops proved that the plantations were orderly and prosperous.[36] As they worked to stress improvements, administrators noted the relative worth of various Europeans and Africans and also made implicit assessments about the utility of men, women, and children. A sharp focus on both labor and defense illuminates the everyday concerns of imperial authorities, just as their discussion of the ability (or not) of various groups to become good colonial subjects belies their ideas about difference and inferiority.

Caribbean governors frequently received correspondence from London demanding to know the composition of island populations and challenging them to make subjective analyses about the worth of island laborers.[37] A typical query requested an assessment of the population and the ability of those present to defend the island: "What numbers of Merchants and Planters—English and Forreigners, Servants and Slaves and how many of them are men able to bear armes?" Additional questions pressed for specificity about the European population and for knowledge about African slaves: "What number of English, Scotch, Irish or Forreignors have for these 7 years last past or any other space of tyme come yearly to Plant and Inhabitt within your Government and also what Blacks or slaves have been brought in within the said tyme and what Rates?"[38] Statistical information regarding the enslaved population mattered for colonial officials, who would use those numbers to legislate their control. Hidden in the quantification was a conflation of the desire to know the numeric landscape of each colony with the need to understand how that terrain affected colonial policies. According to contemporary demographic theories, administrators who connected these two elements of enumeration would become more effective imperial officers.

There was no precise way to count the individuals who lived and labored in the Caribbean, so accounting for the people who inhabited the islands was an impressionistic affair, more art than science. Even those charged with communicating population data to the metropole were aware of the difficulties of ensuring the veracity of their reports. Richard Ligon, who included his assessment of Barbados's population in *A True and Exact History of the Island of Barbados* (1657), acknowledged "it were somewhat difficult to give you an exact account of the number of persons upon the Island." Recognizing this fact did not prevent Ligon from estimating Barbados inhabitants all the same, passing it off as the "true and exact" figure his title proclaimed. He observed that it "has been conjectur'd by those that are long acquainted [with the island] . . . that there are no lesse than 50 thousand soules, besides Negroes."[39] "Conjectur'd" was precisely the right verb to describe Ligon's process: he vastly overstated the numbers of Europeans on Barbados, in all likelihood more than doubling the reality of English success.[40] In 1655 Thomas Povey made a similarly inflated assessment of the enslaved population, noting that the English planters of Barbados "are served with more than 20,000 Negroes."[41] Ligon's and Povey's exaggerations (if colonial officials or others knew it) could be forgiven, for they were all engaged in a process that sought to assess the practices and benefits of colonization. Actual figures that might highlight weaknesses were inconvenient truths.

In 1647, the first surviving questionnaire about Barbados was remitted to London. The account explained that the island's European population consisted of "Inglish, Duch, French, Schots & Irish." In addition, there were about "13,000 Negroes painefull Especially them w[hi]ch come from Angola in color black."[42] "Painefull" here connoted the diligence and assiduousness with which these enslaved Africans labored, indicating that this particular group of laborers worked hard to fulfill the demands of the colony.[43] From the comfort of London, Povey assumed that these laborers were worth the investment, noting that the "20,000 Negroes who subsist merely of the easye fruits of the Earth who by their labour doe rayse 200000lbs sterl. yearly."[44] For him, Africans could be fed with little effort and cost, especially when their prodigious output was taken into consideration.[45] Focusing as it did on the production that resulted, rather than on the expense of supporting such a population, Povey's analysis included a positive assessment of the worth of African laborers, an increasingly popular inclusion in dispatches to London in the decades to come.

Africans were not the only laborers in the Caribbean whose worth had to be assessed. At midcentury the English Caribbean was undergoing a significant demographic shift due to the arrival of those Irish and Scots "sent thither" by Oliver Cromwell. At least as many as ten thousand Irish flooded the Caribbean islands in the 1650s alone. Contemporary reports put the figures higher still, with "12,000 prisoners of warr" arriving in Barbados through the end of the 1650s, the vast majority of whom were from Ireland or Scotland.[46] In 1652, "liberty" (and the promise of a hefty profit) was given to Bristol merchants "Henrie Hazard and Robert Immans . . . to carrie 200 Irishmen from anie port in Ireland to the Caribean Islands."[47] On October 19, 1654, prisoners of war, including those from Ireland, were ordered to be "sent to the Barbadoes, Bermuda or some other of the English plantations in America."[48] And in 1656, twelve hundred men from "Knockfergus in Ireland and Port Patrick in Scotland" were transported to the Americas.[49] Whether the fidelity of these populations could be relied upon was a question that troubled English elites. Counting those who left Ireland or Scotland for Barbados ultimately meant tracking a potentially disloyal and perfidious population into the heart of England's empire.

At the start of the restoration of the Stuart monarchy in England, an anonymous colonial official identified the "severall sorts" of inhabitants of Barbados and arranged them in a hierarchy. "The first and best are the proprietors of the land, whome they call freedhold and who may be effectively five thousand families, the grosse of them are English." Freemen, numbering in the region of five thousand, split equally between English and Scots "and its guessed about one thousand Irish," were listed as the "next sort." They "serve in the country for wages" and "live comfortably." "Christian Servants" followed, numbering around eight thousand men, most of whom, it was alleged, "are Scotts and Irish" sent to Barbados by "the happie success of the Lord Generall Cromwell." At the bottom of the hierarchy came "negroes," who "cannot be lese than twenty thousand who live as absolute slaves to their severall masters."[50] These numbers had important implications following Cromwell's Western Design, when the male, English population of Barbados had been severely depleted as a result of the need to supplement England's forces in Jamaica and Hispaniola. All in all, "for the invasion of the Indies the English took 5,000 men from Barbados."[51] Most of these men had been Protestant English servants, or recent freemen, so their loss seriously affected the ethnic and religious composition of the islands. Desperate for more European servants to replenish the colony's population, English officials were nonetheless wary of embracing non-English servants in their stead.

Though some commentators believed that "people are the foundacon and Improvement of all Plantacons," so that "sending of servants thither" was of utmost importance, authorities disagreed on who precisely should be encouraged to settle the islands.[52] Writers who trusted that the "right sort" of colonists were necessary to create productive settlements were also convinced that the atmosphere in the colonies could be conducive to improving people from less desirable backgrounds.[53] Richard Ligon certainly commented on those European settlers "who began upon small fortunes" but were "now risen to very great and vast estates."[54] Here Ligon hinted at the improvement in status, for some, that could be reached on Barbados. Implicit in his judgment of the island's European population was the promise of advancement and riches that the Caribbean appeared to offer in such abundance to the right sorts of people. Once they had risen in the Americas through their labor, successful indentures were granted their freedom and given land of their own, a stake in colonial society. As a result of these ideas, Barbados planters certainly hoped that "ille wicked and dissolute" Irish and Scots fell into the category of the improvable. In a petition requesting that they pay no customs "for the exportation of necessaries for their subsistence," these planters claimed that they had recently "rendered many thousands of other persons beneficiall to this commonwealth who were noxious whilest they remained [in England, Scotland and Ireland]."[55] Thus, ran the logic, the prisoners of war from Cromwell's expeditions in Ireland and the civil war in England had been remade in the colonies into a better sort of people. In this case, counting the population and surveying and controlling potential malcontents had yielded the desired result, supporting the demographic impulses of colonial officials, who could congratulate themselves that their policies were having a positive effect.

On closer inspection of the records, it seems that while English officials in the Caribbean believed the Scots to be capable of improvement, they were not as confident about the malleability of Irish laborers. The ideas that underpinned parliamentary debates in the metropole hinting that Scots were considered the equal of English indentures appeared to have traversed the Atlantic. A 1667 report sang Scottish praises. "Christian Servants" (in particular Scots) were described as "the nerves and sinews" of a plantation, noted for being "excellent Planters & good Souldiers." The language employed here was targeted: by using a discourse that highlighted the corporeality of the plantation system, the author emphasized the integral importance of Scottish servants to the health of England's imperial project. Nerves and sinews formed essential components in a functioning body; Scottish servants were therefore important signifiers of the island's health and strength. Indeed, the Scots' presence meant that Barbados was now in so "formidable" a position that English colonial officials believed the threat of slave insurrection to be seriously reduced. In 1677, Christopher Jeaffreson, a planter on St. Christopher, concurred, noting that on his island "Scotchmen and Welchmen we esteem the best servants; and the Irish the worst, many of them being good for nothing but mischief."[56] Scottish settlement in the colonies also protected the islands against "invasion from a forraigne Enemy."[57] Unspoken, but crucial to the final part of this calculation, was the Protestantism of the Scots, which would allow these servants to act as a buffer against an internal enemy: Irish Catholics. Governor William Willoughby recorded the reasons for his preferences more directly: "I am for the downright Scot," he wrote to Charles II, "who, I am certain will fight without a crucifix about his neck."[58]

If the Scots contributed to the health of English islands, the Irish threatened to bring disease to the body politic. Ideas about the inherently problematic nature of Irish Catholics arose from both pervasive ideas about Irish inferiority and an interimperial context that suggested that Irish Catholics operated as a fifth column in the heart of the English colonies, willing to side with Spain or France at any given moment.[59] Safe in London, Thomas Povey might have been willing to categorize the Irish as "Christian Servants," but colonial officials in the Caribbean were more resistant to that classification. Governor Willoughby, in his correspondence with administrators in London, was most vociferous in expressing his disdain for Irish servants. In a 1667 report to the Privy

Council he argued that the Lords should "offer a trade with Scotland for transporting people of that nation hither, and prevent any excess of Irish in the future."[60] In 1675 he lamented to the Lords of Trade and Plantations that while Barbados had once been "plentifully furnished with Christian servants from England & Scotland . . . now wee can get few English having no lands to give them at the end of their time." Worse, Willoughby concluded, "Nor have wee many Scotch servants." Instead, Irish servants . . . of small value" continued to flood into the island.[61] Refusing to include the Irish in the category "Christian," Willoughby attacked them on two fronts: first they were religiously suspect; second, they were of "small value" as laborers. The island may have had regenerative effects on some who were "Barbadosed," but for Willoughby the Irish were not counted among those capable of change.

The exaggeration of population statistics in the third quarter of the seventeenth century (combined with assessments of the relative worth of island populations) allowed colonial officials and commentators to demonstrate their good governance of Caribbean islands. But in creating their discourse of improvement, colonial officials were also articulating clear divisions between groups of laborers on the islands. In one category lay those who might become the equals of English subjects. The Scots were a prime example of a formerly recalcitrant population who had been successfully transformed by good English management, despite an environment that was seen as morally and physically deleterious. Africans too held a defined position—officials believed them to be the best of laborers, well suited to the tropical conditions of island sugar plantations, even though a variety of prejudices led them to these conclusions. And despite their place as productive workers, enslaved Africans were also considered property whose status was fixed. The Irish, however, were more difficult to classify. Sometimes they were included in improvable categories, but most often they were locked outside such definitions. As the 1670s came to a close, the Lords of Trade and Plantations demanded an ever-more-exact enumeration of their Caribbean populations. The census returns that resulted continued to obfuscate the problem of Irish Catholics even as they purported to do away with subjective analyses of the worth of island inhabitants altogether.

The Political Anatomy of Caribbean Colonies

In the years 1678 and 1679 the governors and lieutenant governors of Barbados and the Leeward Islands set in motion an accounting of their island populations at a level of accuracy heretofore unseen in the English Caribbean. For the first time, colonial officials attempted to take a precise head count of the population. Responding to demands from the Lords of Trade and Plantations, William Stapleton ordered a comprehensive census in the Leeward Islands that he returned to London in June 1678.[62] Governor Jonathan Atkins instructed officials to begin a similar enumeration in Barbados in 1679.[63] As with William Petty's Down Survey in Ireland, the accuracy of these censuses was questionable, and the supposed objectivity and exactness they claimed were suspect. But the numbers nonetheless had the effect of persuading census analysts that the population had been counted with some degree of precision.[64]

Census making and taking created an idealized elite vision of the Lesser Antilles, one that served to obscure the complex and murky realities of island life. The documents reduced colonial administrators' anxieties about defense and ignored or minimized categories that highlighted the vulnerability of the colonies. More importantly, censuses reveal what English officials, especially those in the Caribbean, thought were important categories to count: who held the land and how many bodies labored upon those plantations. Labor was, after all, central to the colonial endeavor. Without labor, sugar could not be planted, tended, harvested, and processed. Without sugar, the colonies would cease to be productive places, no longer adding vast wealth to the English crown's coffers. Demonstrating the healthy size of their labor force and an ability to keep that force in check was a key goal of colonial officials' counting.

The militarization of the arrangement of the census highlights the ways that colonial elites viewed their mission on the islands, as well as the importance of protection to their success. Counting European men was important beyond their status as property holders because their presence was vital to the security of the colonies. The Barbados census of 1680 recorded the members of the militia, both foot and horse, and the divisions in the Leeward Islands census were arranged according to military division, not parish. The inclusion of these categories, as evidence of a militia ready and able to defend the colony against attack, served to allay concerns about internal and external threats, whether real or imagined. On Barbados challenges to the colonial regime seemed especially potent given the attempted revolt by so-called Cormantee slaves that had taken place in 1675, just one year after Governor Atkins arrived on the island, and the repercussions of the Popish Plot to depose Charles II three years later.[65] Levels of anxiety about the potential for slave revolts were closely linked to the census reports, which laid out in stark terms how many

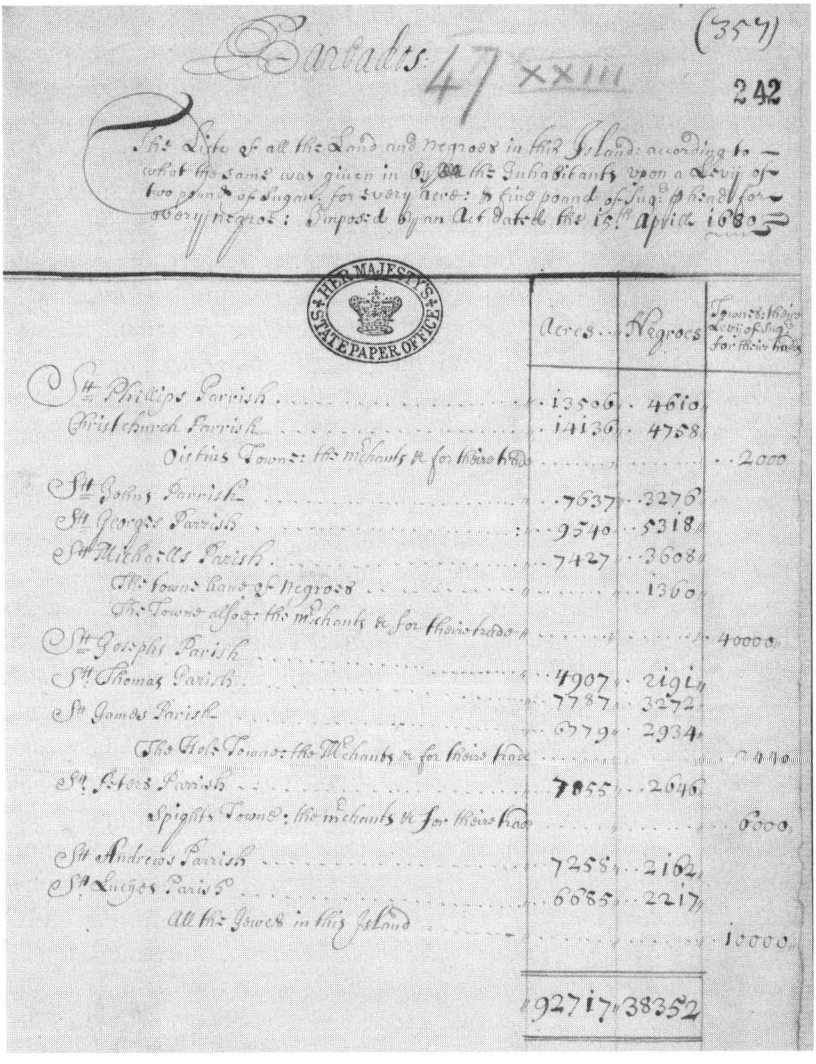

Barbadoes 47 XXIII (357) 242

The Liste of all the Land and Negroes in this Island: according to what the same was given in By the Inhabitants upon a Levy of two pound of Sugar for every acre: & five pound of Sugar p head for every negroe: Imposed by an Act dated the 15th April 1680

	Acres	Negroes	Townes: theire Levy of Sugar for theire trade
St Phillips Parish	13506	4610	
Christchurch Parish	14136	4758	
Oistins Towne: the merchants &c for theire trade			2000
St Johns Parish	7637	3276	
St Georges Parish	9540	5318	
St Michaells Parish	7427	3608	
The towne hand of Negroes		1360	
The Towne alsoe: the merchants &c for theire trade			40000
St Josephs Parish			
St Thomas Parish	4907	2191	
	7787	3272	
St James Parish	6779	2934	
The Hole Towne: the Merchants &c for theire trade			2440
St Peters Parish	7055	2646	
Spights Towne: the merchants &c for theire trade			6000
St Andrews Parish	7258	2162	
St Lucyes Parish	6685	2217	
All the Jewes in this Island			10000
	92717	38352	

FIGURE 4. A summary of the Barbados Census, 1680, with emphasis on land, enslaved Africans, and sugar levies. CO1/44 f. 242. Image reproduced by permission of The National Archives, London.

black bodies were present as a permanent reminder of their threat to the white hierarchy.

Precise figures on a page allowed officials like William Stapleton in the Leeward Islands to make the kinds of mathematical calculations that provided the illusion of security. The systematic method of turning people into numbers had the effect of veiling the threat posed by holding such vast proportions of the islands' populations, whether enslaved Africans or indentured Irish Catholics, in various kinds of bondage. For example, laws were passed encouraging planters to ensure a ratio of one white person for every ten enslaved Africans—on the racial (and racist) calculation that one white body would be sufficient to control ten black bodies, an assumption that both underscored the inherent power dynamic in slavery and implied the inferiority of African-descended peoples.[66] Of course, taking careful note of these numbers could backfire. As Governor Atkins discovered, reporting that the number of men available to fight in the militia was only slightly more than half the number expected by the Lords of Trade and Plantations did not instill confidence in his governance in the metropole.[67] Numbers that should have provided comfort could be sources of anxiety if calculations did not add up favorably.

The risks of incorporating potentially rebellious groups into otherwise trustworthy island populations gave English officials particular pause when it came to Irish Catholics. On Barbados, census takers reduced the visibility of the threat simply by ignoring the Irish presence. Ethnicity was not included as a category in the 1680 census, even though many Irish were living on the islands, some of them small landowners, like Teague Murfee.[68] Murfee's name appears in the entries for St. Peter's Parish, in the northern part of Barbados. Although his Irish status was not noted, his position as landowner records information about his property. He is listed as occupying five acres of land and having five "negroes" in his household.[69] The author of the census is unknown, and it is unclear how he determined what evidence to record and what to omit. Murfee's will, however, is extant. It reveals that he was married to Katherine, had one daughter, Margarett, and had a granddaughter fathered by his recently deceased son, James. The names of the enslaved people he owned are also recorded: Franke, Judy, Loggen, Sheela, and Maria. But whoever was responsible for the St. Peter's census did not think that these were specifics worth noting.[70] Other Irish landowners with slaves on Barbados included Dermon Mollony in St. Philip, Dermon Conniers in St. Joseph, Patrick Browne and Dennis Murfee in St. Lucy, Daniell Maccoline in St. John, Cornelius Bryan in St. James, and, in the same parish as Teague Murfee, Dinis Sullivan.[71]

Certainly the Lords of Trade and Plantations would have been aware of the substantial Irish population on Barbados, even though there was no evidence of the presence of Irish Catholics in the returns Atkins sent to London. These seemingly conscious omissions highlight the difficulties of systemization in a sprawling and jurisdictionally disconnected empire. Irish men like Murfee were absorbed into the planter hierarchy, hidden among the English planters, their potential for rebellion reduced as Murfee and his cohort were counted *for* the defense of the island, not against it. Other religious categories were similarly elided or disregarded in the Barbados census, thus removing the tensions that existed between denominations. For example, Quakers were not marked as such, though their attempts to avoid service in the militia caused much consternation, resulting in steep fines for Friends who refused to serve.[72] Jewish households in Bridgetown were counted, but individual Jews were not: the entire record was relegated to an appendix, removed even on paper from the pages that listed information about their Christian counterparts.[73]

In the Leeward Islands, Governor Stapleton took a different approach to dealing with Irish populations, openly acknowledging the presence of Irish Catholics. The inclusion of the category "Irish" on the Leeward Islands' census of 1678 made clear to the Lords of Trade and Plantations that there would be no choice but to rely on Irish Catholics for the defense of the islands. Indeed, the addition may have been at the behest of Stapleton, who wished to convince London that his fellow countrymen not only were essential cogs in the colonial machine but could be trusted to serve English interests. Whether English officials felt Catholics capable of loyalty became moot. The census revealed that their numbers were too large to be dismissed, their people too omnipresent to be controlled by Protestant colonists. Although all the islands, save Antigua, had significantly larger white than black populations, the proportion of Irish on each was large enough that they would necessarily have to be included in island militias. Irish Catholics accounted for around 25 percent of the white populations of Nevis, St. Christopher, and Antigua, and a dominating 70 percent on Montserrat.[74]

The composition of a number of households on Montserrat demonstrates the importance of the census material for uncovering unusual patterns among island residents, in this case between Irish men. On the island, household after household in the 1678 census was listed with two men at its head, both names recorded, indicating that this arrangement was not a master-servant relationship but rather a partnership between men of equal economic status.[75] Almost three-fifths of the white male population of Montserrat lived this way, and the vast majority of these men were Irish. Some undoubtedly were married or had children; others may have hired indentured servants or participated in the enslavement

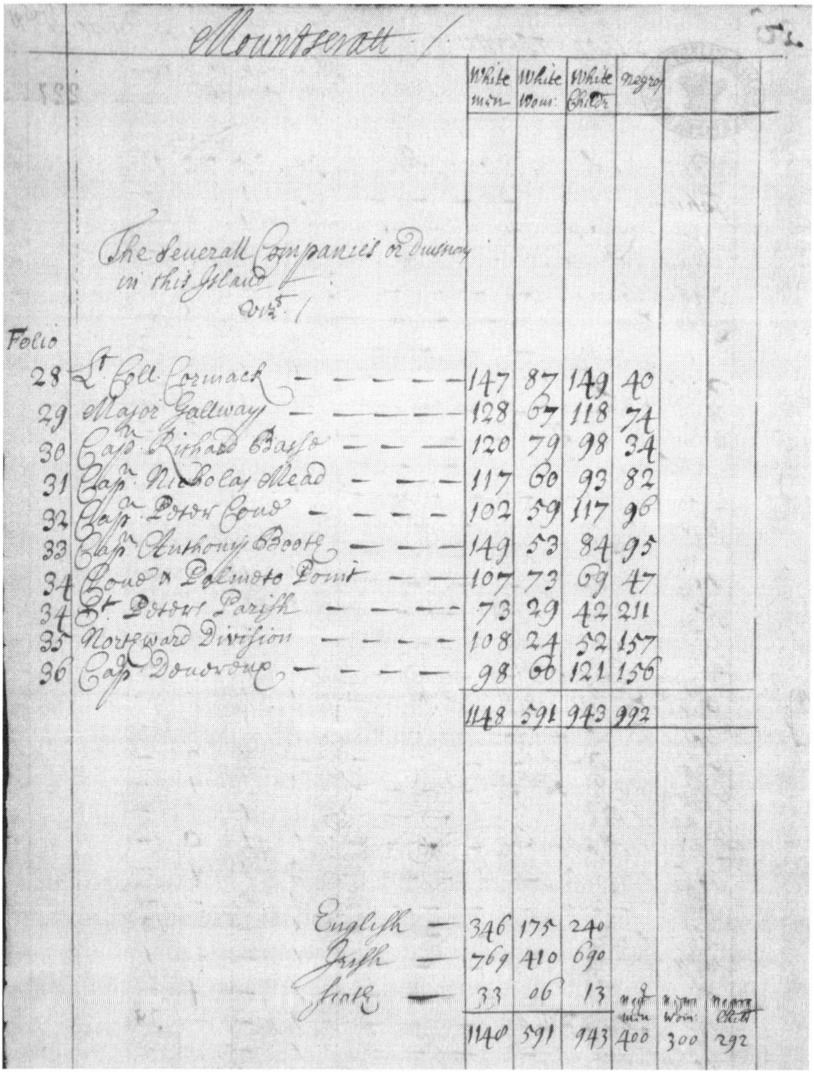

Mountserratt

The Severall Companies or Divisions in this Island Viz^ts

Folio		White men	White Wom:	White Childr	Negroes		
28	Lt Coll Cormack	147	87	149	40		
29	Major Gallway	128	67	118	74		
30	Capt Richard Basse	120	79	98	34		
31	Capt Nicholas Mead	117	60	93	82		
32	Capt Peter Cove	102	59	117	96		
33	Capt Anthony Booth	149	53	84	95		
34	Cove & Palmeto Point	107	73	69	47		
34	St Peters Parish	73	29	42	211		
35	Norteward Division	108	24	52	157		
36	Capt Devereux	98	60	121	156		
		1148	591	943	992		
	English	346	175	240			
	Irish	769	410	690			
	Scots	33	06	13	Negro men	Negro Wom:	Negro Child
		1140	591	943	400	300	292

FIGURE 5. A summary of the Montserrat Census, 1678, with the total numbers of white men, white women, white children, and enslaved Africans for each division included, as well as a breakdown of the total numbers of English, Irish, and Scots on the Island. CO1/42 f. 227. Image reproduced by permission of The National Archives, London.

of Africans. Patrick and Mathew Darcy were brothers who shared land in Colonel Cormack's Division in this manner. The census entry contains little information about the two men. They are named together, but their record, unlike that for some of the larger planters on the island, gives no information as to whether they owned slaves, or were married, or even if any children or women were present in their household at all. The same section of the census lists six households with two English men at their heads that also included two white women and several white children in their domestic unit. This arrangement suggests either that both men were married or that a servant woman was living in the house alongside one couple and their children, with the unmarried man a partner in land ownership. Patrick and Mathew were not included in this group. It does not necessarily follow, however, that both men were single or that they did not own enslaved Africans. At the end of the census, fifty-four white women were listed without any indication of the household to which they belonged. Likewise, 103 white children and forty "negroes old & young of both sexes" were counted but not attributed to any particular dwelling or plantation.[76] Some of these individuals may have been part of Patrick and Mathew's small estate. After all, indentures and enslaved Africans were always present, if not fully absorbed, into the homes of their masters and mistresses. In the Leeward Islands, the division between these groups was quite literal on the census forms, tucked away at the bottom of the returns from each parish, added almost as an afterthought—the important job of noting the names of landowners taking precedent over the recording of any other information.

The inclusion of Irish landowners in the Montserrat returns indicated that perhaps they could be improved. Marking European men as landowners instilled those men with one of the most important markers of early modern masculinity—property—that could be used in life to support their wives and children and in death to provide for future generations. On Montserrat, land was available to more than the very wealthy, thus extending the potential of property ownership to some who had begun their Caribbean careers in the lower echelons of society. Even on Barbados many planters held plots of between only ten and twenty-nine acres.[77] Moreover, land was not the only property that counted: in the Caribbean, property in slaves meant that even the smallest landowner could emulate the elite simply by purchasing a fellow human being, as some of the men in Cormack's Division must have done. The Irish on Montserrat may have lived in somewhat unconventional households in order to achieve a stake in colonial property, but they were now marked as belonging to the most important category on the islands—landowners—and as such were asserting a masculinity understood and recognized by English elites as a marker of belonging to their ranks.

If the recording of landowners was of special importance to census takers, reading the structure of the census can tell us much about how certain groups were ignored or marginalized by colonial officials. Women and children of all sorts were always categorized separately in these reports and were never described in detail. Yet both groups mattered greatly in terms of island demography.[78] Although more Irish men than women entered the colonies, the proportions were much closer than those for English settlers.[79] The enslaved African population was even more balanced: almost as many enslaved women forcibly journeyed across the Atlantic Ocean as enslaved men.[80] Nonetheless, elites recognized neither women nor children as of value to the Caribbean population, even though female indentures and enslaved women labored in the fields alongside their male counterparts.[81] The disregard for women's labor is all the more surprising when considered alongside their reproductive work. Enslaved women "and their increase" literally grew bonded populations, performing labor so important that it was a defining feature of Atlantic slavery.[82]

Details of European women were elided in most enumerations of island populations: these women only sneak into the record occasionally as wives and less often still as property owners in their own right. The inclusion of Honora Burk in the 1678 Montserrat census probably indicated a moment in between spouses for this Irish woman, who was listed along with two "white children" as residing in Palmetto's Division.[83] Perhaps she lived in the town of Plymouth, managing to earn a living in the absence of a spouse by housekeeping for more wealthy settlers. Or she may have worked a small plot of land herself with the aid of her children. The children of European parents (like Burk) were never named and were rarely marked as belonging to a specific household. Burk's experience is unusual because most European women and their children were listed in bulk numbers for each parish, once the details of the heads of household had been recorded, rendering it impossible to tie them to a particular estate or family. These women were considered as surplus to the categories that really mattered: they could neither be bought nor their offspring sold, they performed no military service, and they did not hold positions of imperial authority.

The same kind of elision held for servants (on Barbados) and enslaved Africans across the Caribbean: the categories did not differentiate by sex, simply listing all enslaved Africans, for example, in the column marked "negroes." The effect was to code almost all categories, or at least categories of importance in the census, as male, whatever the reality. Neither women nor children who made up a significant proportion of the total populations of Caribbean islands were counted as individuals.[84] Perhaps because the English considered laboring in the fields to be man's work, and because English planters stated their preference for male slaves, the census also reflected these ideals. Reality, however, did not match preferences. Slave traders, as they worked to empty the holds of their vessels of all captives carried across the Atlantic from Africa, forced planters in Barbados and the Leeward Islands to purchase women and children.[85] Assuming that the servants and slaves who labored on plantations were overwhelmingly male helped officials in the metropole avoid the distasteful idea that their colonial projects were disrupting their ideal gender distinctions. Although women of lower status did perform manual labor in Europe, elite men rarely thought about their actions. Instead they compared the experiences of their own wives (whom they viewed as idle and living a life of ease) to those of African women.[86] Elite men therefore reacted to European women laboring alongside enslaved women as an unnatural corruption, believing that field work was suitable only for barbarous Africans.

Women and children were not the only populations whose inclusion in the census was compromised or contested: other individuals who fit into undesirable categories and thus who threatened careful English differentiations of their island populations were also erased. Both the Barbados and the Leeward Islands censuses failed to categorize people whose biological parents were not of the same category, hiding evidence of sex between Europeans and Africans (or perhaps even, on occasion, Native Americans).[87] In other words, no intermediary categories of race were included in either census. Children of enslaved African women and their European masters disappeared, because of a policy adopted from a Virginia law of 1662 that stated that they would follow the condition of their mothers.[88] In the census, these offspring were hidden in the category "negro children," or perhaps not counted at all. Indeed, their stories emerge only through other archival sources: the census denies their experiences and lives. Thus there is no evidence of John Peers's progeny, even though by 1679 he had fathered four children with enslaved women in Christchurch Parish on Barbados.[89] Neither were the children of enslaved African men and indentured or free European women counted. Ann, the daughter of the unmarked, but presumably English, Mary

Sisnett and "a negro," would have been five years old when the Barbados census was taken, but she does not appear in the records for St. Philip's Parish.[90] English elites no doubt felt uneasy about recognizing the products of sex between English women and African men, given what such liaisons implied about the quality of the woman involved.[91] Similarly, in St. Michael's Parish, free people of color John and Hannah Dally and Charles Cuffee and their children are invisible, hidden by a colonial system that sought to deny that the category of "free negro" could exist.[92] The refusal to acknowledge either intimacy across the color line or the presence of free people of color is an example of English officials' reluctance to complicate categories. Moreover, it demonstrates the resistance to include markers that muddied easy divisions between "negro" and "white," identifiers that were becoming increasingly synonymous with "enslaved" and "free."

The lack of consistency in categories in the various Caribbean censuses demonstrates that even as English officials sought to better regulate island populations they could not create a document that avoided individual interpretation. When Sir William Blathwayt, secretary to the Board of Trade in 1678, read the numbers, he would draw his own conclusions from the information contained in the enumerations. The censuses purported accuracy and objectivity, but authorities subjectively read their contents as explanatory discourses about island productivity and vulnerability. So Blathwayt might have seen the numbers of Irish on Montserrat as a threat, rather than viewing them as essential to the colonial project, as Stapleton appears to have done. Two years later he could have looked at the staggering volume of material that Atkins provided on Barbados and ignored any information that did not jibe with his sense of Barbados as a prosperous sugar-producing island, or he could have read the census as evidence of Atkins's poor management.[93]

The rigidity of census categories forced English ideas about difference to coalesce around an accounting that made landowners and laborers, and therefore whites and blacks, the key distinctions that mattered in the colonies, reflecting in the process the ideology in Petty's *Political Anatomy*. Census taking suggested that categories were distinct and immutable in ways that other forms of differentiating did not. Marking enslaved persons and servants on a census grid as belonging to separate groups was an attempt to make precise distinctions that were not always clearly demarcated in practice, especially in the case of free people of color. Narrowing possible categories allowed officials in the colonies to provide metropolitan authorities with a simple analysis of the populations under their control. It erased potential difficulties caused by the specter of alliances between servants and slaves. In a moment when antipopery in the colonies was rampant, it allowed census readers either to ignore the disturbing presence of Irish Catholics (as in Barbados) or to reconfigure their reputation for being inherently troublesome (in the case of the Leeward Islands), by implying, as Stapleton did, that the Irish had a crucial role to play as loyal subjects in the service of England's colonial enterprise.

* * *

William Petty's desires to render populations knowable and therefore controllable cast a long shadow over the Caribbean. While his goals for Ireland did not come to fruition in the ways he might have hoped, the political arithmetic he advanced did have success of a sort in the colonies. The Scots certainly were believed to have been improved by their experience in the islands and thus came to be considered reliable allies of the English. The Irish fell between categories, sometimes counted, sometimes not, almost always treated with suspicion, the question of their improvement in the Caribbean, as in Ireland, apparently left open. Africans, the central labor force in the colonies, were never considered capable of moving beyond their bonded status. The best that the English could hope for the enslaved was that they would not disturb the peace and that they would continue to be loyal laborers. As time progressed, the census took on forms that reflected these realities.

Perhaps Petty's most far-reaching influence can be found on Montserrat, where a 1730 enumeration of the island's population was titled "The Political Anatomy of Montserrat," mimicking the title of his treatise on Ireland.[94] Unlike the 1678 census, the collators of the "Political Anatomy" did not mark the ethnicity of the heads of household whose names they recorded. But Irish names—Lynch, Kelly, Blake, French, Daly, Gallway— abound in the lists of the colony's propertied inhabitants.[95] Montserrat's "Political Anatomy" was also dissected in greater detail than any previous census in the Caribbean. For each of the four districts—St. Anthony's, St. Patricks', St. George's, St. Peter's—over thirty-one columns were painstakingly filled in, as well as the "names and quality" of each head of household and that person's trade. Additional categories included the kinds of buildings on an estate and the number of men, women, children, servants, and slaves (old and young, men and women, boys and girls). Administrators noted the division of land into acres devoted to sugar,

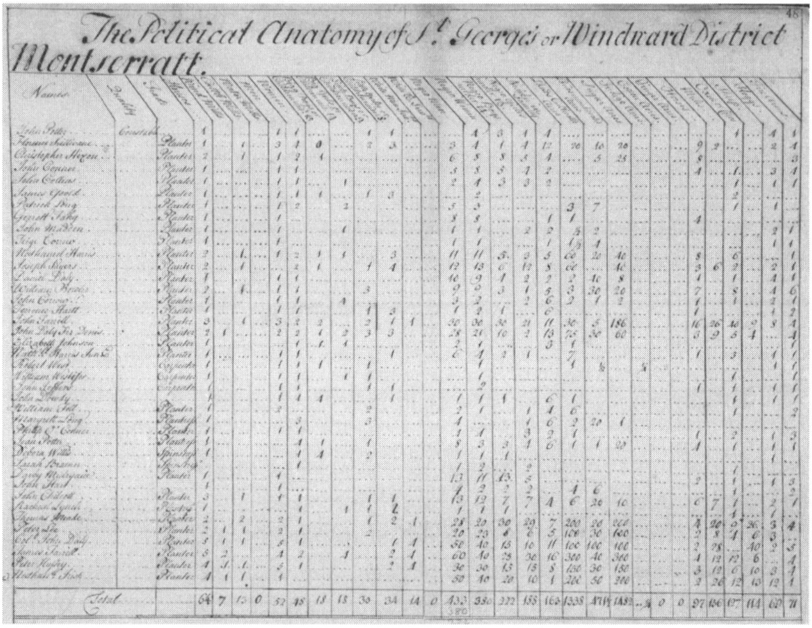
The Political Anatomy of St. George's or Windward District Montserratt.

Total

FIGURE 6. The Political Anatomy of Montserrat, St. George's District, 1730. EXT1/258. The thirty-one columns demonstrate the proliferation of categories counted in the census by the eighteenth century. Image reproduced by permission of The National Archives, London.

indigo, cotton, or ginger, as well as counting some of the livestock. And in a nod to the underlying question of security, the final two columns recorded the number of "fire armes" and "swords" that could be placed in the hands of loyal subjects at times of internal or external conflict. As Britain's Caribbean venture grew, so did the need for knowledge about its imperial holdings. The eighteenth-century accounting of Montserrat reflected its status as a full-fledged slave society, noting its productivity and also its readiness to defend itself against either poor Irish malcontents or the majority slave population of the island.

The process of taking the colonial census affected the people being counted too. Perhaps only landowners were aware of the statistical details recorded—it is possible that servants or enslaved people had little idea of the extent to which their lives were enumerated and categorized. But it seems impossible that they would have been entirely ignorant of the process. They may have seen the churchwardens move from plantation to plantation as they collected information, or they may have overheard their masters and mistresses discussing the census, for such a large operation would surely have been a subject of much conversation and debate among island property holders. The elision of the breadth of experiences present in the early modern English Caribbean in the census poses a problem for historians too. How do scholars get past these census reports whose goal is to erase relationships or remove some of the people who lived and labored on the islands? Asking how enslaved Africans and Irish Catholics viewed difference may be one way of accessing information not contained in the census. Making categories in the colonies was, after all, not an exclusively English affair, even if others who were involved in the process considered their actions to be about finding connections or marking boundaries among and between groups rather than explicitly engaging discourses about difference.

* * *

Cornelius Bryan was pleased when the churchwarden approached his "Mansion House," in St. James. He had expected someone to come and check on the particulars of his plantation—all of Holetown was abuzz with the news that a census of Barbados was being taken. After ensuring that his guest was offered some refreshment (for it was tiring work in the heat of the day to move from plantation to plantation), Cornelius explained proudly that he was settled on fourteen acres of land. The churchwarden asked him about his laborers, carefully noting as Cornelius replied that one hired servant, one indentured servant, and nine negroes were working his sugar estate. Cornelius did not think to provide the names of these servants and slaves, and it did not occur to him that the churchwarden had not asked for those details. Bryan did offer that he had a wife and children, but the churchwarden informed him that those specifics were of little consequence to his current assignment. What did need to be recorded, however, was Cornelius's contribution to the island's defenses. Cornelius was glad that he was able to confirm that he was in Lieutenant Thomas Maxwell's "Troope of Horse." He always felt nervous when talking with English officials, and he hoped that the churchwarden would not mention his infrequent appearances on Sundays at St. James's Church for services. Perhaps, Cornelius reflected, his brogue was enough to quell those kinds of intrusions. He felt quite satisfied with how the meeting had gone as the churchwarden bade him farewell and moved onto the next plantation.

Old Pegg was in the kitchen beyond the main house when the visitor called. She was summoned to provide the stranger with something cooling to drink, and she was glad that she had prepared a beverage with oranges and sugar a few days earlier. Old Pegg had heard some talk that there was to be an accounting of all the people who lived on Barbados, and she wondered if her name would be recorded, and whether they would want to know about her daughter, and namesake, Pegg. She noticed that her master simply mentioned that he had nine negroes without providing names or their connections to each other. And the visitor seemed equally uninterested in that kind of information. She smiled a little when she heard that the wives and children of planters were also of little consequence in these calculations. What strange men were these who ruled the island. What did they think this information they so desperately sought could possibly tell them about the people who lived here when they did not bother to record the kin and family connections that were most important? With the visitor's last question, Old Pegg thought she knew what was really going on. These white men were still so worried about that slave revolt—no wonder they wanted to check whether her master was active in the militia. As the visitor walked out of the house toward the next plantation satisfied with the knowledge he had so carefully recorded, Old Pegg reflected that he had really learned nothing at all.

"To live in perpetuall noise and hurry": Creating
Communities on Caribbean Plantations

In the summer of 1670, Phillip Cheeke, a merchant from England, took
an inventory of his property in the parish of St. Joseph on the island of
Barbados. Bally Tree Hall was a substantial estate. The plantation covered 240 acres. It contained a "dwelling house" furnished with a variety
of luxury goods, a full sugar works (including a windmill, a "boyling
house," a still, a rum cellar, a drying house, and a "Smitths Shopp"), "16
head of meate cattle," eleven "Christian Servants" who were all men, and
"Seaventy two Negroes," including thirty-four men, twenty-nine women,
and nine children.[1] Cheeke's plantation marked him as one of the larger
landowners on Barbados, but in many ways his estate was representative
of the kinds of properties that dotted the soft rolling hills of the island.[2]
At Bally Tree Hall servants and slaves cultivated sugarcane, processing
the ripened crop into both soft, brown, unrefined muscovado sugar and
rum. Cheeke's estate inventory broke down the realities of plantation life
into their constituent parts: "5 prs of canvas drawers" that enslaved Africans would wear in the fields; "8 musketts, 2 blunderbusses, 2 prs of pis
tolls . . . 7 swords with sheaths" for Cheeke or his overseers to maintain
order and control on the plantation; "3 scimmers" that laborers would use
to remove impurities from the refining sugar; and countless other "nec-
essaryes" for the running of the estate. The list of property gives shape
to life on Caribbean plantations; Irish men John Dole, Daniel Dory, and
the other servants headed down to the sugar fields in the morning with
Harry, Giles, Eve, Nanne, Mingo, Jupiter, Ancumma, Caliban, and the

other enslaved Africans who lived and labored on the plantation. They returned together to their homes at night. Between sunup and sundown they worked alongside one another in Cheeke's fields; in the evening they ate, drank, and perhaps even slept together.

Plantations were central to both the construction and the maintenance of hierarchies in the English Caribbean. Estates like Bally Tree Hall were supposed to reinforce developing racial and status differences, with planters ensuring obedience from their laborers through constant supervision and the ever-present threat of violence.[3] On sugar plantations, enslaved Africans and indentured servants were intended to perform analogous functions: they were collectively responsible for the planting, harvesting, and processing of sugarcane.[4] However, they understood, or would come to understand, that their status was not the same, that their positions were not equivalent. It was in that lack of equality that tensions emerged. Over time, indentured servants could become free, as their terms expired: no such official path to freedom was available to enslaved Africans. Nonetheless, for the time that they were all in the fields, or in the boiling houses together, they had to reckon with one another and find ways to endure, if not enjoy, one another's proximity. The connections they made are concealed within records like the Bally Tree Hall inventory, sources whose dry iterations of goods, buildings, machinery, livestock, and laborers work to obscure the vibrant communities forged on plantations.

Uncovering the relationships made by workers requires a new reading of sources like plantation inventories as much for what they do not include as for what was recorded in their production. For example, Cheeke's accounting of his Bally Tree Hall property is a sterile list of buildings, objects, and people that is not even comprehensive, in spite of its seeming attention to detail. Through what he chose to leave out, Cheeke provides a sense of the kinds of circumstances, relationships, and people that planters either believed not worthy of comment or actively chose to elide. In the same way, wills, deeds, Colonial Office records, and the accounts of European travelers and priests all provide fragments of a story about plantation life that, when collected into a whole, provide a rich and layered picture of what it meant to be a laborer in the seventeenth-century Caribbean, even though when read individually each source is found lacking. Only by paying attention to the absences in these sources can the contributions of servants and slaves—their labor, their knowledge, their skills, and their experiences—be seen and understood. Most importantly, shining a light on what exactly everyday life on sugar plantations entailed can produce a more nuanced view of the relationships forged between laborers.

The Caribbean plantation was founded on an oppressive culture of control that servants and slaves had to learn to navigate. English planters, as they worked through their own ideas about difference, hoped to instill a separation between indentured servants and enslaved Africans when it came to their everyday interactions.[5] Reality was more complicated. English ideas about how to distinguish between the people who occupied those two categories were not necessarily adopted by servants and slaves themselves. In the work they did, the violence they suffered, the food they ate, the clothes they wore, and the ways they lived and loved, enslaved Africans (from regions including the Bight of Biafra, the Bight of Benin, and the Gold Coast in the second half of the seventeenth century) and indentured servants (some English, some Scots, most Irish) created alternative ways of relating to one another.[6] Exploring these practices and interactions does not simply bring servants and slaves more fully into view; it demonstrates the co-constitutive process of figuring difference in the early Caribbean as laborers responded to elite attempts to define their place in plantation society.

This chapter explores everyday life on plantations to understand how servants and slaves built a sense of difference separate from those divisions constructed by English elites. The mundane and the repetitious acts that characterized living and laboring on plantations and the intimacy that such proximity created are the key to understanding the connections that laborers made with one another. Spooning soup from a common pot, sharing a blanket, walking together after a hard day's work—these moments made up their daily lives. The nuances that inhabit these spaces of routine demonstrate how the developing race-based hierarchy in the Caribbean was nowhere near as concrete as planters wished. It was in the everyday that the power structures that shaped plantation society were created and sustained, but it was also in these intimate moments that laborers negotiated and made sense of the world in which they lived. Although there may not have been an "emergence of new modes of power" as a result of these interactions between indentured servants and enslaved Africans, the "ruptures" caused by their actions expose alternative, but equally important, structures on plantations.[7] The members of these groups did not need to escape the dominant plantation order; rather they deflected its power in order to create communities of their own and to offer different explanations for their lives.[8]

"All houres of the day and night"

For planters the production of sugar was the means to make profit and maintain their elite status. Considerable political power could be wielded by the men with the most land, but even those with relatively few acres and only a handful of enslaved Africans or indentured servants to tend their crops were marked as members of an elite. Being part of the planter class connoted a certain level of prestige, whatever the size of one's estate. For laborers the production of sugar signified backbreaking work and constant danger—from an accident with a machete in the field, from boiling syrup in the sugar works, or through violence at the hands of a master or overseer. In never-ending cycles enslaved Africans and indentured servants planted cane, weeded fields, harvested the crop, and processed sugar. These repetitive tasks required a great deal of synchronicity, and the cooperation necessitated by such demands pushed laborers on plantations to forge bonds with one another. As workers, they became intimately aware of their commodification: the human elements of a brutal and horrifyingly efficient machine reduced to a financial value.[9] These same roles meant that servants and slaves found themselves in positions of confluence and sympathy that planters would have preferred them to avoid.[10]

The proximities of servant and slave life can be clearly seen in Caribbean plantation inventories. At Bally Tree Hall plantation eleven "Christian" servants worked and lived alongside seventy-two "negroes."[11] On Rice Williams's estate in St. Philip, Cambridge, Pedester, Bashan, and Pugg (all slaves) labored in concert with servants Mary and Bette and Mary's unnamed child.[12] Meanwhile John Ham worked the married enslaved couple Charles and Daddy and the Irish servant Thomas Burke together on his St. James plantation, while in St. John slaves Doll, Marea, Cassy, and Jack and two servants toiled on Christopher Estwicke's land.[13] In these smaller, more intimate, settings it would be impossible for servants and slaves not to interact and willingly or grudgingly collaborate. Indeed, on estates with few acres they might also have worked alongside their masters. Laborers arrived in the Caribbean via different ships, but on plantations their experiences as unfree workers were recognized as equally essential to their owners' success, because "the chiefest Stock of a Planter, consists in his Servants and Slaves."[14] Masters concentrated their distinctions between bonded labor and the owners of that labor, making the lives of servants and slaves more closely resemble each other's than they did the lives of those in the planter class.

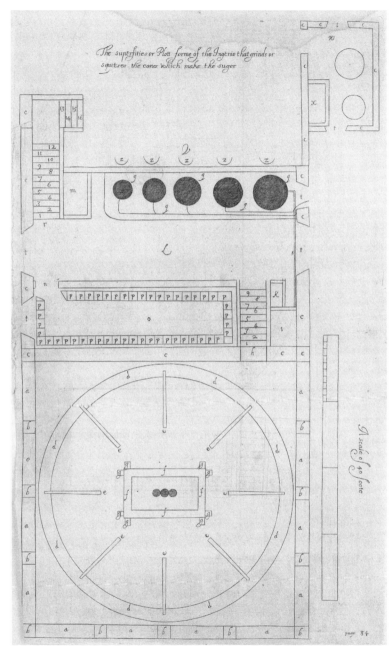

The superfities or Plott forme of the Ingenio that grinds or squizes the canes which make the suger

A scale of 40 foote

page 84

FIGURE 7. Richard Ligon's drawing of a sugar "ingenio," in *A True and Exact History of the Island of Barbados* (1657). Courtesy of the John Carter Brown Library at Brown University.

At Bally Tree Hall, as on plantations across the English Caribbean, sugar provided Phillip Cheeke with the means to furnish his plantation house with the fine goods that announced to any visitor his high standing among island elites. The parlor tables and chairs, "2 carpetts," "pewter dishes," three beds, counterpanes, curtains, and the other furniture and comestibles with which he adorned his home were purchased (at very high prices for luxury imports) with his sweet crop's profits. The central importance of sugar was clear in the detail with which Cheeke recorded all aspects of its production in his estate inventory.[15] The size of his operation attested to the crop's vital role in his economic well-being. First, sugar became profitable through the systems of production that transformed the cane to molasses or crystalline form. The windmill was "compleated with timber, tried & squared for the major part," and included "Rowlers, Carts for Cogg wheeles, &c." The boiling house comprised "8 Sugar Coppers, 1 refining copper, 2 brasse Collers" in which the sugar was heated, and "3 ladles, 3 scimmers" for removing impurities that rose to the top of the vessels. A variety of other materials as well as a range of weights and measures were also included as implements key to processing sugar. In the "Curing House" there were over one thousand pairs of "potts and dipps," as well as various tools for managing sugarcane, and the Still House included "4 stills," "4 wormes" (for boring into sugar cones), "6 cisterns &c," "Bills" for cutting the cane and "Howes" for preparing the ground for planting.[16] These were the necessary tools and equipment for the successful production of sugar and rum on a large Caribbean plantation. But beyond wind power, the production of these machines and instruments was made possible only by the work of unfree laborers. Cheeke's seventy-two enslaved Africans and eleven indentured servants were equally essential pieces of "property." They would ensure that the production of sugar never waned on his 240-acre plantation and that all of the steps in the refining process occurred efficiently and precisely, with the aim of achieving maximum profit.

The enslaved Africans and indentured servants on Cheeke's plantation viewed the estate inventory in a very different light. To them, the lists of tools and equipment were more than an accounting of a set of inanimate objects. The implements connected laborers to the production of sugar in extremely intimate ways. The "Bills" that were used to cut ripe canes "about six inches from the ground" connoted the constant bending and straightening necessary to harvest the crop, as well as the reminder that the sharp tops of the six-foot

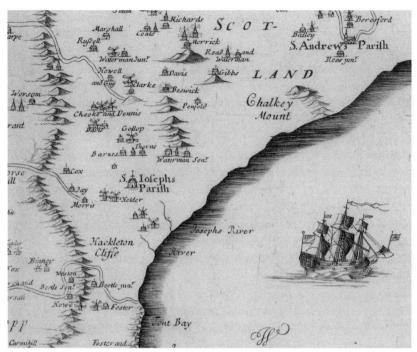

FIGURE 8. Bally Tree Hall Plantation in St. Joseph's Parish, marked here as "Cheeke and Dennis" with two windmills clearly visible. Detail from Richard Ford's 1675 map of Barbados. Courtesy of the John Carter Brown Library at Brown University.

canes had to be safely removed.[17] The "Howes" needed to prepare the ground for planting reminded the enslaved of "a small trench of six inches broad" in which they laid canes end to end so they would sprout within a few months. These tools would also be used to assist in weeding the canes, which (as they matured) became "rough and sharp in the sides" and so would "cut the skins of the Negres" as they worked: "for their bodies, leggs, and feet, being uncloathed and bare," they could not work in the fields "without smart and losse of blood."[18] For plantation owners, these tools ensured an efficient rate of production and a better yield in the fields. For workers, they represented discomfort and pain seemingly without end, as the regular annual harvests of old worlds transformed into a continuous cycle of crop production in the Caribbean.

Neither did the description of the windmill at Bally Tree Hall mention that when the wind was calm two slaves would have to harness "five

Oxen or Horses" to the machinery. The inventory remained silent on the need for "a *Negre*" to feed "the Canes of one side," where "rollers draw them down to the other side," to ensure that all the juice from the cane squeezed out and was collected.[19] The record ignored, too, the young "Negre girles" who removed these flattened canes, carrying them to a large pile by the mill, a task probably performed by Mary, Bess, Joane, and Sue on Cheeke's estate.[20] These kinds of labor required coordination between workers. Harry and Mingo had to work in tandem to guarantee that the pace at which they set the oxen matched the speed with which Mary, Bess, Joane, and Sue removed the crushed sugar stalks. Their rhythm also had to be synchronized with that of the field gangs who cut the canes to ensure that none of the precious crop was spoiled. While Cheeke was careful to note the constituent parts of his property, the very acts that required cooperation between servants and slaves were hidden; these come to light only when we consider the means through which sugar was produced and processed.[21] The dry inventory also masks the decision making, knowledge, and control exerted by servants and slaves as they performed these agricultural tasks.

The inventory for Bally Tree Hall also almost completely obscures the dangers of life on plantations. There is no indication that the work of feeding the canes into the grinder was so hazardous that enslaved people risked losing digits, limbs, or even their lives. It was entirely possible for "a mill feeder [to] be catch't by the finger, his whole body . . . drawn in, and he is squeez'd to pieces."[22] Neither did Cheeke's list impart the hard slog entailed by the long hours that enslaved and indentured laborers worked producing sugar. In the fields, laborers worked from six in the morning until eleven, and then again from one o'clock to six in the evening, being called to and from the fields by the tolling of a bell, and being under overseers' instructions at all times.[23] The use of bells to mark important moments in the day was common in early modern Europe, but while drums may have functioned in a similar fashion in West African societies, it seems likely that indentured servants found it easier to adapt to being called to and from the fields than their enslaved counterparts.[24] The modest two-hour break in the middle of the long day was rarely observed. One commentator imagined that if laborers on a sugar plantation were asked, they would confess that few planters "will admit us above half that time, but hurry us back to work, which proves very injurious to our Health."[25]

Plantation records give the impression of an agricultural factory with the close attention paid to machinery and tools, but they do not reveal the accelerated pace of production at harvest time. To prevent the cane rotting, and to ensure the highest possible yield, the severed sugar stalks had to be sent through the boiling houses within less than forty-eight hours of being cut.[26] This necessity meant that laborers were "forc'd to work so long at the Wind-Mills" that they became "Weary, Dull, Faint, Heavy and Sleepy." Imagining the perspective of an enslaved laborer working under such conditions, Englishman Thomas Tryon noted the effects of exhaustion: "Oft times our Hands and Arms are crusht to pieces, and sometimes most part of our Bodies."[27] While the machines themselves posed dangers, the circumstances under which laborers processed the sugar magnified the threat of disfigurement.

The only piece of information on the Bally Tree Hall inventory that hints at the dangers of plantation life is the inclusion of an enslaved woman named "One Hand" in the list of laborers on the estate. She most likely had worked as a grinder on the plantation and had suffered the loss of her hand as a result of an accident at the sugar works, with her name marking the horrific event.[28] In this world of heavy labor, One Hand's disfigurement brought little attention and attested to the commonplace occurrence of injuries on large sugar plantations. But her fellow workers would have understood her injury, and its meaning both for her life and for the work she could perform, in ways that Cheeke could not. For the ambitious planter, the worth of One Hand was no doubt diminished by her maiming, both in the real monetary value of her physical body and in relation to the more abstract question of her ability to continue to achieve high levels of production. The servants and slaves she worked alongside would have read One Hand's appearance in other ways. Many would have been glad that they had not suffered the same fate. Those who worked similar tasks to One Hand would have had to toil harder to make up for her deficiencies and so may have resented her for causing them to have to perform additional labor. They may even have used the name One Hand as a reminder, a punishment for the woman, and a way to distance themselves from the chance that the same accident could happen to them. One Hand may have been seen as somehow deserving of her fate, perhaps for being careless or for not being quick enough to avoid danger. Others would have shied away from the moniker that further dehumanized the woman, preferring instead to call her by her original name. They would have tended to her disfigured body, taken responsibility for nursing her back to health, perhaps even saved her life in the moments following the accident: someone must have intervened to cut off her hand to prevent her from being pulled further into the rollers. But all of these possibilities are obscured by the sterile plantation inventory.

FIGURE 9. This image depicts the cycle of sugar production on a Martinique plantation in the middle of the seventeenth century. Such scenes were common across the Caribbean. In the background the canes are cut and carried to the Mill by slaves. As two slaves feed the canes into the grinders, another drives oxen to rotate the cylinders that will crush the canes. The resulting liquid moves through a trough into the sugar works itself where two enslaved Africans supervise the boiling process and skim impurities from the tops of the vats. Overseeing the whole enterprise is a single European man armed with a gun. Jean Baptiste du Tertre, *Histoire Generale des Antilles* (Paris, 1667). Courtesy of the John Carter Brown Library at Brown University.

Evidence of the extreme pace of work necessary to keep the plantation functioning efficiently was hidden in other ways: the list entry of the eight sugar coppers could never convey the round-the-clock labor necessary to boil sugar. There is no reason to expect that conditions on Bally Tree Hall were any different from those taking place on other Barbados estates. Tryon noted that the work went on "from Munday morning at one a clock, till Saturday night, (at which time the fire in the Furnaces are put out) all houres of the day and night, with fresh supplies of Men, Horses, and Cattle." On the larger plantations, like Bally Tree Hall, "there [were] six or seven large Coppers or Furnaces kept perpetually boyling" during the week.[29] Molten liquid moved from cistern to cistern, for "the more Coppers it passeth through, the finer and purer it is." Part of the refining process was to remove impurities in the liquid from the top of the coppers using the ladles and skimmers that Cheeke carefully located in the boiling house. With such superheated syrup all around, and with servants and slaves working such long hours, here too lurked considerable dangers. Standing for days in "hot sulpherous Fumes" could result in fatigued workers falling "into the fierce boyling Syrups."[30] Observers noted that "if a Boyler gets any part into the scalding Sugar, it sticks like Glew, or Birlime, and 'tis hard to save either Limb or Life."[31]

To work in a sugar mill was "to live in perpetuall Noise and Hurry." The planter had to carefully control the cycle of production, which never waned, "the whole season of making sugar" lasting almost six months out of every year.[32] Again, as elsewhere, all of this work had to be coordinated, requiring enormous cooperation among and between workers. Servants were often given the position of master boiler, just as Irish sugar boiler James Hanley was on Jacob English's plantation.[33] But one of the more skilled enslaved men could have also held that position, if forever denied the title of "master." Servants and slaves might feed into working patterns dictated by plantation owners. But as they were the ones performing the labor, they no doubt knew the best practices to ensure efficiency. Laborers therefore looked at the means of sugar production in different ways. Servants might have admired the efficiency of the machinery and might have been attentive to how it functioned because they dreamt of profiting from that very system after their terms of indenture came to an end. Enslaved workers would have found it difficult to see these kinds of possibilities. They had to be mindful of how the equipment worked, not because they would one day be able to use the sugar works to their advantage, but because not having knowledge increased the chance of being maimed. For enslaved laborers, plantation apparatus indicated a never-ending cycle of pain and suffering.[34]

Laboring to convert cane into valuable muscovado sugar was not the only part of the profit-making process on sugar estates. Bally Tree Hall was typical of Barbados plantations in that its inventory included rum-making equipment and storage facilities. Nothing was put to waste — impurities skimmed from the boiling house coppers could be turned into valuable liquor.[35] Rum allowed Cheeke an additional avenue for profit, a way to squeeze the maximum benefits out of his sugar plantation investment. For servants and slaves the production of alcohol merely extended the already exhausting production process and added another set of hazards. Rum was "so strong a Spirit" that even a candle brought close to the barrel could set it alight, "burning all about it that is combustible matter." Such conflagrations could incur fatalities. English sojourner Richard Ligon, who managed a plantation on Barbados in the late 1640s, mused that "we lost an excellent Negre by such an accident," who did "not know the force of the liquor he carried."[36] The unnamed man had held a candle too close to the container of alcohol in his hands to better see what he was doing. He burned to death in the accident, following which an order was passed at the plantation prohibiting the movement of spirits at night when flames were used for light. Edward Littleton, another English visitor to the Caribbean, also commented on the dangers of rum production, noting that "if a Stiller slip into a Rum-Cistern, it is sudden death: for it stifles in a moment," a reference to drowning.[37] At every stage of sugar production, laborers risked their lives, working in intensive conditions with little respite and with inadequate succor to provide the strength they needed to complete their tasks. Little wonder that so many laborers died or were maimed in the sugar factories of Caribbean islands.

Enslaved Africans and indentured servants also had to overcome prejudices about their relative abilities to perform field work. One English observer remarked that servants were often "at worke in the parching sun w[i]thout shirt, shoe or stocking" but that enslaved people allegedly coped much better with the heat and humidity as they went about their work.[38] The belief that enslaved people had an easier time laboring in the fields than European servants was not unusual among seventeenth-century travelers. Indeed, in his midcentury account of life on Barbados, Ligon argued that "the servants have the worser lives" as a result of the tropical conditions under which they labored.[39] Of course, Ligon assumed that Africans were more suited to the extremes of heat and the intense sun of the tropics.[40] Reality belied such claims: all those who arrived in the Caribbean found laboring on sugar plantations to be tough, arduous work, as the petition of Rivers and Foyle demonstrates Cheeke's plantation inventory similarly emphasized that planters who wanted their estates to remain productive had no qualms about working servants and slaves together, whatever prejudices they held about the relative endurance of their unfree laborers.

"The whole collection resembles a village"

Daily life beyond the sugar fields or the boiling houses meant very different things to planters and laborers. Planters intervened in this so-called "free" time sporadically to ensure that servants and slaves survived but did not take care to see that they thrived. For laborers, however, such unstructured time provided the opportunity to forge connections, share knowledge, and establish boundaries. All of these essential components of everyday life—whether finding shelter, growing and preparing food, or creating community and family ties—were work, albeit of a different kind from that performed in the fields, and required cooperation with the people one lived alongside. Of course, this closeness bred contempt as readily as it encouraged compassion, but either way laborers made personal and emotional connections with one another. It would be hard for laborers to ignore a sick child, or a family argument, or indeed religious or spiritual rituals when living in such close proximity to one another.

Uncertainty, fear of the unknown, and the violent trauma of being taken from one's homeland affected both indentured servants and African captives, although the extent of the ordeal varied depending on the circumstances under which each group arrived in the colonies. English laborers would have been more comfortable in the Caribbean, as they generally had a degree of choice in their destination and were familiar with societal structures as elites endeavored to create a version of England in the colonies.[41] Scots and Irish were largely forced overseas, although Scottish servants quickly became the more desired group of indentured laborers and accordingly benefited from English preferences. But even the Irish had experience with English customs because of English colonialism in Ireland.[42] Africans might have recognized more of the foodstuffs that were grown on Caribbean islands, but they had no prior experience of surviving life in an English colony and had been forced from their homelands to the Americas. If these groups found a way to share their stories of captivity on plantations, at least the Irish and Africans might have been surprised by the similar circumstances that thrust them into the Atlantic economy—war, prejudice, and greed.

Although the spectacle of the slave auction, with its degrading bodily display and internal inspections, was exclusively reserved for enslaved Africans, the processes by which planters chose an indentured servant or an enslaved African largely mirrored each other, at least in the early years of English colonialism.[43] Ligon described how, on arrival in the Caribbean, servants were assigned to a particular plantation, noting that when a ship arrived at Barbados, planters went on board and bought the most promising servants.[44] Sometimes the purchase of servants was compared to the buying of livestock. Ligon explained an interaction between a planter who had "lately brought a good store of servants," and another who had plenty of provisions to spare but who had a "great want of a woman servant." Here the woman's flesh was bartered against that of an animal. The purchaser proposed: "If you will let me have some of your womans flesh, you shall have some of my hoggs flesh." Ligon insisted that it was common practice for planters "to sell their servants to one another for the time they have to serve."[45] Planters behaved similarly when purchasing enslaved Africans. Ligon described how they "choose them the way they do Horses in a Market; the strongest, youthfullest and most beautifull yield the greatest prices." Moreover, planters also bought Africans straight off the ship, "where they find them stark naked, and therefore cannot be deceived in any outward infirmity."[46] Servants and slaves were treated as akin to domesticated animals and could find themselves bartered or sold on a whim.

Once they had arrived on their masters' plantations, servants and slaves appear to have been left to their own devices when it came to their accommodations. As elsewhere in the English Atlantic, in the Caribbean planters, so careful in their descriptions of other estate buildings, rarely mentioned laborers' living quarters. For example, although the inventory for Bally Tree Hall went into minute detail about the furniture, crockery, and cooking equipment that belonged to the main plantation house, and discussed each part of the sugar works at some length, no mention of slave or servant quarters was included with the list of buildings on the plantation. William Fenwick, who owned 273 acres in St. Philip, created a similarly precise accounting of the edifices on his plantation in the deed that detailed his property, but although he mentioned "the Outhouse for freemen 3 rooms," he too made no references to the accommodations for his unfree laborers.[47] And while William Gibbs listed the "houseings, buildings, sugar mills and all other appurtenances thereunto belonging" as part of his ninety-three-acre estate in St. Thomas, he did not record with any specificity the place where the "negro girle by name Moll," or his other enslaved property lived.[48] Buildings that were so central to the lives of servants and slaves were erased by the records: even the maps of the islands that noted structures tended to mark only plantations houses, sugar works, and the occasional church.[49]

A fuller picture of laborers' accommodations can be found in the extant accounts of travelers Richard Ligon and French Jesuit Father Antoine Biet. Biet in particular is useful because as an outsider he had no investment in subscribing to English owners' versions of life for laborers on their plantations. In the middle of the seventeenth century, Biet informed his readers that enslaved Africans and indentured servants lived alongside one another. The priest painted a vivid picture of the typical scene on a plantation on Barbados. The "houses of indentured servants who are native born English, Irish or Scots and the homes of Negro slaves" were "all close to one another." Such intimacy increased the kinds of interactions that took place among their inhabitants. Biet also provided a sense of familial relationships on plantations, noting that "each household has its own" dwelling. Although the use of "house" and "homes" might suggest a differentiation between the structures in which servants and slaves lived, Biet's final description indicates otherwise. He ended his remarks with the observation that taken together "The whole collection resembles a village."[50] The reference to a "village" connotes community, the creation of social and cultural ties among and between the people who labored together on plantations. Returning to similar dwellings at the end of a hard day of labor and being unable to avoid those you worked alongside would have caused as much strife as it did harmonious interactions. At the same time, by sharing the same living space (Biet does not suggest that there was one area for servants and another for slaves, or that there were separate places for Irish, English, Scots, and Africans) these workers were already upsetting English notions about their inherent differences.

Another way for laborers on plantations to counter English ideas about their differences was to transgress the color line when forming intimate relationships. Of all the relationships obscured by estate inventories, those that involved sex are the most difficult to trace. Laws that prohibited "fornication" between "heathens" and "Christians" existed in the English West Indies, but there is little other evidence in the extant sources that shows the extent to which such bonds were formed. At Bally Tree Hall, for example, there were no female servants, so it is difficult to imagine that the male servants did not engage in sex with any of the twenty-nine enslaved women on the plantation. It is possible that some of the nine children on the estate were the results of such intimacy. Baptism records provide some evidence of sex across the color line, although the status of individuals involved is usually unclear, and the children born to enslaved women who were baptized are few. The only evidence of sex between a European woman and an African man in these records is Ann, the daughter of "Mary Sisnett by a negro," baptized in St. Philip in 1674.[51] There are multiple references to "mulatto" men and women in the parish records, but whether they were the products of relationships between servants and slaves or enslaved women and their masters cannot be determined. Yet given the close quarters in which they lived, such relationships undoubtedly took place.[52]

The close proximity in which indentured servants and enslaved Africans lived and probably forged relationships raises the question of how they communicated with one another and with their masters and mistresses. Although Irish servants would have (like the majority of their compatriots) spoken Gaelic following a renewed adherence to that language as a form of resistance to English colonization, they were also familiar with the language of their colonizers.[53] Enslaved Africans hailing from a variety of West and West Central African regions spoke a variety of languages and dialects. The multilingual nature of the slave populations of the Caribbean meant that newly arrived captives had to find either a common language to use in conversation or another person who came from the same region with whom they could talk. As time passed, enslaved Africans learned English, and this was probably the language in which they communicated with both their owners and the servants they labored alongside. Beyond the fields, however, it seems probable that both Irish and Africans continued to use their own languages when circumstances allowed, using English as a lingua franca only when they spoke with one another.[54] There were, however, multiple occasions when such a need arose, not least when it came to negotiating community formation on plantations.

Laborers had to figure out how to construct the homes that would come to "resemble a village" because masters did not provide instruction in these matters. Construction practices were not self-evident. Ligon wrote that masters who purchased servants would take them to their plantation and order "them instantly to make their Cabins" but that the new arrivals, not knowing where to begin, had to be "advised by other of their servants, that are their seniors." A servant fresh off the boat could not rely on automatic assistance from his or her indentured counterparts. In what may have been an unwillingness to embrace needy new arrivals who demanded time and energy, old hands often refused to help. Ligon explained that if another servant would not show newcomers how to proceed, "then they are to lie on the ground that night."[55] At the end of a long day in the fields, offering a hand to someone may have been beyond the emotional abilities of servants, or they may have resisted an offer of assistance as a way to introduce the fresh arrival to the harsh realities of plantation life. Again, these moments are almost completely lost to us, elided by an inventory that does not acknowledge that laborers had relationships beyond those between themselves and their masters, or the crops they harvested, or the machines they worked. The proximity in which laborers lived would mean that any new arrival, servant or slave, would be obvious to all, so the formalities and customs of welcoming them into the "village" would have been observed by the whole community. Every plantation would have had its own version of these villages, with the atmosphere and norms most probably dictated by those servants and slaves who had survived on the islands the longest and whose life experiences dominated in the living quarters.

The construction of servant and slave accommodations offers a window into potential knowledge sharing between the two groups. The cabins servants erected were made of "sticks, withs and Plantaine leaves" and were located under trees in an effort to keep rain from deluging the structures. Plantain leaves may have been popular because they were suitably large and offered some weatherproofing from tropical rains. But plantains had a particular connotation in Caribbean settings because they were a crucial part of the diet of Africans and were present in Barbados and the Leeward Islands as a result of West African preferences for the fruit.[56] There was therefore probably some African influence in the erection of these structures, albeit not a direct one, with Africans perhaps suggesting the plantain leaves as suitable shelter to servants. Ligon was not as detailed in his account about the construction of the homes of enslaved Africans, but he did comment that they had "many severall divisions . . . in their little houses, and none above six foot square."[57] Marrying Ligon's description with that of Biet demonstrates that indentured servants and enslaved Africans lived in very similar structures. One key difference appears to have been in the manner of sleep, with Africans lying on "boards" and servants resting in hammocks, suggesting that there was not complete overlap in the experiences or preferences of servants and slaves.[58]

Shelter was not the only necessity planters failed to provide: servants and slaves were also largely responsible for growing their food supply. Englishman Thomas Tryon noted that laborers received nothing more than "a small piece of Ground to raise their whole Food and Sustenance." Tryon went on to explain that the production of ample amounts of food was difficult because slave owners would "not allow . . . any sufficient time to manure" the plots during the workweek, so that laborers had to resort to working "upon . . . [the master's] Sabbath day."[59] Enslaved Africans and indentured servants understood that if they did not produce sufficient food to eat, they could not expect help from their owners, though European accounts implied that masters provided for their laborers. For example, Ligon remarked, "I can name a planter there, that feeds daily two hundred mouths," as though it were the landowner, and not those who worked the estate, who produced food rations.[60] European accounts also suggested that masters were the innovators in crop production, but a closer inspection of the record makes clear that the crops that made up substantial portions of laborers' diets were either American or African in origin and that Africans, in particular, brought key knowledge about subsistence plants to the Americas. Europeans learned from their slaves, not the other way around, when it came to growing food on the islands.[61]

The production of food provided additional opportunities for interactions and knowledge sharing between servants and slaves.[62] Ligon specifically noted one Barbadian-grown "Root, of which some of the Negroes brought the Seeds" from Africa. He observed that both the stalks and the roots ("as large as the three biggest Turnips we have in *England*") could be eaten and that the tuber made for especially suitable rations for long sea journeys.[63] Scholars have posited that Ligon was describing taro and that enslaved Africans carried the seeds with them on the Middle Passage.[64] Africans also made innovative uses of crops like plantains that were not native to Africa but that (by the seventeenth century) played a large role in the diet in the West Central region of the continent.[65] When Richard Ligon discussed the kinds of drinks that were imbibed on Barbados, he included a fermented beverage that could be made from plantains, describing it as "farre beyond" the other six drinks on his list in taste and popularity. It is clear that his knowledge about its production came from observing Africans, despite Ligon's adherence to the first-person plural in his account.[66] He wrote that to make the drink it was necessary to harvest the plant when it was "full ripe, and in the height of . . . sweetnesse." Next "we pill off the skin, and mash them in water well boyl'd; and after we have them stay there a night, we strain it, and bottle it up, and in a week drink it; and it is very strong and pleasant drink, but it is to be drunk but sparingly, for it is much stronger than Sack, and is apt to mount up into the head."[67] Given that Europeans were not familiar with plantains, and that according to Ligon the "keeper of the Plantaine grove" was an "able *Negro*," the connections between the production of this beverage and African knowledge are obvious.[68]

There are other clues to African influences in plantation inventories and travelers' accounts. Although listed in the kitchen equipment that would serve the planter's table, the "2 Irons to bake Cussado [cassava]" were perhaps also put to use to prepare the dish for the laborers on Bally Tree Hall plantation.[69] It is unclear which of the twenty-nine enslaved women was tasked with cooking for Cheeke and his family, but she would have brought her knowledge about this food from the slave cabins to the main house.[70] Africans also brought "guinea yams" westward across the Atlantic and became the cultivators and innovators of American crops, especially maize, which had already been established as a subsistence crop in Africa.[71] Sources do not focus on the specifics of shared knowledge between servants and slaves, but it seems probable that Africans helped indentures with subsistence living because of the similarities in the food they ate. Father Biet accused English plantation owners of being peerless in their lack of concern for the quality of enslaved Africans' sustenance, claiming "there is no nation which feeds its slaves as badly as the English," adding that servants were "not much better treated."[72] No doubt each group turned to the other when it came to growing and preparing plants for consumption, just as they had to cooperate when it came to planting, harvesting, and processing sugarcane.

In short, servants and slaves ate remarkably similar food. Potatoes, for example, were a large component of both servant and slave diets. Biet went as far as to claim that enslaved Africans ate little else save the starchy tuber: "For all meals the slaves only get potatoes, which serve them as their bread, their meat, their fish, in fact everything." Irish servants were subjected to no better fare, receiving "only potatoes."[73] Although he concurred that potatoes were a mainstay of servant diets, Ligon expanded their culinary repertoire to include "loblolly and Bonavist," a rustic gruel and a tropical pulse respectively.[74] According to the Englishman, enslaved Africans ate much the same diet, and suffered intestinal discomfort because of it, until they began to plant and eat plantains, a food with which they, and their digestive systems, were more familiar.[75]

There was also a great deal of overlap in foods that servants and slaves did *not* get to eat or at least did not dine on regularly. As a general rule, their diets included very little meat. The exception was the relatively regular inclusion of fish in laborers' diets, although Europeans tended not to recognize such protein as of equivalent value to pork, chicken, or beef. Ligon recorded that enslaved men were allowed "two Maquerels a weeke," while enslaved women were allocated one. Only during holidays, like Christmas, could laborers expect to eat flesh from land-based animals. Biet noted that Christmas Day saw the only respite in the repetitive diet of potatoes—both Africans and Irish ate poultry that had been raised by the enslaved population. In his synthesis of other travel accounts, Richard Blome suggested that meat would be served only on special occasions, such "Christmass, Easter and Whitsontide," when laborers would receive a portion of "Hoggs-flesh, according to the custome of the Island."[76] There were also very occasional rations of beef for servants and slaves. Ligon noted that only if "cattle died by mischance, or by any disease" could servant or slaves expect to receive this kind of meat. Although an overseer would supervise the distribution of the dead animals, it was the laborers who divided the spoils, perhaps according to preferences in taste, or in line with the overseer's perception of hierarchy on the plantation. Servants would "eat the bodies" of the animals, whereas the slaves would take "the skins, head, and intrails."[77] Forced to use these less-than-choice cuts, Irish and Africans would nonetheless have been able to concoct dishes significant to their own communities, offering variation and creativity even within the world of the unfree. Butchering and dividing the dead animal would have been the prelude to a moment of feasting, rare on plantations, but all the more important for being such an unusual occasion. This kind of event may have occurred on Bally Tree Hall plantation if one of the "16 head of meate cattle" died.[78]

Life in new plantation settings forced servants and slaves to adapt their eating habits. Sometimes the foodstuff available to laborers was identical, but the methods of preparation made for divergent final dishes. Underscoring the innovation of Africans when it came to American crops, Ligon noted that Native Americans used maize to make what he described as a kind of bread, but that the enslaved Africans "use the *Mayes* another way, which is, toasting the ears of it at the fire, and so eating it warm off the eare."[79] Servants also ate maize but pounded and boiled the grain until it thickened and then served it with a little salt. In Ireland corn was reserved for feeding horses, not humans, so the Irish may have experimented with the staple both to make it something they would find enjoyable to eat and to reduce the association with animal feed. Given the Irish preference for oatmeal, as noted by Fynes Moryson, Irish servants may have been trying to approximate the dish in the Caribbean.[80] Such an innovation would be one of the few instances where servant adaptations of American foods in the islands become visible. The resulting recipe, called "*Loblollie*," was unpalatable to Africans, who (according to Ligon) were "much discontented, and crie out, *O! O! no more Lob-lob*," when faced with ingesting this particular dish.[81] No doubt exhaustion prevented a good deal of innovation or even choice when it came to the foodstuffs prepared by plantation laborers: taro or potatoes took time to cook; unlike plantains they could not be eaten raw. But it is important to note that when they did have time, servants and slaves worked to create foods that mimicked favorites from home in either taste or texture. These choices in food production are evidence of how, even when the ingredient at hand was the same, Irish and Africans created different final dishes, thus marking a distinction between each other.

Clothing was the other key area of difference in servant and slave plantation experiences. While neither group had much choice in what they wore, a European preference for wearing many layers, even in tropical settings, appears to have prevailed among servants in the islands. Hans Sloane, who spent time in the Caribbean in the latter part of the seventeenth century, noted the particular problems that English settlers faced, "coming from a cold Country." On the islands they continued to "cloth themselves after the same manner as in *England*."[82] Servants on Barbados had "shirts and drawers" available to them, according to Richard Ligon, who also admitted that some masters allowed indentures a change of clothes, so that when they returned from the fields "wet through with their sweating," they could put on something dry.[83] This policy was less a result of the generosity of planters than an acknowledgment on their part of how "the body is infeebled by the great toyle" in the fields and their assumptions about the particular effects of the "Sun's heat" to "exhaust the spirits" of European bodies that were "unaccustomed to it."[84]

If the European preference for clothing continued in the Caribbean, Sloane suggested that the rest of the people who lived "between the Tropics," including "*Negros* and *Indians*," "go almost naked."[85] These differences were reflected in the clothing allowances on plantations. Ligon advocated the purchase of "Irish Ruggs, such as are made at Killkennie, and Irish stockings" for servants to wear. Such garments may have been some small comfort from home for the Irish laborers on plantations, but their distribution may have led to assumptions among other workers that the Irish were being favored in some way.[86] Male "common servants" on plantations would receive six shirts, six "pairs of drawers," and "three *Monmouth* caps" in any given year. For the female servants who worked in the fields, four smocks, three petticoats, and four caps were provided, while those who were house servants received an additional two smocks and three waistcoats per year. Meanwhile, enslaved men would have to survive with only "three pair of Canvas drawers" over the same period, and enslaved women "shall be allowed but two petticoats a piece yearly."[87] These differences translated into planters spending almost £100 on clothing for twenty-four servants and only £35 on clothing for one hundred enslaved Africans over the course of the year, a sharp distinction in terms of economic priorities and cultural difference.[88] Perhaps planters' rationing policies were simply reflections of their embedded assumptions about the appropriate levels of attire that

*An Account of Expences iffuing out yearly for Cloathing , for the Chriftian Ser-
vants, both Men and Women, with the Wages of the principall Overfeer,
which fhall be 50 l. fterling, or the value in fuch Goods
as grow upon the Plantation.*

To the five fubordinate Overfeers,
for each mans cloathing.

	l.	s.	d.
Six fhirts, at 4 s. a piece	1	04	0
Six pair of Drawers, at 2 s.	0	12	0
Twelve pair of fhoes, at 3 s.	1	16	0
Six pair of Linnen or Irifh fto-kings, at 20 d.	0	10	0
Three *Monmouth* Caps, at 4 s.	0	12	0
Two doublets of Canvas, and fix Holland bands	0	15	0
Sum totall for each man	5	9	0
Sum totall for the five Overfeers	27	5	0

To the fourteen common fervants.

	l.	s.	d.
Six fhirts to each man	1	04	0
Six pair of drawers to each man	0	12	0
Twelve pair of fhoes, at 3 s.	1	16	0
Three *Monmouth* caps, at 4 s.	0	12	0
Sum totall to each man	4	04	0
Sum totall, of the fourteen fervants by the year	58	16	0

Now for the ten women fervants, we will difpofe of them, thus :
Four to attend in the houfe, and thofe to be allowed, as followeth
in the firft Columne, *viz.*

The four that attend in the houfe
to each of them

	l.	s.	d.
Six fmocks, at 4 s. a piece	1	04	0
Three petticoats, at 6 s.	0	18	0
Three waftcoats, at 3 s.	0	09	0
Six coifes or caps, at 18 d. a piece	0	09	0
Twelve pair of fhoes at 3 s.	1	16	0
Sum is	4	16	0
Sum totall of the four wo-men that attend in the houfe	19	4	0

The other fix that weed, and do the
common work abroad yearly.

	l.	s.	d.
Four fmocks, at 4 s. a piece	0	16	0
Three petticoats, at 5 s. a piece	0	15	0
Four coifs, at 12 d. a piece	0	04	0
Twelve pair of fhoes, at 3 s.	1	16	0
Sum is	3	11	0
Sum totall of the fix com-mon women fervants	21	06	0

Thirty Rug Gownes for thefe thirty fervants, to caft about them
when they come home hot and wearied, from their work, and to fleep
in a nights, in their Hamocks, at 25 s. a Gown or mantle. — 37 10 0

Now for the Negres, which we will account to be a hundred of both
Sexes, we will divide them equally ; The fifty men fhall be allowed
yearly but three pair of Canvas drawers a piece, which at 2 s. a pair,
is 6 s.

The women fhall be allowed but two petticoats a piece yearly ; at
4 s. a piece, which is 8 s. yearly.

	l.	s.	d.
So the yearly charge of the fifty men Negres, is	15	00	0
And of the women	20	00	0
Sum is	35	00	0

Now

FIGURE 10. Richard Ligon's estimation of the costs for running
a plantation in terms of the probable expenses accrued in providing clothing for indentured servants and enslaved Africans.
From *A True and Exact History of the Island of Barbados* (1657).
Courtesy of the John Carter Brown Library at Brown University.

servants and slaves desired. But they might also be indicative of elite ideas that European bodies must be covered to ensure respectability, whereas leaving black bodies unclothed would reinforce Africans' supposed savage nature.

Considering the foodways and living conditions of servants and slaves brings to light the parallels and overlap between each group's everyday lives and points out the ways in which such interactions were neglected, ignored, or erased by slaveholder records. Although there were clearly moments when masters differentiated between the two categories of laborer (as in the case of the distribution of the body of a dead cow, or the quality and volume of clothing disbursed), indentured servants and enslaved Africans often worked to make their own distinctions in their dress, and sometimes in what they chose to eat. Their insistence on continuing to build community or mark boundaries as they saw fit demonstrated that even in the most oppressive circumstances servants and slaves had the power to make decisions for themselves. Knowledge sharing about how to produce certain foodstuffs, and each group's responsibility to grow subsistence-level crops, built relationships that are never directly acknowledged by extant accounts. Those relationships were nonetheless foundational for forging understandings of similarity and difference among plantation workers.

"Branded with the epithete of white slaves"

For all that servants and slaves found commonalities on plantations, masters and colonial authorities remained determined to enforce hierarchies that would prevent relationships based on solidarity and common experiences from flourishing. Some key ways to implement these kinds of divisions were by treating servants and slaves differently, often through disproportionate punishments. But even here servants and slaves found ways to forge their own understandings of difference, setting relationships on their terms, not those proffered by English planters. These interactions were especially complicated in the connections between Irish servants and enslaved Africans. On the one hand, English derision toward Irish laborers may have drawn them into bonds of sympathy with enslaved Africans. On the other hand, as Irish indentures became free and ended up in supervisory roles over slaves themselves, the bonded populations of the islands rejected any similarities they had formerly shared. So too would freed laborers have been keen to leave behind the social shame of servitude.

Corporeal punishments for alleged transgressions were a defining feature of plantation life for laborers, as planters and overseers brandished
the whip to ensure that the pace of production never waned. Public
executions, floggings, and other kinds of violence were routine in early
modern Europe and the Americas, and torture often accompanied the
interrogation of individuals to encourage them to confess to crimes they
had allegedly committed.[89] That cruelty was a feature of seventeenth-
century Caribbean life is therefore largely unsurprising, although in
colonial settings it took on new forms.[90] Ligon observed an overseer
"beat a Servant with a cane about the head, till the blood has followed,"
and concluded, "Truly I have seen such cruelty there done to servants, as
I did not think one Christian could have done to another," which was less
a commentary on the fact that violence toward servants occurred than
that Caribbean brutality was especially harsh.[91] In the middle of the seventeenth century, Biet observed that the threat of violence under which
enslaved Africans and indentured servants labored was similar in that
"all are treated very badly," noting that beatings were meted out to those
who were deemed too lazy or too slow, servant and slave alike.[92] Meanwhile Ligon suggested that servants who complained about their working conditions were "beaten by the Overseer; if they resist, their time is
doubled." The slightest infraction could incur a beating "for a fault that
is not worth the speaking of." Punishments for enslaved Africans also
shed blood. Hans Sloane wrote that slaves who had not performed to
the levels deemed appropriate by the overseer would be "whipt . . . with
Lance-wood Switches till they be bloody." He went on to explain in
some detail the additional pain that individuals would be subjected to,
which included rubbing salt or pepper into the wounds, or dropping
melted wax on the broken skin, describing these violent perversions as
"very exquisite Torments."[93] Cruelty was such an integral part of life in
slave societies that there was nothing unusual about seeing a servant or
enslaved African with a scar-covered body.

Servants and slaves in positions of skill on plantations usually held
some kind of power over ordinary field workers. On large estates, planters created hierarchy within the slave population by promoting slaves to
the position of driver on the gangs that worked the sugarcane, and men
like James Hanley, the master boiler on Jacob English's plantation, would
have had some control over laborers in the sugar works. These men (and
occasional women) were in charge of work regimens and production and
were empowered to mete out whatever punishments they saw fit. But
of course they could also be subjected to retribution themselves from

overseers or masters on plantations. However, it should not be assumed that an individual who had suffered under the lash would be any more sympathetic to another's sentence than someone who had never been on the receiving end of mandated violence.[94] While most servants would not rise to the status of planter, and thus would not be in a position to enact violence on their own enslaved property, some would become overseers, the men charged with most of the day-to-day punishment of enslaved laborers on plantations. In Ligon's account overseers supervised the division of food, alerted the master to probable domestic violence, and punished laborers in the fields.[95]

The preoccupation of masters and overseers with increasingly horrific methods of exacting pain and humiliation on their laboring populations was tied up in understandings of who could be suitable subjects of such violence.[96] In the 1650s and 1660s it appeared that *all* laborers were potential targets for these kinds of punishments, and the legal system worked to regulate disciplinary measures. For example, Biet noted that the laws of Barbados were such that if "Negro slaves . . . go beyond the limits of the plantation on a Sunday they are given fifty blows with a cudgel."[97] Irish Catholics were subjected to similar restrictions. The Barbados Council passed a law in 1657, just two years after Biet's departure from the island, stating that those of the "Irish nation, freemen and women and servants," who "wander up and down from Plantation to Plantation as vagabonds refusing to Labour" should be "whipt according to the Law."[98] But as time progressed, and as the demography changed, attitudes about the appropriate people to receive such punishments shifted to more narrow definitions.[99]

The nature of violence on plantations increased the likelihood that some of the people who brandished the whip had scars from similar punishments themselves. Overseers who began life as indentured servants might have been flogged in the early years of their colonial experience. Cornelius Bryan, who arrived on Barbados as a laborer, had once suffered "twenty-one lashes on the bare back" for his challenges to the planter class.[100] The ubiquity of punishment did not make Bryan's rise to the position of land and slave owner unusual. Indeed, there is no indication that from the moment he first acquired property Bryan was concerned with anything other than molding himself as a planter, slowly amassing twenty-two acres and thirteen enslaved Africans. He was no doubt comfortable issuing retribution for perceived transgressions that included the use of corporeal punishment. And while he may have delegated the overseeing of the enslaved Africans who labored on his small plot of land to his eldest son, it is much more likely that the intimacies of managing such a small plantation placed Cornelius himself in control of all his property. There is no way to definitively tell if Bryan ever whipped one of his slaves, but if he did not, it would make him a most unusual planter.[101]

The existence of men like Bryan further complicates the kinds of relationships that were forged on plantations. By owning Africans, by enslaving them and putting them to work on his sugar plantation, Bryan was doing his level best to assert his membership in the planter class on the island, despite his Irish background and the rebellious tendencies he had exhibited in his youth. The Bryan of 1656 who was lashed might have felt solidarity with other laborers against planters, including perhaps those from Africa, as he received a punishment with which servants and slaves alike were all too familiar. Or perhaps he simply made connections on an individual basis and did not notice the broader streams of similarity around him. Thirty years later, whatever connections might have been possible appear to have been erased, despite Bryan's inability to remove from his body the scars that marked him as only a recent member of the planter class. Whatever possibilities of solidarity, empathy, or understanding may have existed once in Bryan's life, the dominant forces that determined life in a slave society meant that they no longer applied.

Bryan's case bears some similarity to that of an Irish overseer encountered by Father Biet on Barbados in 1654. The overseer, likely an acquaintance of Biet called Donat Ofaye, was punishing an enslaved man for stealing a pig. Before Biet arrived on the scene, the man had spent a week in irons, receiving a daily whipping from other slaves instructed by Ofaye to mete out the sentence "untill he was all covered in Blood." In addition, Ofaye had severed one of the enslaved man's ears, roasting it in front of his eyes before forcing him to consume the body part. Biet was horrified at the unnatural levels of violence he witnessed, and he worked hard to persuade Ofaye to give up on the rest of the punishment (which would have included more whipping and the removal and roasting of the enslaved man's other ear and nose). Under considerable pressure from Biet, the overseer finally relented, and his victim was released from the irons.[102] It seems impossible to imagine any scenario in which Ofaye and the enslaved man could have found common ground.

The experiences of the majority of Bryan's and Ofaye's compatriots could be found in the sugar fields, working alongside enslaved Africans rather than in a position of power over them. In 1667, English adventurer and soldier John Scott wrote "Some Observations on the Island of Barbados" and sent his conclusions to London. Included among the usual notations about the numbers and kinds of people who inhabited the island was a sentence that provides a brief glimpse of the relationships forged between enslaved Africans and indentured servants. Suggesting that the latter group were "poore men, that are just permitted to live, and a very great part Irish," Scott went on to recount how these Irish men were "derided by the Negroes and branded w[i]th the epithete of white slaves."[103] Contained within this phrase are a host of possibilities about the depicted relationship between Irish servants and enslaved Africans on plantations. The statement can be read straightforwardly as a kind of truth about the position of the Irish, with the use of "white slaves" indicating enslaved Africans' understanding that the place of Irish laborers on plantations was not so very different from their own. At the same time, the use of "derided" suggests an element of contempt on the part of enslaved Africans toward Irish servants. Perhaps the slaves believed Irish laborers saw themselves as superior to workers from Africa and were mocking the reality of the low position they occupied on plantations. Alternatively, the use of irony or black humor may have been in play. In this reading, the slaves would be using the term *white slaves* in jest, (with the term *slave* underscoring the similarity of their positions) and also skewering the Irish (the *white* part of the phrase cementing the space between African and Irish laborers). The enslaved workers may also have tried to draw slaveholders into their banter in recognition of the ways that English planters demeaned Irish laborers. Scott's observation provides no clues besides this brief account as to how the two groups interacted. But in these seven words is one of the very few extant direct references to interactions between servants and slaves of any kind, one that hints at the emotions and relationships of those involved.

Camaraderie may once have been possible between indentured servants and enslaved Africans, but over time divisions between the two groups became more pronounced as the numbers of servants shrank and as the opportunities for servants to rise to the level of overseer or even plantation owner increased accordingly. The disruption of death, sale, or banishment (all so prevalent in the early Caribbean) further jeopardized fragile relations, making common ground all the harder to find and build upon. When some of those who had formerly worked alongside enslaved Africans ended their terms of indenture, acquired a small plot of land, and sometimes became owners of slaves themselves, the dynamics altered dramatically. As the demography shifted, so too did the distribution of corporeal punishment and attitudes toward violence. In part this transformation occurred because there were far fewer servants as the century progressed to experience the punishments that had become a regular feature of plantation living. The numbers of enslaved Africans being transported to the islands exponentially grew. But equally important was the shift in ideology about who could be considered a suitable subject for flogging. African bodies, deemed to be savage by English observers, were appropriate targets for brutal physical punishment—increasingly, European bodies were not. Although large numbers of Irish servants, who were also viewed as less than civil, complicated this transition, by the 1670s the trajectory was set.[104] When it came to corporeal punishment in the late seventeenth-century Caribbean, the whip continued to be in white hands, but those on the receiving end of the lash were almost exclusively black.

* * *

The shutting down of possibilities for empathy and close ties should not be the only lesson taken from an exploration of everyday life on plantations. For every Cornelius Bryan, there were others who took a different message from the constant toil in the fields of plantations, people who were able to create solidarity even from a place of extreme pain and suffering. Surviving on sugar estates in the Caribbean required laborers to overcome the grueling work they were subjected to in the fields and boiling houses and the violence they witnessed or were forced to succumb to on a regular basis. But laborers were also able to use these moments of hardship to forge new ties. Most instances of connection appear as mere glimpses and fragments in elite accounts of island life or are obscured altogether by the construction of sterile inventories. They existed, nonetheless, in a variety of forms, as gaps and absences in a compromised archive.

Paying attention to the everyday lives of plantation laborers brings these layers of erasure into view. It allows us to see the dialogic tension between how English elites wanted to identify and categorize indentured servants and enslaved Africans and how those very laborers, in their response to such constrictions, in turn shaped English ideas and attitudes. The daily interactions between these groups heightened English paranoia, especially regarding threats posed by Irish Catholics and enslaved Africans. But by working to create communities on plantations, laborers appropriated and subverted English attempts to define them and came up with alternative ways of understanding their places in Caribbean hierarchies. The communities they created were not always inclusive. Sometimes elite attempts to mark separations between groups worked, as when food or clothing was distributed unevenly. At other times servants and slaves built separate worlds for themselves by choosing to make and eat different dishes or by insisting on the distinctions in their status. And in still other moments they found comfort by interacting with one another in circumstances that were not dictated by the ringing of plantation bells or the threat of the master's whip.

It was in plantation villages that the proximities of daily life, good and bad, were hardest to ignore. When laborers were able to step back from sugar production, the work they had to perform continued: there were subsistence crops to plant, children to raise, relationships to sustain, and deities to be appeased. The signal moments of life—birth, marriage, and death—occurred in these communal spaces, and here again plantation workers witnessed each other's connection to the supernatural. Men and women who were concerned with finding meaning and comfort in their lives beyond the never-ending toil of laboring in the fields on sugar plantations used religious rites as an alternative way to make sense of their existence, finding multiple ways to survive and thrive that also challenged English perceptions of their inherent difference.

Cornelius rarely thought about his own time under the lash, even when he held a whip in his hand himself. But Tomy had failed to get the crop to the sugar works in Holetown as promptly as he should, and time was of the essence if Cornelius was to bring a profitable harvest to market. Tomy had forced him to pick up the lash, the only way to let his slaves know that challenging him was not an option. He looked down at Tomy's bloody back and for a second his mind flashed to that moment at the Bridge when he had stood, stripped to the waist, waiting for the hangman to commence his sentence. It seemed like another lifetime. It was difficult to know whether the scars were becoming less visible over time. Bryan could only stretch his arms across parts of his back, so he was unsure if the ridges and scar tissue he could still feel had reduced in any way since his wounds first healed. Cornelius decided against rubbing salt in Tomy's wounds, believing the thirty lashes to be enough punishment, for now at least. It wasn't that he was opposed to such actions, more that he wanted to keep something in reserve for worse lapses.

Pegg tried to prevent Young Tomy from seeing what was happening to his father. She had always felt so helpless when she saw her master lift the lash to Old Pegg's back, knowing that she could do nothing to prevent the blows raining down on her mother's body. She explained to Young Tomy that the best thing he could do to help his father was to stay out of sight, to keep them both from the unerasable pain of seeing and being seen whipped in such a humiliating fashion. She told Young Tomy that she would help him prepare some plantains to eat and some Mobbie to drink for when his father came back to their cabin. That way, they could talk of something other than pain, sit together, share food, and allow their minds to take them somewhere else, even if it was only a brief moment of reprieve.

Old Pegg knew Cornelius's secret. She had glimpsed his back once, on one of the rare days that she had known the man to bathe in all the years she had been with him. She had been charged with filling and emptying the tub in which he submerged himself, and she had caught a flash of the telltale criss-cross marks that covered his back. She wondered where and when he had received the lash. She knew plenty of servants who had been punished in that way, had seen too many of her own people with similar marks on their bodies. Whatever had caused Cornelius's back to bear the marks of the whip, Old Pegg had not spoken of it to anyone else in the slave quarters. She did not think it would help if others knew of their master's disfigurement. After all, it did not seem to affect Cornelius's propensity for picking up a whip, and they all knew he had a temper and wouldn't bear any disrespect toward his position of authority.

4 / "Doing their prayers and worshipping God in their hearts": Ritual, Practice, and Keeping the Faith

French Jesuit Father Antoine Biet reflected on the events of the previous week. He had traveled around Barbados in disguise, wary of being uncovered as a priest by the English he encountered. One surprise had been the ease with which he met Catholics eager to hear him perform mass. The Protestants in charge of the island did not seem to care as long as he encouraged worship to take place quietly on some plantation. Just a few days earlier, as he prayed privately in the orange grove of the estate of French planter Cesar de Mesnil, he had been approached by an Irish man who was thrilled to find a Catholic priest on the island. The man had enthusiastically engaged Biet, telling him that there were "many other good Catholics" on Barbados who needed his assistance, men and women who "were in great distress without any spiritual consolation."[1] According to the Irish man, Biet could help by performing baptisms, marriages, and funerals and by preaching mass. But Irish Catholics were not the only true believers on the island in need of a priest. As he explored the island, Biet noted the number of enslaved Africans he encountered who had been converted to Catholicism, many by Portuguese missionaries. He recalled how these slaves were greatly troubled by the circumstances in which they found themselves, telling him that they were "very sorry to see themselves sold in an island of heretics." Not only had the Portuguese taken the captives and transported them across the ocean, but these African Catholics were now subjected to enslavement in

a Protestant colony. It had been so long since they had been in the presence of a priest, Biet reflected, that at this point they were only "tinged"
with Catholicism. He wanted to minister to their needs and help them
find ways to continue to practice secretly in their homes, "worshipping
God in their hearts."[2]

At first glance, Biet's account of the spiritual milieu on Barbados
in 1652 does not seem to offer any surprising insights as to the kinds
of religious fervor a Catholic priest might claim to have found on the
island. His stress on the importance of his presence to Catholics living
in a Protestant setting is in keeping with the records left by other priests
who moved around and through the English Atlantic world, all of whom
tended to exaggerate the numbers of Catholics they encountered and the
extent of their co-religionists' discomfort to emphasize the necessity of
their missions. But Biet's account of his brief time on Barbados raises
a host of possibilities about religious practices among nonelites in the
Caribbean. He moved among some of the most marginalized colonial
subjects, and his descriptions of their experiences demonstrate how
these subordinated people managed to both keep their faith and negoti-
ate the religious hierarchy in the English West Indies, despite a climate
that worked to subdue their own spiritual beliefs, rituals, and rites.

The everyday religious practices of Africans and Irish in the Caribbean were the frameworks through which they made sense of their world
and their place in it. In their spiritual practices, servants, slaves, and free
people (Catholic and otherwise) set their own parameters for community
and belonging. Sometimes their rituals did not change or at least were
not altered significantly by the interactions that took place among different communities on Caribbean islands that, contrary to Biet's account,
showed very little evidence of Christian influence.[3] At other times, Irish
and Africans expressed their ideas about their commonalities and differences—among themselves and English Protestants—by engaging
the Church of England hierarchy. A careful reading of the voluminous
documentation created by parish clerks, Catholic priests, and Protestant
observers, as well as the less prolific archaeological and anthropological evidence, provides an accounting of the religious environment in the
English Caribbean.[4] The connections that nonelites forged in the spiritual realm were subtle, complex, and even on occasion contradictory,
but they were nonetheless emphatic expressions of a worldview that held
importance for its practitioners on an everyday basis.

This chapter focuses on the everyday aspects of religious life to
uncover the endurance of belief and practice on Caribbean plantations,

probing the malleability of such customs and rituals to explore how spiritual practices can demonstrate nonelite ideas about difference. It begins by examining the antecedents of Caribbean religious practices in Africa and Ireland to understand the sorts of traditions that traveled across the ocean and how they survived or changed in new settings. Living in a Protestant society brought its own opportunities and raised new possibilities. Sometimes Irish Catholics used the Church of England to their own ends. Africans, enslaved and free, and island-born creoles also turned to Protestantism on occasion, especially when marking the birth of a child through the sacrament of baptism. When they engaged these systems, however, they were not necessarily embracing English religious dictates. More often they were using the official religion of the island either to hide in plain sight or to invoke the power and protection that endorsing such beliefs might bring. Despite circumstances that restricted and reduced the ability of indentured servants and enslaved Africans to follow their faiths free from interference from masters, overseers, or island authorities, these groups carved out sacred space for themselves on the islands. Irish Catholics continued to cleave to the central tenets of their faith, embracing priests when they appeared in the colonies and finding quiet ways to perform rituals even in their absence. Enslaved Africans brought a rich variety of religious practices with them to the Caribbean and found ways to sustain these beliefs in slavery. Created systems that operated outside English jurisdictions or ran parallel to them could be conscious modes of resistance to the colonial regime but were not necessarily, or merely, examples of such attitudes. Continued and innovated rituals offered Africans and Irish, separately and together, opportunities to maintain their religious distinctions from planters and other elites. Tracing these experiences lays out how these groups understood spiritual difference and forged their own communities of belief in Caribbean society.

"Ringing of Bells and Praying for the Dead"

The religious rituals that became central to the spiritual lives of Caribbean practitioners had their roots in belief systems born in the old worlds of Europe and Africa. Despite the variety and complexity of the various religions followed in West and West Central Africa, it is important to understand the broad contours of the spiritual worlds of the peoples who inhabited those zones. Some captives, especially those from Sierra Leone or Senegambia (but also some from the Gold Coast and Benin) were Muslim.[5] On plantations in the Caribbean they would have quickly worked to orient east and west, all the while troubled by their lack of suitable prayer mats and their inability to always complete the ritual ablutions that preceded prayer. They could perform morning and evening prayers in their quarters, but it would have been difficult, if not impossible, to find a way to pray during the day under the continuous and extensive surveillance provided by masters, mistresses, or overseers. In both Africa and the Americas, a European inability to recognize Muslim worship meant either that many of these practices went unmentioned or that they were mistaken for Christian rites and rituals.[6] And Muslims were not the only Abrahamic religious group to travel from Africa to the Americas. Since the fifteenth century, Catholic missionaries had followed Portuguese explorers down Africa's west coast, achieving considerable success among elites in the Kingdom of Kongo, most of whom converted to Catholicism. By the seventeenth century, Capuchin and Jesuit priests were making some inroads in West Africa too.[7] The extent of conversion is difficult to trace with any specificity, but European observers in Senegambia and along the Gold Coast noted that many Africans were engaging in the Christian sacraments of baptism while continuing to hold onto traditions from their local religions.[8] Some of these rituals, like the consumption of salt or the use of baptismal water, were readily adopted by West Africans because they fit with other African spiritual worldviews.[9]

Most enslaved people who crossed the ocean, however, followed a non-Abrahamic faith, practicing one of a variety of indigenous African religions. The diversity of peoples and religions notwithstanding, there were some broad similarities among the various traditions.[10] A common practice in many West and West Central regions was the use of power objects (called *minkisi* or *nkisi* in West Central Africa, and often referred to as "fetishes" by European observers) that connected the user to a particular spirit.[11] It is difficult to say what precise role such objects played in the spiritual lives of the many peoples of Africa's west coast, but these physical representations of spirits were in widespread use from Senegambia to the Kingdom of Kongo and were utilized on an everyday basis.[12] Some were used for protection or to treat illness. Pieter de Marees, a Dutch Protestant who spent time on the Gold Coast, explained that children were especially likely to have power objects hung on their bodies, "one *Fetisso* being good for sleeping, another against falling, another against vomiting and so on."[13] Further along the coast, French Huguenot Jean Barbot noted that such "fetishes" were imbued with the power to prevent those who wore them from "drowning at sea . . . from being killed in a war; another will give a woman a safe childbirth, another prevent fires, another heal fevers."[14] Power objects in West Africa also appeared frequently during funeral ceremonies, suggesting that the communion between the world of the dead and the world of the living was central to spirituality in the region.[15] De Marees discussed how the closest friends of a deceased inhabitant of the Gold Coast would fashion an object "and pray to it that it may bring the corpse to the other world and not disturb it while traveling." Gold Coast residents believed that "once this has been done, the corpse will be at peace."[16] Keeping one's body, mind, and soul safe in the present was predicated on keeping the ancestral world happy; hence the various offerings Africans made to appease the dead.[17] The adherence to *minkisi* was no different from the practices of the majority of European Christians, who found in the relics of Catholicism a similar connection to the spiritual realm and the ability to protect, to heal, to keep themselves and their families safe.

Other common mortuary practices among West Africans included what one scholar has termed "spiritual inquests."[18] These interrogations were part of the process of appeasing the dead person's spirit and smoothing the transition to the afterlife, allowing mourners to express their anguish at the death of a loved one and to grapple with the meaning of mortality.[19] Following the interrogation of the deceased, the body was laid to rest. Some Africans were buried where they died, or in the home, a way to keep the departed spirit present on a daily basis. Barbot observed that in the southern regions of the Gold Coast "the dead are usually interred in the hut where they died, because they have no cemeteries or special [burial] places."[20] When more formal burials did occur they involved a great deal of grave goods—placed both alongside the deceased and on top of the grave itself. French Huguenot Nicolas Villault described burials at a depth of "four or five feet," with *minkisi* thrown into the grave and where "a good part of the houshold stuff (as his Kettles and Cloaths)" were laid by the deceased's side.[21] De Marees noted that "all . . . [the deceased's] goods, such as his clothes, weapons, Pots, Pans, Stools, Spades and similar chattels which he has used in his lifetime, are brought to the Grave" and buried with the body.[22] In addition, sustenance in the form of palm wine, rice, millet, maize, "and whatever they thought necessary for the life of man" was included so "that he might want nothing whither he was going."[23] On top of the grave a small structure was erected to protect the body from the elements, although eventually it would disintegrate. When the burial was over, the mourners

FIGURE 11. Akan funeral procession. This engraving was included in Pieter de Marees's *Description and Historical Account of the Gold Kingdom of Guinea* (1602) and shows the three stages of an Akan funeral. A and B represent the funeral procession moving towards a covered grave, with mourners playing cymbals and beating gourds; C depicts women weeping and wailing under the grave covering; D shows mourners returning from the water where they have bathed following the funeral. Image shelf mark 566.K.15.(9), 17. © The British Library Board.

returned "weeping and lamenting to their houses," to wash and feast. Death rituals did not end at the moment of interment. An annual pilgrimage to the grave followed: "Once every year they carry meat and drink, and set it at his grave, lest he should be hungry or thirsty in the other world."[24] Between the return to burial sites not in the home and the presence of graves within households, the memorialization of the deceased was ever present, connecting the worlds of the living and of the dead.[25]

With the advent of the transatlantic slave trade, death rituals took on new and important meanings for enslaved Africans. Providing succor to the spiritual world and remaining in conversation with the dead allowed individuals to feel protected in the face of enormous upheavals and change, such as the Middle Passage, during which the trauma endured by captives constituted a form of social death.[26] Moreover, the transportation of captives far away from their birthplaces raised the question of what would happen to their souls when they died. In West Africa, souls were believed to return to their birthplace when death occurred outside a local setting. As a result of the slave trade, the soul would have to make its way across a vast ocean to ensure its final resting place with ancestors in Africa.[27] Such a long journey might necessitate larger quantities of grave goods to provide sufficient succor on the voyage or the inclusion of a sailing vessel, like the small wooden canoe inserted in an enslaved child's grave in South Carolina, to facilitate the spirit on its reverse Middle Passage.[28] Such changes reflect the ways that religious practices morphed as a result of slavery, even as core beliefs did not change.

Religion in Ireland was less diverse than in West Africa, but like the amalgamation of ancient and more contemporary traditions in Africa, the Catholicism practiced by the Irish population was infused with older practices. The Reformation may have had little effect on the Catholic Church in Ireland, but it seems that at least some everyday ceremonies began to resemble English cultural practices as many pre-Christian rites favored by the Irish faded into the background and the effects of the Council of Trent spread. The Elizabethan and Jacobean colonization of Ireland in the late sixteenth and early seventeenth centuries precipitated a considerable upheaval in Irish spiritual life. The Catholic Church continued to allow, and in some cases even encouraged, the performance of certain rites that technically fell outside official church sanction. For example, during baptism Irish parents tied "a little peece of silver to the Corner of the Cloth wherein the Chylde is wrapped" while they also followed the Catholic practice of putting salt "in the Chyldes mouth" as a way to purify the new member of the faith.[29] Church leaders thus provided Irish families with a place to continue traditional practices that provided much comfort.[30]

Ceremonies surrounding death were similarly important signifiers of the religiosity of the Irish: many believed that the spirits of the dead rested with ancestral heroes and that on occasion these spirits might actually appear.[31] Securing the passage of the soul to heaven was a key part of funeral rites, and the practice of keening was an important part of ensuring that the transition was smooth. In 1634 in Dublin, Protestant Englishman William Brereton passed the house of a merchant where a wake was taking place and described hearing a woman within "roaring out as though she were violently distracted."[32] Brereton went on to observe that this display of emotion was "very ordinary with the Irish, and is their custom."[33] Moryson observed that following death those at the bedside "make a monstrous Cry, with shriking, howling and clamp-ping of hands." This practice continued as mourners followed the dead body to the site of burial, with "the Nurse, the daughters, and the Con-cubynes" making the "most vehement" cries.[34] Old English commentator Richard Stanihurst condemned the emotional display he witnessed, stat-ing that Irish women mourners "shout dolefully through swollen cheeks, they cast off their necklaces, they bare their heads, they tear their hair, they beat their brows." Worse still, "they shake the coffin, tear open the shroud, embrace and kiss the corpse," demonstrating what Stanihurst saw as a serious lack of propriety.[35] Despite the obviously critical atti-tudes expressed by these writers, the similarities across accounts suggest the central importance of keening in Irish death rituals.

Burial itself was a fraught issue in many parts of Ireland by the late sixteenth century, and across the island by the middle of the seventeenth century, as formerly Catholic churchyards were seized in the aftermath of English colonization and either turned into Protestant graveyards or deconsecrated and used for secular purposes. There was some degree of collusion between Catholic worshippers and Protestant landowners as Irish Catholics continued to assert their right to the physical space of their former churches, using lay preachers to perform baptisms, mar-riages, and especially burials. For example, one Englishman in County Leitrim in Northwest Ireland who had converted a friary into his home allowed local Catholics to bury their dead in the graveyard attached to the church only after they paid him for the right to do so.[36] At other times, however, Irish Catholics had to resort to using the buildings in secret and burying bodies at night.[37] As in West Central Africa, goods were left at the graveside, although usually after the burial, with wives and children visiting the resting places of deceased loved ones on a regular basis. Moryson noted, "The women espetially and Children doe weekely visit the graves of theire dead frendes, casting flowers and crosses upon them with weeping and many prayers for the dead." Here the confluence of Gaelic and Catholic practices becomes clear: the weeping reminiscent of keening, and the prayer signifying the importance of praying for the safe transport of the soul of the deceased from purgatory to heaven.[38] A Protestant bishop similarly noted the "ringing of bells and praying for the dead, and dressing their graves divers times in the year with flower pots and wax candles."[39] Again two kinds of rituals are blended together, with prayers representing one feature and grave goods being an example of another element of Irish faith. Irish rites surrounding burial were strongly influenced by Gaelic practices in the seventeenth century, but they remained resolutely Catholic nonetheless.[40]

As these accounts attest, Irish women were key actors in ceremonies surrounding mourning. From birth, Irish women took responsibility for the religious education of their children and those they fostered, explaining the rites that were central to securing the souls of loved ones upon death.[41] A second female responsibility was the preparation of the body for burial, cleaning the corpse and wrapping it in a shroud of linen lined with flowers and herbs.[42] Finally, and perhaps most importantly, there was a long tradition in Irish folklore of the place of the *mná caointe*, or wailing women, who cried out both to warn of death and to mourn the deceased.[43] The primary role played by women in death rituals may offer an explanation for the repugnance the church hierarchy exhibited toward mourning practices. Keening and the celebration of the wake enabled church officials to view such excessive displays of anguish as disrespectful to God and as Irish women's usurpation of the power of male priests, a further inversion of a divinely ordered universe.[44] At the same time, Catholic officials grudgingly recognized that women played an important role in the continued success of Catholicism in Ireland. As the seventeenth century progressed, male heads of Irish households increasingly converted to Protestantism as a way to escape prosecution by Protestant English authorities. Tellingly, their wives (and therefore their children) almost never rejected their Catholic faith, demonstrating the extent of female power at home and within the Irish community.[45]

In the middle of the seventeenth century the Cromwellian period sig-naled a dramatic change for open Catholic worship in Ireland. With the celebration of mass and other Catholic rituals forced underground, Irish Catholics had a reduced ability to publicly access older rituals that had become an integral and inseparable part of how they celebrated their faith.[46] English officials worked to accentuate the Catholicism of the Irish, highlighting religious difference as part of a politics of coercion.[47] This crackdown on religious expression of all kinds in Ireland coincided with the mass migration of Irish Catholics sent by Cromwell to Carib-bean colonies.[48] Therefore those who arrived on the western shores of the Atlantic Ocean did so understanding that however strong their faith, outward expressions of devotion to the Catholic Church would have to be subtle or hidden altogether.[49] For enslaved Africans who had suffered the traumas of the Middle Passage, the transfer of religious expression took on different forms. While the specifics of some local practices were lost, the broad parallels that connected West African spiritual expression flourished as groups from a wide range of countries were forced together on Caribbean plantations.[50] The religious milieu that met both groups of laborers also had an effect on the rites and rituals they performed in new settings. Laboring in a Protestant colony held danger for both Africans and Irish, but the risks to the two communities took different forms. For the Irish, paying lip service to the Church of England could be enough to avoid persecution. For enslaved Africans, conversion to Protestantism might provide a pathway to freedom and an escape from bondage altogether. One of the options for religious expression open to both Africans and Irish who arrived in the English Caribbean was to conform to the practices of the Church of England.

"Within the bounds of the Church of England"

While some Irish Catholics and some Africans engaged with Protestant spiritual practices, on the whole neither group seems to have embraced this possibility with much enthusiasm. When they did adopt Church of England rituals, they appeared to do so with very different ends in mind. For the seventeenth-century Caribbean, only Barbados has an extensive collection of the kinds of marriage, baptism, and probate records that note evidence of such spiritual conformity, and even then there are large gaps in the evidence, with information for many parishes not available until well into the eighteenth century. Irish Catholics appear to have largely avoided utilizing the Church of England for baptism and marriage ceremonies, but those with some property to bequeath did write wills, and a careful reading of probate records uncovers some of the ways Irish families circumvented Protestant rituals or used them to their own ends. Enslaved Africans did not leave wills, although they appear frequently in probate records, where they are listed as property. But baptism records do include entries for some enslaved and free people of color who were officially sanctioned members of the Church of England and so provide an opportunity to probe the spectrum of religious options open to at least some Africans in the West Indies.

The baptism of enslaved persons was certainly not a common affair in the English Caribbean, but a perusal of the Barbados baptismal registers indicates that people of color did, on occasion, receive the sacrament. Only four of the eleven parishes on the island have extant baptismal records covering the period up to 1715; just three include entries from before 1650. Even in the parishes of St. Michael, Christchurch, St. Philip, and St. James, entire years of information are missing. So the 185 people of color who took part in a baptism ceremony in one of these four parishes between approximately 1650 and 1715 represent only those included in the extant registers.[51] Out of the thousands of total baptismal records for the period this number is indeed a small fraction of the whole. And other issues are raised by these sources outside the matter of their unrepresentativeness. Using them to determine the rates at which Africans and the children of Africans chose to convert to the Protestant faith is essentially impossible: the records do not state whether the enslaved people who received the sacrament actively sought the process or were forced to comply with their owner's wishes. The motives of the sixty-two confirmed free people of color who were baptized during this period are equally difficult to discern. In addition, the status of over one-third of the people of color listed in the baptismal records is uncertain. The only markers attached to these persons are those of race: forty-one appear simply as "negroes" and twenty-five as "mullatoes," with no further clarification as to whether they were enslaved or free.

A handful of the baptism cases stand out and when cross-referenced with other records provide some insight into the kinds of decisions made by people of color concerning inclusion in the Church of England. In July of 1681, "Thomas Revell and Mary Thomas, negroes," baptized their daughter, Diana, in St. Michael's Parish. A little over a year later, in September 1682, Katherine, "Daughter of Thomas Revel a negro," was also baptized. And six years following, a third daughter, Mary, "of Thomas and Mary Ravell negroes," experienced the same ritual.[52] From the record it is initially difficult to tell whether all three daughters were the issue of Thomas and Mary because Katherine's mother is not named. But between 1681, when "Thomas Revell and Mary Thomas" were listed as the parents of Diana, and 1688, when the younger Mary was born, the elder Mary's appellation in the record had changed to reflect Thomas's last name, indicating that the two had formalized their relationship according to English customs and expectations. Indeed, two days after the younger Mary's baptism, there is a marriage record for a "Thomas Ravell & Mary Ravell, free negroes," in the parish of St. Michael. It appears certain, then, that Thomas and Mary had three daughters together.[53]

The question of whether Thomas and Mary themselves were baptized remains lost to the archive, but a clue to their desire to baptize their daughters comes from their status.[54] Listed simply in the baptismal records as "negroes," they appear in the marriage record as "free negroes," but Thomas, at least, was a former slave. In March of 1669, when his will was proved, another Thomas Revell, an English merchant in the same parish of St. Michael, dictated that the man he described as "my negro Thomas" should be given his freedom "eight years after my death."[55] This Thomas, who was released from slavery in March 1677, taking his former owner's last name in the process, is the Thomas who fathered Diana, Katherine, and Mary. Perhaps Thomas believed that there was a connection between freedom and Christianity, even if official island statutes did not concur.[56] He may have been trying to ensure his free status by embracing the official religion of Barbados.

The Revells had their marriage sanctioned by the church only follow-ing the birth and baptism of their three daughters, an action that again suggests the connection between freedom and conversion to Christian-ity. By legitimizing their daughters in the eyes of the Church of England, the Revells were claiming their spiritual equality with free English colo-nists. The same may have been true for Charles Cuffee, "a negro freed by his master" in the fall of 1677, who baptized his son Thomas and daughter Mary in November of 1689, when they were ten and five years old respec-tively. The later record listed "Charles Cuffy" as a "free Christian negro" and named Andrew Miller and Thomas Alford godfathers and Hannah Lamply and Ellen Hall godmothers to Thomas and Mary.[57] The status and ethnicity of the godparents are not noted, but a careful perusal of the other extant records for this period suggests that they were all English. Why they chose to bear witness to the baptism of Cuffy's children, how-ever, remains unknown.[58] Like Thomas and Mary Revell, Cuffy was mar-ried in the church long after his children were born and five years after they were baptized. In June 1694, the same day that Mary Jones, a "free negro," was baptized, she married a free man of color, "Charles Cuffee."[59] Although the mother of Charles Cuffy's children was not listed in their baptismal records, it is likely that she was Mary Jones, as it was common among communities of color to name children after their parents.[60]

The children of the Revells and the Cuffys were among the sixty or so other people of color marked as "free" who were baptized in the Church of England on Barbados between 1650 and 1715. The records of these ceremonies provide a glimpse of one of the strategies through which a small segment of the free population of color on Barbados legitimized their status as free colonial subjects, in this case through adoption of the official religious practice on the island. If baptism in the church was an active choice by these free people of color, it indicates their desire to reject religion as a signifier of difference between Africans and English. It also speaks, perhaps, to the particular context in which these chil-dren were born and would be raised. Birthrates among the enslaved population of the Caribbean were extremely low throughout the colonial period. The harsh working conditions on plantations account in part for the low fertility of enslaved women, but there is evidence too that enslaved couples actively sought to prevent pregnancies or to terminate those that did occur.[61] For the Revells and the Cuffys, the opportunity to celebrate their children born into freedom could be the key to comprehending free people of color's embrace of baptism. Understanding that their children might have different opportunities as a result of their free status may have alleviated the fraught nature of birthing nonwhite children in a slave society.

Ultimately, however, the baptism of people of color may reveal more about English attitudes toward the links between this sacrament and freedom than anything about the desire and wishes of Africans who became members of the church. Often the connection between freedom and Christianity was made not by the enslaved person but by his or her owner in probate records that dictated the terms of manumission. When Gedeon Goldring of St. Lucy wrote his will in July 1677, he bequeathed twelve enslaved Africans to his wife Katherine. One of the twelve, Goldring's "negro boy Baddue" was ordered to be "sett free by my exec[uto]rs when he shall come to the age of Five and Twenty years." Goldring wanted to guard against the denial of such a request, believing that the "Law of the Land" might prevent Baddue from being granted his freedom. In that eventuality, Baddue was to "be Christencd and sent of[f] the Island," perhaps to Bermuda, where Goldring held additional property.[62] Seven years later, in November 1685, Goldring added a codicil to his will in an attempt to clarify his wishes for Baddue and to "prevent controversie." Instead of asking that Baddue wait until he reached the age of twenty-five to be granted his freedom, now Goldring insisted that he be "sett free immediately after my death" and rejected any notion that Baddue would be "assigned or sent off as a servant" from Barbados.

The common thread in Baddue's manumission instructions was Goldring's repeated request for his slave to be baptized at the moment of freedom.[63] It seems clear that Goldring felt that admittance into the church and emancipation went hand in hand. Because the parish registers containing the baptismal records for St. Lucy do not begin until 1747, there is no documentary trail to prove that Baddue was baptized. Why Goldring was so concerned with Baddue's earthly and spiritual salvation can never be known. It is possible that he was Baddue's father and felt some particular connection to his son, or perhaps having Baddue at his side every day persuaded Goldring of some special quality the boy manifested that necessitated his freedom. Harder to parse is how Baddue felt about Gold-ring's plans. It is easy to imagine that the opportunity to be free was one that Baddue embraced, but even in freedom his master was trying to exert control over Baddue's spiritual choices. And Baddue may even have felt conflicted about being released from enslavement—there were eleven other enslaved people on Goldring's plantation who remained in slavery after their master's death, at least some of whom may have been related to Baddue, either by blood or through kinship ties. These other slaves could also have followed the same faith as Baddue before his introduction to Christianity. Baptism in the Protestant faith and manumission would rupture these relationships, perhaps beyond repair.

In terms of sheer numbers, enslaved people appear no more frequently in the baptism records than men, women, and children who are listed definitively as free, although of course they constituted a much larger proportion of the island's population. Questions arise both about why their masters sought to have these few baptized and about the extent to which those being put through the ceremony had any real engage-ment with Christianity or were willing participants in the services. In the four parishes with records for this period, the use of the actual term *slave* appears for the first time in 1700 in Christchurch, in 1699 in St. James, and not at all in St. Michael; and although there is one reference to a "Jacob son of Phyllis Hyant a slave" in 1666 in St. Philip, the term is not used again in that parish until 1697. Between the mid-seventeenth century and the late 1690s, if the term *negro* had any qualifier that wasn't *free*, the Africans in question tended to be either "at" a particular planta-tion, as in "James mulo. son of negro Mary *at* the Bell Plant[atio]n" in St. Michael, or "of" an owner, as in "Susanna a negro woman *of* John Obsurn" in Christchurch.[64] The shift may simply be a matter of changes in convention for the parish record keepers, or it may indicate that over time planters became more comfortable baptizing people of enslaved status. If "of" is taken as evidence of possession, the rate of recorded baptism for enslaved people does not fluctuate between 1650 and 1715. Perhaps the safest conclusion to be reached from these records is that at least some slave owners believed that baptism did not necessarily lead to freedom, even as others, like Goldring, seemed to find a connection between Christianity and manumission.

Irish Catholics were not enthusiastic about using the Church of Eng-land to baptize their children. Fewer than thirty parents christened their offspring between 1650 and 1715, according to the parish records. But evidence of a more sustained Irish engagement with the official record arises in the arena of death. The probate records for Barbados contain 110 wills for Irish men and a few women who died between 1650 and 1715. For the most part, these wills are formulaic. Their preambles generally give little indication of any religious beliefs, usually stating something to the effect that the deceased was "sicke and weake of Body" at the time they were composed.[65] During the sixteenth and seventeenth centuries, certain standardized preambles became popular and were published extensively in England. To complicate matters further, while it was unlikely that a Catholic would accept a Protestant preamble, or vice versa, neutral preambles were acceptable to people of either religious persuasion: there is plenty of evidence of nondescript preambles in Barbados wills.[66] Moreover, on Barbados, where there was no history of Catholic worship, and therefore probably no tradition of tailoring wills to Catholics, it is likely that those writing the wills used standard preambles, such as those from the *Symbolaeographia*, which were Protestant in their tone.[67] Although referencing Montserrat (and not Barbados), Governor William Stapleton noted that Irish Catholics on the island were content to use Protestant ministers and Protestant churches for the purposes of paperwork, specifically "for licence of marriage, Probatt of Wills."[68] The Irish on Barbados may well have done the same.[69] And despite the difficulties of interpretation, some of the wills proved on the island do provide clues as to religious affiliation.

In their final testaments Irish Catholics of more elite status appeared to embrace Protestantism, asking to be buried in the churches or churchyards of the parishes where they lived. Nicholas Rice was a prosperous merchant from St. Philip; George Rice, his nephew, owned a large plantation in the same parish. Both men were described as coming from "the Citty of Limericke in the Kingdome of Ireland" when their wills were written, in 1677 and 1684 respectively.[70] Nicholas asked to be "decently buryed in the Chancell of the Church of St Philips," and George made the same request, adding that he wished be laid to rest "neere the Corpse of my Uncle."[71] These provisions indicate that the Rices were Protestant. St. Philip was the parish on the southeast coast of Barbados, and to be buried in the interior of the church was in line with the wealth and status of the Rice men, as well as being a common practice among the wealthier members of the Protestant faith.[72] However, Nicholas's further request to leave to "the Roman Catholique Clergy of the Citty of Lymericke where I was borne one hundred and twenty pounds sterling," and George's decision to leave the poor of Limerick £50 and the "poor Irish people" of

FIGURE 12. Insert from Richard Ford's 1675 map of Barbados showing the location of the Rice plantations in St. Philip's Parish. One of the plantations is located at the six paths intersection, the other close to Foul Bay. Courtesy of the John Carter Brown Library at Brown University.

St. Philip "the sum of fourteen Pounds sterl[ing]," suggest that both men still had connections to the Catholic faith and communities in which they had been raised.[73] Indeed, Nicholas left a lasting legacy to the Irish population of St. Philip, donating fifty thousand pounds of "muscovado sugar" immediately, with a further ten thousand pounds a year to follow, "for the onely benefit and advantage of the said Poore of the said parrish," with the hope that others would be similarly generous so that there "may bee sufficient to erect an Hospitall in the said parrish for the poore thereof." Leaving this money was a way to assuage his sins and facilitate a transition from purgatory to heaven, both very Catholic concepts.[74]

Elite men were not those most likely to exhibit the full spectrum of Irish Catholic rituals because they were more invested in mimicking the religious norms of island society. However, even within the Rice family one can glimpse older cultural practices faintly imprinted on the probate records. Nicholas Rice was unmarried and appears to have fathered no children—only nephews, nieces, cousins, and a brother-in-law received bequests in his will—so it is impossible to know how he would have dealt with any progeny. George Rice did have a child, a daughter called Katherine, and the instructions for her future marriage hint at the necessity of following Irish matrimonial traditions. Rice left Katherine his entire estate, including "Plantation houses, land . . . Negroes, Horses, Mares, Cowes, Sheep, Hoggs, Goates, Stock," and the contents of his household, a bequeathal that makes sense given that she was his only child.[75] But Rice also left very specific instructions for Katherine's marriage, asking that she be joined to "one of the name of Rice being of birth and education suitable and not within the sins of consanguinitie." Among the native Irish, marriages allegedly took place among people of closer familial ties than the Catholic Church officially sanctioned, and elites, like the Rices, had adopted the practice.[76] That Rice acknowledged in his will that Katherine's marriage should avoid consanguinity while nonetheless requesting that she marry someone with his last name suggests that he was comfortable with this practice and that melding Gaelic and Catholic rituals was, by this point, second nature in his family. Unfortunately for Katherine, there appears to have been no suitor who met these standards: in 1688 Dominick Rice, a fellow Catholic and likely cousin who also lived in St. Philip, married Catherine Clansey.[77]

There is ample evidence of continued adherence to Irish beliefs in the final testaments of less elite Irish men, despite their ostensibly Protestant preambles. Specifically, the desires of these men become clear in relation to burial responsibilities, which they placed in the hands of the women in their lives, just as they had done in Ireland. Almost half of the wills left by married Irish men whose wives were living at the time of their death listed their wives as executors. And those women were given control over the manner of burial. For example, Patrick Collins, of St. Michael, whose will was proved on 30 April 1681, assigned his wife as his executor and asked for his body to "be decently intered as it shall seem most meet to my executrix."[78] By tasking the organization of this ceremony to his wife, a particularly significant gesture in the Irish Catholic faith, Patrick may have been signaling his continued adherence to Catholicism. In another apparently Protestant preamble, Teague Curreen requested that he "be buried in such decent and Christian manner as to my Executors hereafter named shall deem meet and convenient" and assigned his wife and friends as those responsible for managing the disposal of his estate and his body.[79]

Naming a wife as an executor was not, in and of itself, an unusual practice in the seventeenth century.[80] However, when these probate records are compared to a random sample of the same number of English wills, it becomes clear that only around one-quarter of English men designated their wives to oversee their estates. The differences are more stark with regard to the connections between executors and burial preferences. Over half of all English men (sixty) requested specifically to be buried in the parish churchyard or within the walls of the church itself. Only eight Irish men asked for the same privilege (two of whom were Nicholas and George Rice). The vast majority of Irish men's wills (sixty-nine) made no mention whatsoever of their burial plans, indicating that they were happy to have those they left behind make those decisions for them. Of these, thirty-five included living wives, half of whom were listed as executors. Contrast these numbers to the seventeen English wills that did not make any specific reference to burial, none of which listed wives as executors. Without overstating the importance of these distinctions, one can connect women's crucial role in burial ceremonies in Ireland to their prominence in wills in the Caribbean as suggestive of the fact that this was one way for Irish Catholics to continue to practice aspects of their Catholicism on Barbados, even within a Protestant setting.

Although Africans and Irish both engaged the official religion of the English Caribbean, they did so in different ways and toward different ends. People of color on Barbados who had already earned their freedom chose to embrace the Church of England by baptizing their children and marrying their partners. Their official conversion to Protestantism, even if they continued to engage in other spiritual practices, was an acknowledgment of the reality that emphasizing one's Christianity might make it easier to live as a free person of color in a slave society. Irish Catholics, like the Rices, could also gain something by making an outward show of adherence to Protestantism by attending Church of England services or using Protestant ministers to perform marriages or baptisms. But the testaments they wrote at the end of their lives demonstrate how in death Catholic traditions came to the fore: they may have used the Church of England to gain prestige in their lifetimes, but in death they were determined that their souls would not be damned. The Cuffys or the Revells may have had similar outlooks, returning to older traditions as death neared. Unlike Irish Catholics, however, they had no probate records or other sources to provide glimpses of how the ends of their lives were marked. For Africans and Irish who did not engage with the official religious institutions on the islands, alternative spiritual practices allowed them to keep their faiths.

"Exposing their bodies for the salvation of their souls"

The vast majority of enslaved Africans and Irish Catholics on Barbados and elsewhere in the Leeward Islands did not engage the colonies' official religious institutions at all. English authorities tried to dictate what would pass for acceptable religious practice on the islands by banning Catholic priests and overlooking rituals of enslaved Africans on plantations, "never think[ing] of their slaves' souls" or "speak[ing] to them about any religion or religious exercises."[81] On both counts they failed. The daily expression of religious rites dominated spiritual life on plantations, especially ceremonies surrounding death, an ever-present reality of the Caribbean climate and the process of sugar production on the islands. While most Africans engaged in varied spiritual practices on plantations beyond the watchful eyes of their masters and overseers, some apparently continued to follow the Catholicism they had been introduced to by the Portuguese.[82] Although the presence of priests would always be more important to Irish Catholics than to the few Africans who had undergone baptism in Africa, their continued infiltration in Protestant jurisdictions provided spiritual solace for all who followed the Catholic faith.

In January 1655, the Council of Barbados discussed a worrying rumor that "three Irish priests were landed on this island [from] a ship arrived lately to Spike's Bay."[83] Sixteen months later, the Council banned four Irish priests from the island, giving these men three days to leave Barbados. Cromwell's Western Design against Catholic Spain reinvigorated English anxiety about priests in their midst, despite a general prohibition on their presence, and Barbados was not the only English colony where priests were able to gain a foothold.[84] The proximity of islands under the control of the Catholic empires of France and Spain meant the easy facilitation of the movement of Catholic priests around the Atlantic world. Reports of the arrival of Father Stritch, an Irish priest, in the French part of bijurisdictional St. Christopher in 1650 emphasized the fervor of Irish Catholics, who were ecstatic at being able to access a priest in their midst after being deprived of the chance to worship for so long. Father Jean Baptiste du Tertre, a Jesuit, recorded responses to Father Stritch's arrival. He noted that crowds of Irish appeared to see Stritch, "so fervent that they had no fear about exposing their bodies for the salvation of their souls." Stritch stayed on the island for three months, during which "he remained there constantly occupied in hearing confessions, giving Holy Communion and baptizing and instructing their children."[85]

Father Stritch also visited Montserrat, the island described by a fellow Jesuit, Father Andrew White, as "a noble plantation of Irish Catholiques."[86] Stritch tried to avoid direct confrontation with the authorities and "did not erect a chapel, but served mass in the woods."[87] Providing cover for his actions, Stritch posed as a merchant seeking to purchase wood and spent at least some of his time on Montserrat engaged in exactly that endeavor to forestall English suspicions. In the end, it seems that many on the island were perfectly aware of his status as a priest. Witnesses who were deposed as part of an investigation into a 1655 scandal on Montserrat noted that there was "a priest in the s[aid] Island, called father John." Another man simply referred to Stritch as a "Roman preist" but noted that he was a frequent visitor to the colony.[88] However futile Stritch's attempts at deception may have been, his discovery did not prevent him from successfully ministering to Montserrat's Irish Catholics, and the quiet way in which he went about his mission meant that the English did not feel obliged to banish him as they had the priests who provided similar services on Barbados.

Disguise was a relatively common strategy adopted by priests of all nations. The experiences of Biet, who spent four months on Barbados in 1652, suggested that subterfuge was an important weapon to guard against discovery—Biet dressed as a gentleman throughout his time on Barbados. However, he was clearly recognizable as a priest to those who knew what to look for; perhaps when he was alone he was less cautious about making sure his rosary and the other accoutrements of his faith were hidden. In fact, when Biet encountered the unnamed Irish man in the orange grove on Cesar de Mesnil's estate, something about his appearance allowed the man to feel safe in making "the sign of the cross" to let Biet know that he, too, was Catholic. This bit of theater was not especially convincing to Biet, who was clearly still nervous about confirming his vocation. So the man prostrated himself on the ground, reciting "the Lord's Prayer in Latin, the Hail Mary, the *Credo*, and the *de Profundis* to certify that he believed in the prayer for the dead," proving in the process that he was indeed familiar with the key teachings of the Catholic Church.[89] At the time Biet encountered this unnamed Irish man, he had left his party with the specific purpose of undertaking some private worship. His actions, movements, or words may have marked him as a priest to a careful observer or to a fellow Catholic like the unnamed Irish man.

Secrecy was not only the purview of Catholic priests. Donat Ofaye, an Irish Catholic servant, was one of the first residents of Barbados to greet the ship carrying Father Biet when it arrived on the island.[90] Their meeting does not seem to have been planned, but in an almost unbelievable coincidence the two men had met before and in fact had an acquaintance of some longevity. According to Biet, Ofaye "lived with me [in France for] four or five years, wore the cassock, acting as a clerk in my church."[91] While it is unclear whether Ofaye actually entered the priesthood (he claimed to Biet that he had not "severed his vows to God"), he was "well known to everyone [on Barbados]" and so was perfectly placed to perform religious duties on the island.[92] To do so, Ofaye needed to hide in plain sight, operating under the radar of English authorities, who would not have recognized him as a man of religion. But Irish Catholics would have identified him as occupying the familiar role of leading individual devotions, a frequent occurrence in Ireland when priests were scarce on the ground. Ofaye may have been a bard in his former life, for it was common for bards to receive religious instruction in Europe and then to bring that knowledge back to Ireland to subvert the Reformation.[93] It may be that in the Caribbean Ofaye was an anomaly. However, it appears likely that others like him would have had the knowledge and experience to fulfill similar roles.[94]

Biet's account also demonstrates that Catholics were able to worship in relative freedom on Barbados. Explaining his role on a plantation purchased by members of the French party he traveled with, Biet wrote, "I did the prayers every day, evening and morning. I only said mass on feast days and Sundays . . . whe[n] each one is free to do whatever he wants on the plantation, and to live with whatever religion he wants."[95] He insisted that on Barbados "all are given freedom of belief, provided that they do nothing to be conspicuous in public." The key observation in Biet's description of this seeming flexibility was his statement that "on Sunday one is free to do what one wants in his house, no one bothers to see what he is doing." As far as Biet was concerned, keeping the true faith behind closed doors explained why he was able to carry out his "religious functions with great freedom."[96] Biet was primarily concerned with ministering to those who shared his faith, not fomenting dissent among Catholics, Irish or otherwise, and for this he (and his followers) were largely left alone.

Father Pierre Pelleprat, a French Jesuit who wrote about the order's experiences in the Americas, recorded what happened when secrecy was not maintained. Although Father Stritch was initially successful in ministering to the Irish on St. Christopher, Pelleprat noted that the English soon realized what was happening on the island "and have forbidden all Irish Catholics from going henceforth to the French district" to receive communion.[97] Furthermore, according to Pelleprat, the English were not "content to prohibit the exercise of their religion" and "removed one hundred and twenty five Irish Catholics" who were regarded as the "most angry and most important" to the tiny Isle of Crabs.[98] Pelleprat's description of the events on St. Christopher counters Biet's suggestion that there was great religious tolerance in English colonies and suggests that timing and location was everything for Irish Catholics hoping to receive the sacraments or counsel from their priests.[99]

A similar clampdown on Catholic activity occurred in the late 1680s. On Barbados, almost thirty-five years after Biet had departed the island, another French priest arrived in Bridgetown at the instigation of two recently converted English Catholics. Following the end of James II's reign and the installation of William and Mary as Protestant monarchs, there was an investigation into the role of this French priest on the island. Depositions taken in early 1689 reported that he held Catholic services on plantations and that "those who came to hear Mass . . . were youzally Irish men, and them of the poorer sort and many of them servants."[100] Indeed, of the forty-eight men listed as persons "sawne att Mass att the house of Mr Willoughby Chamberlaine" on Christmas Day, 1688, around half had Irish names.[101] While the discovery of the French priest led to the prosecution of those who had asked him to come to Barbados, the depositions demonstrate that some kind of Catholic community had been sustained on the island, as Irish Catholics refused to let go of the religion they had practiced before crossing the Atlantic Ocean.

The Irish were not the only population on Barbados that priests and English observers suggested might be Catholic. Biet claimed that at least "six Negroes and their wives with their children" were Catholic, and he credited their education in Catholicism to the Portuguese who had forcibly removed the Africans across the Atlantic Ocean.[102] Englishman Richard Ligon also commented on the presence of Africans "bred up amongst the Portugalls," stating that "I have seen some of these *Portugall Negres*, at Collonell *James Draxes*," one of the largest plantations on the island in the early 1650s.[103] Some of the Africans that Biet or Ligon encountered might have been familiar with the basic prayers of the Catholic faith or would have recognized a rosary or a crucifix if they saw one.[104] Indeed, it was Africans like these that Biet described as being "tinged" with Catholicism. Nonetheless, he noted that they kept their faith "the best they can, doing their prayers, and worshipping God in their hearts." This observation suggests that Biet saw some outward expressions of faith from the "Portuguese Christians," perhaps in the prayers they spoke.[105] But these enslaved Africans were forced to keep other aspects of their faith "in their hearts," unable (in the absence of a priest like Biet) to gain access to the kinds of sacraments necessary to maintain their faith.

Of course, it was possible that these African Catholics found ways to worship alongside Irish colonists who held the same faith. Although no "Portuguese Negroes" were mentioned in the depositions about the Catholic mass taking place on Chamberlain's estate, in the very same month the Barbados Council heard that three such Africans "doe openly profess themselves Roman Catholick" and had been "in the time of the Jesuits . . . often seen at Mass," and ordered them to be "sold or transported and sent of this Island to be sold accordingly." It is possible that these men might have been transported to Barbados from nearby French islands. Charles de Rochefort noted that on Guadeloupe and Martinique there were "some Negroes who punctually observe abstinence all the time of Lent, and all the other Fasting-days appointed by the Church."[106] The timing of the order, coming as it did during the investigation into Willoughby Chamberlain's conduct, strongly suggests that these men were part of the Catholic congregation. Perhaps their presence was not sufficiently noteworthy for Dominick Rice and the other deposees. Or maybe they were not asked about non-European participation at the Catholic mass. These three unnamed African men had been freed from bondage just one year previously for proving themselves to be "free borne and Christians."[107] But now the threat they posed by attending mass alongside Irish Catholics was too much to bear. The authorities feared the "ill consiquence" of their "seduceing and drawing of the Negroes and other slaves of this Island" to the Catholic faith, "as well as other wicked attempts and designes [that] might follow thereon."[108]

The communal living and working spaces on plantations discussed in the previous chapter provided opportunities for enslaved Africans and indentured Irish Catholics to observe and perhaps participate in each other's religious observances and rituals. It is likely that the intersection of the religious interests of both groups spilled over into their Sunday downtime, perhaps creating a new set of religious practices that had little in common with any form of Christianity or that drew on common understandings of Catholicism where those existed. Just as Irish women took the lead in baptizing children outside official church institutions, so the "Christianized" African slaves that Biet mentions were "content to baptize their infants in the home," a tantalizing statement that opens up possibilities for what might have occurred between Irish servant women and enslaved African women when a child was born on the plantation.[109] But although ceremonies surrounding birth are one possible area of overlap between Irish and African communities, little extant material describes what these practices looked like on Caribbean islands.

Rituals surrounding death, on the other hand, were much discussed by English observers in the colonies. Richard Ligon recorded his observations of funeral rites on plantations among enslaved Africans, noting, "When any of them die, they dig a grave, and at evening they bury him, clapping and wringing their hands, and making a dolefull sound with their voices."[110] Twenty-five years later, John Taylor observed that when Jamaican slaves died, "they make a great adoe at their burials for having caryed them to the grave in a very mournfule manner.... Both men & women which accompany the corpse sing and howle in a sorrowfull manner in their own language till being come to the grave."[111] Hans Sloane, who was a contemporary of Taylor's on Jamaica, observed that "their country people make great lamentations, mournings, and howlings about them expiring."[112] All of these references parallel the accounts of Barbot and de Marees in Africa, and Moryson, Brereton, and Stanihurst in Ireland.

To note these similarities is not to suggest that burial ceremonies in Ireland and Africa were identical to those that took place in the Caribbean.[113] Irish people found ways to circumvent the lack of consecrated land and often left women in charge of burial in both places, although the means by which they did so had changed. In Ireland, women liaised with lay preachers and negotiated burial (when necessary) on sites that had formerly been consecrated by the Catholic Church. On the other side of the Atlantic Ocean the Irish had to scramble and improvise when it came to their final resting places, with men often naming their wives as their executors in probate records. But on occasion Irish Catholics were able to approach the end of life by more conventional means. On Montserrat in 1654 a man "caryed a Cross before his wive body when she was Caryed to her burial," performing a ritual common in Catholic funerals across the early modern world.[114] This brief glimpse of a more recognizably Catholic ceremony in the Caribbean hints that others might have occurred too. Ultimately, however, the Protestant climate on the islands marked references to such events as rare.

For Africans the move to the Americas had a profound effect on their spirituality. Ligon, Taylor, and Sloane all discussed the beliefs among some of the Africans that on death they would return to Africa: "For they believe a Resurrection, and that they shall go into their own Country again, and have their youth renewed."[115] To help the deceased prepare for this journey, "at their funeral [attendees would] throw in rum and victuals into their graves, to serve them in the other world. Sometimes they bury it in gourds, at other times spill it on the graves." Here the ritual had much in common with practices at African graves, perhaps even referencing the continued use of *minkisi* in the Caribbean. The kinds of materials left at the graveside, however, now had a distinctly American flavor. Some of those "victuals" included "casadar bread, roasted fowles, sugar, rum, tobacco, & pipes with fier to light his pipe withal, and this they doe . . . in order to sustain him in his journey beyond those pleasant hills in their own country whither they say he is now goeing to live at rest."[116]

Unfortunately it is almost impossible to explore these rituals from an African perspective: the goods that entered the ground along with the deceased's body have been buried, quite literally hidden from sight, and the only way to reach them and explore their cultural significance would be a further violation of African bodies. There have been few sites of archaeological exploration involving burial plots of slaves, but one of the most significant areas of investigation has been the Newton plantation in Christchurch Parish, an estate that includes one of the only identified rural slave cemeteries in the English Caribbean. Some of the materials uncovered at Newton demonstrate the continued significance of grave goods in the West Indies. Among the hundreds of enslaved women, men, and children who perished on this sugar-producing plantation over the course of two centuries lay the remains of a man buried in an elaborate fashion around 1700. This individual was most probably a healer or a diviner given the possessions included in his grave. His body was adorned with metal rings around his fingers and bracelets that encircled his forearms. An iron knife and a clay pipe of West African origin were also placed alongside his body. Perhaps most significant were the elements of the necklace that would once have rested around his neck. Dogs' teeth, fish vertebrae, cowry shells, glass beads, and a large carnelian bead were its constituent parts, each signifying an important aspect of the man's spiritual powers.[117] The violence of social death in slavery and the horrors of the Middle Passage affected approaches to spirituality in the Americas, but as the careful burial of the enslaved man on Newton's plantation shows, enslaved laborers continued to seek connection with the world from which they had been wrenched.[118]

Like Africans on plantations, the Irish left goods at the graveside, and it can be assumed that they continued to do the same in the Caribbean. Moreover, a key cultural element of their faith was the expression of sorrow in keening, the kinds of wailing and crying that Ligon, Sloane, and Taylor discussed hearing at African funerals. And Irish Catholics also believed in a journey after death. They may not have thought about it in terms of traversing an ocean or returning to a homeland, but they did believe that prayer, graveside visits, and leaving money to the church and to the poor of the parish were necessary to secure the passage of the deceased's soul from purgatory to heaven. In fact, Nicholas and George Rice's bequests to the Catholic clergy of Limerick were in some sense a means of returning a physical presence to their homeland. While the specific spiritual connotations of each of these practices have obvious differences, there is an overlap in the broad sense, especially in the sentiments each group evoked at the graveside, and it is easy to imagine a mutual recognition, among the different laboring communities on plantations, of the importance of taking care of the deceased's soul and ensuring its safe passage to the realm of the dead.

* * *

Although the religious practices that carried over from Ireland and West Central Africa took on different qualities in the Caribbean, this process of change was not simply a reflection of the mixing of cultural practices but also a natural and inevitable characteristic of systems of belief that were always in flux. Some changes that occurred were closely tied to individuals' exposure to alternative religious rituals, and particularly to the ways in which certain actors understood their place in island hierarchies. It appears that both free people of color and wealthier Irish Catholics viewed a certain degree of outward conformity to the Church of England as a way to signify their differences from enslaved Africans and indentured Irish Catholics respectively. Free people of color used baptism as a way to underscore their freedom and perhaps to ensure that their children would have a better chance of remaining free in the years to come, given the general skittishness of planters when it came to converting their enslaved populations to Christianity. For Irish elites the stakes were different. In many ways they were hoping to have their status as important merchants and planters recognized by island authorities. They wanted to be considered full members in Caribbean society despite their Irish Catholic backgrounds. For them, obscuring the less desirable aspects of their Irishness behind a veneer of Protestantism was key to their acceptance in Barbados and the other Leeward islands. And yet at the ends of their lives these Irish Catholics abandoned conformity to English ways and returned to their religious roots for eternity.

Religious rituals that fell outside official church sanction continued to be the norm for most enslaved Africans and indentured Irish Catholics. In their adherence to certain rites these groups staked claims about what was important to them spiritually and therefore declared how they understood their relationships to each other. An ability to recognize some of the key aspects of one another's funeral rites, such as leaving grave goods, keening and celebrating the loved one's passing, and attempting to keep the worlds of the dead and the living connected, may have forged bonds between Africans and Irish, or at least lessened antipathy between them. Given how prevalent death was in the seventeenth-century Caribbean, such ceremonies would have been very common events. These kinds of interactions on plantations, and those that surrounded labor, and food, and sex, may also have bred as much contempt as they did familiarity. But over the course of the seventeenth century unfree laborers, indentured and enslaved, often found common cause together and worked to challenge colonial authority in more direct ways than those provided by the ordinary experiences of their everyday lives. The relationships they forged through religious practices were important connections that served as the bedrock for more overt resistance to the colonial regime.

Around thirty years after he had arrived on Barbados, Cornelius Bryan decided it was time to make a will. In March 1686, he commended his "soule to God and my body to the earth to be decently buried in my garden," in St. James' Parish, Barbados. Cornelius, despite being "sick in body," was not at all anxious as he prepared to go to his garden grave: he was confident in the knowledge that he had performed the duty expected of a Barbados planter. As he divided his property in land and slaves among his wife and six children, Cornelius wondered whether anyone would notice that he was not asking to be laid to rest in the parish churchyard in Holetown. He had specifically left control over his burial to his wife, Margaret, knowing that she could be trusted to ensure the passage of his soul to the other side through her prayers and keening. It was important to him that the rites surrounding his burial be watched over by Margaret; perhaps she would even be able to find a priest willing to risk performing the ceremony himself. In any case he knew that Margaret would encourage his daughter,

Katherine, to mourn alongside her in the years to come. Cornelius was certain that his soul would be secure and that the Catholicism that had shaped his life would continue to influence his spirit in death.

When she thought about the end of her life, Pegg did not share Cornelius's confidence about what would happen when death finally claimed her. Born on Barbados, she had never known anything other than life in slavery on this island. Old Pegg had told her about the place where she had been born and how different life had been in that distant land, but Pegg found it difficult to conjure up an image of what such an existence must have been like. Old Pegg explained that when she died she would return to her country. Pegg would organize the burial, gather the appropriate foodstuffs to be laid alongside her for the journey, and slip a small wooden canoe into the grave to aid her passage to the land of her ancestors. When she was a child, Old Pegg had made packets with herbs and bones, tying them onto Pegg's wrist or around her waist to better protect her from harm. But despite her mother's teachings, Pegg was not certain about what she would experience when she passed away: she longed to make the journey across the ocean, as her mother would, to be reunited with her ancestors, but as she had no direct connection to the place so far away, Pegg was unsure about whether such a journey would take place. Perhaps she would be trapped on this island for eternity.

5 / "Endeavouring to raise mutinie and sedition": The Challenge to English Domination

The summer of 1692 found Sambo, Sampson, and Ben hopeful. As skilled members of the enslaved community in Barbados, the three men had been moving around the island's western parishes, talking to their fellow "carpenters, Bricklayers, wheelwrights, sawyers, Blacksmiths, Grooms," and other elite enslaved workers. Their conversations were not mere exchanges of kinship and friendship, complaints about the hardships of life on the plantation, or idle gossip about masters, mistresses, and their offspring. Instead, they concerned an audacious plan to overthrow the planter hierarchy on Barbados through a military attack. These discussions were so secret that the plotters would not take their friends into their confidence unless they swore a solemn oath. Following these careful precautions, the three enslaved men had recruited "four or five most capable & those most trusted" enslaved persons on each plantation to their cause. In addition to relying on their enslaved counterparts to step out in the "four Regiments of foot," and mount up in the "two Regiments of Horse," they were counting on another "negro that was an Armourer in the Magazine" to gain access to the necessary firearms by killing the captain in charge of the depot. Enslavement alone did not bind the conspirators: Ben, Sambo, and Sampson also enlisted Irish men to get the soldiers in Needham's Fort drunk.[1] The men plotted for so long that it seemed that the long-anticipated moment of revolt would never come: they had twice postponed the uprising when English naval reinforcements arrived to augment expeditions against the French during King

William's War. Finally, with the fleet set to depart for an attack on Martinique, the three enslaved men felt confident that the moment of revolt had arrived. When it concluded, slavery would be but a distant memory for the participants in the rebellion. Soon they would once again be in charge of their own destiny. As the fall of 1692 approached, Ben, Sambo, and Sampson seasoned their hope with terror of the unforeseen consequences of their actions. The longer they waited to execute their carefully laid plans, the greater the chance that something would go wrong or that someone would betray their confidence.

Revolts planned by unfree laborers had a long history on Barbados, and from the very first instance they worried English authorities. In the 1640s, shortly before Richard Ligon arrived on the island, planters quashed what they presumed to be an island-wide servant uprising. According to Ligon's informants, the servants had tired of their mistreatment, organizing across plantations to kill their masters. On an appointed day the conspirators would "fall on their Masters, and cut all their throats, and by that means, to make themselves not only freemen, but Masters of the Iland." Only a last-minute report by a servant either "failing of his courage, or some new obligation from the love of his Master," revealed this long-plotted conspiracy.[2] Eighteen executions followed; swift, brutal, and intended to intimidate anyone thinking about perpetrating such a rash act in the future. But despite the reminder that the hangman's noose was never terribly far away, plots proliferated on Barbados, exploding in the last quarter of the seventeenth century. In 1675 a group of "Gold Coast Negroes" fell under suspicion of planning to introduce a West African style of government to Barbados. In 1688 Irish and English "Papists" (in conjunction with French priests) stood accused of trying to make the island a Catholic colony. And in 1692, Ben, Sambo, Sampson, and their coconspirators were said to be planning a military assault on the planter class that would make the rebels rulers of their world.

Ascertaining whether these planned uprisings or challenges to English hierarchies actually existed or whether these moments of rebellion should more accurately be viewed as examples of English anxiety run amok is difficult.[3] Reality probably lies somewhere in between—enslaved Africans and Irish Catholics did foment discontent and may have plotted to overthrow slavery or English rule, but the exaggerated responses to these threats on the part of colonial officials magnified their impact on the islands.[4] The choices open to scholars are not as stark as either accepting, for example, the account of the 1692 uprising at face value, or treating the entire episode as simply evidence of English disquiet. It is possible that Ben, Sambo, Sampson, and others hatched a plot to over-throw the planter class *and* that the extent of the plan was exaggerated by English authorities, or indeed by the enslaved men themselves.

This chapter is less concerned with whether any of these individual plots were planned in the way that the records claim they were than it is with the ways that coconspirators chose to explain their alleged schemes to English officials. The power dynamics of archival construction shapes the kinds of narratives that can be told.[5] In the case of the 1675 and 1692 revolts, torture was used to coerce confession. It is not clear whether violence was threatened to extract depositions in the 1688 case, but mili-tia officers asked the questions and so were certainly in a position of authority over their interogees. In all cases the methods under which the accounts were taken severely compromised the sorts of information gleaned by English authorities. These facts do not automatically render the source material useless. In terms of seventeenth-century archives, the records of each of these events provide some of the richest and most detailed descriptions from the perspectives of enslaved Africans and Irish Catholics. They may not necessarily have told interrogators what they really hoped to achieve, or what they actually planned, but in their imagined visions they constructed a narrative that struck fear into the hearts of anxious English officials. Conspirators knew that they would either succeed in their goals or die in the attempt. The moment of capture did not signal the end of their rebellion: hauled before colonial admin-istrators, they made the interrogations themselves a site of continued revolt against the regime. Irish Catholics fed into English stereotypes about their supposed savageness by invoking cannibalism, the drink-ing of blood, and an inversion of the rules of civilized warfare. Enslaved Africans talked of their intention to create an African state, adding fuel to English fears about African challenges to the colonial regime. And in 1692, when the conspirators conjured the image of an intermixed group of Africans and Irish, they underscored the opportunities for solidarity across social, cultural, ethnic, and racial boundaries, despite vigorous English attempts to prevent such collaborations.

The versions of the plots that conspirators presented to English author-ities demonstrate how subordinated peoples understood their perceived inferiority and therefore how they forged their own ideas about differ-ence. This chapter concentrates on the performative aspects of individual conspirators to engage their visions for their lives.[6] By creating space for themselves within English discourses, Africans and Irish (island-born or saltwater slaves) forced themselves into the official record.[7] In the process they upset colonial assertions about control. Their everyday interactions rooted relationships, allowing the alternative understandings rebels had about connection and community to shine through. Since they were the most marginalized groups in Caribbean society, their political power was inevitably curtailed, but what they did have, the power of imagination, they harnessed to dramatic effect, playing on anxious English minds. "Gold Coast" kings were coming to avenge their enslaved countrymen, French priests would rescue Irish Catholics from a heretical government, and a military uprising of Africans and Irish working in concert would set both groups free to run the island as they saw fit. These events drew on the histories of the places from where Irish and Africans had come, and transformed the spaces they now inhabited. Contained in each plot was a vision for a Barbados free from the oppressive yoke of English rule, where alternatives to colonial hierarchies could flourish.

"Hatched by the Cormantee or Gold Coast Negroes"

The year 1675 was tumultuous on Barbados. On the last day of August a devastating hurricane tore across the colony, leaving a swath of death and destruction in its wake. Houses were torn down, island residents were killed, and crops were uprooted. Just a few months before the natural disaster, the colony had been rocked by a human threat: a planned revolt by enslaved Africans.[8] Accounts of the conspiracy can be found in two anonymous pamphlets published the year after the alleged uprising was discovered (*Great Newes from the Barbadoes* and *An Account of the Intended Rebellion of the Negroes in Barbados*), and in the reports that Governor Jonathan Atkins sent back to London in 1675. All agreed on the broad contours of the revolt and on its African dimensions, specifically what English observers noted as "Cormantee" leadership.[9] Governor Atkins described the 1675 participants as "Cormantin Negroes who are much the greater part of Negroes of any one Country and are a warlike and Robust . . . sort of People."[10] Beginning in this period, Europeans in the Americas began to view these Akan speakers as both fierce warriors and hard workers who could be very loyal to those who had earned their respect.[11]

The 1675 conspiracy on Barbados was one of the first in the English colonies to ascribe an African political ideology to a slave revolt, but it was by no means the first time that enslaved people had caused trouble for authorities.[12] In the 1650s the council noted the "divers rebellious &

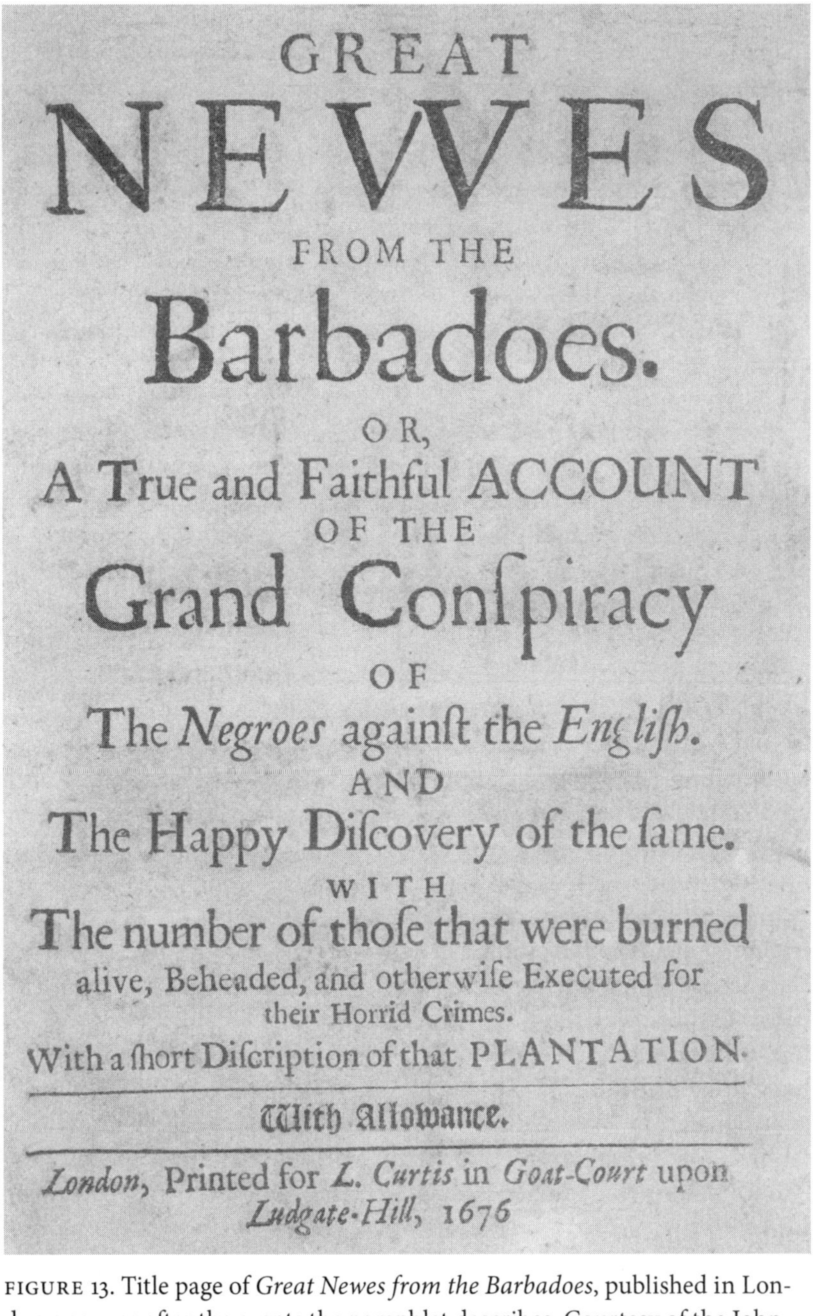

GREAT
NEWES
FROM THE
Barbadoes.

O R,

A True and Faithful ACCOUNT
O F T H E
Grand Conspiracy
O F
The *Negroes* againſt the *Engliſh*.
A N D
The Happy Diſcovery of the ſame.
W I T H
The number of thoſe that were burned

alive, Beheaded, and otherwiſe Executed for
their Horrid Crimes.

With a ſhort Diſcription of that PLANTATION.

With Allowance.

London, Printed for *L. Curtis* in *Goat-Court* upon
Ludgate-Hill, 1676

FIGURE 13. Title page of *Great Newes from the Barbadoes*, published in London one year after the events the pamphlet describes. Courtesy of the John Carter Brown Library at Brown University.

runne away negroes" who "lye lurkeing in the woods and secret places" that adjoined the plantation of Mr. Thomas Moore in the parish of St. Joseph. According to Moore, these runaways were "committinge many violences and attempting to assassinate people to there great Terrour."[13] Barbados topography made it difficult for maroon communities to flourish as they did on more mountainous islands like Jamaica, but in the 1650s there were still some few places in the colony where runaways could conceal themselves, even if just temporarily. English authorities saw considerable danger in such acts of petit marronage. Not only had enslaved Africans removed their essential labor from plantations in the area, but they had also banded together and were collaborating to terrorize planters on the eastern side of the island.

To restore order after individuals ran away, the militia was sent to seek out the "rebellious negroes," inserting the colonial state into the conflict. Those who were captured would be taken to the "Common Gaole to bee proceeded against accordinge to lawe," which could include a number of forms of branding, or having an ear removed, depending on whether or not they were repeat offenders. If any runaways resisted and could not "be taken & subdued," the council allowed that they "maye bee Lawfullye kilde and destroyde."[14] The vehemence of "destroyde" indicated the seriousness of the threat to authority posed by enslaved runaways. To kill individuals was not enough; the entire group would be subject to annihilation.[15] English officials were more willing to risk the destruction of their valuable property than to allow runaways to claim their freedom because they were jeopardizing the entire system of slavery by absconding from the plantation.

With no extant depositions from the 1675 revolt, and only a smattering of references in the official correspondence between London and the colonies, two anonymous pamphlets provide the best accounts of how island authorities treated the enslaved suspects. *Great Newes from the Barbadoes* proudly proclaimed that when the plan was discovered on Justice Hall's plantation, one "young *Negro* Man . . . impeached several, as well his own Master's *Negro's* as others belonging to the adjacent Plantations." Following this initial interrogation, Governor Atkins gave Hall "Commissions to apprehend the guilty and impeached *Negroes*," after which they would be "brought to Tryal at a Court of *Oyer* and *Terminer*." Next they would be subjected to a "strict and due Examination of the matter of Fact of their Conspiracy."[16] The coconspirators were kept "in a stricter manner" as authorities attempted to ascertain what precisely had occurred among enslaved populations on the island.[17] More euphemistic than direct, the meaning was nonetheless clear: conspirators could expect no mercy from island elites. And the careful attention to "Cormantee" details included in *Great Newes* was not simply about adding texture or color to the pamphlet's narrative. In underlining the African elements of the plot, the anonymous author made the protagonists seem all the more foreign, brutal, and frightening in the minds of his English readers. The same sentiment was expressed more directly by the author of the *Account of the Intended Rebellion*, who noted with relief that the English population of the island had been delivered "from the Tyranny and barbarous cruelty of Savage Heathens."[18]

The slaves who were questioned by the magistrates and judges made clear the West African connections to the alleged uprising. Although it may have been English authorities who decided that the plot had been "hatched by the Cormantee or Gold Coast Negroes," enslaved rebels provided the information that they planned to crown one of their own king of Barbados.[19] Intending to "choose them a King, one *Coffee* [Cuffee] an Ancient Gold-Coast *Negro*," the conspirators had set 12 June 1675 as the day of the uprising.[20] Coffee/Cuffee's coronation ceremony would include "a Chair of State exquisitely wrought and Carved after their Mode," and Coffee/Cuffee would witness "Bowes and Arrowes . . . carried in State before his Majesty." The crowning ritual was fundamentally about conferring political supremacy to the revolt's leader: the chair itself was an important representation of power in Akan politics that would also have been understood by English authorities as a symbol of royal authority.[21] The fanfare provided by "Trumpets to be made of Elephants Teeth," would ensure that the whole population knew that a "Cormantee" was now king, and "Gourdes [were] to be sounded on several Hills."[22] The justices who questioned the conspirators had no reason to fabricate the precise descriptions of Akan ceremonies and rituals. Indeed, their inclusion in the report poses the intriguing question of how the plotters expected to acquire these very specific instruments and materials. When the enslaved men put forth this vision, they cemented their distance and distinction from the men who questioned their involvement in the ritual.

The English response to the revolt was typical: almost immediately seventeen men were found guilty and executed in Speightstown in the northwest of the island, "Six burnt alive, and Eleven beheaded, their dead bodies being dragged through the streets." Such conspicuous displays of colonial brutality spoke to English desires to intimidate enslaved people, their scale, more than their content, being a demonstration of the power of English authority.[23] After all, slaves could not have their terms of service extended, they had no property to be confiscated, and they were rarely banished from the colonies, leaving English officials with few threats other than an especially violent enforcement of obedience.[24] At least another sixty slaves were held at the western port of Holetown, the other alleged center of the rebellion; these prisoners, particularly those swept up in island raids, worried that they would suffer the same fate.[25] At first it appeared that such cruelty could encourage conspirators to confess, as when "one of those that were burned alive being chained at the stake, was perswaded . . . *That since he was going to suffer death, Inge-niously to Confess the depth of their design.*"[26] First, the unnamed man asked for some water, "which is a Custome they use before they tell or discover any thing," according to the author of *Great Newes*. Some West Africans did indeed connect drinking with truth telling: if a person lied after taking an oath and drinking some water, then he or she risked death.[27] Before he got a chance to speak, however, another coconspira-tor silenced this unnamed man. Tony, described as "a sturdy Rogue, a *Jew's Negro,*" implored the confessor to think of his fellow countrymen: "*Thou Fool, are there not enough of our Country-men killed already? Art thou minded to kill them all?*" Tony was clearly persuasive, his appeal for solidarity among the people of the Gold Coast enough to sway his fellow suspect to "not speak one word more." Tony drew power from both his status as a rebel and his beliefs. When the crowd taunted him, taking pleasure in that fact that he was about to "fry," Tony responded, "*If you Roast me to day, you cannot Roast me tomorrow,*" safe in the knowledge that he would return to his "own Countrey" when he died.[28]

Both of these moments—water taken as proof that a confessor was telling the truth, and the comfort Tony took from his spiritual belief that death would provide him the freedom earthly life had denied him—are evidence of the West African elements that shaped the planned rebel-lion and its aftermath. The execution, intended as a spectacle that would induce fear in the enslaved people who heard about it or witnessed the event, instead became a source of strength for Tony, and for others who took heart from his show of defiance or who knew that his death would finally send him home. They would recall the event and know that Tony had stood strong and silent in the face of unimaginable pain, and that ultimately he had secured a spiritual freedom, even as his body was reduced to ashes on the Barbados earth.[29] Perhaps his particular punish-ment was an attempt by English authorities to persuade him, and those who watched his execution, that Tony would not actually return to his country because his body was no longer intact.[30] Burning at the stake may also have been a deliberate ploy by authorities to mark slave executions as different and especially disgraceful: this form of capital punishment had rarely been used in England since the Reformation, and formerly it had mostly been reserved for heretics.[31] Or it may simply reflect an English desire to demonstrate their disdain for Tony's supposed atrocities by desecrating his corpse, a common enough occurrence in the broadest sense in England at the time.[32] By killing Tony in such a manner, the authorities were underscoring the severity of his crime and the vast gulf that lay between him and English colonists on the island.

English elites viewed the conspiracy as a plot to overthrow the colonial government aimed largely at destroying the white population. The gourds that would sound the arrival of the new Cormantee king would also be the cue for a "general Rising, with a full intention to fire the Sugar-Canes, and so run in and Cut their Masters the Planters Throats in their respective Plantations whereunto they did belong."[33] Nonetheless, there was still some confusion among island authorities on the final goals of the rebels. The anonymous author of *Great Newes* noted that there were two competing interpretations of what the slaves had planned with regard to the wives and daughters of the planters. In one scenario "they intended to spare the lives of the Fairest and Handsomest Women (their Mistresses and their Daughters) to be converted to their own use." There was, however, an alternative interpretation, one that the writer chose as the more likely: "I am induced to believe that they intended to Murther all the White People there, as well Men as women."[34] Either account was compelling for English elites: in one version English women's lives would be spared, but they would be subjected to the sexual advances of the rebel men. The other reading of the revolt's goals painted the plotters as indiscriminately brutal—showing no mercy to either women or men. Both visions fed into English ideas about the inherent depravity of Africans.[35]

The 1675 revolt also provides evidence of divisions within the enslaved community on Barbados, especially between those who considered themselves "country-men" who plotted the uprising, and those who fell outside those community boundaries and who alerted the authorities.[36] Knowledge of the plot to kill the "Baccarraroes or *White People in the Island within a fortnight*" came to English attention because an enslaved woman named Anna, "a house Negro," informed her master about the brewing conspiracy. Anna was the only enslaved woman named in the historical record as having information about the scheme. The wives of the conspirators had (according to *Great Newes*) been locked out of the plans, although why they were kept in the dark, and why other women were omitted from the record, remains unclear. Perhaps the anonymous author of *Great Newes* could not conceive of a moment of rebellion that included women. Akan politics might have dictated that women remain on the margins of battle. Or the wives of the conspirators may have mostly been island born, and therefore not fully trusted by their husbands. It is also possible that the marriages had been forced by masters and were not consensual, thus diluting the potential bonds of loyalty. Anna was not taken into their confidence, learning of the planned revolt only when she overheard "a Young *Cormantee Negro* about 18 years of age," who was enslaved on the same plantation as she, talk with a fellow conspirator about his reluctance to kill his master. Anna recounted that she had questioned the young man, then gone straight to her "Master and Mistris and discovered the whole truth of what she heard."[37] In *An Account of the Intended Rebellion*, Anna "waited and attended on her mistress" before revealing what she knew, perhaps indicating a certain degree of hesitation on the enslaved woman's part about sharing what she had learned.[38]

Anna's reasons for informing on the conspirators are unclear. The author of *Great Newes* alleged that she had done so because she thought "*that it was great Pity so good people as her Master and Mistriss were, should be destroyed.*"[39] It is entirely possible that Anna did feel a sense of loyalty to her owners. Both accounts of her role in discovering the plot emphasize her status as a house slave who worked closely with Justice Hall's wife. Knowing that there was a conspiracy afoot that would bring violence to her very doorstep may have been enough to persuade Anna that she had to stop the plot before it was put in motion. Some scholars have posited that Anna was an island-born slave and therefore did not have a connection to those plotting to insert a "Cormantee King."[40] If women really were locked out of the planning of the uprising, then Anna may have felt afraid for what would follow. Certainly the position of an enslaved woman in a plantation home was precarious, but perhaps she feared a disruption that could see her worse off than she had been before. Anna may also have hoped to gain favor as a reward for her loyalty. She would have known that faithful slaves who informed on runaways stood to receive payment in the form of muscovado sugar and a badge in the shape of a red cross to wear upon their person.[41] Perhaps she too would receive special treatment if she informed on the conspirators, even though any show of favoritism would mark her as untrustworthy among her fellow slaves.

In the end, Anna received a greater reward than she might have imagined. The members of the Barbados Assembly recommended "the freeing of Fortuna, a negro woman belonging to Mr. Gyles Hall, sent in recompense of her eminent service in discovering the intended rebellion of the negroes."[42] Anna could be the diminutive of Fortuna, or perhaps this woman took the name on gaining her freedom as reminder of her good fortune.[43] In either case, she succeeded where the conspirators had failed by freeing herself from the bonds of slavery, albeit at their expense. She was not the only enslaved woman to be mentioned in the assembly records for 25 November: "Paul Gwynn's negro woman Marrea" was given twenty shillings "for her diligent attending the Assembly." Marrea presumably prepared food and drink and performed other tasks for the assembly members who were, at the same time, debating Anna/Fortuna's fate and the punishments that would befall the conspirators. She therefore witnessed the deliberations of English elites and saw firsthand how authorities parsed out their responses to both Anna/Fortuna and the rebels. What Marrea made of the discussions can only be imagined.[44] If she had connections to the "Cormantee" network, she may have felt aggrieved by Anna/Fortuna's actions. But as someone who also benefited from attending the assembly (she received the twenty shillings, not her owner), she may have understood Anna's actions better than most.

Since Anna/Fortuna was the person responsible for divulging the secrets of the plot, it is all too easy to view her as a traitor. But such an assumption flattens the experiences of enslaved people, reducing woman and men from many different African nations to one allegiance, or taking for granted that all slave experiences on plantations (between field and plantation home, island born and saltwater) were essentially the same.[45] Just as the men who planned the 1675 revolt used their voices to craft a version of events that both engendered fear among English elites and staked a vision of West African political ideology in the Caribbean, so does Anna/Fortuna's decision to speak up provide an equally valid understanding of enslaved politics.[46] Whether it was loyalty to her owners, fear of the unknown, or the desire to separate herself from the conspirators to make her own claim on freedom, Anna/Fortuna took her fate into her own hands. Her assertion of independence proved the lie that all enslaved people acted or thought in the same way or would automatically become part of a conspiracy should the opportunity arise.

Governor Atkins was certain that the intention of the "Damnable Designe" of the "Cormantin Negroes" was "to destroy us all" and that the planned revolt was "farre more dangerous" than the authorities on Barbados had previously believed.[47] Unable to persuade himself that the plot was a contained affair, Atkins instead attributed a unified sentiment and collective action to all enslaved Africans on the island. He was unwilling to grant differentiation among the various groups of bonded laborers. Atkins's claims must have been affected by the anxiety produced by the revolt, because English officials did, in fact, understand that their enslaved populations comprised many nations; they also recognized the differences between saltwater and creole slaves.[48] By 1675 there were more "Gold Coast Negroes" arriving on Barbados, but the slave population was hardly homogeneous.[49] Anna/Fortuna's role in the proceedings, when contrasted with Tony's defiance and suffering, makes clear that there were real divisions in the enslaved community, with the distinction between saltwater and island-born slaves as important as any other differentiation.

"To see the blood of Protestants swim on the ground"

Like the "Cormantee Negroes," Irish Catholic servants and laborers frequently inverted English conceptions of their inferiority both in public and in private. Doing so turned anti-Irish rhetoric intended to diminish the Irish into a positive tool, using the very stereotypes about Irish behavior that English writers had created to muster opposition to the colonial regime. By invoking cannibalism, communicating in the Irish language, and attacking English religious practices, Irish Catholics appropriated the discourse intended to marginalize them in Caribbean society and demonstrated that they could find strength by embracing English ideas about their inherent differences. In fact, their willingness to use the worst fears of the English against them allowed antagonistic Irish to actively distance themselves from the ruling elite.

In 1688 Irish Catholics were accused of being part of a broad Catholic conspiracy on Barbados. In the immediate aftermath of the Glorious Revolution, which saw the fervently Catholic James II replaced by the staunchly Protestant William and Mary in England, some of the colony's most prominent leaders were implicated in a "Roman Catholick" plot with the alleged aim of bringing French rule to Barbados.[50] At the center of the scandal were Sir Thomas Montgomery and Mr. Willoughby Chamberlain, the former the attorney general of Barbados, and the latter a wealthy planter on the island. Both men, as befitted their positions of prominence, were English. Although Edwyn Stede, the Protestant lieutenant governor of Barbados, accused Montgomery and Chamberlain of having recently "turned Papist," they may well have been harboring Catholic sympathies for some time.[52] In late 1688 Montgomery wrote to the "superior Jesuits" of

Martinique, begging them "to send hither some Roman Catholick Priests and Jesuits."[52] If the French would not provide assistance, then Montgomery intended to call upon prominent English Catholics to come to his aid. He was sufficiently confident of his position to write to the Earl of Sunderland, asking him to "Prevaile the sending hither of a roman Catholick Governor for that that Religion could not be soe well propogated under the present Governor of Barbados." Montgomery and Chamberlain succeeded in meeting the first of their goals when "a Jesuit Priest called father Michaell arrived [in Barbados] from Martinicoe." Montgomery's servant Thomas Brown described in his deposition how Father Michael "read and sayd Mass publiquely" in Montgomery's home and how "Sr Thomas was not onely at the Mass but officiated at the service."[53] Such actions demonstrated Montgomery's and Chamberlain's seriousness about their faith and the lengths to which they would go to secure their right to worship.

English Protestants were spurred to new heights of frenzy by the involvement of Irish workers in the plot to install a Catholic governor (French or otherwise) on the island. According to lieutenant governor Stede, who helped to uncover the conspiracy, Montgomery and Chamberlain desired to turn Barbados into "an absolute popish, if not a French Island," with the help of the hands of "the poor Irish servants and freemen in this Island."[54] One deposition was specific about the religious impact of the actions of Montgomery and Chamberlain on the Irish community: "Hee [Montgomery] made greate treat for those who came to hear Mass who were youzally Irish men, and them of the poorer sort and many of them servants."[55] Of the forty-eight men listed as persons "sawne att Mass att the house of Mr Willoughby Chamberlaine" on Christmas Day, 1688, around half had Irish names.[56] The mere presence of large numbers of Irish Catholics at a Christmas mass, even one held at a private house, instilled fear in English Protestants, reminding them of the potential fifth column in their midst. Irish Catholics, who had long held the convictions of their faith, were (in this telling of the plot) the solid backbone responsible for holding the entire scheme together. Here English authorities altered the terms of the discussion, placing large amounts of blame for the conspiracy firmly on Irish Catholics, rather than on the prominent Englishmen who were also intimately involved. Irish Catholics—from the very lowest echelons of society—had, by dint of their faith, played an important role in a plot to unseat Protestant rule on Barbados.

To bolster the case against Montgomery and Chamberlain, Protestant English officials collected a range of testimony showing the depth of Irish Catholic antagonism toward English Protestants on the island. Two Irish servants specifically articulated their wish to harm Protestants, invoking the specter of Irish savagery in the process. An English servant, John Thompson, accused his Irish counterpart, James Jordan, of coming into his room, seeing his Bible, and then cursing him, saying either "Dam you, the English Dogg, or Protestant Dogg"; Thompson was unable to remember which particular insult was used, indicating that the Irish drew on both categories interchangeably. Jordan had gone on to demand, "what doe you read the Devills prayers," before threatening Thompson that he had "a goode mind to cut of your head." Turning physically violent, Jordan then brandished his sword and sliced Thompson on the cheek. The Englishman offered that he could think of no other reason for Jordan's attack except "that he was not of his religion." Indeed, Jordan concluded his assault by shouting that he hoped to see "all the Bibles burnt & all the protestants hanged or killed."[57] Another servant, John Kelly, corroborated Thompson's testimony but added that Jordan had gone on to say, "I hope to have an hundred such English Doggs to bee my slaves ere Long bee."[58] Here Jordan was making a double threat: first that he would do violence to both the sacred Bible and Protestants in general, and next that he intended to make slaves of "English Doggs," the slur compounding the severity of his curse.[59] Coming from a servant on a sugar plantation, this threat was grave indeed, suggesting as it did a turning of hierarchies on their heads.

The violence that Jordan conveyed was picked up by his compatriot Cork Farley, one of the men listed in attendance at mass at Chamberlain's plantation. Farley's threat of harm was doubly dangerous because it was tied to his attempts to spread the Catholic faith on the island. Cesar Crawford testified that he had overheard Farley try to persuade Martha Cuffley to convert to Catholicism for her own safety. Farley had not been particularly subtle in his overtures, indicating that "he hoped to see the blood of Protestants swim on the ground," implying that if Cuffley did not convert, her blood might well be among the bodily fluids spilt.[60] When Cuffley was deposed, she claimed that Farley had gotten into an argument with another servant who was reading a book "called Jacobs Ladder." The unnamed servant told Farley "that he must not worshipe Images," and Farley had "replyed angerly that Bibles where Bookes that caused a great Deall of Differences, & that the Roman Religion was the first Religion that was upon the earth & that it would be the Last."[61] While the violent images contained in these outbursts could be viewed simply as exemplifying anti-Protestant rhetoric, they had a much deeper resonance. Visions of burning Bibles and Protestant blood being spilled in great quantities evoked memories of events in Ulster in 1641, when Irish Catholics had allegedly murdered thousands of Protestant English and Scottish colonists.

Memories of 1641 had their corollary in more local events on Barbados in earlier decades, for Jordan and Farley were not the first Irish men to invoke savagery or a bloodthirsty nature to scare their fellow colonists. In the 1650s the sheer volume of Irish servants and free laborers flooding into Barbados on the heels of Cromwell's expulsion policy meant that the island was a site of tension and unease between recalcitrant Irish and wary English authorities. Recent arrivals from Ireland had fresh memories of the violence and subjugation that had characterized the interregnum period at home, and English authorities in the Caribbean also wanted to curb potential Irish misbehavior. The trepidation about Irish laborers was reflected in the numerous entries about Irish behavior contained in the minutes of the Barbados Council.

When Cornelius Bryan arrived on Barbados in the mid-1650s he quickly found himself in trouble with English authorities on the island. Under the 1652 order passed by the Council and Assembly of Barbados that allowed authorities to "inflict Corporal Punishment on such persons that give out mutinous language," Bryan was sentenced to twenty-one lashes "on the bare back."[62] On the same day that Bryan was sentenced, Irishman Daniell Hallsee was placed "in the pilloryc . . . for the space of two hours" for similarly "scandalizeing the Inhabitants of the Island," while his compatriot Anthony Clarke received the same punishment as Bryan "for endeavouring to raise mutinie and sedition contraye to the peace and quiet of this Land."[63] Twenty months later, Irish servants Teage Dunnshaw and Walter Welsh were said to have "Rebelliously and mutinously behaved themselves" toward their master, Mr. Edward Hollingshead, and his wife, who claimed to be "in fear of their lives by their said servants." The council found the Hollingsheads' testimony persuasive and sentenced the two servants to "thirty one lashes each, soundly laid on their bare backs" and in addition ordered that they be "returned to the Common gaol" for as long as Hollingshead wished them to remain behind bars.[64] Each of these Irish men was accused of threatening the security of English men and women in Barbados.

Amid the general accusations of Irish bad behavior, the report on Bryan's transgression stands out, providing an excellent example of the kinds of calculated insults that Irish Catholics directed at the English around them, usually laborers of a similar social status. According to the evidence placed before the council in Bryan's slander trial, Bryan had been eating a plate of meat when he stated "that if there was as much English Blood in the Tray as there was meat he would eat it." In the same hearing Bryan was ordered under "suspicion of raising a mutiny" to leave the island within one month; failure to do so would see him "proceeded against as a mutineer."[65] Among the Irish men hauled before the Barbados Council, Bryan clearly had a flair for the dramatic: others were accused of slanderous language, or "scandalizeing" the inhabitants of the island, but only Bryan's words were recorded. The specific invocation of cannibalism suggests that Bryan was interested in more than simply offending the English around him. In his *View of the Present State of Ireland*, written at the close of the sixteenth century, Edmund Spenser had discussed what he saw as the Irish proclivity for cannibalism, his allegations focusing on an Irish woman drinking the blood of her son.[66] In 1641 English observers reported that Irish Catholics were cannibalizing their Protestant victims.[67] This shift from eating Irish flesh to consuming English bodies made accusations of the Irish propensity to consume human flesh all the more disturbing. Bryan's bold assertion that he would drink English blood was therefore a specific attempt to terrorize the English within earshot (and those who would listen to the retelling of the incident in the Barbados Council).

In conjuring the image of flesh eating, Bryan was specifically invoking a stereotype he understood and knew to have power.[68] He was not making a literal threat; he was negotiating the confines of an English social and political hierarchy by actively performing savage Irishness. Bryan was determined that the English would not rest easy in his presence, drawing on English anxieties that bubbled just below the surface: it was this knowledge that inspired Bryan to summon the specter of cannibalism. The specific reference to "English blood" implied that some would be spilled—for blood and flesh to be available for Bryan to eat, an English person would have been brutally slain. Moreover, by ingesting English corporeal remains, Bryan would be transgressing boundaries, desecrating an English body and corrupting it by making it part of his own.

Heightening the tensions caused by Bryan's evocation of cannibalism was the link between the Catholic belief in transubstantiation and the consuming of flesh and blood in the form of the body of Christ.[69] Bryan's slander therefore provoked in two ways: first, he reminded English listeners of his supposed barbarous nature; second, he referred, however obliquely, to his Catholic faith. Like Jordan and Farley decades later, the twin threats of violence and Catholicism went hand in hand. Although

Bryan may not have intended to draw the comparison directly when he challenged authority, the English who heard his desire to cannibalize them would have made the connection to his Catholic faith. In a climate where threats from Catholic Europe were foremost in English minds, Bryan's slander referenced the multiple horrors of close contact with perfidious Irish papists.[70]

By the time the Barbados depositions detailing bad Irish behavior were taken in March 1689, William and Mary were safely installed on the English throne. But James II was attempting to mount a challenge from Ireland, and it was thought that the French would soon provide him with support on both sides of the Atlantic. Unsurprisingly, then, the interrogators became curious about potential Irish involvement in bringing the French to Barbados. James Hanley, the Irish sugar boiler on Jacob English's plantation, allegedly suggested to some of his fellow English servants that if the French attacked Barbados, the Irish would "quickly make way for the French to come in."[71] And Darby Lary, who questioned John Brise about his religious beliefs, stated that "there is a Discourse that the French are coming hither and I hope they may for if they are, they shall have five hundred or a thousand [Irish] to side with them."[72] Certainly these Irish men were more than willing to boldly declare their support for France and to claim that they had significant support among their compatriots on the island.

But Irish Catholics pushed English Protestants further still. Not content with merely reminding officials about their willingness to assist fellow Catholics, they exaggerated the English sense of their perfidy by insisting on cleaving to the Irish language as a preferred means of communication. In seventeenth-century Ireland, adherence to the Roman Catholic faith had become synonymous with resistance to English colonial rule.[73] But from the sixteenth century, the use of Irish language also signaled a refusal to acquiesce to English governmental structures or laws and became an explicit way of challenging English imperialism, not least because English observers could not understand the content of conversations between Irish speakers.[74] While James Hanley spoke to his master in English about his desire to assist the French in an attack on Barbados late in 1688, he talked to Edward Macologh "in Irish." Hanley claimed that he made the linguistic switch so that the English around him "understood it not," indicating that he elaborated, or made remarks not for English ears. Macologh, who was interrogated about this exchange, remembered the speech differently, stating that Hanley had related the same words in two languages.[75] Macologh may or may not have been telling the truth about the similarity between

Hanley's comments. Certainly repeating his statement was redundant, suggesting that Hanley took the opportunity when conversing in Irish to embellish his thoughts. Moreover, while there is no indication in the sources that any of the men present spoke *only* Irish, the English lack of comprehension of Irish speech is clear. By using this language Irish women and men could communicate with one another, even about mundane everyday events, in an exclusively Irish space free from English surveillance.[76] This practice had the added bonus of making English colonials uncomfortable (at worst) and terrified (at best), always suspicious that the Irish around them were plotting some nefarious scheme to turn the island Catholic and perhaps to destroy English plantations in the process.

The depositions taken in the case of Montgomery and Chamberlain illustrate perfectly the multiple ways that Irish Catholics kept religious difference and their supposed barbarous nature at the forefront of the minds of English officials who set colonial policy. Coming, as it did, at the end of the century, and during a moment of extreme crisis, the case represents the peak of English anti-Catholicism in the Caribbean. At the same time, Catholicism could (and did) act as a rallying point for those who identified with the same faith, as the collusion between Montgomery and Chamberlain and the "poor Irish servants" suggests. Ultimately, Irish Catholics had forced England's hand in the colonies to the point that the Barbados Council declared that they were "willing rather to trust the Defence of the Island to the few English and their slaves, assisted by the Providence of God and a good cause, than rely in such a case upon the too uncertain and doubtfull hopes of the friendship and fidelity [of the Irish]."[77] Although there is no evidence that the council followed through on this policy, the very fact that they were willing to consider arming slaves indicates how far the Irish had pushed English authorities in this moment. English ideas about the inherent difference of Africans shattered as they entertained the notion of commissioning an interracial force to defend the islands.[78] When an armed interracial group rose up on St. Christopher later that same month, its designs were surely not what elite authorities had in mind.

"Negroes that are Imbodyed with the Irish"

Collusion between Irish and Africans for the purpose of overthrowing English rule reached new and heady heights in the years just preceding the 1692 Barbados uprising. In July 1689 English planters on St. Christopher learned to fear just such an alliance, this time with French

Catholics entering the mix. Edwyn Stede recounted collaboration on St. Christopher between "many of the French, mulattoes . . . & Negroes that are Imbodyed with the Irish."[79] The term *Imbodyed* here connoted a martial relationship among the three groups, but also the tight incorporation of Irish and Africans together.[80] Two years later the English position on the island was still under threat. Englishman Joseph Crisp remembered how "Negros, French & Irish gathering and making up together a formidable Body, discended from the Mountains armed . . . with our own arms taken at times by surprise from us . . . and forced the poor planters to disert their new settlements and retire to the Fort againe for [the] safety of their lives."[81] Viewing their antagonists as being of one body, English authorities merged the religious, nascent racial, and cultural threats posed by Irish, Africans, and Catholics into one unholy entity. In choosing to revolt together, the people that island elites were so concerned with keeping under control refuted the very divisions that the English had attempted to enforce among them. They were Irish, French, African, Catholic, and heathen all at once.[82] And they succeeded, at least in the short term, in overthrowing English rule on St. Christopher.

In October 1692 Barbados officials became aware of Ben, Sampson, and Sambo's plot to overthrow the planter class. As with the 1675 revolt, island elites discovered the conspiracy because "two of them that were talking of this their wicked Design," were "overheard to discourse thereof." The description of the uprising, however, was different. rather than being led by "Cormantee" or African-born slaves who intended to install an Akan-style of polity on Barbados, this plot had been conceived "by the *Negro's* that were born in the Island."[83] Not only were creole slaves in charge of planning the uprising, but they were also willing to include Irish Catholics in their plans, using Irish men to get soldiers drunk so that they could more easily capture Barbados's forts.[84] Like the events of 1675, this conspiracy highlighted fissures within the slave community through the descriptions of the government they planned to put in place once they had achieved their immediate goals of killing white planters, and through their willingness to rely on nonslave allies.

The means through which information about the alleged uprising was gleaned are suspect at best: Ben, Sambo, and Sampson suffered excruciating torture as English authorities attempted to uncover what precisely had been simmering among the enslaved communities on some of the island's most prosperous plantations.[85] The men were told that they would be "hung in chaines on a Gibbett untill you are starved to death, after which your head to be sever'd from your Body & put on a Pole on said Gibbett, your body cutt in quarters and burnt to ashes under said Gibbett." Once this torture began, Sampson apparently died in short order; Ben and Sambo "endured it four daies without any confession," clearly hoping that some of their "confederates" would come to their rescue. When no respite was forthcoming, the men "resolved to make a clear confession of the whole matter" in exchange for their lives. Sambo did not survive to testify, but Ben "discover[ed] the whole truth" of the plot to the authorities.[86] The story Ben told in the face of death may have been the truth, an exaggerated version of the truth, or a fabrication based on telling the authorities what they wanted to hear. Nonetheless, it was an account of a revolt planned with such precision, and with such lofty goals in mind, that it (at minimum) reveals what Ben wanted to present as the horrifying truth to the English audience who heard his confession.

Ben's description of the rebellion stressed that the enslaved plotters intended to take over the island by military might, striking at the heart of English fears about their abilities to control bonded laborers on Barbados. By describing the revolt in European terms (the "regiments of troop" and "regiments of horse" were all too familiar to island elites), Ben put forth a vision that colonial officials understood. But speaking their language did not lessen the severity of the English response. "Many were Hang'd, and a great many Burn'd," for taking part in the plot. The anonymous author of *A Brief, but most True Relation of the late Barbarous and Bloody Plot* specifically noted that "(for a Terror to others,) there are seven Hanging in Chains, alive, and Starving to Death."[87] Just as authorities threatened Ben and Sambo with having their heads displayed publicly on the end of a sharpened post as a reminder to others of the consequences of their actions, so the bodies of the rest of the perpetrators of the 1692 conspiracy were used as tools of intimidation.[88]

The ringleaders of the 1692 plot were island born, not recent arrivals from Africa, and they were the most skilled and trusted laborers. In the estimation of the men who interrogated Ben, the fact that elite slaves were the culprits "add[ed] abundantly to their crimes." Indeed, Ben reported that because they had recruited "four or five of the most capable & those most trusted in each plantation," these slaves would be able to "secretly in the dead of the night first to kill their masters, from thence to goe to the assistance of those in the next plantation."[89] That the revolt was planned by slaves who were believed to be above suspicion by their masters allowed Ben to distance himself from English assumptions about the kinds of relationships that they thought they had with island-born slave populations. "Cormantee Negroes" might be untrustworthy; Ben proved that creole slaves could cause trouble too.

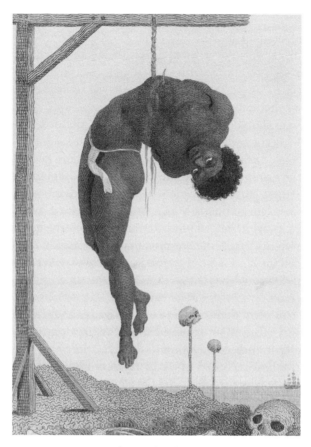

FIGURE 14. *A Negro hung alive by the Ribs to a Gallows*, engraving by William Blake in John Gabriel Stedman, *Narrative of a Five Year's Expedition Against the Revolted Negroes of Surinam*, vol. 1 (London, 1796). This engraving depicts a scene similar to those that occurred during the 1692 slave uprising on Barbados, when enslaved bodies hung on display on the gallows to remind other slaves of the dangers of attempting acts of rebellion. In this instance (based on a 1773 eyewitness report) the victim hung alive for three days, much like Ben and Sambo who endured similar torture for four days in Barbados in 1692. The severed heads on stakes underscore the intended terror such violent images were supposed to instill in the enslaved population at large. Image courtesy of the James Ford Bell Library, University of Minnesota, Minneapolis.

Although the plot by Ben and other Caribbean-born slaves proved their determination to overthrow English rule, he and his coconspirators did not seek solidarity with saltwater slaves. According to *A Brief, but most True Relation*, "No imported *Negro* was to have been Admitted to partake of the Freedom they intended to gain" until one of the creole slaves "who should have been their Masters" decided to free them.[90] Determined, as they were, to avoid collusion with saltwater slaves who might challenge their supremacy, Ben described how he and the other leaders of the group were nevertheless willing to "procure four or five Irish men to their Party" who would be sent to Needham's Fort to get the soldiers drunk. One of the Irish men would then give a "watch word" to let the slaves know it was safe to enter and to open the gate to the garrison. By revealing to his interrogators that the plot included some Irish, Ben expanded the landscape of terror. If uprisings among enslaved Africans deeply disturbed English authorities, plots that included a cross-cultural element sent them into a real panic.

From the moment that Irish servants arrived in the Caribbean in the 1650s, English officials consistently linked their supposed bad behavior and ability to foment rebellion to their relationships with enslaved Africans. The first recorded instance of Irish and African collaboration came in the winter of 1655. The Barbados Council recorded that by the report of Captain Richard Goodhall, Mr. John Jones, and Lieutenant Colonel John Higginbotham there were "several Irish servants & negroes out in Rebellion in the Thicketts & thereabouts." The 1650s had been a decade of general turmoil for English officials. Irish priests had been found roaming the island, servants and laborers were unruly, and now a joint effort between Irish servants and enslaved Africans was under way. The council described the act as one of "Rebellion" but later referred to the malcontents as "run away." These absconders troubled English officials, who wanted to bring them under control by any means possible. Higgenbotham was given permission to "raise any of the companies of Col. Henry Hawly's Regiment" to discover the fugitives; if they made "any opposition & resist his forces & refuse to come in peaceably," then the soldiers were allowed to "suppress or destroy them."[91] By absconding together, Irish and Africans were helping to cement an English notion that they held very similar traits and posed very similar threats. But the risk they took was a collective one, and their decision to flee their plantations as a group demonstrates that they saw benefit in such collaboration and that trust had been forged to make such behavior possible. That their actions reinforced English ideas about their inferiority was not necessarily something that these runaways considered.

Thirty years later, in the mid-1680s, Irish and Africans continued to cause trouble for colonial governments as a result of their collaborations. Governor Edwyn Stede announced that "some Irish servants have been sent to gaol" while others were under surveillance because of suspicions that they were "privy to the late intended rising of the negroes to destroy all masters and mistresses."[92] According to Stede, some of the "Irish Nation" had conspired with enslaved Africans to overthrow English authority on the island. In all, eighteen Irish servants were arrested, but they were freed because there was not enough evidence to punish them, although Stede requested that the constables increase their surveillance on the population.[93] Their enslaved coconspirators were not so lucky: twenty-two men were executed for their part in the alleged plot.[94] And Africans suffered more for their part in the Catholic uprising of 1688, being re-enslaved for participating in Catholic masses, while the Irish were interrogated, freed, or banished to Jamaica. Similarly, in 1692 it was the African leaders of the uprising who were executed; the Irishmen who were supposed to get the soldiers in Needham's Fort drunk were never named, or punished, for their part in the conspiracy.[95] Perhaps the English could not trace the Irish who were accused. They may also have refused to believe that such a collaboration could have taken place under their noses. Here the disproportionate violence meted out to Africans says more about English ideas regarding the difference between Irish and Africans than it communicates anything about how Irish and Africans viewed their relationship. Just as corporeal punishment in the form of whipping became almost exclusively the preserve of Europeans in the last decades of the seventeenth century, so too did execution for alleged participation in treasonous plots seem to become a punishment meted out only to enslaved Africans.

At the end of his 1692 confession, Ben suggested that had he and his coconspirators succeeded in their plan to overthrow island planters, he would have been unsure about what form the new government on Barbados should take. In the list of conspirators drawn up by the interrogators, Ben was listed as the envisioned governor of the island; the commander-in-chief of the military was a slave named Jeffry, while the secretary for the colony was Jack from Brett's plantation.[96] From the content of this document it appears that the leaders of the revolt wanted to continue within the framework of the colonial system already in place. But Ben suggested that "after the conquest over the white people," the conspirators "should have

mett a worse Enemie amongst themselves," indicating that all would not
be harmonious among the rebels. Tensions can be seen even in the way the
creole slaves planned the revolt, including an oath more reminiscent of a
West African past than a Barbadian present. Perhaps strained relationships were developing in the ranks. Ben imagined that the most difficult
moment would have arisen when it came to dividing the spoils of battle,
especially the "white women," the "handsomest" of whom they planned to
marry, with the rest relegated to the positions of "whores, cooks & cham-
bermaids."[97] Certainly the English took Ben's threat about the potential for
sexual violence toward white women seriously. In January 1693 the trea-
surer of Barbados was ordered to pay Alice Mills "the sume of ten pound
ten shill. sterl. for castrating of forty two negroes according to the sentence
and appointment of the Councill impowered to try the Rebellious Negroes
of this island."[98] These valuable slaves would still be able to provide crucial
labor on plantations, but they would no longer pose a sexual threat to the
wives and daughters of Caribbean planters and officials.

Through their refusal to conform to English expectations about their
behavior, Irish Catholics and enslaved Africans alike pushed back against
the constraints of colonial Caribbean society. Although the rise of racial
slavery seemed unstoppable, those who found themselves in slavery, or
skirting the margins of European society, made their own statements about
where they believed their loyalties and sympathies to lie. Sometimes the
actions they took had the power to frighten English officials because of the
religious connotations of Irish Catholics trying to subvert Protestant rule.
On other occasions the threat came from Africans determined to overthrow a system that was the lifeblood of the English Caribbean and central
to its success. And at other times these interests merged. Each moment of
rebellion was profoundly frightening for English officials, who were given
physical proof of the fragile nature of the hierarchies they were trying to
enforce. But for enslaved Africans and Irish Catholics the response must
have been quite the opposite. They felt strength in their solidarity with one
another, and excitement at the power they held when they saw how pan-
icked English authorities and settlers were, not just about the possibility of
a revolt, but about one that involved a mix of races, cultures, and religions
acting in concert against English rule.

* * *

And yet the 1692 conspiracy signaled an end to collaborative action on
the part of enslaved Africans, whether saltwater or creole, and whether

in concert with Irish laborers or not. Apart from a brief scare in 1701, there would not be another attempt to overthrow the planter class on Barbados by enslaved Africans until Bussa's rebellion of 1816. Rebellions were more common in the Leeward Islands in the eighteenth century, most notably the Antigua revolt of 1736.[99] Nonetheless, smaller acts of individual resistance pepper the archival record. In 1698 on Montserrat "a negro man by name Jack" was sentenced to be hanged, drawn, and quartered for running away for three months, and his body was to be displayed as a warning to others contemplating flight. One year later, another enslaved runaway, who had possibly claimed the name John Freeman, was "Condemned to dye . . . by being first broken to pieces and afterwards his limbs and body to be burnt." Cuffee, who had been convicted of stealing twelve pence, was to "be hanged by the neck until he is dead."[100] In Barbados, the landscape of rebellion looked much the same. In 1700 Mr. Frere was compensated for the execution of one of his runaway slaves. Mr. Cole, Mr. Adams, and Lieutenant Colonel Warren received payment to cover the costs of the loss of their slaves, all of whom had been condemned for stealing. Meanwhile, Mr. Martindale and Mr. Maycock were doubly lucky: not only had attempts by their enslaved women to poison them been foiled, but they also received recompense for the loss of their property after the execution of their would-be murderers.[101] In each of these cases, the transgressors signaled their continued resistance to being classified as slaves and property, but now through individual, rather than collective, acts of rebellion.

There were parallels of a horrific kind to the sorts of punishments that those who rebelled could expect to receive. For the charge that he had threatened to drink English blood, Cornelius Bryan received "twenty-one lashes on the bare back," a sentence that caused his own blood to flow. When the specter of sexual violence toward English women was raised, the alleged aggressors were castrated. Africans, whether saltwater or creole, who spoke of their desire to annihilate all English settlers on the islands had their bodies utterly destroyed by the punishments that followed. It would not be enough to simply hang rebellious slaves: English authorities ordered them burned alive, or drawn and quartered, or had their heads placed on spikes as their bodies were reduced to ashes below, to send a message to others and to underscore the severity of their crimes. This dismemberment and destruction of their corporeal remains did not only bring death. English authorities believed that it also threatened West Africans' ability to make the spiritual return to their own countries, thus compounding the violence done to these women and men.[102]

English authorities made distinctions between these enslaved rebels and Irish conspirators, who were never executed for their crimes but instead suffered more modest punishments. Often troublemakers were sent to other islands, most notably Jamaica, following moments of dissent, like the 1688 Catholic conspiracy on Barbados.[103] Despite being found guilty of attempting to "raise a mutiny," Cornelius Bryan was sentenced to banishment, not condemned to death. The English did not see the necessity in destroying Irish bodies as they did those of Africans. The Irish who transgressed in the colonies would be allowed to remain in body and spirit.

Irish and Africans did not accept these English distinctions: they constructed other ways of understanding their connections to, and separation from, one another. In the half century during which moments of collaboration (real or imagined) between these groups flourished, they set forth their own vision of island politics, often directly contradicting English conceptions of difference. Island authorities were more anxious about collusion across racial lines than they were about the propensity of Irish Catholics to cause trouble, or of enslaved Africans to rebel. When servants and slaves worked in concert with one another, finding solidarity in their status as unfree laborers, they were not only challenging English ideas about what constituted difference that were increasingly predicated on developing ideas about ethnic inferiority but also drawing attention to the fiction of race itself. Irish indentures and enslaved Africans who ran away together in the 1650s, or banded together to overthrow colonial rule in the 1690s, sought an alternative way of distinguishing themselves from the colonial hierarchy. The English looked on in horror as together these groups opened up spaces in an attempt to live life on their own terms.

*   *   *

Cornelius Bryan looked over the edge of the bridge at the swamp below. It was January 1656, and the air was warm, the cloudless sky a brilliant blue as the sun shone over the burgeoning town that took its name from the structure on which Bryan stood. Cornelius waited before the common hangman, stripped to the waist, trying to maintain the air of defiance that had seen him sentenced to "twenty-one lashes on the bare back" for suggesting that eating English flesh was a prospect that would give him much joy. He had appeared before the Barbados Council earlier in the month, where someone, he wasn't sure who, had repeated the words he had uttered that fateful dinnertime just a few weeks before. He remembered so clearly look-ing over at the English laborers, smug in their assertions of superiority over him, a mere Irishman, recently arrived on the island, as they ate their food. Before he knew what he was doing he lifted the plate with the tough meat on it and told the assembled throng "that if there was as much English Blood in the Tray as there was meat" he would happily eat it all up. And now here he was, waiting to feel the lash, while a growing crowd eagerly anticipated his cries of pain and the steady flow of blood down his back and onto the ground. Worse still, he had been accused of "raising a mutiny to the dis-turbance of the peace & quiet of this Island." Now he had to find a way off Barbados within the month or risk being "proceeded against as a mutineer."

In the spring of 1675 Pegg was afraid. She had overheard Tomy talking to a slave on an adjacent plantation about plans to bring Cuffee to power on Barbados, and she had listened as he brought Mingo into the plot. They had not realized that she was inside her quarters when they spoke, or she was sure they would have not been so bold. From what she could tell, the plan was for the slaves to the north of Barbados, around Speightstown, to begin the revolt—Cuffee worked on a plantation in that area. They would sound trumpets to signal to the rest of the island that there was to be a new king, and to rise up and cut the throats of their masters. It was clear that there was another set of ringleaders around the Hole, close to where Pegg labored on Cornelius's plantation. She knew that Mingo and Tomy frequently encountered other slaves when they took sugar to Holetown to be processed, and she understood that was where Tomy had first learned of the plot. She tried to imagine what it would be like when slavery was no more. She couldn't be sure that she herself would see freedom. The plotters seemed only to be concerned with including men who had arrived from Africa. Island-born slaves like herself were shut out. She had heard Tomy tell Mingo that he had not even spoken of the plot to his own wife, Betty, to better preserve the secrecy of the matter. Pegg became tense when she thought about the repercussions of the plot. Whenever there was trouble on a plantation it always seemed that more than those who were actually involved were harmed. She worried about what would happen if the mili-tia defended the island, and who would be caught up in the questioning that would follow. Pegg wondered if she might be better off telling her mas-ter about what was afoot. She surely did not want to get Tomy or Mingo into trouble, but perhaps she could gain something from speaking up, bet-ter treatment for herself, or for her mother. Or maybe even freedom itself.

6 / "As quietly and happily as the English subjects": Property, Prosperity, and the Power of Emulation

John Blake sat at his desk in his Bridgetown home preparing to write a letter to his family back in Galway. He needed to respond to charges leveled by his brothers that he had allowed a disreputable Irish servant "whore" into his home. Henry in Montserrat, Thomas and Nicholas in Galway, and even his brother-in-law Robert French had all peppered John with correspondence that accused him of not being in control of his household. John was indignant at their insinuations. Writing to his oldest brother, Thomas, John launched into an impassioned defense of his actions, explaining that the Irish servant woman was crucial to the smooth running of his home. Besides, John argued, she was behaving herself well in Barbados, not least because he was using corporal punishment to keep her in line.[1] Indeed, John had recently acquired that most important of all Caribbean pieces of property: an enslaved woman to work within his home. He was retaining the Irish servant only until she had finished training his slave in the tasks necessary for keeping his house in order. His defense of his actions complete, John blotted the paper with some satisfaction. Surely even his brother Thomas would understand the significance of owning enslaved property, especially a house slave. All the other Bridgetown merchants of any meaningful status had at least one enslaved person in their town houses, and now John could legitimately claim to be among their ranks.[2]

John Blake's life is symptomatic of a larger trend in the experiences of property-owning Irish Catholics who navigated England's colonial world. As the seventeenth century progressed, wealthier Irish Catholics began to see the benefits of following or adopting English ideas about social status, race, and gender in their everyday lives. Men like John Blake proved that some Irish Catholics embraced English imperialism and actively sought a place in the colonial hierarchy by developing a variety of strategies to insert themselves into elite ranks.[3] Purchasing property in both land and slaves was a key part of their success, allowing the Irish Catholics who did so to distinguish themselves from poorer Irish servants and the inferior racial and gendered stereotypes that English observers associated with that class.[4] An equally important task for wealthy Irish Catholics was to overcome English prejudices about their supposed sacrilegious beliefs. So they downplayed their Catholicism, keeping their spiritual lives out of sight of English authorities, and stressed their fealty to the Protestant regime. Whether in the realm of social relations, politics, or religion, propertied Irish Catholics worked to stake their own claims of belonging in the English Caribbean, making their own assertions about difference in the process.

This chapter follows the lives of three Irish men to explore strategies employed by Irish Catholics who wished to become part of the colonial elite, as well as English responses to their choices. It begins by tracing the life of Cornelius Bryan to understand how this initially rebellious Irish piper acquired property and became the owner of a small plantation and a "mansion house."[5] A careful reading of Bryan's will and the disposal of his property suggests how he self-consciously imitated English planters. Property, then, was the minimum requirement for entry into the planter class.[6] More prominent Irish Catholics, like Henry and John Blake, arrived in the Caribbean with sufficient capital to buy a plantation on Montserrat and to set up a merchant business in Bridgetown, Barbados. The brothers' Catholic faith did not bar them from purchasing property immediately upon their arrival in the West Indies. Their story provides insight into the gendered and racialized discourse that some Irish men, most often those of means, used to mark their positions as part of elite society.

Acquiring land and emulating English norms were not the only means to gain power as an Irish Catholic in the Caribbean. One of the most successful Irish men in the English colonies was William Stapleton, governor of Montserrat in the 1670s, and later of all the Leeward Islands. Tracing his rise to power reveals a third strategy that Irish Catholics used to gain favor with English officials: the minimizing of Roman Catholic religious beliefs and practices, and the profession of

Irish loyalty to England. Stapleton's successful tenure as governor was predicated in part on his ability to deflect attention from Catholic practices on the island and in part on his successful management and control of all colonial subjects, Catholics and Protestants alike. The lives of these three individuals and their interplay emphasize the multiple ways that Irish Catholics positioned themselves to become part of the Caribbean hierarchy. It took time, however, for English responses to these disparate cases to be molded into a policy applicable to larger numbers of Irish Catholics. The last part of the chapter uncovers the strategies that English officials employed more broadly to bring certain Irish Catholics into the imperial fold. The solutions they found to neutralize rebellious Irish behavior included appealing to Irish property interests over religious allegiances. This policy showed that more established Irish settlers could be persuaded to support English rule as long as their economic interests were not harmed. Indeed, it proved that it was possible to encourage an entire class of people to embrace English ideas about difference.

"Enjoy my Mansion house with yard and garden"

Cornelius Bryan lost no time in becoming a problem for English authorities on Barbados. While his initial status on the island is unclear, in 1656 he was accused of slander and of attempting to "raise a mutiny" in the colony; he was sentenced to a whipping for the former crime and banishment for the latter.[7] Bryan, then, epitomized the rebellious, perfidious, Irish Catholic, and his supposed exile was in keeping with English policies toward those Irish whom they felt they could not control. Indeed, this version of the story is the one that most scholars have told.[8] But when Bryan died in 1687 he did so on Barbados. Less than a month after he was sentenced to exile, he successfully petitioned to be allowed to remain in the colony providing that he avoided further trouble. The council minutes quietly noted, "Upon the petition of Cornelius Bryan It is ordered that he have two months libertie to staye in the Island provided he give in security for [his] good behaviour."[9] More surprising than the English change of heart was the reversal in fortunes that Bryan himself experienced over the decades between the moment he first appeared in the records, purportedly ready to devour English flesh, and the proving of his last will and testament thirty years later. The will recorded his position as a small planter with a "mansion house," twenty-two acres, and thirteen enslaved Africans listed among his property.[10]

The landowning, slave-owning father of six who died on Barbados in 1687 bore little resemblance to his younger, more rebellious self.

Cornelius Bryan's development as a "planter" can be traced from shortly after his initial confrontation with Barbados authorities to his last land acquisition before his death. As early as 1659 he had amassed "a valuable summe of muscovado sugar" sufficient to purchase seven acres of land in St. Michael's Parish in the southwest of the island.[11] The records are silent on the precise means through which Bryan was able to acquire this property—he was listed as a "piper," an occupation that had connotations of itinerancy and minimal pay, even though he was able to afford the plate of meat on which he based his insult.[12] More likely, Bryan hired himself out as a laborer to island planters; he may even have briefly spent time as an overseer. What is clear is that in three short years Bryan had obtained enough sugar to exchange for a small amount of land. This acquisition of property was Bryan's first step up the island's social hierarchy. Such a move was not altogether unusual for a laborer in the 1650s, but for someone who had acted so antagonistically toward island elites, it was extraordinary indeed.[13]

In 1675, sixteen years after this initial purchase of property, Cornelius and his wife Margaret Bryan sold "ten acres of land be it more or less with the houses, edifices and buildings thereon . . . situate and lying in the said parish of Christchurch."[14] The Bryans received ten thousand pounds of sugar and fifty pounds "lawfull money of England" for their property. At what stage they acquired the land in Christchurch is unclear. Margaret Bryan was described as coming from that parish, and it is possible either that she inherited the land or that it formed part of a dowry upon her recent marriage to Cornelius.[15] The deeds provide no information about when Cornelius sold the St. Michael property. The Bryans were in St. James' Parish by 1680, when the census recorded Cornelius Bryan as holding fourteen acres and having one servant, one hired servant, and nine enslaved Africans in his household.[16] Two years later the Bryans had increased their landholdings to twenty-two acres, buying the excess from property formerly possessed by John Page Clerke and his wife Sarah.[17] The precise nature of the transaction is again murky, but this was the land on which Cornelius would have his "mansion house" and where his enslaved property increased to thirteen enslaved women and men. And it was here that he would die four years later.

These deeds and the census material provide a road map of the practical steps Bryan took in his rise to small landowner.[18] He slowly tripled the amount of land he held. Over time he acquired slaves, and it is likely that

FIGURE 15. Cornelius Bryan's entry in the 1680 Barbados Census, noting his fourteen acres of land, one hired servant, one bought servant, and nine "negroes." CO1/44 f. 148. Image reproduced by permission of The National Archives, London.

the growth in his slave property was due at least in part to the reproductive successes of some of his enslaved women.[19] Perhaps his description as a "planter" in the deeds came at his request, or its inclusion may simply reflect the choice of the person recording the transactions of land, but regardless, such a title conferred legitimacy and prestige. It is from the deeds that his marriage to Margaret becomes visible. This union may have been a means to further improve his property holdings, and if Margaret was English, it may have provided him with a degree of cover and a way to signify that he had left his rebellious Irish nature behind.[20] Sex ratios on Barbados favored a woman's ability to make a good marriage (especially if she was English), so it is possible that Margaret was Irish and Catholic like Bryan, explaining the allure of a match with a man of relatively lowly means when she could, perhaps, have married a wealthier planter. In fact, we know a great deal more about Margaret Bryan than about most women of her rank and status in this period.

For example, one record notes her name before she married Cornelius, a relatively rare inclusion in sources discussing property exchange. She is listed in the deeds as "Margarett Cumberford," which could be an alternate spelling of "Comerford," a popular Irish Catholic name in the seventeenth century.[21] The census records demonstrate that in addition to his enslaved property Bryan had one indentured servant in his household and another servant that he had hired.[22] Thus contained in these documents is the scaffolding of Bryan's life: he was the head of a household, he owned land, he enslaved Africans, he employed servants. Bryan was a Barbados planter, albeit an Irish one.

For a man with a relatively small amount of land, Bryan's description of his home as a "mansion house" indicates his pride in the family residence and provides a glimpse of his aspirations to a better standard of life.[23] Here Bryan may well have been styling himself in the guise of a manorial lord, for it is unlikely that the building was especially grand.[24] His estate was in keeping with the average size of a farm on the island: as late as 1680 the mean size of a farm was only twenty-nine acres, while the median size was smaller still.[25] The rest of his will provides further evidence of Bryan's pride in his property. To his "dearly beloved wife" Margaret he left a third of his estate during her lifetime and ordered that she "enjoy my mansion house with yard and garden . . . during her natural life." His eldest son received all of Bryan's "wearing apparel" and a small amount of money. Despite his small estate Bryan had acquired some luxuries, leaving to his younger daughter, Katherine, "one feather bed and furniture and one cedar chest."[26] His three younger sons and Katherine would ultimately receive the bulk of his estate, splitting between them the "mansion house" and the twenty-two acres he now owned, as well as the majority of his enslaved property. From his will there is every indication that Bryan bought into the emerging social and racial hierarchy on Barbados.[27] He was not leaving a vast estate and endless wealth to his wife and children, but property in land and slaves was no small achievement for a man who had once been threatened with banishment from Barbados and whose Catholicism marked him as an unlikely member of the English colonial hierarchy.

Bryan was not the only Irish man to work his way slowly up the property chain. His neighbors in Barbados, Cornelius Clancy and Garrett Dillon, held similarly small plots of land adjacent to Bryan's estate.[28] The deeds and wills record the experiences of many small planters who held a handful of acres and perhaps an enslaved African or two.[29] These men's experiences demonstrate how property acquisition allowed even

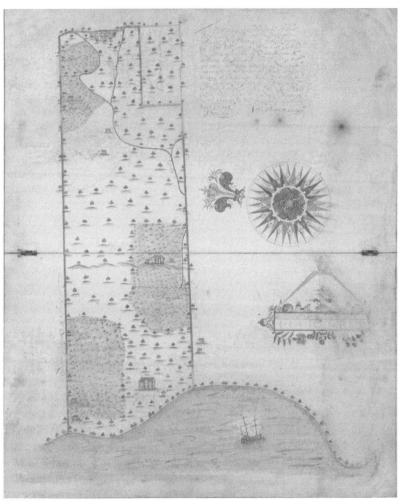

FIGURE 16 This estate plan shows the division of around 300 acres of land in St. James Parish, Barbados. It was surveyed by John Hapcott in October, 1646. The "fallen land" in the upper left had recently been cleared for planting sugar; in the lower left corner was a "potato peece" indicating the importance of that crop. The larger building at the bottom is St. James's Parish church in Holetown. Of interest here are the several smaller plots carved out of the larger estate. In the top right corner, for example, was "Henrie Pirkins" twenty acres; on the left were ten acres belonging to "John Masters," and twenty acres belonging to "Pattrick Rogers." Cornelius Bryan planted a similarly small plot in this parish in the 1670s and 1680s. Courtesy of the John Carter Brown Library at Brown University.

the owners of the smallest estates to gain a stake in the colonial project. As more and more Irish moved from positions of servant or laborer
into a hierarchy that made them the masters of indentures and enslaved
people, the dynamics of difference on Barbados shifted. In these deli-
cately managed transitions from one status to another, the attraction of
landholding and the allure of acquiring both servants and slaves became
clear, underscoring the admission of propertied Irish Catholics into the
ranks of good imperial subjects. Acquiring property went a long way
toward neutralizing English ideas about Irish troublemakers. Holding
enslaved African and indentured servants allowed Irish landowners to
underscore their suitability as colonial planters. Radical transformation
in status was possible for Irish Catholics, as Bryan's case so emphatically
displays.

"Until a Neger Wench I have"

Property ownership may have been the first marker of a person who
had "made it" in colonial Caribbean society, but there were other more
subtle, yet equally pervasive aspects of English life that Irish Catholics
began to emulate and even embrace. Irish men like Henry and John
Blake adopted the same kinds of gendered and racial discourse that
elite English men did when they referred to those they considered to be
their social inferiors. While in and of itself such similarity is unsurprising given that it mirrored divisions among social ranks in Ireland, in
the Caribbean the emulation had a specific purpose: to prove to English
elites that Irish Catholics could be their equals. Unlike Bryan, the Blake
brothers arrived in the Caribbean in the late 1660s with enough capital
to buy a plantation together on Montserrat and to begin a merchant business in Barbados, so they did not struggle like their compatriot to attain
property. Like most of the men who sought fortunes in the Americas,
John and Henry were not first-born sons.[30] The Blakes were one of the so-
called "fourteen tribes" of Galway, a prominent group of Catholics with
Old English ancestry who had been substantial landowners in Galway
until the Cromwellian era of the 1650s, when those lands were confiscated by the Protectorate.[31] Henry and John Blake hoped to profit sufficiently from their overseas investments to buy back land in Ireland that
had been confiscated by Cromwell.[32] In the Caribbean, as in Ireland, they
continued to operate within networks that drew on older associations,
trading and intermarrying with the French and Lynch families, who
also hailed from Galway, making the Irish Blakes similar to English and

Scottish planters, who also drew on transatlantic familial connections in their business relations.[33] Examining a set of letters between the brothers in Barbados, Montserrat, and Galway demonstrates their understanding of, and complicity in, the racial, gender, and social hierarchies of the English colonies.

Henry and John Blake traveled to the Caribbean alone. One brother would remain by himself in the colonies, while the other sent for his wife and daughter. In many ways, their choice of destination dictated their actions: Henry went to Montserrat, an island where Irish Catholics were in the majority, and was able to make a fortune before returning to Ireland and his family; on Barbados, John struggled to find success and ultimately ended up bringing his family out to the Caribbean to be with him, before retreating to Montserrat to take over the family plantation on that island himself. In 1675 his wife crossed the Atlantic, and although their son remained in Ireland for his education, their daughter Catherine later joined her parents in the islands. An Irish servant woman also traveled to Barbados with John's wife; it was this unnamed, unmarried, woman who evidently caused much concern among the Blake brothers.[34] The discussion of her place in John's household spanned the outposts of the Blake family network in Galway, Montserrat and Barbados.[35]

Henry described the servant woman as a "whore" and declared himself "very much troubled" that she had accompanied John's wife to Barbados. He confessed to his older brother Thomas, who had remained in Galway, "I am afraide she may be the occasion of his confusion by her seducem[en]t. I pray God preserve him."[36] Henry was not the only family member to voice concern about the presence of the servant. Both his youngest brother, Nicholas, and his brother-in-law, Robert French, attempted to dissuade John from allowing the unnamed woman to travel with his wife "by telling her quality." It can be gathered from the context that this woman's "quality" was poor. That the brothers were so sure of the servant woman's character might simply indicate that they viewed all servant women as potentially degenerate. But they may also have heard specific tales about this woman's behavior that caused them to speak out. The combined consternation over a lowly servant woman indicates the latter. It also suggests that the family knew that this woman was a direct threat to John. Despite the uproar, John refused to take his brothers' advice, explaining that "the wench came over along with my wife" and that she was indispensable to the running of his household.[37] Henry mused that John's refusal to discharge the woman from his service was "a strange alteration in one that hated the name of a whore as much as any in the world."[38]

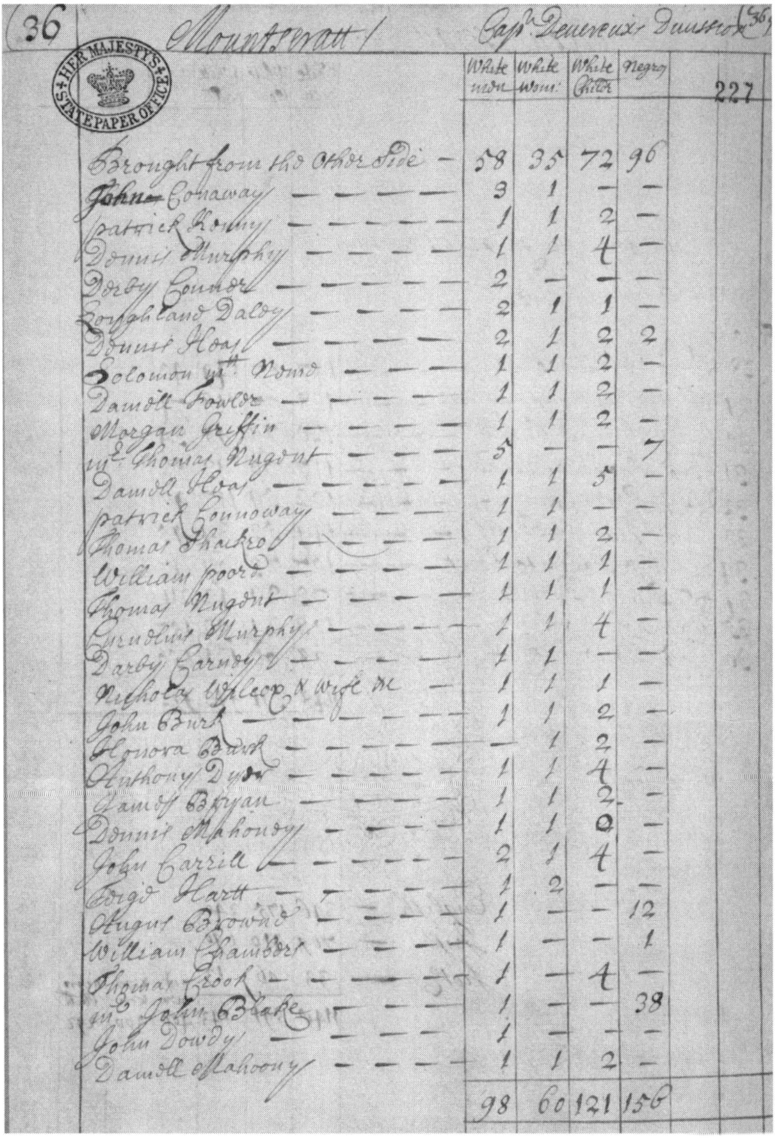

36 Montserratt / Capt. Devereux Division

227

	White men	White Women	White Child	Negroes
Brought from the Other Side	58	35	72	96
John Conaway	3	1	—	—
patrick Romy	1	1	2	—
Dennis Murphy	1	1	4	—
Darby Connor	2	—	—	—
Loughland Daley	2	1	1	—
Dennis Hoas	2	1	2	2
Solomon wth Nome	1	1	2	—
Daniell Fowler	1	1	2	—
Morgan Griffin	1	1	2	—
Mr Thomas Nugent	5	—	—	7
Daniell Hoas	1	1	5	—
patrick Connoway	1	1	—	—
Thomas Shakro	1	1	2	—
William poore	1	1	1	—
Thomas Nugent	1	1	1	—
Cornelius Murphy	1	1	4	—
Darby Carnoy	1	1	—	—
Nicholas Wilcox & wife &c	1	1	1	—
John Burk	1	1	2	—
Elonora Burk	—	1	2	—
Anthony Dyer	1	1	4	—
James Bryan	1	1	2	—
Dennis Mahoney	1	1	0	—
John Carrill	2	1	4	—
Brigd Hartt	1	2	—	—
Angus Browne	1	—	—	12
William Chambers	1	—	—	1
Thomas Crook	1	—	4	—
Mr John Blake	1	—	—	38
John Dowdy	1	—	—	—
Daniell Mahoony	1	1	2	—
	98	60	121	156

FIGURE 17. John Blake's entry in the 1678 Montserrat Census, three lines from the bottom of Captain Devereux's division. John is listed with no white women or white children in his household, but thirty-eight "negroes" are marked as belonging to his estate, making him the third largest slaveowner on the island. CO1/42 f. 227. Image reproduced by permission of The National Archives, London.

Henry felt that he knew the servant woman well enough to state defin-itively that she would be the cause of John's ruin and that she was the sexual aggressor. "Seducement" was active, not something that occurred by accident.[39] There was an additional, more sinister accusation hidden in Henry's letter. The "strange alteration" that the woman had caused in John was, in Henry's eyes, a kind of spell. Her "seducement" had a super-natural quality that transformed John from a man "that hated the name of a whore as much as any in the world" to a man willing to embrace the presence of a servant woman who could "cause his confusion," in other words, his ruin.[40] Henry believed her to have some unnatural power over his younger brother. That John (who as the head of the household was supposed to exhibit a rational masculinity) could be so easily swayed meant that some kind of otherworldly subterfuge had to be afoot. For Henry this was the only reasonable explanation behind John's decision to allow "that woman" to be a permanent figure in his home. This dis-course of seduction also allowed Henry to obfuscate the violence at play in John's interaction with the servant.[41]

The discussion of this woman and her place in John's household illu-minates some of the broader issues that enveloped the lives of the Blake brothers. The servant's reputation as a "whore" was evidently widespread among the male members of the Blake family, but their concern about John's attitude toward her suggests that he may have been the one who had a problem resisting temptation. That each brother felt John was in danger may indicate that they knew he was already involved in some kind of sexual relationship with his servant or had been involved with other similarly positioned women in the past. That John refused to give up the servant woman increased the likelihood that she was suffering physical or sexual abuse. The brothers' lack of faith in John was rein-forced by his unwillingness to acknowledge that there was anything to worry about in his household.

In response to Henry (who feared that John had been bewitched by the servant woman), John insisted that he was "most sensible"—of a clear mind—when it came to understanding her alleged proclivities. In fact, John suggested that the Caribbean itself had provided the circum-stances under which the woman was made "most vitious lesse." Rather than being a site of immorality, Barbados rendered the woman chaste.[42] "Here" John kept the woman under "the most severe correction," an indication that the plantation setting rendered acceptable orders of punishment not tolerated in Ireland.[43] If the servant woman had been immoral or depraved in Ireland, in Barbados she was reformed. John clearly wanted to persuade his brothers that it was more prudent to keep a woman whose alleged vicissitudes he understood than to risk bringing an unknown entity into his home, arguing that he could not do without this particular servant woman because any replacement "may prove ten times worse than her."[44] Whatever the terms of John's relationship with the servant woman, he rested secure that no one in Barbados would have been remotely surprised to find that he was abusing his servant; in fact, it might have been more shocking if he were not.[45] If family members in Galway were not aware of the full consequences attached to keeping a servant woman as part of his Bridgetown household, here John was demonstrating how quickly he had absorbed Caribbean ideologies and practices. He was also educating his brothers in West Indian ways should they desire to venture across the Atlantic Ocean.

John's letter also provided a rationale that laid the blame for the "wench's" presence firmly on his wife. According to John, he was "compelled" to keep the servant because his spouse's "very weak constitution" made her incapable of "keeping the house in good order."[46] When John described his wife's weakness, he laid out the tasks that were beyond her ability, including "washing, starching, [and] making of drink." These chores, which were evidently important for the smooth running of a household in colonial Bridgetown, would have fallen to his servant to perform.[47] In a handful of pages, John indicted his wife's abilities as the manager of his house and declared her unsuitability for the Caribbean climate. But John was also playing the role of the strong head of the household. He refuted his brother's claims about the character of the woman he had chosen as his servant, and by keeping her in his employ he was beginning to form the kinds of domestic relationships that would mark him as a member of the elite.[48] John would brook no objection to his mastery, not even if it came from his elder brothers. Again he was underscoring his understanding of elite etiquette in the Caribbean. His wife may have been incapable of taking on the kinds of tasks performed by the servant herself, but even had she been healthy it is unlikely that John would have wished her to perform such lowly labor.

Using poor Irish women as a foil against which to demonstrate a privileged position continued into the early eighteenth century, when even English governors adopted the model. The younger Christopher Codrington, who like his father held the position of governor of Barbados and the Leeward Islands, was accused by his successor, Colonel Daniel Parke, of profiting directly during war with France in the early years of the eighteenth century.[49] Parke took the opportunity to defame

Codrington by suggesting that one of his character witnesses, an Irish woman named Kate Sullivan, was a former sexual partner of the governor, describing her as "Codrington's wench." According to the Antiguan governor, she had allegedly "layd Two Bastards to him" in addition to "giving him the pox." Parke went on to explain how Codrington had cast Sullivan aside until he needed her to testify to his good character. Although initially willing to swear an oath to the effect that Codrington was an upstanding citizen, Sullivan later "fell sicke and thinkeing she should die she confessed she had perjure[d] herselfe." Parke finished his account of Codrington's relationship with the servant by declaring with some satisfaction that Codrington had "little dream[ed] his Irish Wench had so squeamish a conscience."[50] As far as Parke was concerned, Sullivan's mutability and willingness to lie only proved her "Irishness," while her decision to confess her sins on her deathbed spoke to her Catholic faith. Her declaration of perjury sprang from more than simple religiosity, however, for it was also an indication of her weak womanhood as, fearing death, she threw herself on the mercy of her God and her new governor.

Kate Sullivan may have played a more canny game than either of the powerful men she encountered had imagined her capable of engaging. The fact that Codrington had used her to vouch for his good character indicates that despite her status as "wench" her opinion counted for something. And while Parke painted Sullivan as disloyal and flighty (and his contempt for her is clear in both his description of her as a "wench" and his assumption about the sexually transmitted disease she allegedly passed to Codrington), Sullivan came out on the right side of the current governor in both instances. Each man may have thought he was using her for his own benefit, but she was astute enough to recognize that changing her testimony about Codrington was the pragmatic thing to do under the circumstances, just as her decision to vouch for Codrington in the first place was likely to have been well considered.[51] There is no record of what Sullivan gained in exchange for her testimony on Codrington's behalf, but it seems likely that she was offered some incentive for cooperating, perhaps concerning the upbringing of their children. Similarly, her change of heart on her sickbed might have been prompted by feelings of remorse, but it is easy to imagine Parke making promises to secure Sullivan's retraction of her former statement. Certainly her testimony helped Parke's attempts to confiscate Codrington's estates.[52]

John Blake's unnamed "whore" may have attempted to assert control over her destiny in similar ways to Sullivan. Though the servant woman belonged to one of the lowest orders in the West Indies and so was confined in her choices by her sex and class, she may indeed have pursued a sexual relationship with John. Given that he had a failing wife, who was perhaps not long for this world, she could have hoped to gain favor and become the new Mrs. Blake. At least one visitor to Barbados commented on the ability of young single women to advance socially and economically on the island if they behaved appropriately, even if their virtue was called into question. Visiting the island in 1655, Henry Whistler suggested that "a bawd brought over puts on a demure comportment, a whore if handsome makes a wife for some rich planter."[53] For these very reasons, Barbados planters resisted attempts by Cromwell to export "loose wenches" from the streets of London, believing such policies to be contrary to the colony's interests because of the potential for these women of lesser means to marry themselves into the island's elites. And Barbados was not the only island to suffer such effects. A Montserrat act of 1673 suggested that female servants had been "inveighled by Idle p[er]sons" to come to the island "under the p[re]tence of Marriage" and that once these women discovered that they would not find a husband they were "carelesse of their duties & neglected their service," much to the chagrin of the masters who had purchased their indentures.[54] Despite negative English attitudes toward poor servant women, they continued to arrive on the islands. And some, no doubt, hoped that they would be able to marry well, or at least advance their position, as Cornelius's wife Margaret may have done.

Kate Sullivan and the Blakes' Irish servant may have found ways to use their supposed lower status to their own advantage, and other "wenches" no doubt did the same, but in the end these terms were employed by elite men to continually underscore their superior status as compared to that of the women who worked in their households.[55] By separating the identity of elite women from the labor associated with the domestic realm, prominent men conferred higher status upon themselves. Such verbal and visual strategies became especially important in the case of Irish Catholics, who had to overcome English prejudices about their alleged inferiority. Parke and Codrington unquestionably ranked in the elite, but the same could not be said for John and his brothers. So they used the women in their lives to underscore their membership in the upper echelons of West Indian society. The Blakes came to understand that removing John's wife from everyday domestic labor within the household and calling the character of a female servant into question reinforced the distance between the women in both social and economic terms. They may all have been Irish and Catholic, but that was where the comparison ended.

John's letter revealed one more key component of the Irish Catholic transition to elite status: an investment in the racial hierarchy on the islands. While his own Irish "whore" was considered a potentially troubling addition to his household, thereby making her replacement by another Irish serving woman undesirable, the one sort of person John could effortlessly substitute for his Irish servant was an enslaved woman. From the fragments of archival evidence it is difficult to know when John purchased his desired "neger wench." His letter to Henry in November 1675 suggests that she was present in his household but had yet to be "brought to knowledge" (or trained in the ways of his household), an indication that she had recently arrived on the island.[56] By purchasing this woman John embraced the heart of English Caribbean life: the trade in enslaved property. His actions demonstrate that he knew that there was status attached to his ability to staff his house with enslaved Africans rather than indentured servants.[57]

Cornelius Bryan also saw the importance of owning enslaved Africans, particularly enslaved women, as an announcement of his entry into the Caribbean elite. In the manner of slave owners across the colonies, Bryan classed together the human and animal property he bequeathed to his wife, leaving "one Black guelding" and "one Negroe woman by name Grace" to Margaret to be "at her disposal for ever."[58] The horse was probably the same horse listed in the 1680 census as Bryan's contribution to the defense of the island, while Grace, the enslaved woman, would have been a personal slave for his wife. Bryan left another enslaved woman, Betty, to his eldest daughter, Alice. These specific bequests reveal much about Bryan's attitudes about both the racial hierarchy on the islands and the specific value of enslaved women. Bryan hoped that if he left slave women to his wife and eldest daughter, their potential to reproduce might increase his family's wealth in the future. Moreover, while property in slaves signified a certain level of status, having an enslaved woman working in the home increased a family's level of prestige because the most prominent island planters followed this practice. Bryan may also have assumed that his wife and daughter would be better able to exert control over female, rather than male, slaves.[59] Bryan left the remaining eleven slaves "and their increase" to his four youngest children once they came of age. Asking four of his children to divide eleven slaves between them points to Bryan's assumption that this number would grow naturally, smoothing the division of property. These attitudes were widely held by English planters in Barbados and demonstrate Bryan's absorption of their ideas about race, reproduction, and slavery.[60]

A comparison of the discussion of enslaved women in Bryan's will to the consternation caused by John's Irish servant "whore" or Codrington's "wench" illuminates another layer of hierarchy. Kate Sullivan's illegitimate children and the possible child that might have resulted from John's sexual dalliance with his servant posed particular problems for colonial society. These children, real or imagined, would create a burden on the public to pay for their upbringing and would be a visible reminder of the fornication that had taken place. When enslaved women gave birth they increased their owner's wealth, but their children remained hidden among the ranks of the enslaved. John's sense that he needed an enslaved woman to replace his Irish servant was not simply one of understanding the racial hierarchy in the colonies; it was also caught up in his comprehension of the very different dynamics that would be at work in his household. No family member would accuse an enslaved woman of seducing John and "causing his confusion" because no one would have to recognize the paternity of children produced from such a relationship. In fact, any such children would only increase John's property and his wealth.

By employing the gendered practices and discourses of elite English, and engaging the hierarchies of colonial Caribbean society instead of challenging them, these Irish Catholic men forced English officials to reckon with their presence in the colonies in ways they had not heretofore been pressured to do. Protestant English colonials looked at propertied Irish Catholics and saw men who very much reflected their own families and their own relationships with those they deemed inferior. If they did not readily accept these Irish as their social equals, then English elites would implicitly be calling the entire colonial hierarchy into question. The one distinction that remained was that of religion—no small issue in the seventeenth century. As the specter of Irish perfidy lingered, Irish Catholics found yet anther way to demonstrate their loyalty to England's imperial enterprise.

"The better to governe his Countrymen"

One Irish Catholic who found ways to stress his fealty to the English crown, and who consequently was able to reach the highest levels of government in the Caribbean, was William Stapleton. In the late 1660s, Stapleton was appointed governor of Montserrat, and by the early 1670s he had moved further up the political ladder to become governor of the Leeward Islands. Stapleton's rise to power was predicated on both his loyalty and his ability to reduce the threat posed by his Catholic faith. He demonstrated the former first by supporting the English crown during the war with France in the late 1660s and second by successfully steering the Leeward Islands through a period of relative peace. Issues of revolt, rebellion, and unruly Irish subjects did not arise during Stapleton's time in charge, or if they did, Stapleton chose to omit such information from his missives to London. Part of Stapleton's success was tied to his ability to keep the problems caused by Irish Catholics from bleeding into his correspondences with London. Stapleton never referenced his own faith in his reports to the Lords of Trade and Plantations, and he clearly thought the better of mentioning whatever discontents might have been brewing among the Irish under his charge. Without reading too much into the silences on the subject of religious practices in colonial correspondence, one can see that Stapleton preferred to stress his good governance rather than concentrate on matters of faith. His refusal to discuss the behavior of the Irish Catholics in his charge is a strong example of the ways that elites elided information in the official documents they produced. In this case, Stapleton's actions created an absence in the archive about the Irish on Montserrat, despite their position as the majority population on the island.

Stapleton made a favorable impression on English authorities during the 1667 attempt to wrest control of the English quarters of St. Christopher back from the French. The island, which had been divided into French and English jurisdictions since its settlement in 1624, was a source of consistent antagonism between the two empires, and the territory was often in dispute. Although Major John Scott (an English career soldier who wrote a report of the disastrous attempt to retake the island) blamed much of the military failure on the Irish involved in the expedition, he saved the lion's share of his wrath for the enlisted Irish men. According to the major, "The Irish officers refused [to follow orders] and attempted a Gully, and after some small wounds they were taken, I will not say surrendered to the French, but their souldiers of the same nation by a generall shout surrendered themselves to the enemy, whilst most of the English souldiers found graves."[61] Initially it seemed that Scott was aiming his disapprobation at all Irish participants, including Irish officers like Stapleton, who was in charge of the militia. The description of the "generall shout" with which ordinary Irish soldiers surrendered themselves to French forces conveys not only a sense of joy about their

FIGURE 18. This coastal profile map of Montserrat from 1673 shows the mountainous nature of the island with the major plantations and other sites of note depicted in some detail. In the foreground are three mermaids holding the flags of England, Ireland, and Scotland, a commentary on the primary European settlers in the colony. At the top is the town of Plymouth depicted as it was in 1668 when under attack by the French. The cartographer is anonymous, although it has been speculated that William Stapleton produced the map himself following a circumnavigation of Montserrat. Courtesy of the John Carter Brown Library at Brown University.

situation but also a collective consciousness on the part of Irish soldiers about the benefits of being taken into the custody of their fellow Catholics. Juxtaposed against the image of valiant Protestant English soldiers fighting to the death rather than capitulating, Scott's condemnation of Irish behavior clearly aligned with general English attitudes toward Irish Catholics. However, his thinking on the matter was more nuanced. He differentiated between the Irish officers, who had disobeyed orders but had at least attempted to fight, and ordinary Irish soldiers, who he believed were thrilled at the prospect of being taken prisoner by the French. Scott was making a subtle distinction in his account of the expedition between Irish Catholics of higher status, like the officers, and those of the lower sort, like the enlisted men. The first group might be capable of a kind of loyalty by virtue of their property and emulation of English social and gender norms; the second group, in his estimation, were clearly not. English colonial officials duly followed Scott's careful parsing of the trustworthiness of various kinds of Irish Catholics in the aftermath of the conflict.

When the war with France ended, and when the English parts of St. Christopher and all of Montserrat were returned to English colonial control, William Willoughby, governor of Barbados and the Leeward Islands, discussed the best options for inducing the Irish populations on the islands to remain loyal. Montserrat, the "irish colonie," posed the largest threat. Writing to Joseph Williamson, one of Charles II's closest foreign policy advisors, Willoughby mused that there seemed to be few options available to secure Montserrat from future French attack. He suggested that while the Irish inhabitants did "sweare by Christ they will bee true to his Ma[jesty]," he feared that he could only "believe them till an Enemie appeare."[62] Irish colonists on Montserrat proclaimed their loyalty to Charles II, but as far as Willoughby was concerned, the next overture from a French official would see them all become turncoats. To secure the fidelity of the Irish and ensure the security of Montserrat, Willoughby appointed William Stapleton governor, first because he was "a Gentleman of known valour, good conduct and great Integrity," and second because he was Irish "and therefore understands the better to governe his Countrymen."[63] Like Scott, Willoughby differentiated between kinds of Irish. The faceless majority were considered to be a traitorous group, but prominent Irish like Stapleton had the potential to be truly loyal subjects of the crown because they had proved their fealty in the past and because as landowners they had more to lose.

In fact, William Stapleton was not the first Irish man to be appointed governor of Montserrat: his rise to power came at the expense of the former governor of the island, Anthony Briskett, a man described by Willoughby as "being of the Irish nacon." During the war with France, Briskett had allegedly been eager to "accept a commission from the French King" to govern "most especially the Irish inhabitants of the Leeward side" of Montserrat, precisely because of his Irish background.[64] When the island was returned to English control in 1668, the Montserrat Assembly confiscated Briskett's lands. Briskett defended his actions in the war, claiming that he had accepted the French commission "for the preservation of yo[u]r Majestys most distressed subjects," who would otherwise "by the fury of barbarous bloody Indians, and others . . . undoubtedly [have] been utterly destroyed."[65] Briskett provided testimony from "severall considerable inhabitants and planters" of Montserrat who claimed that his actions had come at their request: these English men were worried about the "fury of the Rebellious Irish" and wanted Briskett to "preserve them from danger."[66] Briskett's appeal to keep his lands now that the English had regained control of Montserrat drew on two long-standing anxieties held by English officials—the untrustworthiness of the Irish and the savagery of Caribbean Indians. But Briskett's petition to have his lands reinstated failed. Willoughby instead kept two plantations for the crown and gave the remaining 525 acres at "Waterworke" to William Stapleton as a reward for his loyalty. While Briskett had been dallying with the French, Stapleton had been risking his life in service of the English empire.

Complicating matters further, Briskett was a Protestant, not a Catholic. For the English, this should have made him *more* trustworthy—the ideal person to govern the island as an Irish man who was of the right religion as far as authorities in London were concerned. Willoughby's tone of skepticism about Briskett, and the record of wartime events, however, demonstrated that Briskett's Protestantism had not been enough to make him a loyal subject of the English crown. The petitions written by English settlers may have saved Briskett from accusations of treason, but they were not sufficiently convincing to effect his reinstatement as governor.[67] Accounting for Briskett's fall from power and Stapleton's rise is difficult because Willoughby offered no direct explanations for his decisions. He viewed the Irishness of both men as important enough to note, but he seems to have concluded that national background worked for each in different ways. Briskett's Irishness served as an explanation for his perfidy; Stapleton's Irishness marked him as someone suitable to govern others from that land. Here Briskett's purported Protestantism became a disadvantage. A Protestant who had potentially lapsed and who was seduced by a Catholic enemy was more dangerous than a Catholic who at least had the courage of his convictions. Stapleton was considered to be more appropriately Anglophilic, and therefore the right man to control the Irish population on Montserrat, an assignment at which he seemed to excel during his tenure as deputy governor of the island.

After Stapleton proved his loyalty to England in the war with France, he appears to have used his Catholicism to gain support from the Irish inhabitants on Montserrat. Unfortunately many of his specific actions are lost to the archive: the Montserrat Assembly minutes are sparse, and additional materials held in the Stapleton family papers are similarly brief.[68] His correspondence with London officials is equally unedifying—Stapleton discussed the composition of island populations, explained various laws that were passed, referenced incidents of disease and death, and made requests for aid and support, but he wrote little on the question of religion.[69] The laws of Montserrat also have very little to say on the matter. The only act that touched on the subject at all was passed shortly after Stapleton became the governor of Montserrat in 1668. "An Act for the raising a Maintenance for a preaching Minister" suggested that as a result of the war the island of Montserrat had been "much destitute of a preaching Minister," causing "Breaches of the Sabbath, and a general Neglect of publick Worship." This lack of religious instruction was "to the Dishonour of Almighty God, and scandalizing of the Protestant Religion." Stapleton's remedy was to request that "an able preaching Orthodox Minister be procured" who would perform church services and administer the sacraments "according to the Canons of the Church of *England*, and the known Laws of the said Realm."[70] From this law, it would seem that Stapleton actively encouraged Protestant worship on Montserrat. But a closer look indicates that what he was actually doing was assuaging London's anxieties about the large population of Irish Catholics on the island. One minister, while a start, would not be sufficient for the whole population of the island, and although Church of England preachers seemed always to be in short supply in the English Caribbean, the fact that not a single Protestant minister could be found on Montserrat suggests that the majority Catholic population were managing perfectly adequately in their absence.[71]

This law was not the only indication of the way Stapleton attempted to avoid shining a spotlight on the religious practices of Irish Catholics on Montserrat. When he was appointed governor of the Leeward Islands, Stapleton became responsible for sending reports back to London answering scores of questions from the Lords of Trade and Plantations about how the islands functioned. In 1676, Stapleton was asked specifically about the religious persuasions of the populations of each Leeward island. First Stapleton admitted that the "Protestant Tenett or perswasion is not prevalent and professed in all the Islands." Although he indicated that "in Mounserrat there the most part are Roman Catholiques," he went on to say that "they give noe scandal to the Protestant Church which is the prevalent perswasion, for the minister when any comes preaches as in any other Island, every Licence of marriage, Probatt of wills, and all other Ecclesiasticall Acts are done according to the Cannons of the Church of England."[72] Though "the Romish in Montserratt is six to one Protestant," official religious practices and (more importantly) births, marriages, and deaths occurred under the auspices of the Church of England, at least on paper if not in practice. This law (and Stapleton's description of religious practices on Montserrat) indicates that the governor wanted to impress on London that the most significant life events were being sanctioned by Church of England clergy. Stapleton's strategy facilitated a reading in London that while there were few Protestants present on Montserrat in need of religious instruction, Catholics on the island were willing to accept the Church of England as a valid entity when it came to baptizing children, marrying, and proving wills. By emphasizing his engagement with Protestant norms, Stapleton subordinated his own Catholicism and that of the Irish on the island, who made up the majority of the population.[73]

Evidence suggests that Stapleton was allowing Catholic practices to continue on Montserrat, a factor that probably contributed to his successful tenure as governor. During James II's reign, Irish Catholics on the island felt emboldened by the accession to the throne of a fellow coreligionist to petition the king for the right not to pay tithes to Protestant churches so that they might be able to support their own clergy. When they demanded absolution from the requirement to finance Protestant churches they referenced "the Clergy under whose case wee were" the Catholic priests who were living among them on the island.[74] Although Stapleton was dead by the time this petition was written, it is clear from the context of the petitioners' plea that Catholic clergy had been present on Montserrat for some time. They would have been part of the island's infrastructure at a moment when Stapleton was in charge, either as governor of Montserrat itself or as governor of the Leeward Islands. By avoiding discussions about religion on the islands as much as possible, Stapleton nursed the impression of Irish Catholics as willing participants in England's colonial project, a strategy aimed at reducing English anxiety about Irish Catholics as a fifth column in their midst. Unlike the hand-wringing that had been the hallmark of most prior correspondence between the colonies and London about Irish Catholics' presence in the empire, Stapleton's strategic silences did not aggravate anti-Catholic sentiment in the metropole, and in return imperial officials did not pose many questions about this subject.[75]

Similar attempts to downplay faith can be found in the words of Cornelius Bryan and John and Henry Blake. Like many Irish Catholic men who commissioned wills on Barbados, Bryan asked to be buried in his garden at the discretion of his executors, who included his wife, Margaret.[76] In Ireland women were in charge of burial rituals, so asking to be laid to rest in such a manner might have been Bryan's way of reconciling his Catholic faith with his status as planter. Requesting burial on his land also removed any questions about churchyards, which on Barbados at this time were all Church of England. Although Bryan left no other clues as to his religious affiliation, he ensured that English officials who remained wary of Catholicism did not have their attention drawn to his family. The Blakes said even less about their religious practices. John and Henry both asked to be remembered "to Father Daniell," the family priest in Galway, but nothing else about the way they practiced their religion has made it into the record.[77] It seems probable that they simply kept their faith to themselves on Barbados and practiced quietly on Montserrat under Stapleton's rule.

Stapleton's success in softening the rebellious aspects of Irish Catholicism helped him promote a way of living that other landowning Irish men could emulate. By avoiding discussions of religious practice as much as possible and in all other ways acting as a model planter, Stapleton allowed English officials to ignore or to forget that he too was a Catholic. His good governance of the Leeward Islands lasted over a decade, until his death in 1686. He profited from being in the graces of the English crown: the 525 acres that Willoughby had granted him in 1668 grew to include plantations on each of the major Leeward Islands. At his death he left each of his daughters, Anne and Louise, over one thousand pounds sterling. His widow remained on the Nevis plantation for the duration of her life, while his executors received his St. Christopher estate. The Montserrat and Antigua properties went to his sons, James and Miles, respectively.[78] Stapleton's large estates were not the only aspect of his life that mirrored the lives of wealthy English planters. He also assigned family members to political positions and married his daughters off to other prominent Irish men in the Caribbean. Both of Stapleton's brothers, Redmond and John, were appointed deputy governor of Montserrat during his tenure in charge of the Leeward Islands. Irishman James Cotter, who had been one of Stapleton's fellow officers in the 1668 attack on St. Christopher, also rose to the position of governor of Montserrat for a short time and married Stapleton's daughter, Margaret.[79] Like the Irish governor, John Blake used his position as landowner to further the family's political aspirations and to secure a good marriage for his daughter. By 1681 he was speaker of the assembly in Montserrat, and his daughter,

Catherine, was wed to Nicholas French, an Irish man who held both property and a position of political power on Antigua.[80] Little wonder that elite English men could look at their Irish counterparts and see an image that closely reflected their own.

The success of Stapleton could be described as an anomaly. Certainly some English colonial officials wished to see him as such. Charles Wheeler, who succeeded Willoughby as governor of the Leeward Islands, grudgingly admitted that he was "sure of [Stapleton's] fidelity" but advised the Council for Foreign Plantations that "his majesty would take special care that after Col. Stapleton's time . . . not only an English Governour be always instituted [on Montserrat], but that there be some Cittadell and small Garrison of English in pay."[81] Wheeler was cleaving to his belief that the only true way to subdue Irish Catholics was to place English Protestants in all significant positions of power. Wheeler's pleas ultimately fell on deaf ears, but his sense that Irish Catholics, even prominent ones, were generally not to be trusted illustrates the difficulties English officials had in overcoming and altering the attitudes they had held toward the Irish for generations. Wheeler's discussion can also be read in another way: that the categories colonial officials were so keen to impose were not distinct and impermeable. It was perfectly possible for an Irish Catholic like Stapleton to be a loyal subject of the English crown, while an Irish Protestant like Briskett could not be trusted. The blanket categories of "English," "Irish," "Protestant," and "Catholic" did not always make sense when applied to individual cases. Bryan, the Blakes, and Stapleton all proved the slippage that could occur. Their demonstrations of loyalty through their holding of land, their understanding of gendered and racial hierarchies, and the dilution of their faith helped to draw them into island elites despite their background. The key to elite Irish success going forward would be to find a way to have their place recognized in the aggregate and not simply on the individual level.

"To live happily and with esteeme among us"

As the seventeenth century drew to a close, English officials searched for ways to make their interactions with a handful of Irish Catholics applicable to a broader swath of the Irish population in an effort to reduce the Irish threat once and for all. Tensions during moments of interimperial or civil war raised the stakes associated with such attempts. As news of the accession of Protestant William and Mary and the flight of Catholic James II into exile reached the colonies, nuanced understandings of the potential for Irish Catholic loyalty seemed to fall away and older rhetoric about untrustworthy papists returned to the fore. The governor of Barbados and the Leeward Islands Christopher Codrington the Elder spent much of 1689 and 1690 frantically trying to prevent uprisings on a number of islands. To save Nevis and Antigua from falling into French hands, he rounded up Irish men suspected of being the ringleaders of schemes to turn the colonies over to the French and banished them to Jamaica.[82] Plots to overthrow English rule appeared to be coming from all directions. Even Barbados, previously the safest of all eastern Caribbean colonies, appeared to be under threat from the French and the "Papists" on the island.[83] Montserrat, the island with the largest Irish Catholic population, loomed as the greatest cause for concern. The lieutenant governor of the island, Colonel Nathaniel Blakiston, a Catholic loyal to the English crown, feared that it would not be long before the Irish on the island decided, as the English felt they had done in the 1660s, that they preferred a Catholic French to a Protestant English regime. He wrote to Codrington asking for advice. Should he banish prominent Irish leaders? Confiscate their lands?[84]

In this crucible of war, and on the brink of losing all of England's Leeward colonies, Codrington (a man not known for his sympathy toward Catholics of any sort, least of all those from Ireland) suggested a policy to save Montserrat that not only was counter to much of the prevailing wisdom about how to deal with Irish Catholics but also would radically change the landscape of English interactions with Irish subjects in the future. In his correspondence with London, Codrington took a hard line, laying much of the blame for the conflict in the Caribbean firmly at the door of "Irish Papists." This correspondence was in keeping with Codrington's general disdain for the Irish, whom he viewed as inherently aggressive and culturally inferior.[85] But in his interisland communications, the governor argued for a more pragmatic approach to dealing with the diverse "enemies" that threatened English authority on the islands.[86] Responding at length, and in great detail, to Blakiston's request for advice on how to best protect the English inhabitants of Montserrat from Irish treachery, Codrington asked two questions: first, whether anything could be done to "give sufficient security of the fidelity of the Irish in case your island be attacqued," and second, "if there cannot, what is best and fittest to be done for the honour of their maj[esties] and the interests of the English subjects in your island?"[87]

According to Codrington, the answer to the first of these questions was not (as he had been suggesting to London) simply that the Irish were categorically untrustworthy and therefore should not be given the benefit of the doubt when it came to matters of war and loyalty. He rather observed that "the Irish of Montserat do there enjoy their estates and Livelyhoods as quietly and happily as the English subjects do." In making such a connection, Codrington stated something about Irish Catholics that no English governor had dared express before, namely their similarity to English settlers on the islands. This direct comparison demonstrated Codrington's faith in the power of property on the western shores of the Atlantic to secure Irish good behavior. He believed that "there are but few men so desperately wicked that will gratify their Revenge at the Expense of their own Ruine and I believe fewer so very generously virtuous and pious, at least wise on this side of the Tropick, that will either hang or starve for their Country or Religion."[88] Here Codrington emphatically stated that the religious beliefs that had long divided Irish Catholics from English Protestants mattered no more, or at least had been seriously reduced in importance. The spoils of sugar simply proved too attractive for religion to act as a bar to planters' desires to protect their property. This was true even at moments of civil strife when the French encouraged the Irish to revolt.

Appeals to the profit motives of planters were not Codrington's sole consideration. He did not presume that all Montserrat property owners were craven, greedy individuals. The situation was more complicated than profit trumping piety. To reduce the allure of living under Catholic French jurisdiction, Codrington asked Blakiston to impress upon the Irish that they had no guarantees of French support, whereas "by cordially uniting with us they may rationally promise to themselves to secure the island and for the future to live happily and with esteeme among us, and even as to theire Religion may have some toleration and allowance."[89] In arguing for such a solution, Codrington appealed to both Irish property interests *and* the religious concerns of the inhabitants of Montserrat. He recognized that not all Irish were the same: some could be as pragmatic as the English elite, at least on matters of economics, as long as their religious practices were protected. Better still, the Irish were not merely to be tolerated—they would get to live "happily with esteeme among us" if they followed Codrington's plan. Codrington was not talking about the Irish populations of Montserrat as a whole; rather, he was singling out those with property to lose—the landowners and merchants of the colony, many of who resided in Plymouth or Kinsale.[90] The English governor may have hoped that by promising religious toleration he would entice more than the wealthy to remain loyal, but the main constituents for such an appeal were island planters. John Blake was exactly the sort of Irish property-owning man who would be attracted to Codrington's proposal. As one of the largest slave owners on Montserrat, and someone who held positions of authority in the island's assembly, Blake would have had much to lose by backing a failed attempt by the French.[91]

Codrington's approach proved to be persuasive. On 17 March 1690 he reported to the Committee on Trade and Plantations in London: "At Monserrat I at large layd before the Irish the ruine in all respects they would certainly bring upon themselves should they prove treacherous to the Government, and on the other hand the advantage of behaving themselves like good subjects. . . . They then with great appearance of joy promised faithful obedience to their maj[esties] Government."[92] The gamble paid off: Montserrat remained an English colony. No doubt the fact that the request for loyalty had come from a fellow Catholic helped to ensure Irish fealty. Blakiston after all had previously persuaded the Irish who supported the French to "lay down their Arms."[93] Overtures from the French were ignored, and Irish planters on the island—large and small—decided that it was more in their interest to remain loyal to Protestant English rule than to risk the uncertainties of an alliance with France.

The full import of Codrington's success on Montserrat could not have been understood in the moment. But even at the time, the fact that Montserrat, the "irish colonie," had not rebelled must have signaled to contemporaries a sea change in Irish Catholic behavior beyond that which could be effected by individual Irish men like Stapleton. That most of the Irish population on Montserrat owned land probably accounted for the success of Codrington's proposal. It mattered little that the majority of the men who lived on the island worked only on very small plots. They were nonetheless more invested in the maintenance of their property rights than those who had no land and no slaves.[94] Colonial officials remained wary of drawing too many conclusions on the basis of this one small victory. But by persuading those Irish Catholics of higher social and economic standing to remain loyal to the Protestant crowns of William and Mary they changed forever the way that English Protestants and Irish Catholics interacted in the islands.[95]

✳ ✳ ✳

Ideas about who could be considered part of the elite and who could not fell more along class than religious or ethnic lines in the English

Caribbean by the start of the eighteenth century, with wealthy Irish Catholics being very much accepted as part of the upper echelons of island societies. Crucially, the avenues to prestige were almost always confined to Irish men: Irish women became pawns in their rise to power, like the unnamed Irish servant woman who served John Blake, or Kate Sullivan, whose testimony was used by two different governors in their fight for supremacy. Central to distinguishing among kinds of Irish Catholics was property ownership in the form of plantations and enslaved Africans. Cornelius Bryan, Henry and John Blake, William Stapleton, and other small Irish landowners on both Barbados and Montserrat increasingly participated in this most American of institutions, the buying and selling of African women and men whose labor would be used to produce wealth in the form of sugar. It was not simply ownership of slaves, however, that allowed Irish property holders to join the ranks of the elite. These men had to adopt the kinds of racial and gendered discourse that demonstrated their suitability for the upper strata of island society. By working within the hierarchies of the colonial Caribbean instead of trying to subvert them, these men encouraged English officials to rethink their former antipathy toward anyone hailing from Ireland.

Tempering fears about their Catholicism was crucial to these planters' successes in more closely resembling English elites. Poorer Irish Catholics may recently have participated in secret masses on plantations or might have been involved in cross-racial religious ceremonies or celebrations, but these wealthy Irish men did not fraternize with the lower orders and knew how to keep their faith without antagonizing English Protestants. Moreover, neutralizing Irish religious practices went hand in hand with the emergence of a growing class of propertied Irish Catholics who built their success by inserting themselves into the structure of England's imperial empire. Peace on Montserrat during Stapleton's tenure meant that Irish landowners on the island were able to increase their property in land *and* in enslaved persons, thus accelerating the process by which large numbers of Irish Catholics were able to enter the planter class in English colonial society.

* * *

In May 1687 Cornelius lay on his deathbed. His wife Margaret was by his side, and his children came for a short visit every morning. Weak as he was, Cornelius wanted to make sure that his final wishes were carried out to perfection. Feeling proud of his accomplishments, he reflected on his good fortune: less than one month after he had been sentenced to banishment from the island, the council had decreed that he might stay on Barbados as long as he no longer gave English settlers any trouble. Now, three decades later, Cornelius felt that he had found success in the colony. He had twenty-two acres and a "mansion house" that he was leaving to his wife, four sons, and two daughters. But more than the acquisition of land accounted for his contentment. He also owned thirteen enslaved Africans, the true mark of the Barbados planter he considered himself to be. And like the rest of his property, they would be divided among his children. Cornelius felt proud that he could leave his children substantially more property than he had ever dreamed possible. He hoped that at least one of the women, Pegg perhaps, or Nell, would have a child before his youngest children came of age. That would help to smooth the division of his property. But even if they did not, he reflected, giving a young, healthy slave girl to one of the children, along with a similarly fit young man, would be the best way to approach the issue: surely they would breed and increase the overall value of the estate he left behind.

News of their master's impending death spread to the slave quarters via Grace. She had been monitoring Cornelius's condition for the last year, ever since the will had been written, and she moved quickly to tell the rest of the workers on the plantation that he was close to leaving this world. Pegg was distressed at the possibility of being separated from her aging mother. She knew that Old Pegg was not worth much in the eyes of her master and that she would probably be considered no better than a refuse slave. Grace had brought information about the contents of the will to the slave quarters a year earlier after she had overheard Cornelius discussing its contents with Captain Robert Kelly, one of the men he knew from the militia who had signed his name to the document. She knew that Cornelius planned to divide eleven of his slaves between four of his children and that she and her mother were in that group. Understanding the mathematical impossibility of dividing eleven people four ways, Pegg knew she would be expected to bear a child, to "increase" Cornelius's property to ensure that each child got an equal share of his estate. She wondered if in the years to come she would be separated from her son or daughter to pay off a future debt, or as part of another division of property upon the demise of her new master or mistress. Therefore as Cornelius's health declined, and the certainty of his death was sealed, Pegg's fears about her unknown future grew.

Epilogue

The construction of difference was always a multifaceted process in which the dynamics of power were in constant flux between officials in London and the people who lived and labored in the Caribbean. Whether based on ethnicity, labor, religion, or gender norms, differences on the plantation and across the islands were refined and challenged in continuous motion. When Irish Catholics and enslaved Africans related to one another in ways that challenged the expectations of English officials, they forced colonial authorities to work harder to enforce English preferred hierarchies and categorization. Together Irish Catholics and enslaved Africans ran away, plotted against the colonial regime, made food and drink, buried their dead, and remarked upon their relative positions of servitude. Yet ultimately the allure of the slave society, with all of its attendant violence and perversion, proved too strong to resist for some Irish Catholics who confounded English ideas about difference by claiming membership among the elite. They became landowners in the English model. They purchased slaves and used corporeal punishment to keep them in line. They sided with the English against the French, thus making their religion-based perceived perfidy a nonissue altogether. The possibilities open to Irish Catholics and enslaved Africans cut more than one way in the island colonies. They could offer an alternative to elite-imposed hierarchies, or they could provide space to imagine a different way of forging bonds. But as the seventeenth century drew to a close, the ability to counter elite ideologies appeared to collapse altogether.

* * *

By the start of the eighteenth century, constructions of difference in the English Caribbean coalesced around developing understandings of racial difference. The demography of the islands shifted considerably in the last decades of the seventeenth century and the first decades of the eighteenth. Africans now accounted for more than half the populations on Antigua, Montserrat, Nevis, and St. Christopher and made up over 80 percent of Barbados residents.[1] Distinctions between English and Irish blurred as Irish Catholics like Bryan, the Blakes, and Stapleton found ways to make themselves indispensible to broader English ambitions on the islands. Property ownership—in either land or slaves—became the main signifier of elite status, creating a collective understanding among Europeans, from wherever they hailed, that they had much more in common with one another than not. As increasing numbers of Irish Catholics availed themselves of opportunities to own slaves and land, they escaped their ambiguous status and melted into the upper echelons of Caribbean society. Even the smallest acreage allowed former servants and laborers to turn a profit, find security, purchase a slave, and so have an investment in the colonial system.

Of course not all Irish Catholics became landowners: many continued to flood into the islands as indentured servants. Promulgating the fiction of islands populated by worthy Irish Catholics who would remain loyal to a Protestant English empire required officials to wrestle with lower-status Irish who did not automatically support slave societies. Authorities found solutions to this problem all the more difficult to determine because the security of the islands was still at risk: a growing enslaved population maintained the threat of rebellion as ever present in anxious English minds. To help provide for the militia and for slave patrols, colonial governments instituted laws that ordered island planters to keep at least one "white servant to every Twenty negroes living."[2] But this law raised the question of who could (or would) be considered "white" in this context.

While their more wealthy counterparts might have adopted the sorts of English gender, religious, and status norms that made them equal partners in England's colonial venture, poorer Irish Catholics were no longer, as far as English authorities were concerned, capable of improvement. Conflating these cultural markers and marginal economic worth with developing ideas about race, English colonists did not recognize these Irish as white. Lower-status laborers continued to cleave to their

Catholicism and were perceived by the English to be unreliable defend-
ers of the islands. So in September 1699 the Antigua Assembly, noting
that "the importation of Irish Roman Chatholick servants for these last
nine months past" might in the end "prove of very evill consequence,"
declared that these laborers should not be encouraged to settle on the
island, specifically excluding them from the numbers counted in the
"act for incouragement and settlement of this island with white People."[3]
Planters did not count Irish Catholics when they sent forth their quo-
tas for filling island militias: in contrast, the Scots were included for the
defense of the colonies. By 1701 the status of Scottish servants and settlers
was formally set when authorities announced that every Scot was to be
"accounted as an Englishman" in Barbados and the Leeward Islands.[4]
The lines were clear: English authorities banned Irish Catholic servants
because of their religious and ethnic backgrounds; they encouraged English and Scots (even those from the lower orders) to settle because they
considered them appropriate members of the white, Protestant island
communities who would be invested in controlling enslaved Africans.

　　Where Antigua led, the rest of the Leeward Islands followed. In October 1701 the colonial agent for Nevis, Colonel Joseph Jory, reported to the
Lords of Trade and Plantations that an act had passed preventing Catholics from settling on that island "for the future and the better governing
of those papists already settled." To protect Nevis from the threat of Irish
servants' treachery, planters would not be "inforced" to buy Irish servants
sold on the island. Jory linked this law with events from eleven years earlier, when Nevis had "expected dayley to be attacked by the French, the
Irish Papists &c joining in conflict together." Regardless of that community's actual social composition, in 1701 Jory placed blame on lower-class
Irish laborers. Later the same month, the attorney general of the Leeward
Islands prohibited all "Papists and reputed Papists" from settling in any of
the islands. This act, which aimed to reinforce prohibitions on Irish servants, would also shut out men of means like Stapleton and the Blakes.[5]

　　If the laws of the late seventeenth and early eighteenth centuries reveal
the practical steps taken by English authorities to incorporate wealthy
Irish Catholics into island hierarchies and to exclude those Irish deemed
beyond redemption, then the census taking in the Leeward Islands in
the early 1700s reflects how these policies created categories of difference
that were more racially based. "English," "Negro," and "Servant," were
the key identifiers recorded in the Barbados census of 1680; "English,"
"Irish," and "Negro," were the main markers that populated the Leeward Islands census of 1678. The enumeration that took place in the first

decades of the eighteenth century told a different story. Both censuses were less detailed than those taken earlier. The category "Irish" disappeared from the returns that Leeward Island officials sent back to the metropole. In Barbados the central categories continued to be "White" and "Negro"; here the category of "Servant," present in 1680, disappeared.[6] Although the composition of the islands' enslaved populations had significantly increased in the thirty or so years between the two sets of census data, servants and free people of all colors continued laboring on the islands. The laws of the late 1690s made clear, moreover, that Irish Catholics were still present in the islands in significant numbers. Reflecting this demographic reality mattered less than imposing English colonial ideologies. So the early eighteenth-century censuses consciously created the impression that all labor was performed by enslaved Africans and that differences among Europeans no longer mattered. The illusion generated by ink on paper allowed English authorities to congratulate themselves on their successful management of Caribbean populations. It also assuaged colonial fears about the threats from within their society in a way that laws or demonstrations of force never could.

For all that the English attempted to present a society that had no troublesome subjects (at least on paper), individuals who fell into undesirable categories continued to make their presence felt. On Montserrat, Irish Catholics like laborer John Gallway provoked English inhabitants and reminded Protestants that many Irish remained loyal to the former king, James II. In October 1699 Gallway's accusation that "the English were Rebells and had dealt unkindely in dethroning James II" caused him to appear before the Montserrat Assembly, who fretted about the consequences of his sentiments as war with France once more reared its head.[7] Other poor Irish Catholics demonstrated that they were still present in numbers significant enough to frighten English officials on the island. In July 1698 Irish laborers Hugh McDaniell, Catherine McDaniell, Jemima Morphey, Dennis Deacey, Catherine Dowdey, and Teigue Dowdey were alleged to have "committed a Riott" when they took cattle from Montserrat's deputy provost marshall.[8] Two months later, two unnamed runaway Irish "servant women" who had stolen a canoe to effect their escape were rounded up on Montserrat and sentenced "to be whipt on the bare back not exceeding thirty-nine lashes" before being returned to their master to completed their years of service, plus additional time in recompense for the time during which they had absconded. Once they had served out their indentures with their original master, they were ordered to be "sould by the Marshall for four years longer" to another island planter.[9]

These servants would go on to become poor laborers on the island, their descendants filling out the 1730 "Political Anatomy of Montserrat," where they were noted with no land and no occupation in the less salubrious surroundings of St. Patrick's and St. Peter's districts.[10]

Montserrat was not the only place that severely challenged English attempts to create clean and distinct categories. A Barbados case from 1697 shows how the presence of individuals who were of indeterminate status also troubled English elites. In February of that year, a "mallatto named Jervis" aboard the sloop *The Flag of Truce* was captured as a suspected runaway. The council claimed that Jervis "belong[ed] to Mr Reynold Alleyn," a planter in the colony, and that Jervis posed a danger to the security of the island, "it being probable hee came to seduce our Negroes."[11] Jervis's mixed-race status was not his only offense. The alleged runaway was also suspected of being a Catholic who was loyal to the French. Two French shipmates spoke to the assembly on Jervis's behalf, relating that his father had been a white merchant on Martinique, while his mother was a woman of color. The men acknowledged that they "know . . . not whether shee was free, or a slave," but argued that regardless of the status of his mother, Jervis had been "Free from his Birth," and moreover that he was a Christian, "for all are Baptized, Negroes as well as free People at Martinique."[12] As a Roman Catholic, as a recipient of the sacrament of baptism, and as a man of mixed race, Jervis threatened the established English hierarchy on Barbados in at least three different ways. Barbados authorities had no need to voice the fear engendered by Jervis's profound discrepancy with their ideal of white Protestantism. Instead they simply removed him from the island's jurisdiction.

Authorities in the colonies erased populations who complicated a simpler narrative in which only enslaved Africans required controlling and English planters alone exercised the power to control. Eighteenth-century censuses omitted economic distinctions beyond the size of plantations, sometimes noted with the attendant inferences of relative wealth. But the changes to racial and ethnic categories in the eighteenth century had the effect of collapsing economic distinctions into those of race. According to the censuses taken at this time, to be "white" and male would define an individual as a landowner; "white women" and "white girls and boys" indicated the wives and children of these landowners. Thus anyone who was not noted as white was a "negro" and therefore enslaved. In these new colonial countings, Irish servants disappeared from the census altogether; Irish planters large and small became subsumed into the category "white." Thus Darby Murphy, Daniell and

Elizabeth Mallony, William Clansey, Tym Donovan, Daniel McCoy, and Dennis McCarty were all listed in the Barbados census, but their ethnicity was not marked.[13] English colonial officials had finally categorized their island populations in a way that reflected the broad shifts that had taken place over the second half of the seventeenth century. Their creations reflected an idealized English construction of difference and hierarchy in the colonies. After struggling for fifty years over where to place Irish Catholics within their island hierarchies, English authorities could now see how, at least on paper, they had found a solution. As Irish landowners were absorbed into the colonial elite, and Irish servants disappeared from official island records, divisions that emphasized race, not religious or other myriad cultural distinctions, took hold. Yet these seemingly rigid markers of black and white were no more fixed than the cultural divisions that had preceded them. Defining difference in the eighteenth-century English Atlantic did not replicate the processes of the seventeenth, but the course was just as messy and complex as what had come before. Imperial officials may have increasingly desired to insert their colonial subjects into immutable racial categories, but such societal bifurcation could only ever exist as an impossible ideal given the realities of everyday life in the Caribbean.

* * *

If this book has been about the possibilities of the past, it is also about the possibilities open to scholars who write about the peoples in those pasts. By probing archival spaces and fissures, this book has moved marginalized historical actors closer to the center of the historical narrative. This reorientation challenges how we understand the processes through which difference was constructed in the early Caribbean. The arrangement of the archive certainly works to constrain our focus, encouraging a concentration on the actions and writings of the elite. It becomes all too easy to work within the comfort of an abundance of material rather than to push at the edges, peer beyond the written, and craft questions that illuminate the lives of the less visible people of the past. But it is only by taking such an approach that we can consider the narratives of people like Cornelius and Pegg. We learn from their stories that the powerful forces that shaped life in the colonies were created anew every day through the interactions of ordinary people.

And we see too the unrealized possibilities that might have been. Cornelius began his Caribbean sojourn on the margins of English colonial society, resentful of island authorities: his body bore the scars that proved his antipathy toward English colonists. He might have gone on to forge bonds with others who bore similar disfigurements. Cornelius could have been a part of the group of "Irish and Negroes" who were "out in Rebellion" in the late 1650s. But instead of ending his days as an Irish troublemaker, Cornelius began to slowly accumulate property, first in sugar, then in land, finally in slaves. As one of the enslaved women he owned, Pegg's possibilities on Barbados were always more constrained than those of her master. She may have formed bonds with the other enslaved women and men with whom she labored and may have found comfort in having her mother close at hand. But ultimately Pegg's bondage trapped her in the drudgery of plantation life. As a woman, and as a slave, she was reduced to property, valuable to her master for her productive and reproductive labor alone. Cornelius ably moved beyond his status as an Irish laborer because he acquired property, including this enslaved woman. Pegg's only release from a lifetime of labor on Barbados, however, would be death itself.

Cornelius's life is hard to uncover, and the lives of his children are even less visible in the archival traces. The Bryan offspring do not appear in the 1715 Barbados census. They are also absent in the probate records for the island. It is possible, however, that at least three of the children—Alice, Katherine, and Daniel—moved from St. James to St. Michael. The marriage records for that parish note that three Bryans with these first names were wed in the last decade of the seventeenth and the first of the eighteenth century, when Cornelius's children would have been around the right age to marry. Daniel became the husband of Joyce Yeates in January 1694. In June 1697 Alice married John Davies. And Katherine and John Harris's nuptials took place in September 1704.[14] If these were indeed Cornelius's children, then they were not the only people who moved after his death. Alice would have taken the "negroe woman named Betty" with her to St. Michael. Daniel and Katherine were each bequeathed a quarter share of the rest of the estate's slaves, so they too would have had enslaved property to bring with them to their new homes. The lives of these individuals are elided altogether. Accessing the stories of the Bryan children exposes the fundamental problem of the colonial archive that has been a central concern of this book: nonelites who inhabited seventeenth-century Barbados, from Irish Catholics to enslaved Africans, remain frustratingly elusive.

Attempting to write a history of marginalized people about whom so little is known, people like Cornelius, Pegg, and thousands of unnamed others, can itself become an act of violence: "straining against the limits of the archive" to try to salvage the unrecoverable necessitates making choices that remain confined within already compromised parameters that work to erase the lives of these men and women altogether.[15] Yet to ignore the possibilities of their experiences is equally problematic. It was through the everyday lives of nonelites that hierarchies of power and discourses about difference were inscribed in colonial settings. So it becomes imperative to pay attention to the circumstances of the lives they led. Rather than assume that a fragmented source base is a barrier to historical investigation, this book has examined the presence of absences to consider the silences contained there. By engaging the many lines of inquiry and possibility that emerge, scholars can begin to counter the power of the archive and redress the imbalance always already present in colonial sources. The erasures and the absences remain, but their authority is diminished. Embracing possibilities, including their contradictions, complexity, and ambiguities, offers a way to write a history of everyday life in the early English Caribbean.

* * *

When Pegg's master died, things had, at first, remained much the same on the small St. James plantation. The mistress and the children remained on the estate, and so did Pegg and her fellow laborers, continuing their daily grind of planting, tending, and harvesting sugar. Another slave revolt caused some excitement, with George lucky to escape the rounding up of island-born slaves accused of being part of the conspiracy, for Pegg knew that he had at least had foreknowledge of the plot. So despite the violence that accompanied the aftermath of the 1692 revolt, it was not until the mistress died that Pegg's world was turned upside down for the first time. Tomy and Mingo were sold almost immediately to pay off some debts. Pegg and her mother were separated according to the provisions of Cornelius's will. Pegg, along with Grace and George, went with Katherine; Old Pegg became Daniel's property. A second upheaval followed in short order when Old Pegg died, leaving her daughter bereft of blood kin. Pegg understood that she would probably not remain long in Katherine's household. From the snatches of conversation she overheard, it seemed that finances continued to be in flux for her mistress: selling Pegg would provide some respite, however brief, for the family. What she suspected came to pass. Shortly following the move to St. Michael came proof of the loss of the Harris's tenuous financial security, and the anxiety and terror of an auction block in Bridgetown.

Notes

Introduction

1. BPL, January 15, 1656, Lucas MSS, reel 1, fol. 179; BDA, RB6/40, p. 398.

2. Monahan, *Creolizing Subject*, 75–76.

3. Beckles, "Riotous and Unruly Lot." For work that briefly discusses the Irish and that stresses the anxieties they generated among English elites, see Menard, *Sweet Negotiations*, 44; Dunn, *Sugar and Slaves*, 69; Bridenbaugh and Bridenbaugh, *No Peace*, 112.

4. Akenson, *If the Irish Ran the World*. Akenson's work serves as a strong counterpoint to more popular texts that present Irish Catholics only as victims of Cromwell's policies of transportation and describe their status in the Caribbean as akin to that of enslaved Africans without differentiating sufficiently between slavery and servitude; see, for example, O'Callaghan, *To Hell or Barbados*. While a work of historical fiction, McCafferty's *Testimony of an Irish Slave Girl* offers a similar perspective. Other scholars have analyzed the Irish presence more broadly, most frequently in terms of their place on the smaller Leeward Islands and with respect to the late seventeenth- and early eighteenth-century censuses. Zacek discusses the significance of the Irish populations of the Leeward Islands (*Settler Society*, especially 46–120). Berleant-Schiller analyzes the 1678 census to explain the composition and distribution of the Irish population on Montserrat ("Free Labor"). The geographer Lydia Pulsipher has also explored the Irish presence on Montserrat in her dissertation ("Cultural Landscape"). Scholars who have investigated the Irish beyond the English Caribbean include Quinn, *Ireland and America*; Lorimer, *English and Irish Settlement*; Cullen, "Irish Diaspora"; Block and Shaw, "Subjects without an Empire." Some recent scholarship explores later eighteenth- and nineteenth-century associations between Irish Catholics and African slavery: Rodgers, *Ireland, Slavery*; O'Neill and Lloyd, *Black and the Green*.

5. Jamaica, in the western Caribbean, and removed geographically and (until 1670) politically from England's other tropical colonies, is not a part of this study. It did not rise to prominence in the English Atlantic world until well into the eighteenth

century. A close look at the Colonial Office sources from the second half of the seventeenth century as well as the Jamaican census records demonstrates that Irish Catholics were few and far between on Jamaica and were never the subjects of discussion among English elites to the extent that they were on Barbados and the Leeward Islands in the same period. For the Jamaican census of 1680, see TNA, CO1/45, no. 1, i–xiv; for discussions of trouble in the 1660s concerning servants and slaves that do not mention the Irish, see TNA, CO140/1, fols. 18–20, 36–37, 85–86, 91–92; for legislation in the same vein, see TNA, CO139/1, fols. 66–75. While certainly some Irish Catholics found themselves on the island, either by accident or design, in the period under review, the shifts and transitions that frame the hallmarks of their existence in Barbados and the Leeward Islands do not have their corollary on Jamaica.

6. The classic interpretation of the English Caribbean in the seventeenth century is still Dunn's *Sugar and Slaves*. Dunn suggests that the transition to racial slavery was swift and absolute. Sheridan outlines a similar trajectory (*Sugar and Slavery*), as do Bridenbaugh and Bridenbaugh (*No Peace*). More recently Amussen has pointed to the 1661 slave code as having determined the differentiation between white and black and free and slave (*Caribbean Exchanges*, 129–35).

7. On the rise of the international slave trade, see Eltis, *Rise of African Slavery*. Beckles charts the shift from servitude to slavery on Barbados (*White Servitude*). For the Atlantic transition to African slavery, see Galenson, *White Servitude*, and Menard, *Migrants, Servants and Slaves*. Menard suggests that the rise of sugar influenced the shift away from servitude and toward slavery (*Sweet Negotiations*, 39–41). For more on the difference between "slave societies" and "societies with slaves," see Berlin, *Many Thousands Gone*, prologue and sections I and II.

8. Kidd, *British Identities*, 9–13. The inclusive nature of the Mosaic understanding of history also gave rise to biblical justifications for slavery, most famously the Curse of Ham. See Braude, "Sons of Noah"; Haynes, *Noah's Curse*. Kidd's analysis is a caution against anachronistic uses of modern conceptions of difference that have their roots in the scientific racism of the nineteenth century.

9. A similar trajectory can be traced in seventeenth-century Virginia; see Brown, *Good Wives*; Goetz, *Baptism of Early Virginia*; Breen and Innes, *Myne Owne Ground*. Walsh complicates this picture, arguing that as early as the middle of the seventeenth century plantation owners in Virginia were actively choosing to pursue the enslavement of Africans (*Motives of Honor*, 20–21).

10. Kidd, *British Identities*, especially chs. 6 and 7; Muldoon, "Indian as Irishman"; Muldoon, *Identity*, 66–67, 79–81, 89–92. Building on his earlier work, Kidd has broadened his exploration of the connections between race and religion (*Forging of Races*). See also Canny, *Elizabethan Conquest of Ireland*, 119. For more on Irish social and sexual relationships, see Laurence, "Cradle to the Grave." The question of which came first, slavery or racism, absorbed scholars for much of the twentieth century. Overviews of these debates can be found in Frederickson, *Racism*, and D. Davis, "Constructing Race." The 1997 *William and Mary Quarterly* special edition on race provides other strong examples of scholarship focused on cultural productions of difference between the sixteenth and eighteenth centuries. See especially J. Morgan, "Some Could Suckle"; Kupperman, "Presentment of Civility"; Chaplin, "Natural Philosophy." For book-length projects that engage similar questions, see Kupperman, *Indians and English*; Chaplin, *Subject Matter*. Scholars who have paid particular attention to the

intersections of Europeans, Africans, and Americans in the English Atlantic include K. Fischer, *Suspect Relations*; John Sweet, *Bodies Politic*; Kopelson, *Faithful Bodies*; K. Brown, *Good Wives*, especially chs. 1–4.

11. Kussmaul, *Servants in Husbandry*, 5–9.

12. Scholars' estimations of the numbers of Irish who found themselves shipped to the Caribbean vary widely. Some claim that upwards of fifty thousand were "sent beyond the seas" in the 1650s alone, but estimates that range from ten thousand to twenty-five thousand are more likely to be accurate. For the lower figure, see Akenson, *If the Irish Ran the World*, 19. For the higher estimate (which includes Virginia as well as the Caribbean), see Smyth, *Map-Making*, 161–62. Canny and Cullen have contended that between twenty thousand and forty thousand Irish arrived in the Americas over the second half of the seventeenth century; Canny, "English Migration," and Cullen, "Irish Diaspora," 64, 139.

13. Servants expected to receive ten acres of land on completion of their indenture, but by the 1660s on Barbados such arrangements were no longer being fulfilled because of a lack of land. Servants instead received sugar and became hired laborers, or they tried their luck on islands where land was more plentiful, like Montserrat. Some traveled to the North American mainland instead, or returned to Europe (Dunn, *Sugar and Slaves*, 52–53; Beckles, *White Servitude*, 161–66). There is a vast literature on the subject of indentured servitude in the Americas, especially in the English colonies. Kenneth Morgan, in *Servitude and Slavery*, provides an overview of the subject matter and historiographical trends in the field. Canny has edited a similarly useful volume, *Origins of Empire*. See also Menard, *Migrants, Servants and Slaves*. On servants and the choice of destination, see Galenson, *White Servitude*, 81–116. Donoghue has recently argued that we need to deconstruct the category "indentured servant" for the seventeenth century and instead focus on the multiple "slaveries" experienced by bonded laborers in the English Atlantic world ("Out of the Land").

14. J. Morgan, *Laboring Women*.

15. On the place of religion in politics and society in Africa, see Thornton, *Africa and Africans*, part I; Law, "Religion, Trade."

16. Kupperman, *Providence Island*; Gragg, *Englishmen Transplanted*; Gragg, *Quaker Community on Barbados*; Sensbach, *Rebecca's Revival*; Beasley, *Christian Ritual*; Pestana, *Protestant Empire*; Block, *Ordinary Lives*.

17. Smallwood, *Saltwater Slavery*, 52–64. Seeman discusses the importance of death to everyday life in the Americas (*Death in the New World*). Vincent Brown has shown the way that mortality affected life in slavery in the English Caribbean (*Reaper's Garden*). Both works discuss the belief that on death Africans would return to their home.

18. This ideology of everyday life is most clearly articulated in Certeau's *Practice of Everyday Life*. Certeau suggests that "a tactic is determined by the *absence of power* just as a strategy is organized by the postulation of power" (38). For Certeau's explication of strategies and tactics, see *Practice of Everyday Life*, xix–xx, 34–39.

19. Fumerton, "Introduction," 12.

20. Gardiner, *Critiques of Everyday Life*, 168. See also Highmore, who argues that for Certeau "the everyday exists 'between the lines.' . . . Attending to the everyday will also mean attempting to rescue the traces, the remainders of the overflowing unmanageability of the everyday" (*Everyday Life*, 26).

21. Trouillot, *Silencing the Past*, 25, 51–53.

196 / NOTES TO INTRODUCTION AND CHAPTER 1

22. Certeau, *Practice of Everyday Life*, 21.

23. For the unnamed servant woman, see Oliver, *Caribbeana*, 1:55–56. For the baptism in St. Michael, see BDA, RL1/1, p. 259, 3 July 1681; BDA, RL1/1, p. 275, 5 September 1682; BDA, RL1/1, p. 378, 9 October 1688. For the religious ceremony on Drax's plantation, see Ligon, *True and Exact History*, 50. For the Irish man who was lashed, see BPL, Lucas MSS, reel 1, fol. 179, 15 January 1656.

24. N. Davis, *Return of Martin Guerre*, 5. Davis's book about the experiences of three early modern women has also been very influential on this study (*Women on the Margins*).

25. On issues of recreation of events despite a problematic archive, I have drawn on the work of Hartman, *Scenes of Subjection*; Hartman, "Venus in Two Acts." Also useful has been Bennett's work on the ways historians fetishize the archive and the specific problems this raises for writing the history of Africans and the enslaved, "Subject in the Plot."

26. In *Unredeemed Captive*, Demos, arguing that speculation is important, fills in the gaps between sources when discussing the subjectivity of Eunice/A'ongote as she debated whether to remain in the Mohawk village of Kahnawake (108). I agree with Demos that such an attempt is important, despite its risks. Richter has similarly invoked imagination in his reading of early European sources from an indigenous perspective in *Facing East*, 11–40. He asserts that "only imagination can put Indians in the foreground of these scenes" (13).

27. Putnam, "To Study the Fragments/Whole."

28. Price, *Alabi's World*. In a discursive footnote Price suggests that following twenty years of work with Suriname materials, he can "permit my educated imagination to construct probabilities" (285). He draws on the work of fellow anthropologist Clifford Geertz, arguing that his approach is "an imaginative way of seeing through experience."

29. Scholars of microhistory whose work has inspired me include Natalie Zemon Davis, Carlo Ginzburg, and Robert Darnton. Hoffman, Sobel, and Teute's edited collection *Through a Glass Darkly* has also been useful for thinking through both the scope and the limitations of microhistorical approaches. I am grateful to Kristen Block for shared conversation about both the question of silences in archives and the subject of microhistory, which she engages in her monograph *Ordinary Lives*, especially 6–9.

30. Cornelius Bryan's experience is culled from his appearance before the Barbados Council (BPL, Lucas MSS, reel 1, fol. 179, 15 January 1656), the deeds that chart his property acquisition (BDA, RB3/8, fol. 534; RB3/9, p. 89; RB3/11, p. 573, RB3/3, p. 720), and his will (BDA, RB6/40, p. 398). For the rest of his story I have drawn on Rivers and Foyle, *Englands Slavery*; BPL, Lucas MSS, reel 1, fol. 211, 21 May 1656; Biet, *Voyage*; Ó'Siochrú, *God's Executioner*. The references to Pegg, Old Pegg, and the other enslaved Africans are based on information in Bryan's will, but their experience of life in the sugar fields draws on Dunn, *Sugar and Slaves*, Mintz, *Sweetness and Power*, and Ligon, *True and Exact History*.

1 / "An Heathenishe, Brutish and an uncertaine, dangerous kind of People"

1. HL, BL 369, "An Act for the Better Ordering and Governing of Negroes," Barbados, 27 September 1661, 1. The 1661 slave code can also be found in TNA, CO 30/2, fols. 16–26. For the act governing servants, see *Acts of Assembly*, 21–27. These codes

are also discussed by Dunn (*Sugar and Slaves*, 238–40) and Amussen (*Caribbean Exchanges*, 129–35). Beckles analyzes the servant code of 1661 (*White Servitude*, 80–85).

2. Noonan argues that the Irish became the "touchstone against which to define Englishness" ("Cruell Pressure," 168).

3. Ohlmeyer, "Seventeenth-Century Ireland," 460. See also Canny, "Ideology of English Colonization"; Andrew, Canny, and Hair, *Westward Enterprise*; Quinn, *Ireland and America*; Smyth, *Map-Making*, 421–40.

4. On English sartorial, comestible, and architectural preferences in Barbados that matched those at home, see Dunn, *Sugar and Slaves*, especially ch. 8; Puckrein, *Little England*. For the Leeward Islands, see Zacek, *Settler Society*, ch. 1.

5. Amussen makes the point about the increase in slave labor in the 1650s (*Caribbean Exchanges*, 130). For Irish transportation, see Dunn, *Sugar and Slaves*, 56–57, 69; Beckles, *White Servitude*, 52–54.

6. Canny, *Making Ireland British*, 59. The Gaelic Irish and Old English found common ground and created a common identity in opposition to English colonization in the late sixteenth and early seventeenth centuries (Caball, "Faith, Culture and Sovereignty," 125–27).

7. For more on the idea that legal statutes respond to events on the ground, see Crane, *Witches, Wife Beaters*, especially 8, 15; Kopelson, "Sinning Property."

8. Amussen makes this point (*Caribbean Exchanges*, 122).

9. Pestana, *English Atlantic*, 210–12. Pestana notes that Rivers, and possibly Foyle, had managed to return to England from Barbados and wrote their petition on behalf of all transported royalists. Donoghue has contextualized the voluminous pamphlet production of this period, noting that almost all pamphlets conflated the tyranny of government with slavery ("Out of the Land," 954–55).

10. There is a vast historiography on the English Civil War, sometimes referred to as the English Revolution or the Wars between the Three Kingdoms. Of influence here have been Hill, *World Turned Upside Down*; D. Smith and Little, *Parliaments and Politics*; Ohlmeyer, *Civil War and Restoration*; Pestana, *English Atlantic*.

11. Rivers and Foyle, *Englands Slavery*, title page.

12. Amussen, *Caribbean Exchanges*, 127–28. See also Pestana, *English Atlantic*, 211.

13. Amussen, *Caribbean Exchanges*, 127–28. See also Donoghue, "Out of the Land," 970–71.

14. Rivers and Foyle, *Englands Slavery*, cover. Quotation is from Exodus 26:1.

15. Ibid., 5.

16. Ibid., 8, 17. The quotation is translated as "How long, oh Lord, how long?" in this case asking how long Parliament will allow the petitioners to suffer.

17. Ibid., 7. Pestana suggests that unfavorable comparisons with Turks were common in this period (*English Atlantic*, 211).

18. Ibid. Pestana notes that the case reinforced public perceptions that the Protectorate was tyrannical. Amussen argues that the use of the term *slavery* in the pamphlet was more a way to underscore the illegal machinations of government than a useful way to get at how the petitioners thought about African slavery (*Caribbean Exchanges*, 127–28). While I agree with Pestana and Amussen that issues of status would have garnered sympathy from parliamentarians of similar rank and thus would have aided the success of the petition, like Beckles I believe it is important to explore the similarities

between the experiences that Rivers and Foyle recount and those endured by enslaved Africans ("English Parliamentary Debate," 346–47).

19. Beckles, "English Parliamentary Debate," 346–47.

20. Rediker, *Slave Ship*, 73–75.

21. Rivers and Foyle, *Englands Slavery*, 21.

22. Smallwood, *Saltwater Slavery*, 86–94. Rediker, *Slave Ship*, 167–70. Even the period of two weeks that the prisoners spent languishing aboard ship off the coast of England before the *John* departed has its mirror in the ways that slave ships lingered just off the coast of Africa, ensuring that their cargo holds were as full as possible at the time of departure.

23. Rivers and Foyle, *Englands Slavery*, 4. Smallwood points out that men and women were segregated on slave ships, locked in separate areas, even when they were allowed on deck once land was out of sight (*Saltwater Slavery*, 72–76); see also Rediker, *Slave Ship*, 120.

24. Rivers and Foyle, *Englands Slavery*, 22; Rediker, *Slave Ship*, 265–70.

25. Rivers and Foyle, *Englands Slavery*, 15.

26. J. Morgan, *Laboring Women*, 50, 104; Smallwood, *Saltwater Slavery*, 171–72, 196. The issue of language comprehension was not just between English and Africans but among Africans too. Although writing over a century later, Olaudah Equiano commented that from the moment he was kidnapped "I always found somebody that understood me till I came to the sea coast," (*Interesting Narrative*, 35). Rediker has argued that the language barrier among Africans has been overstated in the literature (*Slave Ship*, 276–77).

27. Those responsible for guarding Rivers and Foyle and their counterparts were also English. In the African trade, on the other hand, Gold Coasters were often used as security on ships, responsible for watching over people from other polities (Smallwood, "African Guardians," 679–716).

28. Rivers and Foyle, *Englands Slavery*, 17. Prominent in the minds of English members of Parliament may have been similar accounts of Englishmen being sold as captives in Algiers. Captain John Smith was captured and taken to Istanbul, where he spent two years in slavery (J. Smith, *True Travels*). Although the account was written after this debate took place, William Okeley's experiences in Algeria were representative of experiences of those English sold into slavery in the Muslim world. Recounting how he and his fellow captives were examined like animals, Okeley noted that those with good teeth would fetch a higher price (*Eben-ezer*, 9–11). See also R. Davis, *Christian Slaves*; Matar, *Turks, Moors*.

29. For a discussion on the selling of slave cargoes in "lots" that ensured the sale of every enslaved person, see Smallwood, *Saltwater Slavery*, 171–76.

30. Rivers and Foyle, *Englands Slavery*, 5.

31. Beckles makes a similar point ("English Parliamentary Debate," 345).

32. Rosenberg, "Thomas Tryon," 616. Donoghue argues that Tryon and his cohort, while not arguing for an end to slavery altogether, nonetheless put forth the kinds of arguments that eighteenth-century abolitionists used when combating the institution. He posits that the similarities between seventeenth- and eighteenth-century abolitionism are more revealing than their differences ("Out of the Land," 946–47).

33. Equiano and Prince were enslaved Africans who spent time in the Caribbean in the eighteenth century before gaining their freedom on moving to England. Their

autobiographies are some of the earliest antislavery writings and are significant as examples of eighteenth-century enslavement.

34. Pestana argues as much, noting that when members of Parliament addressed the petition they were horrified by the idea of slavery, but only insofar as it affected English subjects (*English Atlantic*, 212–13).

35. Stock, *Proceedings and Debates*, 1:256.

36. Ibid.

37. Ibid, 1:260.

38. Rivers and Foyle, *Englands Slavery*, 10.

39. Stock, *Proceedings and Debates*, 1:253.

40. Ibid, 1:254.

41. Ibid, 1:257.

42. Pestana makes a similar observation (*English Atlantic*, 211–12). See also Beckles, "English Parliamentary Debate," 344–52.

43. Stock, *Proceedings and Debates*, 1:256.

44. Zacek suggests that there were relatively few Scots in the Leeward Islands prior to the eighteenth century (*Settler Society*, 10). Dunn compares the small numbers of Scots who labored as indentured servants on Barbados to Irish Catholics (*Sugar and Slaves*, 69); Beckles stresses the English preference for Scottish servants (*White Servitude*, 39, 69, 98).

45. Kew, "Irish Sections," 38. For an overview of Moryson's journeys and travel writing, see Mancall, "Introduction," 1–9.

46. Spenser, *View*, 55. A boolie was a temporary structure; see Oxford English Dictionary Online, s.v. "bowly, adj.," www.oed.com/view/Entry/22270?redirectedFrom= boolie (accessed 11 October 2011). Although written in 1596 and circulated widely in manuscript form, Spenser's tract was not published until the 1630s (Canny, *Making Ireland British*, 57–58). The *View* is written in the form of a dialogue between two Englishmen: Eudoxus, a recent arrival on the island, and Irenius, a resident of who has spent considerable time in Ireland and therefore is more practical about the measures necessary to "civilize" the Irish than his politically naive friend.

47. Davies, *Discovery*, 169–70.

48. Kew, "Irish Sections," 107, 109.

49. K. Brown, *Good Wives*, 33–34.

50. Kupperman, "Presentment of Civility," 193–228.

51. Spenser, *View*, 57. For a thorough discussion of English attitudes toward the Irish mantle, see A. Jones and Stallybrass, "Rugges of London," 128–35.

52. Speed, *Theatre of the Empire*, bk. 4, 138.

53. Moryson, *Itinerary*, 236.

54. Spenser, *View*, 58. For more on the connections between Irish dress and sexual behavior, see A. Jones and Stallybrass, "Dismantling Irena," 151–71. See also Suranyi, *Genius*, 115–18.

55. Spenser, *View*, 58.

56. Kew, "Irish Sections," 105. Jennifer Morgan notes that European women only began to use corsets in the sixteenth century and that "only then did the elevated breasts of corseted women become a marker of refinement, courtliness, and status" (*Laboring Women*, 206 n. 17). Kathleen Brown has explored the language of cleanliness with regard to Moryson's assessment of Irish barbarism (*Foul Bodies*, 32).

57. Spenser, *View*, 85.

58. Kew, "Irish Sections," 111.

59. Canny, "Ideology of English Colonization," 583. For more on the lay practice of Catholicism in early modern Europe, see Thomas, *Religion*; Gillespie, *Devoted People*; Cameron, *Enchanted Europe*; Seitz, *Witchcraft and Inquisition*.

60. Priests who worked in line with Catholic Reformation teaching were remarkably tolerant in their acceptance of rites that closely resembled ancient practices. For example, Father Bonaventure Ó Hussey deliberately adopted bardic traditions in his religious writings, turning the catechism into a series of easy-to-remember traditional mnemonic metrical stanzas in the Irish language, making church teachings more readily accessible and understandable to Irish Catholics (Meigs, *Reformations in Ireland*, 82). For more on the use of Irish language in the Catholic Renewal, see Canny, *Making Ireland British*; Gillespie, *Devoted People*, 12–13; Palmer, "Interpreters."

61. Noonan, "Cruell Pressure," 157; Takaki, "*Tempest* in the Wilderness," 895.

62. For a broad sketch of the events of 1641, see R. Armstrong, *Protestant War*, chs. 1 and 2.

63. Hundreds of pamphlets and woodcuts on the massacre were produced and disseminated by English Protestants across the Three Kingdoms (Ó Siochrú, "Atrocity"). Carey notes a similar phenomenon relating to Sir Henry Sidney's battles in Ireland in the late sixteenth century. John Derricke created a number of woodcuts that championed English violence toward the barbarous Irish as a model for future English success in the island (Carey, "Icons of Atrocity").

64. Noonan, "Cruel Pressure," 161–63.

65. Fitzpatrick, *Bloody Bridge*, 89, 138. Kathleen Brown argues that incidents of alleged cannibalism by the Irish led English observers to believe them "capable of any barbarism" (*Good Wives*, 35–36). McCabe makes a similar point, noting that cannibalism was seen as "the ultimate index of racial inferiority" and that "to drink blood in a ritualistic manner is to compound the abomination by enacting a sort of savage Eucharist, a demonic antitype of the Christian sacrament" (*Spenser's Monstrous Regiment*, 59–60). Whether any of these incidents of cannibalism actually took place is another question; see Greenblatt, who argues that eyewitness testimony has been used as evidence of the barbaric nature of alien cultures since Herodotus (*Marvellous Possessions*, 123–29).

66. Noonan, "Cruel Pressure." For more on the popularity of Temple's text, see Barnard, "1641." For a discussion of the effects on the Protestant psyche, see Ford, "Living Together." Stanwood notes the importance of the events of 1641 on antipopery in the colonies (*Empire Reformed*, 7).

67. Cronon, *Changes in the Land*, 55–58; Daunton and Halpern, *Empire and Others*; Muldoon, "Indian as Irishman."

68. On the Scottish Highlanders, see Kidd, *British Identities*, ch. 8; Dawson, "Gaidhealtachd." For English engagement with Indian cultural practices, see Kupperman, *Indians and English*. On both West African and Native American cultural practices, see K. Brown, "Native Americans."

69. Thornton has explored the changes in African dress in the Americas, noting the presence of a Kongolese mantle in Mexico in the seventeenth century (*Africa and Africans*, 231–34). Probably the most famous mantle in the early Americas was the cloak that was said to have belonged to an Algonquian leader in the Chesapeake, Powhatan.

For a discussion of the significance of Powhatan's mantle, see Waselkkov, "Maps," 453–57.

70. In *Laboring Women*, Jennifer Morgan notes that Amerigo Vespucci painted Native American women as cannibals, connecting their savagery to their propensity to ingest the flesh of their human enemies (19). Law has covered a European obsession with alleged instances of cannibalism in Africa dating back to the fifteenth century ("Human Sacrifice"). Of course the comparison cut both ways. In their slave narratives, both Olaudah Equiano and Quobono Ottobah Cugoano discuss the possibility of being eaten by white men (Equiano, *Interesting Narrative*, 38–39; Cugoano, *Thoughts and Sentiments*, 8–9).

71. For an Irish example, see Kew, "Irish Sections," 108. For the African (and to a lesser extent, indigenous American) context, see J. Morgan, "Some Could Suckle"). Kathleen Brown discusses the Irish and Indian experiences of childbirth (*Good Wives*, 35, 58).

72. Dunn, *Sugar and Slaves*, 18–19, 118–19; Akenson, *If the Irish Ran the World*, 21–22, 28–30; Boucher, *Cannibal Encounters*, 39–48.

73. Fickes, "They Could Not Endure," 58–61. Ligon notes the presence of Indian slaves on Barbados (*True and Exact History*, 54–55).

74. There is very little pre-Restoration Caribbean legislation to analyze: the vagaries of the archive mean that most extant legislation dates from the latter part of the seventeenth century. Acts from later periods often reference previous laws but do not go into any detail about their precise language (Dunn, *Sugar and Slaves*, 238; Amussen, *Caribbean Exchanges*, 130). The main exceptions are the Barbados Acts from 1652, published in London for distribution "at the India Bridge" in 1654 so that all literate colonists would know the parameters of the law (*Acts and Statutes*).

75. TNA, CO154/1, no. 49. Unlike Barbados, Antigua and the other Leeward Islands had small indigenous populations, so it is not surprising that the Antigua Assembly included "Indian" as a possible category in their discussion of sex between "Christians and Heathens." See also Dunn, *Sugar and Slaves*, 228; Goetz, *Baptism of Early Virginia*, ch. 3.

76. TNA, CO154/1, no. 49.

77. Ibid.; K. Brown, *Good Wives*, 195; Kopelson, *Faithful Bodies*.

78. According to Jennifer Morgan, whites feared sexual and social contact because it "belied the fixity of their own whiteness" (*Laboring Women*, 72). See also C. Jones, *Engendering Whiteness*, 27–29.

79. A similar attempt to control servant women's sexuality can be found in the 1652 Barbados Act, which "priced" sexual relations with women servants out of the reach of their fellow servants by increasing time in service both for the women and for the men who fathered their children (Amussen, *Caribbean Exchanges*, 126; see also Pestana, *English Atlantic*, 186).

80. TNA, CO154/1, no. 49. Fields notes the inherent problem with biological understandings of race whereby a white woman can give birth to a black child, but a black woman can never give birth to a white child ("Ideology and Race," especially 149).

81. Christian men who were married or free paid fines and received small prison sentences or worked off their punishment in public service. Male servants could expect to be whipped like their female counterparts, but they did not spend additional time as indentures and were not banished from the island; serving one year in public service

was the only additional penalty for their crime (TNA, CO154/1, no. 49). Pestana also notes this distinction (*English Atlantic*, 186). For more on the connections between extended service and reproduction, see K. Brown, *Good Wives*, 134; J. Morgan, *Laboring Women*, 76; K. Fischer, *Suspect Relations*, 102.

82. K. Brown, *Good Wives*, 197.

83. The act states two ways of ascertaining paternity. First, when the child was one month old, the council or the justice of the peace examined the child to determine "whether they conceive the child to have bin begotten of a white man, Indian, or negroe." Second, a pregnant African or Native American woman could name the father while she was in the final throes of labor, in much the same way as in other instances of adultery that did not traduce boundaries of faith (K. Brown, *Good Wives*, 98; Gowing, *Common Bodies*, 160–62). This shift is all the more surprising when one probes the reasons behind the idea that a birthing confession contained an essential truth: in European cases, a belief that the pain of childbirth and the very real possibility of death rendered a woman incapable of lying. Yet by giving credence to the words of an African or Native American woman in the same situation, colonial officials were unintentionally suggesting that these women too experienced pain during birth, thus contradicting the idea that they were exempt from the Curse of Eve, a belief that had helped shape the view of these same women as outside a Mosaic understanding of humanity in the first place.

84. TNA, CO154/1, no. 49. Kathleen Brown discusses a similar set of circumstances involving the children of enslaved women and European men in Virginia (*Good Wives*, 131–32).

85. TNA, CO154/1, no. 49. Goetz argues that the tracing of legitimacy through fathers by English custom accounts for the discrepancy between how the children of Christian men and the children of Christian women were treated (*Baptism of Early Virginia*, ch. 3).

86. HL, BL 369, "An Act for the Better Ordering and Governing of Negroes," 3. See also Amussen, *Caribbean Exchanges*, 131–32. Amussen argues that the 1661 slave code "created an entirely new judicial system" on Barbados by ignoring the precedent of trial by jury that characterized the system in England.

87. HL, BL 369, "An Act for the Better Ordering and Governing of Negroes," 8–9. Dunn also discusses this marking of the arm (*Sugar and Slaves*, 241). Of course the badge of the cross did more than identify slaves perceived to be loyal to the English: it also allowed other enslaved Africans to see those among them who might not be trustworthy. It was a stark contrast to the branding of runaways, which involved physical disfigurement.

88. The red cross also evokes the Templar cross of the Crusades. Although its precise connotations would not have reflected a direct link to the medieval past, the specific description of this cross nonetheless invokes an earlier moment and a crusade to overcome infidels. The symbol of the red cross also plays an important part in book 1 of Spenser's *Faerie Queene*. The "Redcrosse Knight" bears the emblem of St. George and is later revealed to be the real St. George.

89. Just a few years later, elites in London ordered that the enslaved population should be educated in the Christian faith to the extent that those who would "arrive at a competent knowledge therein, [would] be admitted to the sacrament of Baptisme" (TNA, CO1/21, no. 15, Instructions for the Lord Willoughby of Parham, 4 February

1667). To prevent baptism from becoming an avenue to freedom for enslaved Africans (as many slaveholders feared), they went on to pass a law specifically prohibiting such a challenge. Most plantation owners still preferred not to educate their enslaved populations in Christian doctrine, continuing to fear that baptism paved a road to freedom (see Gomez, *Exchanging Our Country Marks*, 57).

90. TNA, CO154/2, fols. 107–8, 26 May 1675, Nevis. See also Dunn, *Sugar and Slaves*, 244.

91. Pincus, *Protestantism and Patriotism*, ch. 10.

92. Firth, *Narrative of General Venables*, cited in Block and Shaw, "Subjects without an Empire," 47.

93. Block has explored the religious and political implications of Cromwell's Western Design, noting that its failure destroyed hopes of a pan-Protestant attack against Catholicism in the Caribbean as ordinary English men were shut out of opportunities to profit from their service (*Ordinary Lives*, part III).

94. BPL, Lucas MSS, reel 1, fols. 161–62, 6 November 1655.

95. BPL, Lucas MSS, reel 1, fol. 368, 22 September 1657.

96. BPL, Lucas MSS, reel 1, fol. 361; BPL, Lucas MSS, reel 1, fols. 161–62; BPL, Lucas MSS, reel 1, fol. 179.

97. TNA, CO1/21, no. 55, "Major Scott's Relation," 12 July 1667. See also Zacek, *Settler Society*, 80–82.

98. Hall, *Acts Passed*, 103–4. See Trevor-Roper, *From Counter-Reformation*, 237. While the conspirators in the so-called "Popish Plot" of 1678 (who allegedly intended to assassinate Charles and bring his Catholic brother James to the throne) were executed, Charles rejected subsequent calls by certain factions in the English Parliament to exclude James from the succession (Monod, *Power of Kings*, 231).

99. See Zacek, *Settler Society*, 83; Akenson, *If the Irish Ran the World*, 101. Both note that Irish Catholics could take the test and remain loyal to the Catholic faith. Zacek points out that even those who "accepted the tests and oaths with less than perfect sincerity were making a public performance of their loyalty to Crown and Church."

100. Stock, *Proceedings and Debates*, 1:250.

101. Beckles notes that the work that the petitioners and enslaved Africans performed was the same, and he suggests that Parliament was not convinced by Noell's protestations to the contrary ("English Parliamentary Debate," 345, 347).

102. TNA, CO31/1, fol. 366, Assembly to Governor Dutton, 30 March 1681.

103. *Acts of Assembly*, 118. See also Amussen, *Caribbean Exchanges*, 139.

2 / "An exact account of the number of persons upon the Island"

1. The Leeward Island census material is located at TNA, CO1/42.

2. An exception would be the meticulous records from the 1620s in Virginia that listed the names of the living and dead following the 1622 Indian attack, and a short census of the colony taken two years later (Hotten, *Original Lists*; Dorman, *Adventurers of Purse*).

3. Dunn, *Sugar and Slaves*, 84–16, 126–31; Beckles, *White Servitude*, 125–26, 130–34; Akenson, *If the Irish Ran the World*, 105–16; Zacek, *Settler Society*, 46–65; Berleant-Schiller, "Free Labor."

4. J. Morgan, "Demographic Logics." I thank Jennifer for sharing her work in progress and permitting me to draw on it in this study. See also Poovey, *History of the*

Modern Fact; McCormick, *William Petty*; Cohen, *Calculating People*; Buck, "Seventeenth-Century Political Arithmetic"; Sussman, "Colonial Afterlife."

5. Certeau, *Practice of Everyday Life*, xvii, xx.

6. Wilson, "Rethinking the Colonial State"; Cohen, *Calculating People*, 44.

7. Quotation in McCormick, *William Petty*, 10.

8. Sussman argues that "demography and colonial expansion may not be intrinsically connected, but they have been historically intimate in a way that is seldom recognized" ("Colonial Afterlife," 98).

9. For Cohen, "Numbers also assumed a reputation for reality and objectivity and introduced into Western thought the idea that it is possible to remove values from anything that can be quantified" (*Calculating People*, 46).

10. Jennifer Morgan refers to these as "obscene abstractions" ("Demographic Logics," 3).

11. Petty, *History of the Survey*, 13–14. Ostensibly his charting of Ireland enabled Cromwell's conquering army to be self-sufficient: those who had financed the war effort in Ireland would be rewarded in land. Petty himself was to benefit enormously from his position as a surveyor, gaining fifty thousand acres of Irish land valued at around £6,700 by 1685. Poovey notes that Petty's own advancement, and the charges that he had indeed been acting in self-interest when he assessed Irish lands, led to one of his biggest contributions to quantification as he abandoned qualitative descriptions that could be seen as "interested" for quantitative ones that were viewed as impartial (whatever the reality might have been) (*History of the Modern Fact*, 122–24).

12. Petty, "Survey of Ireland," BL, Add MSS 72875–76.

13. On the question of the accuracy of the numbers Petty employed in the service of impartiality, see Poovey, *History of the Modern Fact*, 130.

14. Buck, "Seventeenth-Century Political Arithmetic," 73–74. For a discussion of Petty's philosophical influences and mentors, see Poovey, *History of the Modern Fact*, 93–96; McCormick, *William Petty*, especially chs. 1 and 2; Barnard, "Petty, Sir William."

15. Petty, *Political Arithmetick*, preface (no page number).

16. Petty, *Tracts Chiefly Relating to Ireland*, 288.

17. Petty, *Political Arithmetick*, preface.

18. See Cohen, *Calculating People*, 30–33, for more on Petty's evolution as mathematician and statistician. See also Wilson, "Rethinking the Colonial State," 1299.

19. The connections between the body politic and medicine would develop over the course of the eighteenth century when even more explicit connections between medicine and politics would be made (Miller, "Body Politic"; see also Schiebinger, *Nature's Body*, ch. 5; Chaplin, *Subject Matter*).

20. Poovey, *History of the Modern Fact*, 136.

21. Petty, *Economic Writings*, 561–62.

22. Petty, *Political Anatomy*, 29–30.

23. Ibid., 31. McCormick argues that Petty's dislike of Catholicism had less to do with religion than with the political and social implications of allowing the church to control the calendar, people's diet, and how and when they married, all factors that could affect the productivity of the Irish population (*William Petty*, 245). Petty does not elaborate on where he hoped to find English priests.

24. Poovey, *History of the Modern Fact*, 135.

25. Ibid., 136; McCormick, *William Petty*, 199–201; Sussman, "Colonial Afterlife," 103.

26. Petty, *Political Anatomy*, 30.

27. Ibid., 30–31.

28. McCormick, *William Petty*, 200–201.

29. Ann Jones and Peter Stallybrass note that for Spenser's conception of relation-ships between the Irish and Old English to make sense, all the Irish had to be women, and all the Old English, men. Moreover, the Irish were "untransformable"; the Old English, "permeable" ("Dismantling Irena," 163–64).

30. Ohlmeyer has recently discussed Petty's plans as part of the attempt to make Ireland English (*Making Ireland English*, 170).

31. Poovey suggests that while "there is no necessary connection between [abstractions] and the kind of brutality expressed in Petty's solution to the Irish problem," "such abstractions do permit—if they do not encourage—the formula-tion of policies that overlook the well-being of the individuals they theoretically represent" (*History of the Modern Fact*, 137). I would suggest that the abstractions do, in fact, encourage the birth of systems that are brutal and that there is a direct connection between abstractions made in the name of political economy and the enactment of violence.

32. Petty, *Political Anatomy*, 21.

33. Poovey asserts that Petty, in his *Political Arithmetick*, valued "male and female adults equally but at twice the rate of children" (*History of the Modern Fact*, 130–31).

34. Enslaved Africans, and not the Irish, were the population who would ultimately be subjected to the reductive conclusions of Petty's analysis. Jennifer Morgan makes this point most astutely, suggesting that "a population valued or undervalued solely for its labor is a population that can easily be extracted from particular geographies and located elsewhere to benefit the state" ("Demographic Logics," 12).

35. See, for example, Hariot, *Brief and True Report*; Smith, *True Relation of Occur-rences*; Percy, *True Relation*; Ligon, *True and Exact History*; Shrigley, *True Relation of Virginia*; Clarke, *True and Faithfull Account*.

36. Cohen, *Calculating People*, 44–45, 69–74.

37. The English approach here was in contradistinction to the Spanish *Relaciones Geográficas*, the royally decreed questionnaires sent by the Spanish crown to their American colonies. The Spanish were more concerned with mapping the region and assessing its resources than with assessing their colonial populations (Mundy, *Map-ping of New Spain*).

38. These were queries posed to William Stapleton, governor of Montserrat, by the Lords of Trade and Plantations in 1676 (TNA, CO153/2, fols. 176–77, 19 August 1676).

39. Ligon, *True and Exact History*, 43.

40. Dunn, *Sugar and Slaves*, 74–75.

41. BL, Add MSS 11,411, fol. 17, T. Povey, Register of Letters relating to the West Indies, 1655–1661, n.d., but probably 1655.

42. Ferrar Papers, no. 1117, answers 51 and 3, VCA, Ferrar Papers, 1590–1790, www.amdigital.co.uk/m-collections/collection/virginia-company-archives. For more on John Ferrar's life, see Ransome, "Ferrar, John."

43. The etymology of *painefull* in the Oxford English Dictionary Online also sug-gests that the term was often used as a description for bonded labor ("painful, adj.,"

Oxford English Dictionary Online, www.oed.com/view/Entry/136063?isAdvanced=fa lse&result=5&rskey=i7fpue& [accessed 6 October 2008]).

44. BL, Add MSS 11,411, fol. 17, T. Povey, Register of Letters Relating to the West Indies, 1655–61, n.d., but probably 1655.

45. Block notes a similar comment by Henry Whistler during the Western Design (*Ordinary Lives*, 136).

46. BL, Add MSS 11,411, fol. 17, T. Povey, Register of Letters Relating to the West Indies, 1655–61, petition of Barbados planters to Cromwell, n.d. (but likely 1655).

47. TNA, SP 25/31, no. 93, London, 20 August 1652, Order of the Council of State. *Liberty* meant the ability to "act or function without hindrance or restraint" ("liberty, n. 1," Oxford English Dictionary Online, www.oed.com/view/Entry/107898?rskey=JS 4mBC&result=1 [accessed 19 March 2012]).

48. TNA, SP 25/75, no. 586, London, 19 October 1654.

49. TNA, SP 25/77, no. 141, 22 May 1656. While the orders to transport prisoners or those believed to be troublemakers were sometimes vague (sending them to any of the Caribbean islands) and sometimes specific (naming Barbados, Jamaica, or Bermuda as the destination), in reality many prisoners would have disembarked on Barbados, the first port of call for virtually all English shipping entering the waters of the Caribbean (Dunn, *Sugar and Slaves*, 18; Smallwood, *Saltwater Slavery*, 147–48).

50. BL, Eg 2395, fol. 625, "An Estimate of the Barbadoes and of the now Inhabitants there."

51. Calendar of State Papers, Venetian, vol. 30, 1655–56, Venetian Ambassador to the Doge and Senate, 3 March 1656.

52. BL, Eg 2395, fol. 277.

53. BL, Add MSS 11,411, fol. 17.

54. Ligon, *True and Exact History*, 43.

55. BL, Add MSS 11,411, fol. 17.

56. Jeaffreson, *Young Squire*, 2:207, cited in Zacek, *Settler Society*, 89; Beckles, "'Riotous and Unruly Lot," 511.

57. TNA, CO 1/22, no. 20, 1667, "An Account of the English Sugar Plantations."

58. BL, Stowe MSS, 16 September 1667. For more on Willoughby's attitude, see Beckles, "Riotous and Unruly Lot," 508–10.

59. Block and Shaw, "Subjects without an Empire," 33–60.

60. TNA, CO1/21, no. 162, 16 December 1667.

61. TNA, CO29/2, fol. 34, 24 November 1675, Barbados, Lord William Willoughby.

62. TNA, CO 1/42, fols. 45–59.

63. TNA, CO 1//44, fols. 142–379. The census was sent to London in April 1680 and is therefore most often referred to as the 1680 census (Dunn, *Sugar and Slaves*, 84). See also Dunn, "Barbados Census of 1680," 3–30.

64. In addition to counting colonial subjects and providing precise population statistics, Atkins was ordered to produce information about the judiciary, the militia and defense of the island, the revenue made from sugar, the numbers of enslaved people imported onto Barbados, and a map of the island (TNA, CO29/2, fols. 283–85, 26 July 1679).

65. Atkins reported back to London about the revolt (TNA, CO1/35, no. 29, Atkins to Secretary Joseph Williamson, Barbados, 3–13 October 1675). Accounts of the revolt can also be found in *Great Newes*.

66. Jennifer Morgan notes that when determining demographic practices seventeenth-century mathematicians failed to make a "clear distinction between those who count and those who are *only* always counted" ("Demographic Logics," 14).

67. Dunn, *Sugar and Slaves*, 87. Atkins reported that there were 5,588 men in the island militia, a sharp reduction in number from the 10,000 he had estimated who were able to bear arms in 1676.

68. Wills and deeds from this period demonstrate the presence of Irish men and women on the islands, as does Colonial Office correspondence that describes the composition of island populations, or that outlines the threat posed by Irish Catholics (BDA, RB6 [wills], and RB3 [deeds]). Occasionally an Irish person is marked in the 1680 census. For example, the list of burials for St. Michael's Parish includes an entry for an unnamed "Irish woman" (TNA, CO1/44, no. 47, iv).

69. TNA, CO1/44, no. 47, xxi.

70. Murfee's will can be found at BDA, RB6/40, fol. 525. The will was written four years after the Barbados census was taken, and it was proved three years later, in 1687.

71. TNA, CO1/44, no. 47, x, xii, xv, xvi, xvii, xxi.

72. Gragg, *Quaker Community on Barbados*, 79–80.

73. Dunn, *Sugar and Slaves*, 105, 106.

74. TNA, CO1/42. See also Dunn, *Sugar and Slaves*, 126–31.

75. Lydia Pulsipher noted this unusual phenomenon and labeled these units male-partner households ("Cultural Landscape of Montserrat," 64). Berleant-Schiller built on this analysis and expertly broke down the importance of these groups for Irish life on the island ("Free Labor"). Comparisons to the Chesapeake region may explain the existence of these households. On completing their term of indenture, newly minted landowners in Maryland often could not afford to produce enough tobacco individually, so often went into partnership together to reduce costs, using an economy of scale to improve profits (Carr and Menard, "Immigration and Opportunity").

76. TNA, CO1/42, nos. 46–47.

77. Dunn, *Sugar and Slaves*, 89.

78. Initially there were as many as nine English men for every English woman in the colonies (Dunn, *Sugar and Slaves*, 326).

79. Akenson notes that Irish men on Montserrat were more likely to be married than English men, suggesting that there were larger numbers of Irish women on the island (*If the Irish Ran the World*, 115). Although there are virtually no extant passenger lists for ships that traveled from Ireland to Barbados in the seventeenth century, the record for the *Abraham*, which traversed the ocean in 1636/7, is somewhat informative. Of the fifty-seven Irish servants on board, seventeen were women, a ratio of just under two and a half men for every woman. The distribution of the servants is also interesting. The indentures of forty men were sold to just five planters; the seventeen women were sold to twelve planters, most of whom were purchasing only one servant (TNA, HCA 30/636, no. 7, 28 January–29 April 1637).

80. Over 40 percent of all Africans who experienced the Middle Passage in the last three decades of the seventeenth century were women, about 50 percent were men, and the rest were children (J. Morgan, *Laboring Women*, 177–79; see also J. Morgan, "Slavery and the Slave Trade," 25; Eltis and Engerman, "Was the Slave Trade Dominated").

81. J. Morgan, *Laboring Women*, ch. 5; Bush, *Slave Women*, 36–39.

82. J. Morgan, *Laboring Women*, 82–83; Burnard, *Mastery, Tyranny*, 214–15.

83. TNA, CO1/42, no. 64.

84. Smallwood, *Saltwater Slavery*, 164.

85. Smallwood discusses the selling of slaves in lots to ensure that all cargo was purchased (*Saltwater Slavery*, 169–76).

86. Fletcher, *Gender, Sex*, 223–24.

87. None of the census material for the islands notes the presence of Native Americans, although Caribs are occasionally referred to on St. Christopher, usually appearing in the sources during moments of interimperial tension. For example, the French were often accused of being in league with Native Americans when they attacked St. Christopher and Montserrat in the 1660s and 1670s (BL, Eg 2395, fol. 459; TNA, CO153/2, fol. 105, "The past and present state of the Leeward Caribee Islands &c."). Native Americans on Antigua are mentioned briefly in 1668 in relation to an agreement reached between them and the English "to make peace" to make the settlement of the island easier (TNA, CO29/1, fol. 115, 9 July 1668, Lord William Willoughby to the King's Council).

88. Henning, *Statutes at Large* (2:170).

89. BDA, RL1/17, fol. 123, 13 August 1683. Although the dates of the baptisms listed here are after the 1679/80 census was taken, at least four of the children had already been born. The enslaved women and children who were the property (and in some cases the progeny) of John Peers, one of Barbados's largest planters, are the subject of an article in progress. The Lords of Trade and Plantation in London did allude to the fact that "mollatos" might exist in the English Caribbean, asking, "What number of whites, blacks, or Molattos have been borne and Christen'd for these seaven yeares last past or any other space or tyme?" In doing so they were implicitly acknowledging sex across the color line (TNA, CO153/2, fols. 176–77, 19 August 1676).

90. BDA, RL1/22, fol. 32, January 1674.

91. C. Jones, *Engendering Whiteness*, 20–23.

92. BDA, RL1/1, fol. 215, 9 September 1676; RL1/1, fol. 255, 3 April 1681. Again, while the dates do not correlate directly to the census, there is evidence that both Dallys and Cuffee lived in St. Michael before and after the census was taken.

93. Dunn notes that Atkins's behavior, specifically his inability to keep the metropole informed about events on the island, and his proclivity for passing laws disagreeable to the crown, troubled the Lords of Trade. It was their discomfort with Atkins that led to their demands for extensive information about Barbados, and his response did ultimately result in his downfall (*Sugar and Slaves*, 86–87).

94. TNA, CO152/18, Board of Trade, Original Correspondence, 1730. The oversized pages of the "Political Anatomy" must be called separately and can be found under TNA, EXT 1/258. I thank one of the press's readers for encouraging me to incorporate this source.

95. Zacek notes the inclusion of Irish names in her analysis of the "Political Anatomy." She suggests that those who had no land and no listed occupation probably continued to cause trouble on the island. She argues that "these impoverished islanders, marginalized within the political, social, and economic realms, had little to lose by openly professing their Catholicism" (*Settler Society*, 91–93, quotation on 93).

3 / "To live in perpetuall noise and hurry"

1. BDA, RB3/8, fols. 105–8, 14 December 1670. In the deed that includes the inventory

of Bally Tree Hall, Cheeke was granting Richard Dorys, another Barbados merchant, "and his heyres for ever One Quarter part of all that Plantation." There are few extant estate inventories in the Barbados deeds. Cheeke was the only one to assign a name to his plantation.

2. Dunn used the 1680 census of Barbados to categorize planters as "big," "middling," or "small, " according to the number of enslaved Africans they counted among their property. In Dunn's analysis, planters with over sixty slaves were "big," while "middling" planters owned between twenty and fifty-nine bondspeople (*Sugar and Slaves*, 90–93, table on 91).

3. Foucault, *Discipline and Punish*, part III, 1.

4. Scholars who look more closely at the overlap between servants and slaves include Sobel, *World They Made Together*; Beckles, *White Servitude*. Philip Morgan investigates interactions between whites and enslaved people in Virginia and the Lowcountry but broadens his categories of whites beyond servants to include all "plain folks" (*Slave Counterpoint*, 300–317). Edmund Morgan has also commented on how servants' and slaves' lives in colonial Virginia had considerable overlap (*American Slavery*, 319).

5. E. Morgan, *American Slavery.*, 332–37.

6. Philip Morgan has written what is probably the most extensive analysis of the role of the everyday for the creation of black culture in the eighteenth century (*Slave Counterpoint*).

7. Sewell, *Logics of History*, 14.

8. Certeau, *Practice of Everyday Life*, xiii, 30–31. Price discusses the "ultimate capacities of the oppressed to respond, resist, create," in his discussion of torture and violence in Caribbean slave societies, even as European dominance appeared completely overwhelming ("Dialogical Encounters").

9. Smallwood, *Saltwater Slavery*, 35–36. Hauser uses everyday life to explore slave economies on plantations and their links to uprisings against the planter class, arguing that "the apparatus of control was never all encompassing" ("Of Earth and Clay," 165–68, quotation on 166).

10. See Sobel, *World They Made Together*, for a comparison of this process in eighteenth-century Virginia.

11. BDA, RB3/8, fols. 105–8, 14 December 1670.

12. BDA, RB6/10, p. 1, 12 January 1668.

13. BDA, RB6/10, p. 87, 2 December 1668; BDA, RB6/15, p. 176, 16 April 1662.

14. Blome, *Description of the Island*, 85. Blome did not visit the colonies but rather collected the writings of other travelers into his own synthesized accounts (Mendyk, 'Blome, Richard").

15. Roberts argues that by the late eighteenth century Barbados plantations grew a more diverse set of crops than historians have previously acknowledged and that the enslaved men and women that labored upon them held a variety of skilled positions ("Working between the Lines"). The Bally Tree Hall inventory does not provide details of slave occupations, but the list of buildings and tools strongly suggests that sugar was the sole cash crop grown on the estate. However, Cheeke's servant and slave population were no doubt responsible for the production of their own food in much the same way as slaves on the Newton and Seawell plantations in Roberts's study.

16. BDA, RB3/8, fols. 105–8, 14 December 1670.

17. Ligon, *True and Exact History*, 89.

18. Ibid., 88.

19. Ibid., 90.

20. BDA, RB3/8, fols. 105–8, 14 December 1670.

21. Dunn provides an overview of sugar production in the Caribbean (*Sugar and Slaves*, 192–201). See also Amussen, *Caribbean Exchanges*, 75–82; Menard, *Sweet Negotiations*, 17–19, 29–30; Beckles, *White Servitude*, 128–29.

22. Littleton, *Groans of the Plantations*, 19–20. Using male pronouns as a default was common among writers in this period, so it should not be assumed that only male slaves performed this particular task.

23. Ligon, *True and Exact History*, 44.

24. Servants who were familiar with field work would have been used to working long days with only a break for a midday meal (Sobel, *World They Made Together*, 21, 24).

25. Tryon, *Friendly Advice*, 95. Tryon, an Anabaptist who spent time on Barbados in the 1660s, wrote *Friendly Advice* as an indictment of the treatment of enslaved Africans, from their perspective. Despite his predisposition to stress the cruelties of slavery, Tryon's account matches those of other European observers—his innovation was to force the reader to place him- or herself in the position of an enslaved African—and so his account remains useful beyond its place as an early antislavery treatise.

26. Mintz, *Sweetness and Power*, 21; Guitar, "Boiling It Down."

27. Tryon, *Friendly Advice*, 89.

28. BDA, RB3/8, fols. 105–8, 14 December 1670. Citing W. L. Mathieson, Mintz notes how workers who became tired might find their hands or arms caught in the grinder and that there was an ax on hand to sever the injured limb (*Sweetness and Power*, 50). See also Menard, *Sweet Negotiations*, 15; Dunn, *Sugar and Slaves*, 192 Amussen, *Caribbean Exchanges*, 98. Burnard notes that Africans were more likely to name people for events than Europeans and that sometimes those names could be demeaning or satirical ("Slave Naming Patterns," 336).

29. Tryon, *Friendly Advice*, 300.

30. Ibid., 90.

31. Littleton, *Groans of the Plantations*, 20; Amussen, *Caribbean Exchanges*, 98–99.

32. Tryon, *Friendly Advice*, 301.

33. TNA, CO28/37, no. 7, xv, 24 March 1689.

34. Vincent Brown discusses how sugar production consumed enslaved bodies ("Eating the Dead").

35. Dunn, *Sugar and Slaves*, 196–97.

36. Ligon, *True and Exact History*, 93.

37. Littleton, *Groans of the Plantations*, 19. *Stifle* has a number of meanings in the early modern period, but among the most common are "suffocate" and "drown" ("stifle, v. 1," Oxford English Dictionary Online, www.oed.com/view/Entry/190225?rskey=O70iQp&result=3&isAdvanced=false [accessed 20 November 2011]).

38. TNA, CO1/21, no. 170.

39. Ligon, *True and Exact History*, 43.

40. Ibid, 27.

41. Gragg, *Englishmen Transplanted*, ch. 6. For the choices (or lack thereof) open to English servants, see Galenson, *White Servitude*, 81–96.

42. Canny, *Making Ireland British,* 450–55.

43. Amussen, *Caribbean Exchanges,* 142.

44. Ligon, *True and Exact History,* 44.

45. Ibid., 59.

46. Ibid., 46. See also Smallwood, *Saltwater Slavery,* 161–62.

47. BDA, RB3/10, fols. 104–9, 22 April 1685, inventory of estate completed 7 March 1685.

48. BDA, RB6/10, p. 53, 15 July 1668.

49. Map of Barbados, 1675, and Map of Montserrat, 1673, both in the John Carter Brown Library Map Collection.

50. Biet, *Voyage,* 289. Biet uses *la case* to describe the homes of indentured servants and the more common *les habitations* to refer to slave dwellings. The 1694 edition of the *Dictionnaire de l'Académie française* notes that while "the house" is the most literal translation of *la case,* it was not current or proper usage for the time and indicated a more casual reference. Thanks to Christian Crouch for her suggestions in parsing Biet's language. For more on Caribbean plantation villages, see D. Armstrong, *Old Village,* 62–68. More recently, Armstrong has posited that the artifacts found at Seville Plantation in Jamaica reveal the mixing of European and African cultures in the plantation village ("Reflections on Seville," 80–85). Upton discusses the development of slave quarters as social spaces in eighteenth-century Virginia ("White and Black Landscapes," 63–64).

51. BDA, RL1/22, fol. 32.

52. On the Virginia comparison, see Sobel, *World They Made Together,* 149. Brown describes numerous court cases that demonstrate the existence of such relationships (*Good Wives,* 131–33, 194–201). For historical fiction that explores a sexual relationship between a female Irish servant and an enslaved man, see McCafferty, *Testimony of an Irish Slave Girl.*

53. On the use of both Gaelic and English in Ireland, see Bliss, "English Language," 509–42.

54. On language retention and change in the Americas, see Thornton, *Cultural History,* 315–441. Equiano noted that it took some months for him to pick up rudimentary English (*Interesting Narrative,* 45).

55. Ligon, *True and Exact History,* 44.

56. Carney and Rosomoff, *In the Shadow,* 114–17.

57. Ligon, *True and Exact History,* 47. Drawing on the work of John Mitchell Vlach, Sobel discusses how similar these structures were to those found in parts of West Central Africa (*World They Made Together,* 123–24). Philip Morgan makes a similar observation about Lowcountry housing (*Slave Counterpoint,* 104).

58. Ligon, *True and Exact History,* 47, 44.

59. Tryon, *Friendly Advice,* 94. Note that in this context *manure* meant "cultivate," from the Latin *manus* (hand). This need for Sunday labor was an affront that only served to underscore, for Tryon, the lack of care that planters had for the immortal souls of their laboring populations.

60. Ligon, *True and Exact History,* 55; Carney and Rosomoff, *In the Shadow,* 117.

61. Ligon, *True and Exact History,* 55.

62. For a broader discussion of the cultural significance of food and foodways in early America, see LaCombe, *Political Gastronomy.*

63. Ligon, *True and Exact History*, 99–100.

64. Carney and Rosomoff, *In the Shadow*, 106. Rice is probably the most famous African crop to be brought by slaves to the Americas before being cultivated on an industrial scale on Carolina plantations (Carney, *Black Rice*). African women also were instrumental in indigo production in South Carolina (Knight, "In an Ocean of Blue").

65. Carney and Rosomoff, *In the Shadow*, 114–17.

66. Ibid., 117.

67. Ligon, *True and Exact History*, 32.

68. Also note that while plantains are not African in origin (they moved first from Asia to Africa) they were such an important part of West African foodways by the time of European incursions down the African coast that their particular uses made them African (Carney and Rosomoff, *In the Shadow*, 43).

69. BDA, RB3/8, fols. 105–8, 14 December 1670.

70. Ligon also discussed the account of an "antient Captain" on Barbados who claimed that the provenance of some cooking pots found on the island was Africa, specifically referring to bowls "fetcht from *Angola*." Ligon concurred with his assessment, stating that he was "willing to believe . . . that the Negres brought some pots thither" and that they were "very fine and artificially made" (*True and Exact History*, 23).

71. Carney and Rosomoff, *In the Shadow*, 112.

72. Biet, *Voyage*, 290. Dunn concurs that slaves ate badly but notes that the main distinction was between the eating habits of the upper classes and laborers (*Sugar and Slaves*, 278). See also Amussen, *Caribbean Exchanges*, 97–98.

73. Biet, *Voyage*, 290.

74. Ligon, *True and Exact History*, 43.

75. It should be noted that Ligon did not explain why he thought that servants ate a worse diet than enslaved Africans given that they ate almost exactly the same food. Over time, however, Ligon noted an improvement in servants' diet and living conditions and described how they came to eat meat once or twice a week and had a dry change of clothes to put on at the end of a wet workday (*True and Exact History*, 44).

76. Blome, *Description of the Island*, 86.

77. Ligon, *True and Exact History*, 37.

78. BDA, RB3/8, fols. 105–8, 14 December 1670.

79. Ligon, *True and Exact History*, 31.

80. Kew, "Irish Sections," 110.

81. Ligon, *True and Exact History*, 31.

82. Sloane, *Voyage to the Islands*, 1:47.

83. Ligon, *True and Exact History*, 44.

84. Ibid., 45.

85. Sloane, *Voyage to the Islands*, 1:47. *Naked* in the seventeenth century did not mean that people were entirely unclothed, but rather that they were wearing considerably fewer garments than their English counterparts (Kupperman, *Indians and English*, 49–55).

86. Ligon, *True and Exact History*, 109.

87. Ibid., 115. See also Dunn, *Sugar and Slaves*, 282–84.

88. For these figures, see the tables in Ligon, *True and Exact History*, 116.

89. On criminal proceedings in seventeenth-century England, see Gaskill, *Crime and Mentalities*. For a discussion on the place of torture as practiced by the state in Europe in the same period, see L. Silverman, *Tortured Subjects*. Silverman makes the point that although we may view public executions, floggings, maimings, and so forth as forms of torture, people in the early modern world did not (4–5). She also argues convincingly that torture had real cultural meaning in the early modern period, and that contemporaries believed that "the infliction of pain could indeed draw truth from the body just as a knife draws blood" (22). For a broader discuss of the place of pain in the everyday, see Scarry, *Body in Pain*, especially part 1.

90. Amussen, *Caribbean Exchanges*, 147–48.

91. Ligon, *True and Exact History*, 44.

92. Biet, *Voyage*, 290.

93. Sloane, *Voyage to the Islands*, 1:57. Amussen notes that Colonel James Drax did distinguish punishments between servants and slaves, putting the former in stocks and subjecting the latter to whipping (*Caribbean Exchanges*, 97).

94. Smallwood notes how Europeans employed Africans to control enslaved populations in the transatlantic slave trade and how they did not necessarily feel solidarity with their captives ("African Guardians").

95. Ligon, *True and Exact History*, 37, 47; Amussen, *Caribbean Exchanges*, 123–29.

96. Foucault, *Discipline and Punish*, part III.

97. Biet, *Voyage*, 290.

98. BPL, Lucas MSS, reel 1, fol. 374, 22 September 1657. See also Beckles, "Riotous and Unruly Lot," 515–17. English authorities on Barbados may have been reminded of poor vagrants who wandered the English countryside looking for work and who were viewed with suspicion and contempt by the inhabitants of the towns and villages they entered (Wrightson, *English Society*, 142).

99. Arguments over who could be whipped spanned the Caribbean. In 1774 an enslaved man named Raymond on Saint Domingue whipped a white peddler in the marketplace. The peddler turned on Raymond and tried to hit him with a cane. The case that resulted was debated in the highest echelons of the French colonial administration (Ogle, "Natural Movements"). Vidal discusses the tension between private and state violence and how ethnicity could be deployed in either case in colonial Louisiana ("Private and State Violence"). Dawdy explores the use of a black executioner in 1730s New Orleans to heighten the disgrace of white punishment ("Burden of Louis Congo").

100. BPL, Lucas MSS, reel 1, fol. 179.

101. Although concentrating on the antebellum U.S. South, Glymph has written eloquently on what slave ownership did to slave owners (*Out of the House*).

102. Biet, *Voyage*, 291.

103. TNA, CO1/21, no. 170. See also Beckles, "Riotous and Unruly Lot," 511.

104. Burnard makes a similar point when explaining Thomas Thistlewood's continued use of extreme violence to punish enslaved Africans in eighteenth-century Jamaica as Enlightenment thinking increasingly argued for a move away from corporeal punishment (*Mastery, Tyranny*, 104–5).

4 / "Doing their prayers and worshipping God in their hearts"

1. Biet, *Voyage*, 275–76. An English translation of part of Biet's experiences in Barbados has been edited by Handler ("Father Antoine Biet's Visit").

2. Biet, *Voyage*, 292.

3. Rather than accept that all those who encountered Christian missionaries converted, scholarship has tended to focus on the nuanced nature of religious syncretism in the Atlantic world. For missionizing to Native Americans, see, for example, D. Silverman, *Red Brethren*; Bross, *Dry Bones*; Greer, *Mohawk Saint*. For discussion of African religious practices in the early modern era that emphasizes continuities, see Gomez, *Exchanging Our Country Marks*; James Sweet, *Recreating Africa*; Young, *Rituals of Resistance*; James Sweet, *Domingo Álvares*. Thornton has written extensively about the creation of African forms of Christianity. See, for example, Thornton, "Development" [1997], *Kongolese Saint Anthony*, and *Africa and Africans*, ch. 9. There has generally been less scholarship on Irish religious practices in the Americas in the seventeenth century. Some works that explore the question broadly include Akenson, *If the Irish Ran the World*; Zacek, *Settler Society*; Johnston, "Papists in a Protestant World."

4. James Carson suggests that to overcome the asymmetries in the source material between the Americas, Africa, and Europe we should "subject Europeans to the same limitations as the other continental literatures." In other words, he proposes an approach where discussions of Christianity take their cues about the level of specificity engaged from African or American religions (*Making an Atlantic World*, 3). Determining what precisely constituted the belief systems of such a diverse group of people is difficult because rituals performed on an everyday basis are not the sorts of events that individuals note (Gillespie, *Devoted People*, vii).

5. Gomez notes that both scholars and contemporaries fail to make the right connections between various African practices and the influence of Islam, especially in Senegambia. He suggests that after Senegambia, Sierra Leone was the region with the second-highest proportion of Muslims to send slaves to the Americas (*Exchanging Our Country Marks*, 60–61, 87). See also James Sweet, *Recreating Africa*, 87–91; Ryan, "African Muslim Spirituality."

6. Gomez, *Exchanging Our Country Marks*, 67.

7. Heywood and Thornton, *Central Africans*, 99–103, 171–76.

8. De Marees, *Description*, 72; Barbot, *Barbot on Guinea*, 1:150. Barbot makes a similar point when he writes about his experiences in Sierra Leone (221–22).

9. According to Young, Kongolese often assumed that by consuming salt they were warding off bad spirits rather than receiving God's salvation (*Rituals of Resistance*, ch. 2, especially 52–56, 65, 76–78, 85). See also James Sweet, *Recreating Africa*, 195. In his most recent work, James Sweet notes the parallels between Christian baptism and vodun initiation (*Domingo Álvares*, 50).

10. James Sweet, *Recreating Africa*, 104–5.

11. MacGaffey, "Art and Spirituality"; James Sweet, *Domingo Álvares*, 76.

12. Seeman, *Death in the New World*, 18.

13. De Marees, *Description*, 69.

14. Barbot, *Barbot on Guinea*, 1:85, letter 8. Barbot's writings are complicated. Although he traveled to the Gold Coast twice in the late 1670s and early 1680s, his account draws heavily from Olfert Dapper, a Dutch scholar who wrote an account of Africa in 1668 despite having never left Holland (Law, "Jean Barbot").

15. James Sweet, *Recreating Africa*, 186; V. Brown, *Reaper's Garden*, 65–66.

16. De Marees, *Description*, 69–70.

17. Thompson and Cornet, *Four Moments*, 37. For more on the development of discourse on West African fetishes, see Pietz, "Problem of the Fetish, I" and "Problem of the Fetish, II." In "Problem of the Fetish, IIIa," Pietz argues that European descriptions of power objects and their uses in Africa served to underscore the perverse nature of African society by being couched in terms of the ludicrous and superstitious.

18. V. Brown, *Reaper's Garden*, 66–68; James Sweet, *Recreating Africa*, 176–79.

19. Seeman, *Death in the New World*, 19.

20. Barbot, *Barbot on Guinea*, 1:640. Archaeological surveys bear out the suggestion that burials within homes were common, as evidenced by excavations carried out in Elmina (DeCourse, *Archaeology of Elmina*, 187–88). Seeman draws on the account of Andreas Ulsheimer, a German surgeon who spent a year on the Gold Coast, to explain the significance of in-home burial, suggesting that it was about "maintain[ing] a daily connection with the spirit world" (*Death in the New World*, 21).

21. Villault, *Relation of the Coasts*, 194.

22. De Marees, *Description*, 182.

23. Ibid.; Villault, *Relation of the Coasts*, 194 (quotation from Villault).

24. Villault, *Relation of the Coasts*, 194–95.

25. Seeman, *Death in the New World*, 21–22.

26. On social death and the Middle Passage, see Smallwood, *Saltwater Slavery*, 52–61.

27. Seeman, *Death in the New World*, 188.

28. Smallwood, *Saltwater Slavery*, 190–191.

29. Kew, "Irish Sections," 109.

30. Gillespie, *Devoted People*, chs. 1–2; Meigs, *Reformations in Ireland*; Palmer, "Interpreters."

31. Gillespie, *Devoted People*, 110.

32. Brereton, *Travels in Holland*, 142.

33. Ibid.

34. Kew, "Irish Sections," 110.

35. Stanihurst, "On Ireland's Past," 157.

36. Tait, *Death, Burial*, 78–79; See also Walsham, *Reformation of the Landscape*, 175–76.

37. Meigs, *Reformations in Ireland*, 135–38.

38. For more on the place of purgatory in Catholic death rituals, see Tait, *Death, Burial*, 140–42.

39. Marmaduke Middleton, Bishop of Waterford and Lismore, 20 July 1580, in *Calendar of State Papers*, 229.

40. Meigs, *Reformations in Ireland*, 137–38.

41. On fostering, see Laurence, "Cradle to the Grave," 76–78, and Kew, "Irish Sections," 109. For a discussion of women's roles in religious instruction, see O'Dowd, *History of Women*, 156; Gillespie, *Devoted People*, 12–13.

42. Fry, *Burial in Medieval Ireland*, 124–26.

43. Partridge, "Wild Men"; Tait, *Death, Burial*, 36.

44. Tait, *Death, Burial*, 37.

45. O'Dowd, *History of Women*, 159; Gillespie, *Devoted People*, 13.

46. Catholics were also excluded from the educational sphere, forbidden to take

positions at universities, as schoolteachers, or in private service lest their devotion to the pope supersede their loyalty to Parliament (Corish, *Irish Catholic Community*, 47).

47. Canny, *Making Ireland British*.

48. Catholic priests tended to flee to continental Europe, while others remained in Ireland, disguised as tradesmen. Some European-bound priests found employment as soldiers in the Spanish Netherlands, but large numbers spent their time as scholars in the seminaries of France and Spain (Canny, "Formation of the Irish Mind," 94).

49. For a broader discussion of the retentions of non-Christian rituals, see Tait, *Death, Burial*. On the blended nature of Irish religious practices, see Gillespie, *Devoted People*; Laurence, "Cradle to the Grave." For a more general discussion of the intersections between Christian and non-Christian religious practices, see Thomas, *Religion*.

50. On the transfer of the central elements of African religious practices, see Seeman, *Death in the New World*, 22.

51. BDA. For St. Philip, see RL1/22; for St. Michael, see RL1/1 and RL1/2; for St. James, see RL1/46; and for Christchurch, see RL1/17. Gragg counts 135 baptisms of people of color in Barbados in the seventeenth century (*Englishmen Transplanted*, 164).

52. BDA, RL1/1, p. 259; BDA, RL1/1, p. 275; BDA, RL1/1, p. 378, 9 October 1688.

53. BDA, RL1/1, p. 378, 11 October 1688.

54. Ibid.

55. BDA, RB6/10, p. 123, 4 March 1669.

56. Beasley, *Christian Ritual*, 82–83.

57. BDA, RL1/1, p. 215, 9 September 1677; BDA, RL1/1, p. 391, 17 November 1689.

58. Andrew Miller, Thomas Alford, and Hannah Lamply all appear in Sanders's collected volumes of the baptism, probate, and marriage records of Barbados, *Barbados Records: Baptisms*; *Barbados Records: Wills*; and *Barbados Records: Marriages*. Beasley notes the expectation that godparents would have been baptized so that they could sincerely promise to raise their charges in the ways of the church but that masters might baptize the children of enslaved parents without regard to the status of their mothers and fathers (*Christian Ritual*, 74).

59. BDA, RL1/1, p. 485, 25 June 1694.

60. Handler and Jacoby, "Slave Names."

61. J. Morgan, *Laboring Women*, 113–14.

62. BDA, RB6/40, p. 260.

63. The codicil to Goldring's will can be found at BDA, RB6/40, p. 347. Goldring's will was proved almost a year after the codicil was added on 30 September 1686. We do not know what age Baddue was by the time Goldring died, but given that eight years had passed since Goldring's first will, it is likely that he was in his teens.

64. BDA, RL1/1, p. 371, 3 April 1668; BDA, RL1/17, p. 111, 24 November 1678.

65. See, for example, BDA, RB6/11, 373. Alternative brief preambles are "being sicke and weake of body but of a good sound and p[er]fect comembrance praised be God" (BDA, RB 6/14, 352), "being indisposed in body but of sound and p[er]fect mind and memory" (BDA, RB6/5, 383), and "being sensible in my minde and weake in body" (BDA, RB6/11, 561). Larry Gragg investigates wills more broadly for the clues they contain about the religious beliefs of the testators (*Englishmen Transplanted*, 80–83).

66. Alsop has pointed out that in the early modern period will making was a cultural ritual and that the majority of wills contained either brief or noncommittal statements like those cited above ("Religious Preambles," 19).

67. West's *Symbolaeographia* was first published in 1590 and was reprinted, with alterations, eleven times up to 1632. See also Spufford, "Religious Preambles."

68. TNA, CO153/2, fols. 187–88.

69. Johnston suggests as much in her dissertation, "Papists in a Protestant World," 247.

70. Nicholas Rice's will can be found at BDA, RB6/13, fol. 398, proved 14 July 1677. George Rice's will can be found at BDA, RB6/40, p. 215, proved 1 July 1686.

71. BDA, RB6/13, p. 398, and RB6/40, p. 215.

72. As Cressy has argued: "Protestants knew that no spiritual advantage attached to being buried in one piece of holy ground rather than another, but proximity to the altar and location within the chancel or aisle still mattered for social reasons" (*Birth, Marriage*, 461).

73. BDA, RB6/13, p. 398, and RB6/40, p. 215. Akenson makes a similar argument (*If the Irish Ran the World*, 76).

74. Burgess, "By Quick and by Dead," 837–58.

75. Rice did make provision that if "Elizabeth Rice to whom I was marryed, be now or shall hereafter be with child whether with male or female," "for reasons best known to my self" that said child would receive "onely five shillings sterl[ing]" in lieu of any claim to his lands. Leaving instructions in a will about how a child, especially a daughter, should marry was not unusual in this period (Wrightson, *English Society*, 48–60). What is unusual about George Rice's actions is the way he continued to endorse practices that were both Irish and Catholic.

76. Laurence, "Cradle to the Grave," 70–71. Moryson was typically hyperbolic in his discussion of Irish marriage practices, drawing on Camden's reports to discuss what he saw as the Irish propensity for incest, bastardy, concubinage, and divorce (Kew, "Irish Sections," 107).

77. BDA, RL1/65, Marriage Index, 1643–1768. Dominick Rice was one of the men who recorded the people present at Willoughby and Chamberlain's Christmas mass in 1688: TNA, CO28/37, no. 7, xxx, 24 March 1689.

78. BDA, RB6/14, 207.

79. BDA, RB6/41, 359. O'Dowd, *History of Women*, 157. For a broader discussion of the role of women in religious practices in the seventeenth century, see Strasser, *State of Virginity*; Dinan and Meyers, *Women and Religion*. Quakers, another group persecuted for their religious beliefs, largely requested burial at the discretion of their friends and executors and, given that they also refused burial in churchyards, have interesting parallels with Irish Catholics discussed here (Cressy, *Birth, Marriage*, 418). See also Block, *Ordinary Lives*, chs. 10–12.

80. Wrightson, *English Society*, 94.

81. Biet, *Voyage*, 292.

82. Thornton has argued that despite evidence of "syncretism" in Kongolese Christianity, the Catholicism practiced by the Kongolese was recognized as legitimate in Rome as an African Christianity and had become "the national religion of Kongo" by the sixteenth century ("Development" [1984], 161). Sweet challenges the degree to which ordinary Kongolese converted to Christianity, suggesting that it would "strip them of their spiritual core" to reduce all Kongolese religious practices to Catholicism (*Recreating Africa*, 109–15, quotation on 112). See also Young, *Rituals of Resistance*, 57–59, for further critiques of Thornton's position.

83. BPL, Lucas MSS, reel 1, fols. 79–80, 26 January 1655. "Spike's Bay" is present-day Speightstown on the west coast of Barbados.

84. BPL, Lucas MSS, reel 1, fol. 211, 21 May 1656. At least twenty-one priests were sent from Carrickfergus to the Caribbean in 1654, and countless others were no doubt rounded up from other parts of Ireland (TNA, SP 28/4).

85. Du Tertre, *Histoire Generale*, 4:299.

86. White, *Voyage to Maryland*, 33.

87. Du Tertre, *Histoire Generale*, 4:310.

88. TNA, CO1/12, no. 31, i and iii.

89. Biet, *Voyage*, 275–76. We know from his account that he had brought his vestments, rosaries, and other necessary adornments with him but that these were supposedly secreted away in a case.

90. In his translation of extracts from Biet's *Voyage*, Jerome Handler reads the "f" in Ofaye as a long "s" and so suggests that Biet may have meant the Irish name O'Shea ("Father Antoine Biet's Visit," 58).

91. Biet, *Voyage*, 270.

92. Ibid.

93. For more on the place of bards in post-Tridentine Catholicism in Ireland, see Meigs, *Reformations in Ireland*, 81–84, 133–38.

94. Ofaye holds many of the traits identified by Ira Berlin as characteristic of the Africans he labeled "Atlantic Creoles": linguistically skilled; familiar with "cultural conventions"; able to mediate between, on one hand, the French settlers who traveled with Biet and, on the other, English planters and officials. For a fuller discussion of the concept of Atlantic creoles, see Berlin, *Many Thousands Gone*, 17–46.

95. Biet, *Voyage*, 278.

96. Ibid., 293, 294.

97. Pelleprat, *Relation des Missions*, 42–43.

98. Ibid., 43.

99. Ibid., 37–40.

100. TNA, CO28/37, no. 7, xix, Examination of Thomas Brown, Barbados, 7 March 1689. As Johnston has shown in her detailed examination of the Catholics who were present at Chamberlain's mass, Stede's assertions that most of the Irish present were poor is not borne out ("Papists in a Protestant World," 54–56).

101. TNA, CO28/37, no. 7, xxx, Examination of Dominick Rice, Barbados, 20 March 1689.

102. Biet, *Voyage*, 277, 292.

103. Ligon, *True and Exact History*, 52.

104. James Sweet, *Recreating Africa*, 192.

105. Biet, *Voyage*, 271, 291–92.

106. Rochefort, *History of the Caribby-Islands*, 2:201.

107. BPL, Lucas MSS, reel 2, fol. 383.

108. BPL, Lucas MSS, reel 2, fol. 497, 11 March 1689.

109. Biet, *Voyage*, 292. Beasley suggests that a good proportion of all baptisms took place within homes in the islands (*Christian Ritual*, 66–67).

110. Ligon, *True and Exact History*, 50.

111. Taylor, *Second Part of the Historie*, 544.

112. Sloane, *Voyage to the Islands*, 1:xlviii.

113. Mintz and Price note the dangers of accepting a complete cultural transference from the eastern to the western sides of the Atlantic Ocean (*Birth of African American Culture*, 52–60).

114. TNA, CO1/12, no. 31, i and iii. See also Johnston, "Papists in a Protestant World," 135.

115. Ligon, *True and Exact History*, 50–51.

116. See Sloane, *Voyage to the Islands*, 1:xlviii; Taylor, *Second Part of the Historie*, 544. For a more in-depth discussion of the archaeological artifacts that bear out some of these rituals, see Handler and Lange, *Plantation Slavery in Barbados*.

117. Handler performed extensive archaeological digs on the Newton Plantation, the most thorough for any plantation site in the English Caribbean. A number of interesting graves point to African religious practices on Barbados, including that of a woman laid prone in her resting place, which Handler attributes to her possible identity as a witch ("Prone Burial"). For more on the analysis of the enslaved man buried on Newton Plantation, see Handler, "African-Type Healer/Diviner." A broader analysis of archaeological finds in slave communities on Barbados can be found in Hander and Lange, *Plantation Slavery in Barbados*.

118. Smallwood, *Saltwater Slavery*, 190–91.

5 / "Endeavouring to raise mutinie and sedition"

1. TNA, CO28/1, fols. 203–4, 20 January 1693. Mullin notes that later in the eighteenth century a spate of revolts occurred in the Caribbean that were planned and led by acculturated, skilled, enslaved men, making this 1692 revolt perhaps the first in this long trajectory (*Africa in America*, 215–16). Beckles discusses the Irish role in the 1692 rebellion in some detail ("Riotous and Unruly Lot"). Sharples puts the 1692 rebellion in the context of the larger Atlantic framework of what he terms "conspiracy panics" ("Flames of Insurrection," introduction and ch. 1). See also Handler, "Barbados Slave Conspiracies"; Handler, "Slave Revolts."

2. Ligon, *True and Exact History*, 46.

3. I agree with Gaspar, who argues that although the torture that authorities used to extract confessions compromises accounts of conspiracies, scholars can use slave testimony as long as they are cautious about the conclusions they draw (*Bondmen and Rebels*, 12). Similarly helpful has been Sidbury, who argues (in the context of the Denmark Vesey plot), that conspiracy accounts are "collective fictions . . . shaped by white magistrates, but most of whose details were invented by enslaved Charlestonians" ("Plausible Stories," 182). For an alternative view, see P. Morgan, "Conspiracy Scares." There is a considerable scholarship on the anxiety that slave owning produced in white planters and on the violence used in slave interrogations. Of influence here are Jordan, *Tumult and Silence*; Mat Johnson, *Great Negro Plot*; Lepore, *New York Burning*; Martínez, "Black Blood"; Michael Johnson, "Denmark Vesey"; Sharples, "Flames of Insurrection."

4. Gaspar, *Bondmen and Rebels*, 5–6.

5. Trouillot, *Silencing the Past*, 1–30.

6. Thinking critically about agency and slavery has a long genealogy; see Hartman, *Scenes of Subjection*, 11–12; W. Johnson, "On Agency." Jennifer Morgan develops a critique of gendered agency in *Laboring Women*, 6–7. Fuentes builds on this work in "Power and Historical Figuring" and questions the utility of the concept of agency

altogether. Recently Walter Johnson has made a similar point ("Agency"). Also useful for thinking about the tensions between slave resistance and politics is V. Brown, "Social Death."

7. On the contemporary use of the term *saltwater*, see Smallwood, *Saltwater Slavery*, 7–8.

8. Governor Jonathan Atkins reported back to London about both the revolt and the hurricane (TNA, CO 1/35, no. 29, Atkins to Secretary Joseph Williamson, Barbados, 3–13 October 1675). For more on the effects of this natural disaster, see Mulcahy, *Hurricanes and Society*, 17, 72, 76, 85–87, 101, 104, 107, 130–32.

9. "Coromantee/Cormantee" was a category invented by Europeans, originally used to describe Akan speakers from the Gold Coast (Wilson, "Performance of Freedom," 67). See also Kopytoff, "Development."

10. TNA, CO 1/35, no. 29, Atkins to Secretary Joseph Williamson, Barbados, 3–13 October 1675. Dunn briefly discusses this uprising (*Sugar and Slaves*, 257–58). See also Amussen, *Caribbean Exchanges*, 159–61.

11. Thornton, "War, the State." Thornton notes that even the term *Akan* is anachronistic—a nineteenth-century creation. James Sweet also discusses the problems with assigning names to early modern West African nations and suggests that some of these identities became forged in diaspora ("Mistaken Identities?"). Sharples argues that colonists ascribed ethnic identity to what was a shared linguistic association ("Flames of Insurrection," 72–73).

12. Enslaved "Cormantees" were allegedly involved in numerous plots across the seventeenth- and eighteenth-century English Atlantic. Jamaica was the site of the most frequent Cormantee-led uprisings, beginning in 1673 (which may indeed account for some of the English anxiety in this period). For more on Jamaica, see Dunn, *Sugar and Slaves*, 260. See also Thornton, "War, the State," 196–97. On the Jamaican Maroon Wars, see Kopytoff, "Development," and Wilson, "Performance of Freedom."

13. TNA, PRO31/17/44, p. 231, 23 June 1657.

14. Ibid.

15. "Destroyed" in this context implied the slaying of an entire group, a degree of overkill ("destroy, v.," Oxford English Dictionary Online, www.oed.com/view/Entry/51103?redirectedFrom=destroyed [accessed 26 March 2012]).

16. *Great Newes*, 11.

17. *Continuation of the State*, 19.

18. Ibid. For more on the connections colonists made between Indian Wars and slave insurrections (as evidenced by this pamphlet), see Sharples, "Flames of Insurrection," 59–60.

19. Thornton notes that there was not necessarily a connection between the "coronation" of a Cormantee king in the Americas and a slave conspiracy, even though the two were often connected in the minds of European observers ("War, the State," 195).

20. Handler posits that "Coffee" was really "Cuffee," the Akan word for "Friday" and a common name for enslaved men ("Barbados Slave Conspiracies," 315).

21. Handler, "Barbados Slave Conspiracies," 315; Thornton, "War, the State," 195–96; Gaspar, *Bondmen and Rebels*, 6, 90–91; Smallwood, *Saltwater Slavery*, 22.

22. *Great Newes*, 10. The trumpets were probably to be made of ivory tusks, rather than the actual teeth of elephants.

23. V. Brown, *Reaper's Garden*, 135–36; Martínez, "Black Blood," 479.

24. For this point, see Edmund Morgan's *American Slavery*, 311–13.

25. *Great Newes*, 12–13.

26. Ibid., 12, italics in original.

27. Shumway, *Fante*, 114–15. Handler suggests that oaths were an important part of slave conspiracies across the Caribbean and that this kind of swearing fealty had West African origins ("Slave Revolts," 25). See also Bilby, "Swearing by the Past," and V. Brown, "Spiritual Terror."

28. *Great Newes*, 12.

29. V. Brown, *Reaper's Garden*, 131–35.

30. Ibid., 133–34; Egerton, "Peculiar Mark of Infamy."

31. I am grateful to an anonymous reader for making this point. The last person burned at the stake in England was Anabaptist Edward Wightman in 1612 (Atherton and Como, "Burning of Edward Wightman"). David Fischer notes that only two people were burned at the stake in Massachusetts in the seventeenth century—both of them female slaves (*Albion's Seed*, 194–95). In 1741 in New York City fourteen slave conspirators were also burned at the stake for their alleged part in a plot to burn key city storehouses (Mat Johnson, *Great Negro Plot*).

32. Seeman, *Death in the New World*, 196. For the display of enslaved bodies, see Paton, "Punishment, Crime."

33. *Great Newes*, 10.

34. Ibid.

35. Martínez, "Black Blood," 481–82.

36. Other moments of slave resistance had similar trajectories. Referencing a moment of rebellion from 1649, Richard Ligon explained how some "high spirited and turbulent" slaves had decided to burn a boiling house and sugarcane fields but how other slaves within the community "who hated mischiefe" had told their master, who "brought in so many witnesses against them, as they were forc't to confesse" (Ligon, *True and Exact History*, 53). For the comparison in Virginia, see Sidbury, *Ploughshares into Swords*.

37. *Great Newes*, 10–11.

38. *Continuation of the State*, 19.

39. *Great Newes*, 11, italics in original.

40. Handler, "Slave Revolts," 15; Craton, *Testing the Chains*, 109; J. Morgan, *Laboring Women*, 175.

41. HL, BL 369, "An Act for the Better Ordering and Governing of Negroes," 8–9. See also chapter 1 above.

42. TNA, CO31/2, no. 201, Journal of Assembly, 25 November 1675.

43. Block, *Ordinary Lives*, 176. Handler notes that it would not have been uncommon for the enslaved woman to go by two names ("Barbados Slave Conspiracies," 313).

44. Jennifer Morgan suggests that while Anna/Fortuna testified and gained her freedom, Marrea's voice is silenced, an indication of the breadth of women's responses to their enslavement (*Laboring Women*, 175–76).

45. Wilson, "Performance of Freedom," 48.

46. W. Johnson, "On Agency"; V. Brown, "Social Death."

47. TNA, CO 1/35, no. 29, Atkins to Secretary Joseph Williamson, Barbados, 3–13 October 1675.

48. As early as 1647 Ligon noted the linguistic diversity among slaves as a deterrent to revolt (*True and Exact History*, 46).

49. Smallwood, *Saltwater Slavery*, 3–5.

50. TNA, CO28/37, no. 7. For a discussion of the discourse surrounding the Glorious Revolution in the colonies at large, see Stanwood, "Protestant Moment."

51. TNA, CO29/4, fol. 107, Stede to Lord Shrewsbury, 30 May 1689.

52. TNA, CO28/37, no. 7.

53. TNA, CO28/37, no. 7, xix, Examination of Thomas Brown, Barbados, 7 March 1689.

54. TNA, CO29/4, no. 107, Barbados, 30 May 1689, Colonel Edwyn Stede to the Lord of Shrewsbury; TNA, CO29/4, no. 162, Barbados, 11 March 1689, Lieutenant Governor and Council to the Prince of Orange.

55. TNA, CO28/37, no. 7, xix, Examination of Thomas Brown, Barbados, 7 March 1689.

56. TNA, CO28/37, no. 7, xxx. Johnston traces the backgrounds of all the Catholics listed at the mass and argues that they came from a broad range of socioeconomic backgrounds ("Papists in a Protestant World," 54–56).

57. TNA, CO28/37, no. 7, v, Barbados, deposition of John Thompson, 23 February 1689.

58. TNA, CO28/37, no. 7, vi, Barbados, deposition of John Kelly, 23 February 1689. John Bowen of St. Thomas Parish gave similar sworn testimony (TNA, CO28/37, no. 7, vii).

59. *Dog* was used as a term of abuse to indicate contempt in this period (Oxford English Dictionary Online, www.oed.com.libdata.lib.ua.edu/view/Entry/56405?rskey=Ip2T2j&result=1#eid [accessed 21 September 2012]).

60. TNA, CO28/37, no. 7, xvi, Barbados, deposition of Cesar Crawford, 24 March 1689.

61. TNA, CO28/37, no. 7, xvii, deposition of Martha Cuffley, 4 March 1689.

62. BPL, Lucas MSS, reel 1, fol. 179, 15 January 1656. The law can be found at BL, *Acts and Statutes*. Beckles also discusses these cases ("Riotous and Unruly Lot," 512–14).

63. TNA, PRO31/17/43, p. 121, 15 January 1656.

64. BPL, Lucas MSS, reel 1, fol. 361, 1 September 1657.

65. BPL, Lucas MSS, reel 1, fol. 179, 15 January 1656.

66. Spenser, *View*, 66.

67. Fitzpatrick, *Bloody Bridge*, 89, 138.

68. Hulme, *Colonial Encounters*, 13–87; Greenblatt, *Marvelous Possessions*, 44–47; Lestringant, *Cannibals*.

69. For an analysis of Protestant "holy horror" ("sainte horreur") at this Catholic practice, see Lestringant, *Sainte horreur*. Tashiro discusses the Protestant relationship to the Eucharist in "English Poets."

70. A classic interpretation of the violence of the wars of religion in Europe is N. Davis, "Rites of Violence."

71. TNA, CO28/37, no. 7, xv, Barbados, depositions of Mr. Jacob English, William Griffith, and Edward Macologh, 24 March 1689.

72. TNA, CO28/37, no. 7, viii, Barbados, deposition of John Brise, 9 March 1689. Despite the likelihood that exaggeration, prejudice, and fear all contributed to the creation of the depositions and examinations, it seems plausible that these accounts are broadly accurate.

73. Tait, *Death, Burial*, 78–79; Meigs, *Reformations in Ireland*, 82.

74. See Canny, *Making Ireland British;* Gillespie, *Devoted People;* Meigs, *Reformations in Ireland;* Palmer, "Interpreters."

75. TNA, CO28/37, no. 7, xv, Barbados, depositions of Mr. Jacob English, William Griffith, and Edward Macologh, 4 March 1689.

76. Linebaugh discusses the power of the Irish language to frighten English observers in eighteenth-century London (*London Hanged,* 291–92).

77. TNA, CO152/37, no. 22, 31 July 1689.

78. Slaves would eventually be used in the British military, but not until the mid-eighteenth century. See Buckley, *Slaves in Red Coats;* Bollettino, "Slavery, War."

79. TNA, CO28/37, no. 11, Barbados, 16 July 1689 (from Edward Stede).

80. "Embodied | imbodied, adj.," Oxford English Dictionary Online, www.oed.com/view/Entry/60904?rskey=FWMaD9&result=2&isAdvanced=false (accessed q14 April 2012).

81. TNA, CO28/37, no. 31, Barbados, deposition of Joseph Crisp Gent., 2 July 1691.

82. Similar worries about the kinds of disorder caused by Irish and African collaborations can be found on Bermuda in 1660. "John Meclarie, an Irishman," was accused of having "presumptuouslie undertaken to deliver a caske of rumbullian to the Governor's Negro woman, Sarah Simon . . . and thereby having occasioned great disorder and drunkennesse amongst the Governors negroes and others" (BA, CR III: 181A, November 1660, Council Meeting).

83. *Brief, but most True Relation.*

84. TNA, CO28/1, 203–4: Board of Trade, Barbados, 20 January 1693; Beckles, "Riotous and Unruly Lot," 518. Dunn mentions the 1692 conspiracy but suggests that it was a "replay" of 1675 (*Sugar and Slaves,* 258). See also Handler, "Barbados Slave Conspiracies"; Handler, "Slave Revolts."

85. Gaspar, *Bondmen and Rebels,* 12.

86. TNA, CO28/1, 203–4, Board of Trade, Barbados, 20 January 1693.

87. Ibid.; *Brief, but most True Relation.* Amussen discusses the English backlash in some detail (*Caribbean Exchanges,* 162–63).

88. V. Brown, *Reaper's Garden,* ch. 4, especially 135–36.

89. TNA, CO28/1, 203–4, Board of Trade, Barbados, 20 January 1693.

90. *Brief, but most True Relation.*

91. BPL, Lucas MSS, reel 1, fols. 161–62, 6 November 1655; Beckles, "Riotous and Unruly Lot," 515–17.

92. TNA, CO31/1, fol. 675, Minutes of the Barbados Council, 1 March 1686.

93. BPL, Lucas MSS, reel 2, fol. 160. In Virginia, just one year later, authorities accused indentured servant John Nickson of leading a revolt of servants and slaves against his master, Ralph Wormeley II, in Middlesex County (Zacek, "John Nickson"). Parent notes that this incident marked one of the last moments of interracial cooperation in Virginia (*Foul Means,* 147–49).

94. TNA, CO31/1, fol. 675, Minutes of the Barbados Council, 1 March 1686; Beckles, "Riotous and Unruly Lot," 517–18.

95. TNA, CO28/1, fols. 203–4: Board of Trade, Barbados, 20 January 1693.

96. TNA, CO28/1, fol. 205, 3 November 1692, Kendall to the Lords of Trade and Plantations.

97. TNA, CO28/1, fol. 204, 20 January 1693. For an alternative view, see Sharples, "Flames of Insurrection," 78–81.

98. TNA, CO31/4, fol. 397, Minutes of the Council of Barbados, 24 January 1693. Martínez notes that in the 1612 conspiracy in Mexico City the plotters planned to execute all Spanish men except those of the religious orders, who would be castrated instead so that they would not be able to reproduce ("Black Blood," 481–82).

99. Gaspar, *Bondmen and Rebels*, especially part 1.

100. TNA, CO155/2, Minutes of the Assemblies of the Leeward Islands, fols. 536, 543, 545.

101. TNA, CO31/5, fols. 527–28.

102. V. Brown, *Reaper's Garden*, 135–36.

103. TNA, CO152/37, no. 30, Col. Codrington to the Committee for Trade and Plantations, Nevis, 15 August 1689; TNA, CO152/37, no. 35, Mr. Carpenter and Mr. Belchamber to the Committee of Customs, Nevis, 19 August 1689; TNA, CO152/37, no. 41, Col. Codrington to the Committee for Trade and Plantations, Antigua, 19 September 1689.

6 / "As quietly and happily as the English subjects"

1. These letters can be found in two places: Oliver, *Caribbeana*, 1:51–57; Blake, *Blake Family Records*.

2. Dunn, *Sugar and Slaves*, 88.

3. In his study of the Irish on Montserrat, Akenson poses the question of what would have happened "if the Irish ran the world" and concludes that an Irish empire would much resemble that of the English (*If the Irish Ran the World*).

4. Ibid., 73.

5. BDA, RB 6/40, p. 398.

6. Akenson suggests that property in land was most important to New World settlers (*If the Irish Ran the World*, 78). I agree that land ownership was key for those with elite aspirations, but I contend that property in slaves was especially important for those who wanted to reach the highest echelons of the colonial elite.

7. BPL, Lucas MSS, reel 1, fol. 179, 15 January 1656.

8. Beckles, "Riotous and Unruly Lot," 513; Dunn, *Sugar and Slaves*, 69.

9. TNA, CO31/17/43, fol. 127, Barbados Council Minutes, 6 February 1656. Most scholars have stopped their discussion of Bryan at his initial moment of rebellion and his appearance before the council. Beckles, for example, says that Bryan was deported ("Riotous and Unruly Lot," 513). Dunn does not comment on Bryan's life after his rebellion (and does not even mention him by name) (*Sugar and Slaves*, 69). Gragg references Bryan as an example of an untrustworthy Irish Catholic but does not develop his story further (*Quaker Community on Barbados*, 31).

10. BDA, RB 6/40, no. 398.

11. BDA, RB3/5, fol. 720, 16 March 1659.

12. BPL, Lucas MSS, reel 1, fol. 179, 15 January 1656. Pipe players were "associated with travelers, vagrants, etc." ("piper, n. 1," Oxford English Dictionary Online, www.oed.com/view/Entry/144404 [accessed May 30, 2012]). Beckles describes Bryan as an "Irish wage-servant," in contrast to the other "indentured servants" in his discussion ("Riotous and Unruly Lot," 513). Dunn does not specifically mark Bryan, but the context of his reference suggests that he believes him to be an indentured servant (*Sugar and Slaves*, 69).

13. Beckles comments on the ability of European laborers to move up the social ladder in Barbados by acquiring land (*White Servitude*, 151–59).

14. BDA, RB3/9, fol. 89, 21 May 1675.

15. Ibid.

16. TNA, CO1/44, no. 47, ii.

17. BDA, RB3/11, fol. 573, 20 October 1682.

18. Dunn classifies "small planters" on Barbados as those who held more than ten acres and between zero and nineteen enslaved Africans (*Sugar and Slaves*, 91).

19. Bryan's will records his ownership of six enslaved women (Betty, Grace, Old Pegg, Venus, Pegg, and Nell), four enslaved men (George, Mingo, Jack, and Cain), and three other enslaved people whose sex cannot be determined by name or by how they are referenced in the will (Tomy, Young Tomy, and Anah) (BDA, 6/40, no. 398). Given that Bryan had only nine slaves listed in the 1680 census, it is possible that two of the additional four slaves he owned by 1686 were the children of his older slaves. For more on "forced breeding" of enslaved women and men and the attempts by planters to increase their wealth through the reproduction of their slaves, see J. Morgan, *Laboring Women*, 82–83.

20. BDA, RB2/9, fol. 89, 21 May 1675. There is no corresponding marriage record in the Barbados records. In marrying Margaret, Cornelius was perhaps following the common experiences of poorer settlers in Virginia, who often married a wealthy widow or daughter of a wealthy landowner as a way to move up the social ladder (K. Brown, *Good Wives*, 92–93).

21. O'Hart, *Irish Pedigrees*, 1:815, 838–39.

22. TNA, CO1/44, no. 47, ii.

23. The term *mansion house* had more than one meaning at this time. In using the term, Bryan may have simply been referring to the dwelling in which his family lived, or he could have been suggesting that the structure was more grand ("mansion, n.," Oxford English Dictionary Online, www.oed.com/view/Entry/113651?rskey=nxcR71& result=1&isAdvanced=false [accessed May 24, 2008]). In Ireland, there was increasing status attached to having the right kind of abode (Barnard, *Making the Grand Figure*, 36); Stephen Primatt's *The City and Country Purchaser and Builder* (London, 1667) contained an "H-Plan" for a mansion house, a style that "became common on both sides of the Atlantic" (Reinberger and McLean, "Isaac Norris's Fairhill," 254–55). Certainly by the time he dictated his last will and testament Bryan would have spent sufficient time in Barbados to go through the three stages of home development that Cary Carson et al. describe (primitive shelters, to temporary, impermanent buildings, to "fayre houses") ("Impermanent Architecture," 140).

24. I thank Lorena S. Walsh for corresponding with me on this issue and accept her suggestion that someone like Bryan who aspired to greater things would have compared himself to a manorial lord and so may have meant "manor house."

25. Dunn, *Sugar and Slaves*, 88–91. The number of slaves that Bryan owned was also in keeping with the size of his estate—on average most planters had one enslaved field worker for every two acres of land they owned (67).

26. BDA, RB 6/40, no. 398.

27. For many European men who had served out their terms of indenture, gaining land on Barbados was difficult especially after midcentury. Many former servants (or free men with little means) chose to move to other islands, like Montserrat, where resources could be more easily pooled. Some stayed on Barbados and like Bryan were able to farm smaller plots of land in the less fertile and less desirable locations on the

island (Bridenbaugh and Bridenbaugh, *No Peace*, 14, 111–13; Dunn, *Sugar and Slaves*, 66–67).

28. BDA, RB3/9, fol. 89, 21 May 1675.

29. See, for example, BDA, RB 3/9, fols. 76–93; RB 3/8, fols. 23–29; RB 6/40, nos. 262, 297, 348, 349, 363.

30. For examples, see Hatfield, *Atlantic Virginia*; Games, *Migration*; Hancock, *Citizens of the World*.

31. See Canny, *Making Ireland British*, 412–14, 456, 553; Bradshaw and Keogh, *Christianity in Ireland*, 81. For more on the movement of members of the Fourteen Tribes to the Caribbean, see Cullen, "Galway Merchants," 69–70.

32. Akenson, *If the Irish Ran the World*, 69.

33. Oliver, *Caribbeana*, family tree, 1:53–54.

34. There is very little literature on the experiences of Irish servant women in the Caribbean because (as with all servant women) their lives are so hard to trace and reconstruct. Some few women appear in census material as heads of households because of their status as widows, but their last names are those of the men they married. The most focused examination of Irish servant women is McCafferty's work of historical fiction, *Testimony of an Irish Slave Girl*. As the title suggests, however, the book equates Daley's experiences too directly with that of enslaved women and follows many of the exaggerated accounts of Irish women as "breeders" espoused in works like O'Callaghan's *To Hell or Barbados* (115–16).

35. As Kathleen Brown has noted, the presence of the servant "wench" allowed a hierarchy of labor to develop within the households of the elite or those who aspired to become the elite (*Good Wives*, 101).

36. Oliver, *Caribbeana*, 1:55, Montserrat, 29 May 1675.

37. Ibid., 55–56, Bridgetown, Barbados, 5 November 1675. The threat posed by this servant woman was tied up with her unmarried status (K. Brown, *Good Wives*, 104).

38. Oliver, *Caribbeana*, 1:55, Montserrat, 29 May 1675.

39. In the seventeenth century, *seducement* connoted both the act of seducing someone and an insidious temptation ("seducement, n.," Oxford English Dictionary Online, www.oed.com/view/Entry/174725?redirectedFrom=seducement [accessed 4 October 2010]).

40. *Confusion* in this case refers to John's possible ruin or destruction ("confusion, n.," Oxford English Dictionary Online, /www.oed.com/view/Entry/39014?redirectedFrom=confusion [accessed 28 October 2010]).

41. Hartman, *Scenes of Subjection*, 89–90.

42. "Vitious lesse" or "viciousless" here means "without immorality" ("vicious, adj.," Oxford English Dictionary Online, /www.oed.com/view/Entry/223179?rskey =EJvR4p&result=5&isAdvanced=false [accessed 9 January 2012]). Zacek notes that although the English at that time thought of the Caribbean as licentious environment, those in the Leeward Islands (at least) sought to paint white women as "immaculate characters" who "upheld both the purity of the white race and the legitimacy of colonial authority" (*Settler Society*, 169–73, quotation on 171). While the servant woman was of a class of women not usually viewed in such a light, it is possible that John thought of her this way.

43. Although the earlier usage of "correction" in this context indicated disciplining a person or possibly chastising them, by the seventeenth century it had come to refer

quite specifically to corporal punishment or even flogging ("correction, n.," Oxford English Dictionary Online, March 2012, www.oed.com/view/Entry/41910?redirectedF rom=correction [accessed 4 October 2010]).

44. Oliver, *Caribbeana*, 1:55–56, Bridgetown, Barbados, 5 November 1675.

45. Kathleen Brown discusses the incidence of infidelity among Virginia's planter class, and in particular William Byrd II's predilection for sexual activity with servant women, whom he invariably described as "wenches." Brown notes that in Byrd's affairs with white women not of his social rank, "often the sexual relationship accompanied an economic one. When Byrd engaged a woman to wash his linens and provide him with meals, it seems to have been understood that she would also become his lover" (K. Brown, *Good Wives*, 331). It seems entirely possible that John's relationship with his servant woman was similar to Byrd's with his "wenches."

46. Oliver, *Caribbeana*, 1:55–56, Bridgetown, Barbados, 5 November 1675.

47. Ibid. For more on the way that the organization of space within homes began to separate elite women and men from the labor necessary to make a home run efficiently, see K. Brown, *Good Wives*, 250–52. For the kinds of labor involved in "washing, starching," see K. Brown, *Foul Bodies*, 30–31; on preparing drinks, see Ligon, *True and Exact History*, 31–32.

48. J. Morgan, *Laboring Women*, 148; Norton, *Founding Mothers and Fathers*, 10, 29–30, 57, 77.

49. Christopher Codrington the Younger became governor in 1699 following his father's death (Mandelbrote, "Codrington, Christopher"). See also Zacek, *English Settler Society*, 221.

50. TNA, CO 152/8, no. 41.

51. For a fuller discussion of Codrington's feud with Parke, see Zacek, "Death in the Morning," 223–25.

52. Parke eventually paid the ultimate price for his abuses of power and was murdered in December 1710 (Zacek, *Settler Society*, 228–34).

53. Whistler, *Journal*, 145–47.

54. JRL, Stapleton MSS, box 1, fol. 5, "An Act against Inveigling Women Servants." See also Berleant-Schiller, "Free Labor," 558–59.

55. K. Brown, *Good Wives*, 87–88.

56. Oliver, *Caribbeana*, 1:55–56, Bridgetown, Barbados, 5 November 1675. For more on the experiences of enslaved women in the Caribbean, see J. Morgan, *Laboring Women*; Beckles, *Centering Women*; Bush, *Slave Women*.

57. While the connection between status and the presence of household slaves would become more pronounced in the eighteenth and nineteenth centuries, there is evidence that such a link was being made much earlier, as John's letter suggests. See J. Morgan, *Laboring Women*, 148–50, for more on enslaved women and domestic labor. See also Beckles, *Natural Rebels*, 57–58.

58. For a more sustained discussion of the ways in which planters discussed enslaved property and animal property, see Weaver, *Medical Revolutionaries*, 82.

59. Sturtz, "'Dimduke' and the Duchess."

60. J. Morgan, *Laboring Women*, 82–83.

61. TNA, CO1/21, no. 55, "Major Scott's Relation," 12 July 1667.

62. TNA, CO1/22, no. 60, Willoughby to Joseph Williamson, 3 April 1668.

63. TNA, CO29/1, fol. 119, 9 July 1668.

64. TNA, CO1/24, no. 71. This Anthony Briskett was the son of a former governor of Montserrat who had the same name. The elder Briskett spent time in Ireland under the tutelage of the lord deputy Sir Henry Sidney, who held lands in Wexford. He was the son of Lodowick Bryskett, who had come to England from Italy in the early sixteenth century. For a fuller discussion of Briskett's background and his families ties to Ireland, see Akenson, *If the Irish Ran the World*, 50–56. See also Richard A. McCabe, "Bryskett, Lodowick."

65. TNA, CO1/24, no. 70, Petition of Anthony Bryskett to the King, 17 June 1669.

66. Ibid., no. 71.

67. Ibid. Briskett had also been party to one of the bigger scandals of the 1650s. In 1654 Irish governor Roger Osborne ordered his brother-in-law, Samuel Waad, to be executed and laid claim to lands owned by Waad's widow, who was also Briskett's mother. In the war of words that followed, Osborne ultimately prevailed, although Briskett would eventually become governor himself (Zacek, *Settler Society*, 75–77).

68. JRL, Stapleton MSS, boxes 1 and 2.

69. TNA, CO153/3, fol. 119, Stapleton to the Lords of Trade and Plantations, Nevis, 29 March 1684; TNA, CO1/29, no. 15, "An Account of the Leeward Islands," transmitted 17 July 1672.

70. TNA, CO176/1, The Laws of Montserrat.

71. On the lack of Church of England ministers, see Gragg, *Englishmen Transplanted*, 69–70.

72. TNA, CO153/2, fol. 187, Stapleton to the Lords of Trade and Plantations, 19 August 1676, answer to question 20.

73. Zacek also discusses Stapleton's support for Anglican churches (*Settler Society*, 83–84). Akenson notes that Stapleton chose to remain silent on his own religious beliefs when communicating with London (*If the Irish Ran the World*, 102).

74. TNA, CO1/63, no. 70, Petition of Roman Catholicks, Montserrat, 23 November 1687.

75. Examples of the ways that Irish Catholics were discussed before and after Stapleton's tenure can be found in the minutes of the Council of Barbados and the Colonial Office records. See BPL, Lucas MSS, reel 1, fol. 368, 22 September 1657; TNA, CO152/37, no. 10, 10 June 1689; TNA, CO28/37, no. 21, 2 September 1689; TNA, CO31/4, fol. 339, 20 April 1693.

76. BDA, RB 6/40, no. 398.

77. Oliver, *Caribbeana*, 1:55, Montserrat, 29 May 1675, and 1:55–56, Bridgetown, Barbados, 5 November 1675.

78. JRL, Stapleton MSS, box 2, no. 1, fol. 4.

79. Neal Garnham, "Cotter, Sir James"; HL, Blathwayt Papers, BL364, 15 April 1681.

80. HL, BL 364, 15 April 1681.

81. TNA, CO 1/27, no. 52, 9 December 1671. Wheeler's tenure as governor of the Leeward Islands was cut short because of his ineffective management of the islands, and William Stapleton was promoted to his position in recognition of his good governance of Montserrat.

82. For Codrington's decisions to send Irish Catholic "ringleaders" to Jamaica, see TNA, CO152/37, no. 30, Col. Codrington to the Committee for Trade and Plantations, Nevis, 15 August 1689; TNA, CO152/37, no. 35, Mr. Carpenter and Mr. Belchamber to the Committee of Customs, Nevis, 19 August 1689; TNA, CO152/37, no. 41, Col. Codrington to the Committee for Trade and Plantations, Antigua, 19 September 1689.

Codrington may have calculated that the dissidents he sent to Jamaica would not be coming back to haunt him. And as Jamaica was under a different colonial jurisdiction, he was merely following an older English practice of transporting troublemakers out of his area of immediate authority.

83. See TNA, CO28/37, no. 7, i–xix.

84. The letter that Blakiston sent to Codrington has not survived, but the content is clear because of Codrington's point-by-point response (TNA, CO152/37, no. 83, viii, Antigua, 18 February 1690).

85. Zacek, *Settler Society*, 98.

86. Some examples of Codrington's letters to London are in TNA, CO125/37, no. 22, Antigua, 31 July 1689; TNA, CO152/37, no. 30, Nevis, 15 August 1689; and TNA, CO152/37, no. 41, Antigua, 19 September 1689.

87. TNA, CO152/37, no. 83, VIII, Antigua, 18 February 1690.

88. Ibid.

89. Ibid.

90. Berleant-Schiller, "Free Labor," 548.

91. Blake, *Blake Family Records*; see also HL, Blathwayt Papers, box 1, BL 368, "An Account of the Carybee Islands," and TNA, CO1/42, for the Leeward Islands Census, fols. 218–27 for Montserrat.

92. TNA, CO152/37, no. 83.

93. *Full and True Account*, 2. Zacek discusses the role of Blakiston in preventing Irish insurgency in more detail (*Settler Society*, 87–88).

94. TNA, CO1/42, for Montserrat census material from 1678.

95. James Cotter, who had profited from his role defending English assets in the Caribbean, became one of the few prominent Irish Catholics from the region who did *not* support William and Mary. However, his case rather proves the point because it was upon the loss of his lands on Nevis that Cotter declared himself firmly for James II, even being described as "now in Rebellion & actually in arms under the late King James in Ireland" (TNA, CO152/37, no. 50, 11 June 1689). Cotter had returned to Ireland in 1682, leaving his wife and sons in charge of his Caribbean landholdings. On their deaths, he reasserted his claim to the land, but his plantation was confiscated. Thus he no longer had a stake in appeals by the English to his property rights, although his long-held fealty to the Stuart monarchs no doubt played a role in his support of James II. For more on Cotter's life, see Ó Cuív, "James Cotter," 135–59.

Epilogue

1. TNA, CO176/1, no. 19, Christopher Codrington, Leeward Islands, 1693; TNA, CO29/5, no. 165, 23 March 1695, Barbados; TNA, CO153/6, no. 33, Antigua, 11 November 1696; TNA, CO155/2, no. 319, Antigua, 16 September 1699; TNA, CO 152/4, no. 54, Nevis, 12 October 1701.

2. TNA, CO152/4, no. 53, 1701.

3. TNA, CO 155/2, no. 319, St. John's, Antigua, 16 September 1699, the Gentlemen of the Assembly to the Deputy Governor and Council.

4. TNA, CO 152/4, no. 27, 4 June 1701, Whitehall, Lords of Trade and Plantations answer to Col. Codrington's queries.

5. TNA, CO 152/4, no. 54, 1701, To the Lords of Trade and Plantations.

6. For the 1708 Leeward Island census, see TNA, CO318/2, no. 7; for the 1715 Barbados census, see TNA, CO28/16.

7. TNA, CO155/2, fol. 546, 25 October 1699.

8. TNA, CO 155/2, fol. 535, 12 July 1698.

9. TNA, CO 155/2, fol. 535, 12 July 1698.

10. TNA, CO152/18; EXT 1/258.

11. TNA, CO31/5, fol. 194, 25 February 1697.

12. Ibid. The French Code Noir specified that any child born of an enslaved woman and a French man should be freed upon birth; it also stipulated that the parents of the child be married. Obviously these mandates were not always followed or enforced, but it does explain why the status of Jervis's mother would have been of little consequence to his claim of freedom.

13. TNA, CO28/16.

14. BDA, RL1/1, p. 497, 10 January 1694; BDA, RL1/1, p. 537, 6 June 1697; BDA, RL1/2, p. 37, 28 September 1704.

15. Hartman, "Venus in Two Acts," 11.

Bibliography

Archival Sources

Barbados

Barbados Department of Archives, Black Rock (BDA)
Bridgetown Public Library, Bridgetown (BPL)
Barbados Museum and Historical Society

Bermuda

Bermuda Archives (BA)

England

British Library, London (BL)
John Rylands Library, Manchester (JRL)
National Archives, Kew, London (TNA)

Ireland

National Library Ireland, Dublin
National Archives Ireland, Dublin

United States

Folger Shakespeare Library, Washington, D.C.
Huntington Library, San Marino, California (HL)
John Carter Brown Library, Providence, Rhode Island
John D. Rockefeller Library, Williamsburg, Virginia

Published Primary Sources

Acts and Statutes of the Island of Barbados Made and Enacted since the Reduce-ment of the same, unto the Authority of the Common-wealth of England, 7th September 1652. London, 1654.

Acts of Assembly Passed in the Island of Barbados From 1648 to 1718. London, 1732–39.

Barbot, Jean. Barbot on Guinea: The Writings of Jean Barbot on West Africa, 1678–1712. Ed. P. E. H. Hair, Adam Jones, and Robin Law. London: Hakluyt Society, 1992.

Biet, Antoine. Voyage de la France Equinoxiale en L'Isle de Cayenne, entrepris par les François en l'anné'e M.DC.LII . . . Paris, 1656.

Blake, Martin J. Blake Family Records: 1300–1700. A Chronological Catalogue with Notes, Appendices, and the Genealogies of Many Branches of the Blake Family. London: Elliot Stock, 1905.

Blome, Richard. A Description of the Island of Jamaica With the Other Isles and Territories in America to which the English are Related. London, 1672.

Brereton, William. Travels in Holland and the United Provinces, England, Scot-land and Ireland. London: Chetham Society, 1844.

A Brief, but most True Relation of the late Barbarous and Bloody Plot of the Negro's in the Island of Barbados on Friday the 21 of October, 1692. London: Printed for George Croom in Thames-street, 1693.

Calendar of State Papers, Ireland, 1574–1585. London: Longmans, Green Eader and Dyer, 1867.

Clarke, Samuel. A True and Faithfull Account of the Four Chiefest Plantations of the English in the Americas. London, 1670.

A Continuation of the state of New-England being a farther account of the Indian warr, and of the engagement betwixt the joynt forces of the United English col-onies and the Indians, on the 19th. of December 1675: with the true number of the slain and wounded, and the transactions of the English army since the said fight: with all other passages that have there hapned from the 10th of Novem-ber, 1675. to the 8th. of February, 1676: together with an account of the intended rebellion of the negroes in the Barbadoes. London, 1676.

Cranford, James. The Teares of Ireland. London, 1642.

Cugoano, Quobono Ottobah. Thoughts and Sentiments on the Evil and Wicked Traffic of the Slavery and Commerce of the Human Species Humbly Submitted to the Inhabitants of Great-Britain. London, 1787.

Davies, John. Discovery of the True Causes Why Ireland was Never Brought Under Obedience of the Crown of England. Dublin, 1666.

de Marees, Pieter. Description and Historical Account of the Gold Kingdom of Guinea, 1602. Ed. A. van Danzig and Adam Jones. Oxford: Oxford Univer-sity Press, 1987.

Dorman, John F. Adventurers of Purse and Person, Virginia, 1607–1624/5. Balti-more: Genealogical Publishing Company, 2005.

Du Tertre, Jean Baptiste. *Histoire Generale des isles de S. Christophe, de la Gua-deloupe, de la Martinique et autres dans l'Amerique*. Paris, 1654.

Equiano, Olaudah. *The Interesting Narrative of the Life of Olaudah Equiano, or Gustavus Vassa, the African, Written by Himself*. Ed. Werner Sollors. New York: W. W. Norton, 2001.

Firth, C. F., ed. *The Narrative of General Venables*. London, 1900.

Fitzpatrick, Thomas. *The Bloody Bridge, and Other Papers Relating to the Insurrection of 1641*. Dublin, 1903.

A Full and True Account of the Besieging and Taking of Carrickfergus by the Duke of Schomberg, as also a Relation of what has lately pass'd in the Islands of Antego, Mevis, and Montserrat in the West-Indies, Where Their Majesties have been Solemnly Proclaim'd. London: Printed for Richard Baldwin, 1689.

Great Newes from the Barbadoes. London: Printed for L. Curtis in Goat-Court upon Ludgate Hill, 1676.

Hall, Richard. *Acts Passed in the Island of Barbados, 1643–1762*. London: Printed for Richard Hall, 1764.

Hariot, Thomas. *A Brief and True Report of the New Found Land Virginia*. London, 1588.

Henning, W. W. *The Statutes at Large; Being a Collection of All the Laws of Virginia from the First Session of the Legislature in 1619*. Richmond, VA: Samuel Pleasants, 1810.

Hotten, J. C. *Original Lists of Persons of Quality: Emigrants, Religious Exiles, Political Rebels, Serving Men Sold for a Term of Years, Apprentices, Children Stolen, Maidens Pressed, and Others, Who Went from Great Britain to the American Plantations, 1600–1700*. Blowie, MD: Heritage Books, 2006.

Jeaffreson, John Cordy, ed., *A Young Squire of the Seventeenth Century from the Papers (A.D. 1676–1686) of Christopher Jeaffreson*. London: Hurst and Blackett, 1878.

Ligon, Richard. *A True and Exact History of the Island of Barbados*. London, 1657.

Littleton, Edward. *Groans of the Plantations: Or a True Account of their Grievous and Extreme Sufferings by the Heavy Impositions upon Sugar, and Other Hardships Relating More Particularly to the Island of Barbados*. London, 1689.

Moryson, Fynes. *The Itinerary of Fynes Moryson in Four Volumes*. Glasgow: MacLehose, 1908.

Okeley, William. *Eben-ezer: Or, a small monument of great mercy, appearing in the Miraculous Deliverance of William Okeley, John Anthony, William Adams, John Jephs, John Carpenter, from the miserable slavery of Algiers, with the wonderful means of their escape . . .* London, 1676.

Oliver, Vere Langford, ed. *Caribbeana: Being Miscellaneous Papers Relating to the History, Genealogy, Topography, and Antiquities of the British West Indies*. London: Mitchell, Hughes and Clark, 1910–19.

Pelleprat, Pierre. *Relation des Missions des PP de la Compagnie de Jesus dans les Isles & dans la terre ferme de L'Amerique Meridionale.* Paris, 1655.

Percy, George. *A True Relation of the proceedings and occurrents of moment which have hap'ned in Virginia from the time Sir Thomas Gates was shipwrack'd upon the Bermudes, anno 1609, until my departure out of the country, which was in anno Domini 1612.* London, 1612.

Petty, William. *The Economic Writings of William Petty.* Ed. Charles Henry Hull. Cambridge: Cambridge University Press, 1899.

———. *The History of the Survey of Ireland, Commonly Called the Down Survey.* Ed. Thomas Aiskew Larcom. 1851. Reprint, New York: A. M. Kelly, 1967.

———. *Political Anatomy of Ireland.* London, 1691.

———. *Political Arithmetick.* London, 1690.

———. *Tracts Chiefly Relating to Ireland.* Dublin, 1769.

Rivers, Marcellus, and Oxenbridge Foyle. *Englands Slavery, or Barbados Merchandize Represented in a Petition to the High Court of Parliament.* London, 1659.

Rochefort, Charles de. *The History of the Caribby-Islands, VIZ Barbados, St Christophers, St Vincents, Martinico, Dominico, Barbouthos, Montserrat, Mevis, Antego, &c. in Two Books.* London, 1666.

Sanders, Joanne McRee, ed. and comp. *Barbados Records: Baptisms, 1637–1800.* Baltimore: Genealogical Publishing Company, 1984.

———, ed. and comp. *Barbados Records: Marriages, 1643–1800.* Vols. 1–2. Baltimore: Genealogical Publishing Company, 1982.

———, ed. and comp. *Barbados Records: Wills, 1639–1725.* Vols. 1–3. Baltimore: Genealogical Publishing Company, 1981.

Shrigley, Nathaniel. *A True Relation of Virginia and Maryland.* London, 1669.

Sloane, Hans. *A Voyage to the Islands Madera, Barbados, Nieves, S. Christophers and Jamaica: In Two Volumes.* London, 1707.

Smith, John. *A True Relation of Occurrences and Accidents in Virginia.* London, 1608.

———. *The True Travels, Adventures, and Observations of Captaine John Smith in Europe, Asia, Africke, and America.* London, 1630.

Speed, John. *The Theatre of the Empire of Great Britain.* Book 4. London, 1612.

Spenser, Edmund. *The Faerie Queene.* Ed. Thomas P. Roche and C. Patrick O'Donnell. Reissue ed. New York: Penguin Classics, 1979.

———. *A View of the State of Ireland.* Ed. Andrew Hadfield and Willy Maley. Oxford: Blackwell, 1997.

Stanihurst, Richard. *On Ireland's Past.* In Colm Lennon, *Richard Stanihurst the Dubliner, 1547–1618: A Biography with a Stanihurst Text, On Ireland's Past.* Dublin: Irish Academic Press, 1981.

Stock, Leo Francis, ed. *Proceedings and Debates of the British Parliaments respecting North America.* Vol. 1. *1542–1688.* Washington, DC: Carnegie Institution, 1924.

Taylor, John. *Second Part of the Historie of his Travels in America*. London, 1688.

Tryon, Thomas. *Friendly Advice to the Gentlemen-Planters of the East and West Indies In Three Parts*. London, 1684.

Villault, Nicholas. *A Relation of the Coasts of Africk Called Guinee: With a Description of the Countreys, Manners and Customs of the Inhabitants, of the Productions of the Earth, and the Merchandise and Commodities it Affords, with Some Historical Observations Upon the Coasts: Being Collected in a Voyage Made by the Sieur Villault, Escuyer, Sieur de Bellefond, in the Years 1666, and 1667*. London, 1670.

West, William. *Symbolaeographia. Which May be termed the Art, Description, or Image of Instruments, Covenants, Contracts etc*. London, 1590.

Whistler, Henry. *Journal of the West Indies Expedition*. Ed. C. H. Firth. London: Longmans, 1900.

White, Andrew. *Voyage to Maryland*. Ed. and trans. Barbara Lawatsch-Boomgaarden with Josef IJsewign. Wauconda, IL: Bolchazy-Carducci, 1995.

Secondary Sources

Akenson, Donald Harman. *If the Irish Ran the World: Montserrat, 1630–1730*. Toronto: McGill-Queen's University Press, 1997.

Alsop, J. D. "Religious Preambles in Early Modern English Wills as Formulae." *Journal of Ecclesiastical History* 40 (1989): 19–27.

Amussen, Susan Dwyer. *Caribbean Exchanges: Slavery and the Transformation of English Society, 1640–1700*. Chapel Hill: University of North Carolina Press, 2007.

Andrew, K. R., Nicholas P. Canny, and P. E. H. Hair, eds. *The Westward Enterprise: English Activities in Ireland, the Atlantic and America, 1480–1650*. Liverpool: Liverpool University Press, 1978.

Armstrong, Douglas V. *The Old Village and the Great House: An Archaeological and Historical Examination of Drax Hall Plantation, St. Ann's Bay, Jamaica*. Urbana: University of Illinois Press, 1990.

———. "Reflections on Seville: Rediscovering the African Jamaican Settlements at Seville Plantation, St. Ann's Bay." In *Out of Many, One People: The Historical Archaeology of Colonial Jamaica*, ed. James A. Delle, Mark W. Hauser, and Douglas V. Armstrong, 77–101. Tuscaloosa: University of Alabama Press, 2011.

Armstrong, Robert. *Protestant War: The "British" of Ireland and the Wars of the Three Kingdoms*. Manchester: Manchester University Press, 2005.

Atherton, Ian, and David Como. "The Burning of Edward Wightman: Puritanism, Prelacy, and the Politics of Heresy in Early Modern England." *English Historical Review* 120 (2005): 1215–50.

Barnard, Toby. *Making the Grand Figure: Lives and Possessions in Ireland*. New Haven: Yale University Press, 2004.

———. "1641: A Bibliographical Essay." In *Ulster, 1641: Aspects of the Rising*, ed.

Brian MacCuarta, 173–86. Belfast: Institute of Irish Studies, Queen's University, 1993.

Beasley, Nicholas M. *Christian Ritual and the Creation of British Slave Societies, 1650–1780*. Athens: University of Georgia Press, 2009.

Beckles, Hilary M. *Centering Women: Gender Discourses in Caribbean Slave Society*. Kingston: Ian Randle, 1999.

———. "English Parliamentary Debate on 'White Slavery' in Barbados, 1659." *Journal of the Barbados Museum and Historical Society* 36 (1982): 344–52.

———. *Natural Rebels: A Social History of Enslaved Black Women in Barbados*. New Brunswick: Rutgers University Press, 1989.

———. "A 'Riotous and Unruly Lot': Irish Indentured Servants and Freemen in the English West Indies, 1644–1713." *William and Mary Quarterly*, 3rd ser., 47 (1990): 503–22.

———. *White Servitude and Black Slavery in Barbados, 1627–1715*. Knoxville: University of Tennessee Press, 1989.

Bennett, Herman. "The Subject in the Plot: National Boundaries and the 'History' of the Black Atlantic." *African Studies Review* 43, no. 1 (2000): 101–24.

Berleant-Schiller, Riva. "Free Labor and the Economy in Seventeenth-Century Montserrat." *William and Mary Quarterly*, 3rd ser., 46, no. 3 (1989): 539–64.

Berlin, Ira. *Many Thousands Gone: The First Two Centuries of Slavery in North America*. Cambridge, MA: Harvard University Press, 1998.

Bilby, Kenneth. "Swearing by the Past, Swearing to the Future: Sacred Oaths, Alliances, and Treaties Among the Guianese and Jamaican Maroons." *Ethnohistory* 44, no. 4 (1997): 655–89.

Bliss, Alan J. "The English Language in Early Modern Ireland." In *A New History of Ireland III: Early Modern Ireland (1534–1691)*, ed. Theodore W. Moody et al., 546–60. Oxford: Clarendon Press, 1976.

Block, Kristen. *Ordinary Lives in the Early Caribbean: Religion, Colonial Competition, and the Politics of Profit*. Athens: University of Georgia Press, 2012.

Block, Kristen, and Jenny Shaw. "Subjects without an Empire: The Irish in a Changing Caribbean." *Past and Present* 210 (2011): 34–60.

Bollettino, Maria Alessandra. "Slavery, War, and Britain's Atlantic Empire: Black Soldiers, Sailors, and Rebels in the Seven Years' War." PhD diss., University of Texas, Austin, 2009.

Boucher, Philip P. *Cannibal Encounters: Europeans and Island Caribs, 1492–1763*. Baltimore: Johns Hopkins University Press, 1992.

Bradshaw, Brendan, and Dáire Keogh, eds. *Christianity in Ireland: Revisiting the Story*. Dublin: Columba Press, 2002.

Braude, Benjamin. "The Sons of Noah and the Construction of Ethnic and Geographical Identities in the Medieval and Early Modern Periods." *William and Mary Quarterly*, 3rd ser., 54 (1997): 103–42.

Breen, T. H., and Stephen Innes. *Myne Owne Ground: Race and Freedom on Virginia's Eastern Shore*. New York: Oxford University Press, 1981.

Bridenbaugh, Carl, and Roberta Bridenbaugh. *No Peace beyond the Line: The English in the Caribbean, 1624–1690.* Oxford: Oxford University Press, 1972.

Bross, Kristina. *Dry Bones and Indian Sermons: Praying Indians in Colonial America.* Ithaca: Cornell University Press, 2004.

Brown, Kathleen M. *Foul Bodies: Cleanliness in Early America.* New Haven: Yale University Press, 2009.

———. *Good Wives, Nasty Wenches, Anxious Patriarchs: Gender, Race, and Power in Colonial Virginia.* Chapel Hill: University of North Carolina Press, 1996.

———. "Native Americans and Early Modern Concepts of Race." In *Empire and Others: British Encounters with Indigenous Peoples, 1600–1850,* ed. Martin Daunton and Rick Halpern, 79–100. London: UCL Press, 1999.

Brown, Vincent. "Eating the Dead: Consumption and Regeneration in the History of Sugar." *Food and Foodways* 16, no. 2 (2008): 117–26.

———. *The Reaper's Garden: Death and Power in the World of Atlantic Slavery.* Cambridge, MA: Harvard University Press, 2008.

———. "Social Death and Political Life in the Study of Slavery: Between Resistance and Oblivion." *American Historical Review* 114, no. 5 (2009): 1231–49.

———. "Spiritual Terror and Sacred Authority in Jamaican Slave Society." *Slavery and Abolition* 24, no. 1 (April 2003): 24–53.

Buck, Peter. "Seventeenth-Century Political Arithmetic: Civil Strife and Vital Statistics." *Isis* 68, no. 1 (1977): 67–84.

Buckley, Roger Norman. *Slaves in Red Coats: The British West Indian Regiments, 1795–1815.* New Haven: Yale University Press, 1979.

Burgess, Clive. "'By Quick and by Dead': Wills and Pious Provision in Late Medieval Bristol." *English Historical Review* 102, no. 405 (1987): 837–58.

Burnard, Trevor. *Mastery, Tyranny, and Desire: Thomas Thistlewood and His Slaves in the Anglo-Jamaican World.* Chapel Hill: University of North Carolina Press, 2004.

———. "Slave Naming Patterns: Onomastics and the Taxonomy of Race in Eighteenth-Century Jamaica." *Journal of Interdisciplinary History* 31 (2001): 325–46.

Bush, Barbara. *Slave Women in Caribbean Society, 1650–1838.* Bloomington: Indiana University Press, 1990.

Caball, Marc. "Faith, Culture and Sovereignty: Irish Nationality and Its Development, 1558–1625." In *British Consciousness and Identity: The Making of Britain, 1533–1707,* ed. Brendan Bradshaw and Peter Roberts, 112–39. Cambridge: Cambridge University Press, 1998.

Cameron, Euan. *Enchanted Europe: Superstition, Reason, and Religion, 1250–1750.* Oxford: Oxford University Press, 2010.

Canny, Nicholas P. *The Elizabethan Conquest of Ireland: A Pattern Established, 1565–76.* New York: Harper and Row, 1976.

———. "English Migration into and across the Atlantic during the Seventeenth and Eighteenth Centuries." In *Europeans on the Move: Studies in European Migration, 1500–1800*, ed. Nicholas Canny, 39–75. New York: Oxford University Press, 1994.

———. "The Formation of the Irish Mind: Religion, Politics and Gaelic Irish Literature, 1580–1750." *Past and Present* 95 (1982): 91–116.

———. "The Ideology of English Colonization: From Ireland to America." *William and Mary Quarterly*, 3rd ser., 30, no. 4 (1973): 575–98.

———. *Making Ireland British, 1580–1650*. New York: Oxford University Press, 2001.

———. *Oxford History of the British Empire*. Vol. 1. *The Origins of Empire: British Overseas Enterprise to the Close of the Seventeenth Century*. Oxford: Oxford University Press, 1998.

Carey, Vincent. "Icons of Atrocity: John Derricke's *Image of Irelande* (1581)." In *World-Building and the Early Modern Imagination*, ed. Allison B. Kavey, 233–54. New York: Palgrave Macmillan, 2010.

Carney, Judith A. *Black Rice: The African Origins of Rice Cultivation in the Americas*. Cambridge, MA: Harvard University Press, 2001.

Carney, Judith A., and Nicholas Richard Rosomoff. *In the Shadow of Slavery: Africa's Botanical Legacy in the Atlantic World*. Berkeley: University of California Press, 2010.

Carr, Lois Green, and Russell R. Menard. "Immigration and Opportunity: The Freedman in Early Colonial America." In *The Chesapeake in the Seventeenth Century: Essays in Anglo-American Society and Politics*, ed. Thad W. Tate and David L. Ammerman, 206–42. New York: W. W. Norton, 1979.

Carson, Cary, Norman F. Barka, William M. Kelso, Garry Wheeler Stone, and Dell Upton. "Impermanent Architecture in the Southern American Colonies." *Winterthur Portfolio* 16, nos. 2/3 (1981): 135–96.

Carson, James Taylor. *Making an Atlantic World: Circles, Paths, and Stories from the Colonial South*. Knoxville: University of Tennessee Press, 2007.

Certeau, Michel de. *The Practice of Everyday Life*. Trans. Steven Rendall. Berkeley: University of California Press, 1984.

Chaplin, Joyce E. "Natural Philosophy and an Early Racial Idiom in North America: Comparing English and Indian Bodies." *William and Mary Quarterly* 54, no. 1 (1997): 229–52.

———. *Subject Matter: Technology, the Body, and Science on the Anglo-American Frontier, 1500–1676*. Cambridge, MA: Harvard University Press, 2001.

Cohen, Patricia Cline. *A Calculating People: The Spread of Numeracy in Early America*. Chicago: University of Chicago Press, 1982.

Corish, Patrick J. *The Irish Catholic Community in the Seventeenth and Eighteenth Centuries*. Dublin: Helicon, 1981.

Crane, Elaine. *Witches, Wife Beaters, and Whores: Common Law and Common Folk in Early America*. Ithaca: Cornell University Press, 2011.

Craton, Michael. *Testing the Chains: Resistance to Slavery in the British West Indies*. Ithaca: Cornell University Press, 1982.

Cressy, David. *Birth, Marriage and Death: Ritual, Religion and the Life-Cycle in Tudor and Stuart England*. London: Oxford University Press, 1997.

Cronon, William. *Changes in the Land: Indians, Colonists, and the Ecology of New England*. 2nd ed. New York: Hill and Wang, 2003.

Cullen, Louis M. "Galway Merchants in the Outside World, 1650–1800." In *Galway Town and Gown, 1484–1984*, ed. Diarmuid O'Cearbhaill, 63–89. Dublin: Gill and Macmillan, 1984.

———. "The Irish Diaspora of the Seventeenth and Eighteenth Centuries." In *Europeans on the Move: Studies in European Migration, 1500–1800*, ed. Nicholas Canny, 113–49. New York: Oxford University Press, 1994.

Daunton, Martin, and Rick Halpern, eds. *Empire and Others: British Encounters with Indigenous Peoples, 1600–1850*. Philadelphia: University of Pennsylvania Press, 1999.

Davis, David Brion. "Constructing Race: A Reflection." *William and Mary Quarterly*, 3rd ser., 54 (1997): 7–18.

Davis, Natalie Zemon. *The Return of Martin Guerre*. Cambridge, MA: Harvard University Press, 1984.

———. "The Rites of Violence: Religious Riot in Sixteenth-Century France." *Past and Present* 59 (1973): 51–91.

———. *Women on the Margins: Three Seventeenth Century Lives*. Cambridge, MA: Harvard University Press, 1995.

Davis, Robert C. *Christian Slaves, Muslim Masters: White Slavery in the Mediterranean, the Barbary Coast, and Italy, 1500–1800*. New York: Palgrave Macmillan, 2003.

Dawdy, Shannon Lee. "The Burden of Louis Congo and the Evolution of Savagery in Colonial Louisiana." In *Discipline and the Other Body: Correction, Corporeality, Colonialism*, ed. Steven Pierce and Anupama Rao, 61–89. Durham: Duke University Press, 2006.

Dawson, Jane. "The Gaidhealtachd and the Emergence of the Scottish Highlands." In *British Consciousness and Identity: The Making of Britain, 1533–1707*, ed. Brendan Bradshaw and Peter Roberts, 259–300. Cambridge: Cambridge University Press, 1998.

DeCourse, Christopher R. *An Archaeology of Elmina: Africans and Europeans on the Gold Coast, 1400–1900*. Washington, DC: Smithsonian Institution Press, 2001.

Demos, John. *The Unredeemed Captive: A Family Story from Early America*. New York: Alfred A. Knopf, 1994.

Dinan, Susan E., and Debra Meyers, eds. *Women and Religion in Old and New Worlds*. New York: Routledge, 2001.

Donoghue, John. "'Out of the Land of Bondage': The English Revolution and the Atlantic Origins of Abolition." *American Historical Review* 115 (2010): 943–74.

Dunn, Richard S. "The Barbados Census of 1680: Profile of the Richest Colony in English America." *William and Mary Quarterly*, 3rd ser., 26, no. 1 (1969): 3–30.

———. *Sugar and Slaves: The Rise of the Planter Class in the English West Indies, 1624–1713*. Chapel Hill: University of North Carolina Press, 1972.

Egerton, Douglas R. "A Peculiar Mark of Infamy: Dismemberment, Burial, and Rebelliousness in Slave Societies." In *Mortal Remains: Death in Early America*, ed. Nancy Isenberg and Andrew Burstein, 149–60. Philadelphia: University of Pennsylvania Press, 2003.

Eltis, David. *The Rise of African Slavery in the Americas*. Cambridge: Cambridge University Press, 2000.

Eltis, David, and Stanley Engerman. "Was the Slave Trade Dominated by Men?" *Journal of Interdisciplinary History* 23 (1992): 237–57.

Fickes, Michael L. "'They Could Not Endure That Yoke': The Captivity of Pequot Women and Children after the War of 1637." *New England Quarterly* 73 (March 2000): 58–81.

Fields, Barbara J. "Ideology and Race in American History." In *Region, Race, and Reconstruction: Essays in Honor of C. Vann Woodward*, ed. J. Morgan Kousser and James M. McPherson, 143–77. New York: Oxford University Press, 1982.

Fischer, David Hackett. *Albion's Seed: Four British Folkways in America*. Oxford: Oxford University Press, 1989.

Fischer, Kirsten. *Suspect Relations: Sex, Race, and Resistance in Colonial North Carolina*. Ithaca: Cornell University Press, 2002.

Fletcher, Anthony. *Gender, Sex and Subordination in England, 1500–1800*. Bath: Bath Press, 1999.

Ford, Alan. "Living Together, Living Apart: Sectarianism in Early Modern Ireland." In *The Roots of Sectarianism in Early Modern Ireland*, ed. Alan Ford and John McCafferty, 1–23. Cambridge: Cambridge University Press, 2005.

Foucault, Michel. *Discipline and Punish: The Birth of the Prison*. 2nd ed. Trans. Alan Sheridan. New York: Random House, 1995.

Frederickson, George. *Racism: A Short History*. Princeton: Princeton University Press, 2002.

Fry, Susan Leigh. *Burial in Medieval Ireland, 900–1500: A Review of Written Sources*. Dublin: Four Courts Press, 1999.

Fuentes, Marisa J. "Power and Historical Figuring: Rachel Pringle Polgreen's Troubled Archive." *Gender and History* 22, no. 3 (2010): 564–84.

Fumerton, Patricia. "Introduction: A New New Historicism." In *Renaissance Culture and the Everyday*, ed. Patricia Fumerton and Simon Hunt, 1–17. Philadelphia: University of Pennsylvania Press, 1999.

Galenson, David W. *White Servitude in Colonial America: An Economic Analysis*. Cambridge: Cambridge University Press, 1981.

Games, Alison. *Migration and the Origins of the English Atlantic World*. Cambridge, MA: Harvard University Press, 1999.

Gardiner, Michael E. *Critiques of Everyday Life*. London: Routledge, 2000.

Garnham, Neal. "Cotter, Sir James (*d.* 1705)." In *Oxford Dictionary of National Biography*, ed. H. C. G. Matthew and Brian Harrison. Oxford: Oxford University Press, 2004.

Gaskill, Malcolm. *Crime and Mentalities in Early Modern England*. Cambridge: Cambridge University Press, 2000.

Gaspar, David Barry. *Bondmen and Rebels: A Study of Master-Slave Relations in Antigua*. Baltimore: Johns Hopkins University Press, 1985.

Gillespie, Raymond. *Devoted People: Belief and Religion in Early Modern Ireland*. Manchester: Manchester University Press, 1997.

Glymph, Thavolia. *Out of the House of Bondage: The Transformation of the Plantation Household*. Cambridge: Cambridge University Press, 2008.

Goetz, Rebecca A. *The Baptism of Early Virginia: How Christianity Created Race*. Baltimore: Johns Hopkins University Press, 2012.

Gomez, Michael A. *Exchanging Our Country Marks: The Transformation of African Identities in the Colonial and Antebellum South*. Chapel Hill: University of North Carolina Press, 1998.

Gowing, Laura. *Common Bodies: Women, Touch, and Power in Seventeenth-Century England*. New Haven: Yale University Press, 2003.

Gragg, Larry Dale. *Englishmen Transplanted: The English Colonization of Barbados, 1624–1660*. Oxford: Oxford University Press, 2003.

———. *The Quaker Community on Barbados: Challenging the Culture of the Planter Class*. Columbia: University of Missouri Press, 2009.

Greenblatt, Stephen. *Marvelous Possessions: The Wonder of the New World*. Chicago: University of Chicago Press, 1991.

Greer, Allan. *Mohawk Saint: Catherine Tekakwitha and the Jesuits*. New York: Oxford University Press, 2006.

Guitar, Lynne. "Boiling It Down: Slavery on the First Commercial Sugar Ingenios in the Americas (Hispaniola, 1530–45)." In *Slaves, Subjects, and Subversives: Blacks in Colonial Latin America*, ed. Jane G. Landers and Barry M. Robinson, 39–82. Albuquerque: University of New Mexico Press, 2006.

Hancock, David. *Citizens of the World: London Merchants and the Integration of the British Atlantic Community, 1735–1785*. Cambridge: Cambridge University Press, 1997.

Handler, Jerome S. "An African-Type Healer/Diviner and His Grave Goods: A Burial from a Plantation Slave Cemetery in Barbados, West Indies." *International Journal of Historical Archaeology* 1, no. 2 (1997): 91–130.

———. "The Barbados Slave Conspiracies of 1675 and 1692." *Journal of the Barbados Museum and Historical Society* 36, no. 4 (1982): 312–33.

———. "Father Antoine Biet's Visit to Barbados in 1654." *Journal of the Barbados Museum and Historical Society* 32 (1967): 56–76.

———. "A Prone Burial from a Plantation Slave Cemetery in Barbados, West Indies: Possible Evidence for an African-Type Witch or Other Negatively Viewed Person." *Historical Archaeology* 30, no. 3 (1996): 76–86.

———. "Slave Revolts and Conspiracies in Seventeenth-Century Barbados." *Nieuwe West-Indische Gids* 56, nos. 1/2 (1982): 5–42.

Handler, Jerome S., and JoAnn Jacoby. "Slave Names and Naming in Barbados, 1650–1830." *William and Mary Quarterly*, 3rd ser., 50, no. 4 (1993): 727–42.

Handler, Jerome S., and F. W. Lange. *Plantation Slavery in Barbados: An Archaeological and Historical Investigation*. Cambridge, MA: Harvard University Press, 1978.

Hartman, Saidiya V. *Scenes of Subjection: Terror, Slavery and Self-Making in Nineteenth-Century America*. New York: Oxford University Press, 1997.

———. "Venus in Two Acts." *Small Axe* 26 (2008): 1–14.

Hatfield, April. *Atlantic Virginia: Intercolonial Relations in the Seventeenth Century*. Philadelphia: University of Pennsylvania Press, 2007.

Hauser, Mark W. "Of Earth and Clay: Locating Colonial Economies and Local Ceramics." In *Out of Many, One People: The Historical Archaeology of Colonial Jamaica*, ed. James A. Delle, Mark W. Hauser, and Douglas V. Armstrong, 163–82. Tuscaloosa: University of Alabama Press, 2011.

Haynes, Stephen R. *Noah's Curse: The Biblical Justification of American Slavery*. New York: Oxford University Press, 2002.

Heywood, Linda M., and John K. Thornton. *Central Africans, Atlantic Creoles, and the Foundation of the Americas, 1585–1660*. Cambridge: Cambridge University Press, 2007.

Highmore, Ben. *Everyday Life and Cultural Theory: An Introduction*. London: Routledge, 2002.

Hill, Christopher. *The World Turned Upside Down: Radical Ideas during the English Revolution*. New York: Maurice Temple Smith, 1972.

Hoffman, Ronald, Mechal Sobel, and Fredericka J. Teute, eds. *Through a Glass Darkly: Reflections on Personal Identity in Early America*. Chapel Hill: University of North Carolina Press, 1997.

Hulme, Peter. *Colonial Encounters: Europe and the Native Caribbean, 1492–1797*. London: Routledge, 1992.

Johnson, Mat. *The Great Negro Plot: A Tale of Conspiracy and Murder in Eighteenth-Century New York*. New York: Bloomsburg, 2007.

Johnson, Michael P. "Denmark Vesey and His Co-Conspirators." *William and Mary Quarterly*, 3rd ser., 58 (2001): 915–76.

Johnson, Walter. "Agency: A Ghost Story." In *Slavery's Ghost: The Problem of Freedom in the Age of Emancipation*, ed. Walter Johnson, Eric Foner, and Richard Follett, 8–30. Baltimore: Johns Hopkins University Press, 2011.

———. "On Agency." *Journal of Social History* 37, no. 1 (2003): 113–24.

Johnston, Shona Helen. "Papists in a Protestant World: The Catholic Anglo-

Atlantic in the Seventeenth Century." PhD diss., Georgetown University, 2011.

Jones, Ann Rosalind, and Peter Stallybrass. "Dismantling Irena: The Sexualizing of Ireland in Early Modern England." In *Nationalisms and Sexualities*, ed. Andrew Parker, Mary Russo, Doris Sommer, and Patricia Yaeger, 151–71. New York: Routledge, 1992.

———. "'Rugges of London and the Deuills Band': Irish Mantles and Yellow Starch as Hybrid London Fashions." In *Material London, ca. 1600*, ed. Lena Cowen Orlin, 128–35. Philadelphia: University of Pennsylvania Press, 2000.

Jones, Cecily. *Engendering Whiteness: White Women and Colonialism in Barbados and North Carolina*. Manchester: Manchester University Press, 2007.

Jordan, Winthrop D. *Tumult and Silence at Second Creek: An Inquiry into a Civil War Slave Conspiracy*. Baton Rouge: Louisiana State University Press, 1993.

Kew, Graham. "The Irish Sections of Fynes Moryson's Unpublished 'Itinerary.'" *Analecta Hibernica*, no. 37 (1995–96): 1–137.

Kidd, Colin. *British Identities before Nationalism: Ethnicity and Nationhood in the Atlantic World, 1600–1800*. New York: Cambridge University Press, 1999.

———. *The Forging of Races: Race and Scripture in the Protestant Atlantic World, 1600–2000*. Cambridge: Cambridge University Press, 2006.

Knight, Frederick. "In an Ocean of Blue: West African Indigo Workers in the Atlantic World to 1800." In *Diasporic Africa: A Reader*, ed. Michael A. Gomez, 28–44. New York: NYU Press, 2006.

Kopelson, Heather Miyano. *Faithful Bodies: Race and Religion in the Puritan Atlantic*. New York: New York University Press, forthcoming.

———. "Sinning Property: Race, Religion, and Unlawful Sex in Early Bermuda." *William and Mary Quarterly*, forthcoming, spring 2013.

Kopytoff, Barbara K. "The Development of Jamaican Maroon Ethnicity." *Caribbean Quarterly* 22 (1976): 33–50.

Kupperman, Karen Ordahl. *Indians and English: Facing Off in Early America*. Ithaca: Cornell University Press, 2000.

———. "Presentment of Civility: English Reading of American Self-Presentation in the Early Years of Colonization." *William and Mary Quarterly*, 3rd. ser., 54 (1997): 193–228.

———. *Providence Island, 1630–1641: The Other Puritan Colony*. London: Cambridge University Press, 1993.

Kussmaul, Ann. *Servants in Husbandry in Early Modern England*. Cambridge: Cambridge University Press, 1981.

LaCombe, Michael A. *Political Gastronomy: Food and Authority in the English Atlantic World*. Philadelphia: University of Pennsylvania Press, 2012.

Laurence, Anne. "The Cradle to the Grave: English Observation of Irish Social Customs in the Seventeenth Century." *Seventeenth Century* 3 (1988): 65–78.

Law, Robin. "Human Sacrifice in Pre-colonial West Africa." *African Affairs* 84 (1985): 53–87.

———. "Jean Barbot as a Source for the Slave Coast of West Africa." *History in Africa* 9 (1982): 155–73.

———. "Religion, Trade, and Politics on the 'Slave Coast': Roman Catholic Missions in Allada and Whydah in the Seventeenth Century." *Journal of Religion in Africa* 21 (1991): 42–77.

Lepore, Jill. *New York Burning: Liberty, Slavery and Conspiracy in Eighteenth-Century Manhattan*. New York: Vintage, 2006.

Lestringant, Frank. *Cannibals: The Discovery and Representation of the Cannibal from Columbus to Jules Verne*. Trans. Rosemary Morris. Berkeley: University of California Press, 1997.

———. *Une sainte horreur, ou Le voyage en Eucharistie, XVIe–XVIIIe siècle*. Paris: Presses universitaires de France, 1996.

Linebaugh, Peter. *The London Hanged: Crime and Civil Society in the Eighteenth Century*. Cambridge: Cambridge University Press, 1992.

Lorimer, Joyce, ed. *English and Irish Settlement on the Amazon River, 1550–1646*. London: Hakluyt Society, 1989.

MacGaffey, Wyatt. "Art and Spirituality." In *African Spirituality: Forms, Meanings, and Expressions*, ed. Jacob K. Olupona, 235–43. New York: Crossroad, 2000.

Mancall, Peter C. "Introduction: What Fynes Moryson Knew." *Journal of Early Modern History* 10 (2006): 1–9.

Mandelbrote, Scott. "Codrington, Christopher (1668–1710)." In *Oxford Dictionary of National Biography*. Oxford: Oxford University Press, 2004–. Accessed 22 September 2008. www.oxforddnb.com/view/article/5795.

Martínez, María Elena. "The Black Blood of New Spain: Limpieza de Sangre, Racial Violence, and Gendered Power in Early Colonial Mexico." *William and Mary Quarterly*, 3rd ser., 61, no. 3 (2004): 479–520.

Matar, Nabil. *Turks, Moors, and Englishmen in the Age of Discovery*. New York: Columbia University Press, 1999.

McCabe, Richard A. "Bryskett, Lodowick (c.1546–1609x12)." In *Oxford Dictionary of National Biography*. Oxford: Oxford University Press, 2004– Accessed 25 September 2008. www.oxforddnb.com/view/article/3817.

———. *Spenser's Monstrous Regiment: Elizabethan Ireland and the Poetics of Difference*. Oxford: Oxford University Press, 2002.

McCafferty, Kate. *Testimony of an Irish Slave Girl*. New York: Viking Penguin, 2002.

McCormick, Ted. *William Petty and the Ambitions of Political Arithmetic*. Oxford: Oxford University Press, 2009.

Meigs, Samantha A. *The Reformations in Ireland: Tradition and Confessionalism, 1400–1690*. London: Macmillan, 1997.

Menard, Russell R. *Migrants, Servants and Slaves: Unfree Labor in the Colonial British America*. Aldershot: Ashgate, 2001.

———. *Sweet Negotiations: Sugar, Slavery, and Plantation Agriculture in Early Barbados*. Charlottesville: University of Virginia Press, 2006.

Miller, Jacquelyn C. "The Body Politic and the Body Somatic: Benjamin Rush's Fear of Social Disorder and His Treatment for Yellow Fever." In *A Centre of Wonders: The Body in Early America*, ed. Janet Moore Lindman and Michele Lise Tarter, 61–74. Ithaca: Cornell University Press, 2001.

Mintz, Sidney W. *Sweetness and Power: The Place of Sugar in Modern History*. London: Penguin, 1986.

Mintz, Sidney W., and Richard Price. *The Birth of African American Culture: An Anthropological Perspective*. Boston: Beacon Press, 1992.

Monahan, Michael J. *The Creolizing Subject: Race, Reason, and the Politics of Purity*. New York: Fordham University Press, 2011.

Monod, Paul Kléber. *The Power of Kings: Monarchy and Religion in Europe, 1589–1715*. New Haven: Yale University Press, 1999.

Morgan, Edmund S. *American Slavery, American Freedom: The Ordeal of Colonial Virginia*. New York: W. W. Norton, 1975.

Morgan, Jennifer L. "Demographic Logics and Early Modern English Colonialism." Work in progress, presented to the Columbia Seminar on Early American History and Culture, February 2011.

———. *Laboring Women: Reproduction and Gender in New World Slavery*. Philadelphia: University of Pennsylvania Press, 2004.

———. "Slavery and the Slave Trade." In *A Companion to American Women's History*, ed. Nancy Hewitt. Oxford: Blackwell, 2003.

———. "'Some Could Suckle over Their Shoulder': Male Travelers, Female Bodies, and the Gendering of Racial Ideology, 1500–1770." *William and Mary Quarterly*, 3rd ser., 54 (1997): 167–92.

Morgan, Kenneth. *Servitude and Slavery in North America, 1607–1800*. Edinburgh: Edinburgh University Press, 2000.

Morgan, Philip D. "Conspiracy Scares." *William and Mary Quarterly*, 3rd ser., 59, no. 1 (2002): 159–66.

———. *Slave Counterpoint: Black Culture in the Eighteenth-Century Chesapeake and Lowcountry*. Chapel Hill: University of North Carolina Press, 1998.

Mulcahy, Matthew. *Hurricanes and Society in the British Greater Caribbean, 1624–1783*. Baltimore: Johns Hopkins University Press, 2008.

Muldoon, James. *Identity on the Medieval Irish Frontier*. Gainesville· University of Florida Press, 2003.

———. "The Indian as Irishman." *Essex Institute Historical Collections* 111 (1975): 267–89.

Mullin, Michael. *Africa in America: Slave Acculturation and Resistance in the American South and the British Caribbean, 1736–1831*. Urbana: University of Illinois Press, 1992.

Mundy, Barbara E. *The Mapping of New Spain: Indigenous Cartography and the*

Maps of the Relaciones Geográficas. Chicago: University of Chicago Press, 1996.

Noonan, Kathleen M. "'The Cruell Pressure of an Enraged, Barbarous People.'" *Historical Journal* 41, no. 1 (1998): 151–77.

Norton, Mary Beth. *Founding Mothers and Fathers: Gendered Power and the Forming of American Society.* New York: Alfred A. Knopf, 1996.

O'Callaghan, Sean. *To Hell or Barbados: The Ethnic Cleansing of Ireland.* Dingle, County Kerry: Brandon Books, 2000.

Ó Cuív, Brian. "James Cotter, a Seventeenth-Century Agent of the Crown." *Journal of the Royal Society of Antiquaries of Ireland* 89, no. 2 (1959): 135–59.

O'Dowd, Mary. *A History of Women in Ireland, 1500–1800.* London: Longman, 2004.

Ogle, Greg E. "Natural Movements and Dangerous Spectacles: Beatings, Duels, and 'Play' in Saint Domingue." In *New World Orders: Violence, Sanction, and Authority in the Colonial Americas,* ed. John Smolenski and Thomas J. Humphrey, 226–48. Philadelphia: University of Pennsylvania Press, 2005.

O'Hart, John. *Irish Pedigrees, or, The Origin and Stem of the Irish Nation.* 5th ed. Dublin: James Duffy, 1892.

Ohlmeyer, Jane H. *Civil War and Restoration in the Three Stuart Kingdoms: The Career of Randall MacDonnell, Marquis of Antrim, 1609–1683.* Cambridge: Cambridge University Press, 1993.

———. *Making Ireland English: The Irish Aristocracy in the Seventeenth Century.* New Haven: Yale University Press, 2012.

———. "Seventeenth-Century Ireland and the New British and Atlantic Histories." *American Historical Review* 104 (1999): 446–62.

O'Neill, Peter D., and David Lloyd, eds. *The Black and the Green Atlantic: Cross-Currents of the African and Irish Diasporas.* London: Palgrave Macmillan, 2009.

Ó'Siochrú, Micheál. "Atrocity, Codes of Conduct and the Irish in the British Civil Wars, 1641–1653." *Past and Present* 195 (2007): 55–86.

———. *God's Executioner: Oliver Cromwell and the Conquest of Ireland.* London: Faber and Faber, 2008.

Palmer, Patricia. "Interpreters and the Politics of Translation and Traduction in Sixteenth Century Ireland." *Irish Historical Studies* 33, no. 131 (2003): 257–77.

Parent, Anthony S. *Foul Means: The Formation of a Slave Society in Virginia, 1660–1740.* Chapel Hill: University of North Carolina Press, 2003.

Partridge, Angela. "Wild Men and Wailing Women." *Eigse* 18 (1980): 25–37.

Paton, Diana. "Punishment, Crime, and the Bodies of Slaves in Eighteenth Century Jamaica." *Journal of Social History* 34, no. 4 (2001): 923–54.

Pestana, Carla Gardina. *The English Atlantic in an Age of Revolution, 1640–1661.* Cambridge, MA: Harvard University Press, 2004.

———. *Protestant Empire: Religion and the Making of the British Atlantic World.* Philadelphia: University of Pennsylvania Press, 2009.

Pietz, William. "The Problem of the Fetish, I." *RES* 9 (Spring 1985): 5–17.

———. "The Problem of the Fetish, II." *RES* 13 (Spring 1987): 23–45.

———. "The Problem of the Fetish, IIIa." *RES* 16 (Autumn 1988): 105–22.

Pincus, Steven C. A. *Protestantism and Patriotism: Ideologies and the Making of English Foreign Policy, 1650–1668.* New York: Cambridge University Press, 1996.

Poovey, Mary. *A History of the Modern Fact: Problems of Knowledge in the Sciences of Wealth and Society.* Chicago: University of Chicago Press, 1998.

Price, Richard. *Alabi's World.* Baltimore: Johns Hopkins University Press, 1990.

———. "Dialogical Encounters in a Space of Death." In *New World Orders: Violence, Sanction, and Authority in the Colonial Americas,* ed. John Smolenski and Thomas J. Humphries, 47–66. Philadelphia: University of Pennsylvania Press, 2005.

Puckrein, Gary A. *Little England: Plantation Society and Anglo-Barbadian Politics, 1627–1700.* New York: New York University Press, 1984.

Pulsipher, Lydia. "The Cultural Landscape of Montserrat, West Indies, in the Seventeenth Century: Early Environmental Consequences of British Colonial Development." PhD diss., Southern Illinois University at Carbondale, 1977.

Putnam, Lara. "To Study the Fragments/Whole: Microhistory and the Atlantic World." *Journal of Social History* 39 (2006): 615–30.

Quinn, David Beers. *Ireland and America: Their Early Associations, 1500–1640.* Liverpool: Liverpool University Press, 1991.

Ransome, David R. "Ferrar, John (c.1588–1657)." In *Oxford Dictionary of National Biography.* Oxford: Oxford University Press, 2004–. Accessed 6 October 2008. www.oxforddnb.com/view/article/60958.

Rediker, Marcus. *The Slave Ship: A Human History.* New York: Viking, 2007.

Reinberger, Mark, and Elizabeth McLean. "Isaac Norris's Fairhill: Architecture, Landscape, and Quaker Ideals in a Philadelphia Colonial Country Seat." *Winterthur Portfolio* 32, no. 4 (1997): 254–55.

Richter, Daniel K. *Facing East from Indian Country: A Native History of Early America.* Cambridge, MA: Harvard University Press, 2001.

Roberts, Justin. "Working between the Lines: Labor and Agriculture on Two Barbadian Sugar Plantations, 1796–97." *William and Mary Quarterly,* 3rd ser., 63 (2006): 551–86.

Rodgers, Nini. *Ireland, Slavery and Anti-Slavery. 1612–1865.* London: Palgrave Macmillan, 2007.

Rosenberg, Philippe. "Thomas Tryon and the Seventeenth-Century Dimensions of Antislavery." *William and Mary Quarterly,* 3rd ser., 61, no. 4 (2004): 609–42.

Ryan, Patrick J. "African Muslim Spirituality: The Symbiotic Tradition in West Africa." In *African Spirituality: Forms, Meanings, and Expressions,* ed. Jacob K. Olupona, 284–304. New York: Crossroad, 2000.

Scarry, Elaine. *The Body in Pain: The Making and Unmaking of the World*. New York: Oxford University Press, 1985.

Schiebinger, Londa. *Nature's Body: Gender in the Making of Modern Science*. New York: Beacon Press, 1993.

Seeman, Erik R. *Death in the New World: Cross-Cultural Encounters, 1492–1800*. Philadelphia: University of Pennsylvania Press, 2010.

Seitz, Jonathan. *Witchcraft and Inquisition in Early Modern Venice*. New York: Cambridge University Press, 2011.

Sensbach, Jon F. *Rebecca's Revival: Creating Black Christianity in the Atlantic World*. Cambridge, MA: Harvard University Press, 2006.

Sewell, William H. *Logics of History: Social Theory and Social Transformation*. Chicago: Chicago University Press, 2005.

Sharples, Jason T. "The Flames of Insurrection: Fearing Conspiracy in Early America, 1670–1780." PhD diss., Princeton University, 2010.

Sheridan, Richard. *Sugar and Slavery: An Economic History of the British West Indies, 1623–1775*. Baltimore: Johns Hopkins University Press, 1973.

Shumway, Rebecca. *The Fante and the Transatlantic Slave Trade*. Rochester: University of Rochester Press, 2011.

Sidbury, James. "Plausible Stories and Varnished Truths." *William and Mary Quarterly*, 3rd ser., 59 (2002): 179–84.

———. *Ploughshares into Swords: Race, Rebellion, and Identity in Gabriel's Virginia, 1730–1810*. Cambridge: Cambridge University Press, 1997.

Silverman, David J. *Red Brethren: The Brothertown and Stockbridge Indians and the Problem of Race in Early America*. Ithaca: Cornell University Press, 2010.

Silverman, Lisa. *Tortured Subjects: Pain, Truth, and the Body in Early Modern France*. Chicago: University of Chicago Press, 2001.

Smallwood, Stephanie E. "African Guardians, European Slave Ships, and the Changing Dynamics of Power in the Early Modern Atlantic." *William and Mary Quarterly*, 3rd ser., 64 (2007): 679–716.

———. *Saltwater Slavery: A Middle Passage from Africa to American Diaspora*. Cambridge, MA: Harvard University Press, 2008.

Smith, David L., and Patrick Little. *Parliaments and Politics during the Cromwellian Protectorate*. Cambridge: Cambridge University Press, 2007.

Smyth, William J. *Map-Making, Landscapes and Memory: A Geography of Colonial and Early Modern Ireland, c. 1530–1750*. Cork: Cork University Press, 2006.

Sobel, Mechal. *The World They Made Together: Black and White Values in Eighteenth-Century Virginia*. Princeton: Princeton University Press, 1987.

Spufford, Margaret. "Religious Preambles and the Scribes of Villagers' Wills in Cambridgeshire, 1570–1700." In *When Death Do Us Part: Understanding and Interpreting the Probate Records of Early Modern England*, ed. Tom Arkell, Nesta Evans, and Nigel Goose, 144–57. Oxford: Oxford University Press, 2000.

Stanwood, Owen. *The Empire Reformed: English America in the Age of the Glorious Revolution*. Philadelphia: University of Pennsylvania Press, 2011.

———. "The Protestant Moment: Antipopery, the Revolution of 1688–89, and the Making of an Anglo-American Empire." *Journal of British Studies* 46 (2007): 481–508.

Strasser, Ulrike. *State of Virginity: Gender, Religion, and Politics in an Early Modern Catholic State*. Ann Arbor: University of Michigan Press, 2004.

Sturtz, Linda L. "The 'Dimduke' and the Duchess of Chandos: Gender and Power in Jamaican Plantation Management." *Revista/Review Interamericana* 29 (1999): 1–11.

Suranyi, Anna. *The Genius of the English Nation: Travel Writing and National Identity in Early Modern England*. Newark, NJ: Rosemont, 2008.

Sussman, Charlotte. "The Colonial Afterlife of Political Arithmetic: Swift, Demography, and Mobile Populations." *Cultural Critique* 56 (2004): 96–126.

Sweet, James H. *Domingo Álvares, African Healing, and the Intellectual History of the Atlantic World*. Chapel Hill: University of North Carolina Press, 2011.

———. "Mistaken Identities? Olaudah Equiano, Domingo Álvarez, and the Methodological Challenges of Studying the African Diaspora." *American Historical Review* 114, no. 2 (2009): 279–306.

———. *Recreating Africa: Culture, Kinship, and Religion in the African-Portuguese World, 1441–1770*. Chapel Hill: University of North Carolina Press, 2003.

Sweet, John W. *Bodies Politic: Negotiating Race in the American North, 1730–1830*. Baltimore: Johns Hopkins University Press, 2003.

Tait, Clodagh. *Death, Burial and Commemoration in Ireland, 1550–1650*. London: Palgrave, 2002.

Takaki, Ronald. "*The Tempest* in the Wilderness: Indians and Others in Early America." *William and Mary Quarterly*, 3rd. ser., 53 (1996): 892–912.

Tashiro, Tom T. "English Poets, Egyptian Onions, and the Protestant View of the Eucharist." *Journal of the History of Ideas* 30 (1969): 563–78.

Thomas, Keith. *Religion and the Decline of Magic: Studies in Popular Beliefs in Sixteenth and Seventeenth Century England*. New York: Oxford University Press, 1971.

Thompson, Robert Farris, and Joseph Cornet, eds. *The Four Moments of the Sun: Kongo Art in Two Worlds*. Washington, DC: National Gallery of Art, 1981.

Thornton, John K. *Africa and Africans in the Making of the Atlantic World, 1400–1800*. 2nd ed. Cambridge: Cambridge University Press, 1998.

———. *A Cultural History of the Atlantic World, 1250–1820*. Cambridge: Cambridge University Press, 2012.

———. "The Development of an African Catholic Church in the Kingdom of Kongo." In *Christianity and Missions, 1450–1800*, ed. J. S. Cummins, 237–58. Aldershot: Ashgate, 1997.

———. "The Development of an African Catholic Church in the Kingdom of Kongo, 1491–1750." *Journal of African History* 25, no. 2 (1984): 147–67.

———. *The Kongolese Saint Anthony: Beatriz Kimpa Vita and the Antonian Movement.* 2nd ed. Cambridge: Cambridge University Press, 1998.

———. *Warfare in Atlantic Africa, 1500–1800.* London: University College London Press, 1999.

———. "War, the State, and Religious Norms in Coromantee Thought." In *Possible Pasts: Becoming Colonial in America,* ed. Robert Blair St. George, 181–200. Ithaca: Cornell University Press, 2000.

Trevor-Roper, Hugh. *From Counter-Reformation to Glorious Revolution.* Chicago: University of Chicago Press, 1992.

Trouillot, Michel Rolph. *Silencing the Past: Power and the Production of History.* Boston: Beacon Press, 1995.

Upton, Dell. "White and Black Landscapes in Eighteenth-Century Virginia." *Places* 2 (1984): 59–72.

Vidal, Cécile. "Private and State Violence against African Slaves in Lower Louisiana during the French Period, 1699–1769." In *New World Orders: Violence, Sanction, and Authority in the Colonial Americas,* ed. John Smolenski and Thomas J. Humphries, 92–110. Philadelphia: University of Pennsylvania Press, 2005.

Walsh, Lorena S. *Motives of Honor, Pleasure, and Profit: Plantation Management in the Colonial Chesapeake, 1607–1763.* Chapel Hill: University of North Carolina Press, 2011.

Walsham, Alexandra. *The Reformation of the Landscape: Religion, Identity, and Memory in Early Modern Britain and Ireland.* Oxford: Oxford University Press, 2011.

Waselkkov, Gregory A. "Maps of the Colonial Southeast." In *Powhatan's Mantle: Indians in the Colonial Southeast,* 2nd ed., ed. Tom Hatley, Gregory A. Waselkkov, and Peter H. Wood, 435–502. Lincoln: University of Nebraska Press, 2006.

Weaver, Karol K. *Medical Revolutionaries: The Enslaved Healers of Eighteenth-Century Saint Domingue.* Urbana: University of Illinois Press, 2006.

Wilson, Kathleen. "The Performance of Freedom: Maroons and the Colonial Order in Eighteenth-Century Jamaica and the Atlantic Sound." *William and Mary Quarterly,* 3rd ser., 66, no. 1 (2009): 45–86.

———. "Rethinking the Colonial State: Family, Gender, and Governmentality in Eighteenth-Century British Frontiers." *American Historical Review* 116, no. 5 (2011): 1294–1322.

Wrightson, Keith. *English Society, 1580–1680.* London: Routledge, 1982.

Young, Jason R. *Rituals of Resistance: African Atlantic Religion in Kongo and the Lowcountry South in the Era of Slavery.* Baton Rouge: Louisiana State University Press, 2007.

Zacek, Natalie A. "A Death in the Morning: The Murder of Daniel Parke, Antigua, 1710." In *Cultures and Identities in Colonial British America*, ed. Robert A. Olwell and Alan Tully, 223–43. Baltimore: Johns Hopkins University Press, 2005.

———. "John Nickson (fl. 1687)." In *Encyclopedia Virginia*, ed. Brendan Wolfe. Virginia Foundation for the Humanities. Accessed 18 January 2012. www.EncyclopediaVirginia.org/Nickson_John_fl_1687.

———. *Settler Society in the Leeward Islands: 1670–1776*. Cambridge: Cambridge University Press, 2010.

Index

1641 Uprising, 30–33, 39, 41, 143, 144, 200

Account of the Intended Rebellion, 132, 135, 138
Africa, regions: Gold Coast, 73, 103–5, 130, 132, 135, 136, 140; Kingdom of Kongo, 104, 214, 217; Senegambia, 103, 104, 214; West Africa, 6, 33, 78, 87, 104–7, 109, 125, 130, 135, 136, 139, 152, 153, 200, 215, 217, 220, 221; West Central Africa, 86, 103–4, 108, 126, 211
African ethnicities in diaspora: Akan, 106, 132, 135, 138, 147, 220; Cormantee, 132, 135, 137–8, 139, 140, 147, 148, 220; Kongolese, 104, 214, 217
Africans: and English perception of as inferior, 17–18, 33–34, 37, 65, 93, 137, 194–95, 200–201, 202; in Africa, 6, 11, 18, 21–22, 33, 78, 86, 87, 88, 89, 101–2, 104–7, 119, 122–25, 195, 200–201, 212, 213, 214–15, 217, 220, 221. *See also* captives, African; enslaved; religious practices, in Africa; slave trade
Akan. *See* African ethnicities in diaspora
Akenson, Donald Harman, 3, 193, 195, 207, 224
Amussen, Susan Dwyer, 19, 194, 197, 201, 202
Anna/Fortuna (1675), 137–40
Annesley, Alexander, 24
Antigua, 35–37, 38, 44, 61, 153, 168, 178–79, 180, 186, 187, 201, 208

Atkins, Jonathan, 58, 60, 66, 132, 134, 139–40, 206, 207, 208

Baddue, 113–14
baptism, 85, 101, 103, 104, 107, 108, 110–14, 118, 119, 126, 189, 202–3. *See also* religious practices
Barbados, 1–3, 4, 8, 9, 12–14, 15, 18–26, 34, 38, 40–41, 43, 45, 52–61, 63–67, 69–70, 71, 75, 77, 80, 81, 82, 83, 85, 87, 88, 91–93, 95, 96, 97, 101–2, 110–18, 119–23, 127, 128, 129–55, 156, 158–63, 164, 166–67, 169, 171, 174, 178, 180 183, 184, 189, 190–92; population of, 6, 33, 34, 45, 52–58, 59–61, 64, 65–67, 186–88, 190
Barbados Assembly, 9, 15, 17, 39, 41, 43
Barbados Council, 1, 12, 39, 95, 119, 123, 143, 144, 146, 150, 154
Barbadosed, 5, 19, 26, 33, 43, 57.
barbarism, 5, 26, 28, 30, 31, 50, 199, 200. *See also* civility/civilized; heathen; savagery
Barbot, Jean, 104–5, 124, 214
bastardy, 27, 28, 168. *See also* children, illegitimate; fornication
Beake, Major Robert, 24
Beckles, Hilary, 3, 193, 197
Ben (1692), 8, 129–30, 131, 147–50, 151–52
Biet, Father Antoine, 84–85, 87, 89, 94, 95, 96, 101–2, 120–21, 122–23, 124
Blake, Henry, 156, 157, 163–64, 166, 170, 177, 178, 183

Blake, John, 156–57, 163–67, 168–71, 177–78, 182, 183

Blake Family, 8, 156, 163–64, 166–67, 186

Blakiston, Nathaniel, 180, 181, 182

Blathwayt, Sir William, 66

Boscowan, Edward, 23

Brief but Most True Relation, 148, 150

Briskett, Anthony, 174–75, 179

Bryan, Cornelius, 1–2, 3, 9–10, 12–13, 38, 43, 60, 69, 95–96, 98, 99–100, 127–28, 143–45, 153, 154–55, 157, 158–63, 169, 170–71, 177–78, 179, 183–84, 186, 190–92, 224, 225

Bryan, Margaret, 1, 127–28, 159–61, 169, 170, 178, 183–84

Bryan Family, 1, 69, 159, 161, 170–71, 178, 191.

burials: and Africans, 105–7, 124–25, 126, 215, 219; and Irish, 107–9, 117–18, 126, 127–28, 177–78, 207. *See also* funerals; grave goods; keening; religious practices

cannibalism: African fears of, 22, 201; English perceptions of Irish, 31, 33, 131, 140, 141, 144–45, 200, 201

captives, African, 3, 18, 21–23, 33, 65, 83, 86, 101, 103–4, 106–7. *See also* slave trade

castration, 31, 152, 153

Catholicism/Catholic: and Africans, 101–2, 104, 109, 119, 122–23, 147, 151, 189, 217; and English, 40, 122, 130, 140–42, 146, 179–80; and Irish, 1–4, 6, 8, 11, 13, 16–18, 30–31, 45, 48, 60–61, 95, 101, 103, 107–9, 114–18, 119–22, 124, 126–27, 128, 130, 140–45, 146–47, 152, 154, 156–57, 158–61, 163–64, 169, 171–78, 183, 185–88, 190, 193, 200; perceived as inferior by English, 2–3, 16–18, 25–26, 30–31, 33–34, 38–40, 46, 48–50, 56, 57, 60, 67, 98–99, 131–32, 142–45, 146, 154, 171, 179–82, 183, 186–87, 215–16. *See also* Jesuits; priests; Purgatory

census, 7, 10, 46–47, 57, 58, 65–67, 68–69, 193; Barbados 1680, 1, 9, 45, 57–58, 59–61, 65–66, 69, 159–61, 171, 187; Down Survey, 45, 48, 49, 58; eighteenth-century census, 187–90, 191; Leeward Islands 1678, 44–45, 57–58, 61–64, 66, 165, 187; Political Anatomy Montserrat, 67–68, 189. *See also* enumeration; quantification

Chamberlain, Willoughby, 122–23, 140–42, 146

Charles I, of England, 19

Charles II, of England, 39–40, 56, 58, 174

Cheeke, Phillip, 71–72, 76–78, 79, 81–82, 88, 209

childbirth, 27, 28, 35–36, 104–5, 112–13, 123–24, 171, 201; and Curse of Eve, 33, 202

children, 8, 22, 31, 35–37, 46, 61, 64, 65, 67, 99, 165, 168; enslaved, 13, 22, 37, 64, 65–66, 71, 85, 107, 122, 123, 125, 128, 171, 183–84; free black, 8, 85, 111, 112–13, 114, 126; illegitimate, 35–36, 65–66, 168, 171; in Africa, 104–5; Irish, 1, 9, 27, 28, 31, 33, 35, 50, 61, 63, 64, 69–70, 108–9, 114, 117, 120, 123, 127, 161, 170–71, 183–84, 191, 192. *See also* bastardy

Christianity: as basis for difference, 6, 17, 36–38, 41, 123, 126; as criterion for civility, 17, 21, 31, 34, 36–38; as criterion for freedom, 17, 36, 110–14, 118, 126. *See also* Catholicism/Catholic; Church of England; Protestantism/Protestant

Church of England, 102, 103, 110–19, 126, 176–77, 178. *See also* Christianity; Protestantism/Protestant

Civil War, English, 18, 19, 33, 55; and Cavaliers, 19, 24–25; and Roundheads, 19, 25; and Salisbury Rising, 19, 22, 23

civility/civilized, 5, 16, 20, 26, 27, 30, 31, 33, 35, 38, 49, 131, 194. *See also* barbarism; heathen; savagery

clothing, 18, 27–29, 33, 91–93, 99, 120; and distinctions between servants and enslaved, 91–92, 93, 99; mantles, 28–29, 33, 200–201

Codrington, Christopher (the elder), 180–82

Codrington, Christopher (the younger), 167–68, 169, 171

conspiracy, 130, 132, 134, 137–138, 139, 140–41, 147–48, 151, 152, 154, 192, 219. *See also* rebellion/revolt

conversion, religious: to Catholicism, of English, 40, 122, 142; to Christianity, of Africans, 101–2, 104, 110–14, 126, 214, 217; to Protestantism, of Irish, 50–51, 109; as strategy, 109, 111, 112–13, 126, 142, 202–3

Cormantee. *See* African ethnicities in diaspora

Cotter, James, 178, 229

Cranford, James, 32

creoles, African, 103, 140, 147, 148, 150, 152–53, 218
Cromwell, Oliver, 19, 26, 33, 38, 39, 43, 47–48, 54, 55, 109, 119, 143, 163, 169
Cromwellian regime, 12, 19, 24, 26, 109, 163
Cuffee/Coffee (1675 revolt), 135, 155
Cuffley, Martha, 143
Cuffy, Charles, 66, 112
Cuffy, Mary, 112
Cuffy, Thomas, 112
Cumberford, Margaret. See Margaret Bryan

Davies, John, 27, 30, 31, 35, 49
Davis, Natalie Zemon, 9, 196
De Marees, Pieter, 104–6, 124
deeds, 8, 9, 72, 84, 159–61
demography. See census; enumeration; quantification
depositions, 31, 122, 123, 131, 134, 141–43, 145–46. See also testimony
difference: cultural, 2, 16–17, 22, 27–33, 87, 91–92, 195–95; English ideologies of, 5, 18, 26, 33–34, 41, 46, 52, 73, 140, 146, 151, 154, 190, 192; ethnic, 2, 26–27, 30–32, 41; non-elite influence on, 2–3, 4, 7, 8, 69, 73, 85, 93, 98–99, 102–3, 112, 126, 131, 140, 146, 154, 157, 158, 185, 186, 190, 192; racial, 2, 3, 6, 17, 37 38, 66, 72, 187, 188; religious, 5–6, 17, 30–31, 34, 35–37, 41, 109, 146; sexual, 27–28, 35–37; status 2, 16, 72, 140
drink, 1, 3, 10, 37, 70, 88, 100, 106, 131, 136, 139, 144, 153, 167, 185
Du Tertre, Father Jean Baptiste, 80, 119

England, 5, 25, 33, 39, 40, 41, 44, 48, 50–51, 57, 71, 83, 91, 115, 137, 140, 146, 158, 159, 173, 175; and imperial ambitions, 2, 4, 5, 8, 16, 18, 36, 38, 54, 55–56, 67, 177, 180, 183, 186. See also English
Englands Slavery or Barbados Merchandize, 19–20
English: colonial officials/authorities, 1–5, 7, 8, 10, 16, 26, 33, 34, 35, 36, 38, 39, 40, 44–47, 49, 52–53, 54–58, 59, 60, 61, 64–66, 69, 93, 103, 109, 119, 120, 121, 123, 126, 130, 131, 132, 134, 135, 136, 137, 139, 140, 141, 143, 145–48, 150–54, 157, 158, 159, 171, 172, 174, 175–79, 180, 182, 183, 185, 186, 187, 188, 189, 190, 191; colonists,

1, 3, 4, 16, 17, 30, 31, 112, 137, 186, 191; elites, 1, 2, 3, 6–9, 11, 12, 16–18, 23, 26, 28, 34, 42, 46, 58, 63–64, 65, 66, 73, 74, 76, 83, 98, 99, 103, 135, 137, 139, 140, 146, 147, 148, 157, 159, 163, 169, 170, 171, 179, 181, 182, 183, 189, 190; in Ireland, 26–32; Members of Parliament, 22, 23–26. See also difference, English ideologies of; England; planters; servants
enslaved, 4, 6, 16, 34, 37, 38, 40, 41, 45, 47, 51, 53, 54, 57, 60, 65–69, 71–72, 74–82, 86, 92, 94–96, 97, 129–32, 134, 140, 147–50, 151, 153–54, 158, 159, 161, 163, 183, 186, 187, 188, 191; children, 1, 13, 36–37, 65–66, 113, 114; and children as "increase," 6, 64, 159, 170–71, 184, 222; and commodification, 6, 44, 83–84; and community, 6, 8, 10, 83, 85, 86, 87, 93, 102, 129, 132, 137, 140; Englishmen as, 10, 18–26; as marker of difference, 2, 3, 5, 6, 7, 10, 17, 40, 41, 73, 93, 98, 152, 185, 189; men, 1, 64, 65, 81, 89, 130–31, 134, 135–37, 170; and quarters, 10, 84–85, 86–87; women, 1, 8, 9, 12, 36, 64, 65, 91, 113, 137–39, 156, 160, 170–71, 191. See also captives, African; rebellion/revolt; religious practices in Africa; runaways; slavery
enumeration, 10, 44–47, 53, 57–58, 64, 66, 67, 187. See also census, quantification
Equiano, Olaudah, 23, 198–99
estate, 1, 3, 8, 14, 63, 64, 67, 69, 71–72, 74, 76, 78–82, 84, 85, 88, 94, 98, 101, 117–18, 120, 123, 125, 161–63, 165, 168, 178, 181, 184, 191, 192. See also plantation
everyday life, 4, 7–9, 18, 46–47, 72–73, 83, 93, 98, 127, 157, 190, 192, 195–96
executions, public, 94, 130, 136–37, 147–49, 151, 153. See also punishment; violence

family: African, 70, 83, 104–5, 111–13; English, 31, 50, 88; Irish, 1, 8, 27, 48, 64, 116 17, 156, 161, 164, 166–67, 170–71, 176, 178, 192.
Farley, Cork, 142–43, 144
food, 3, 7, 22, 73, 83, 87–91, 93, 95, 99, 100, 127, 139, 155, 185; and adaptations by servants and enslaved, 91, 99; and African knowledge, 88–89; and distinctions between servants and enslaved, 90–91, 93, 99; as grave

goods, 105, 107; production of, 88, 139; subsistence, 87–89, 93, 99. *See also* maize; plantains; potatoes
fornication, 35, 85, 171. *See also* bastardy; sex and sexual
Foyle, Oxenbridge, 19–21, 23–26, 35, 40, 41, 82. *See also* Barbadosed; prisoners of war; Marcellus Rivers
France and French, 11, 34, 39, 40, 43, 44, 47, 54, 56, 119, 121, 122, 123, 129, 130, 132, 140–41, 145, 146–47, 167, 172–75, 180–82, 185, 187, 188, 189
free people of color, 8, 11, 36, 46, 66, 103, 110–14, 118, 123, 126, 139, 153, 188, 189
funerals: and African, 8, 105–7, 124–25, 126; and Catholic, 101; and Irish, 107, 126. *See also* burials; grave goods; keening; religious practices

gender roles: connection to race, 6, 35–37, 137, 152, 170–71; corruption by women 28, 50, 164–66, 168, 169; masculinity and property, 62–63, 157, 159–62, 163–67, 170–71, 174, 183; and difference, 3, 5, 6, 26, 28, 31, 33–34, 35–37, 64, 137, 152, 157, 170–71, 174, 179, 185; and labor divisions, 64–65, 138, 167, 169–70; and religion, 108–9, 117–18, 123–24, 178
Gewen, Thomas, 24
Goldring, Gedeon, 113–14
grave goods, 105–7, 108, 125, 126, 127. *See also* burials; funerals
Great Newes from the Barbadoes, 132 133, 134–35, 136, 137–38

Hanley, James, 81, 94, 145–46
Haslerigge, Sir Arthur, 24
heathen, 5, 15, 17, 18, 21, 30, 33, 34, 35–37, 85, 135, 147. *See also* barbarism; civility/civilized, savagery
Hispaniola, 38, 55

indentured servants. *See* servants
Indians. *See* Native Americans
interracial alliances, 37–39, 97, 123–24, 129, 146–47, 150–51, 153, 154, 191
Ireland, 5, 10, 11, 12–13, 16, 18, 19, 28, 30–33, 35, 41, 42, 43, 45, 46, 54, 58, 90, 103, 107–9, 117, 118, 121, 124, 126, 145, 163–64, 166, 178, 180, 103: English colonization of, 16–17, 25–26, 27, 30, 33, 45, 47–52, 55, 67, 83, 107, 109, 143, 145; training ground

for Americas, 16, 26, 33, 35, 39, 52, 57. *See also* Irish
Irish, 1–4, 5, 8, 9, 16, 25, 41–42, 43, 44–46, 54–57, 68–69, 81, 83, 101, 119, 127, 185, 188; in colonies, 1–5, 8, 16–17, 25–26, 34, 35, 38, 54, 60–67, 68, 81, 85–98, 101–3, 110, 114–18, 119–22, 123–24, 126, 174–79, 180, 182; in Ireland, 1, 16, 26–34, 46, 47–52, 83, 90, 107–9; rebellious, 1, 8–9, 38–40, 43, 56–57, 68, 96, 129, 130, 131, 132, 140–46, 147, 150–51, 152, 154–55, 172, 175 191. *See also* difference; planters; religious practices in Ireland; servants
Irish Rebellion, The, 31
Islam. *See* Muslim

Jamaica, 4, 38, 55, 124, 134, 151, 154, 180, 193–94
James II, of England, 122, 140, 145, 177, 179, 188
Jesuits, 31, 84, 101, 104, 119, 120, 121, 123, 140–41. *See also* Catholicism/Catholic; priests
Jewish, 61
Jones, Mary, 112
Jordan, James, 142–43, 144
Jory, Colonel Joseph, 187

keening, 107–8, 109, 126, 127. *See also* burials; funerals
kin/kinship, 47, 70, 114, 129, 192.
Knight, Major, 25
Kongolese. *See* African ethnicities in diaspora

labor: and status, 3, 5–6, 15, 17, 18, 41, 55, 64–66, 167, 169, 183, 100, and sugar production, 4–5, 22, 58, 64, 74–83, 183; in the Caribbean, 2–3, 4, 5, 10, 11, 16, 17, 21–23, 38, 40–41, 45–46, 47, 52–57, 64–65, 67, 71–73, 74, 76, 79, 81, 82–99, 110, 125, 126, 127, 134, 140, 143, 148, 152, 155, 167, 169, 188, 191; in Ireland, 49–52. *See also* enslaved; servants
land: English views of, 5, 18, 26–27, 28, 46, 48–50, 52, 58–59; and Indians, 33; in Ireland, 18, 26–27, 33, 49, 163; as marker of status, 1, 3, 13, 55, 60, 62–63, 64, 67–68, 74, 95–96, 97, 127, 157, 159–62, 174–75, 179, 182, 186, 191. *See also* transhumance

landowners: English, 44, 66, 68, 71, 87, 189; in Ireland, 108, 163; Irish, 44, 60, 63–64, 159, 163, 174, 178, 181, 183, 185, 186, 190. *See also* planters

laws, 15–18, 24, 38–39, 41, 43, 60, 112, 145, 176–77, 186; and servitude, 15–16, 95, 187–88; and sex, 17, 35–36, 85; and slavery; 15–17, 37–38, 41, 65, 95, 113, 134.

Leeward Islands, 3, 4, 6, 18, 33, 34, 44–45, 52, 57, 58, 59, 61, 63, 65, 67, 87, 119, 127, 153, 157, 167, 172, 174, 176, 177–80, 187–88. *See* also Antigua; Montserrat; Nevis; St. Christopher

Lenthall, Sir John, 23, 25.

Ligon, Richard, 53, 55, 75, 82, 83–84, 86, 87–88, 89–90, 91–92, 94–95, 122, 124, 126, 130

Lords of Trade and Plantations, 44–46, 57, 58, 60–61, 172, 176, 182, 187.

Louis XIV, of France, 40

maize, 89, 90, 105

mantle. *See* clothing

manumission, 113–14

marriage, 11, 46, 99, 101, 108, 110, 115, 118, 169, 176–77, 191; between English women and Irish men, 46, 50, 52; among enslaved, 137–38; and free people of color, 111–12; among Irish, 117, 159–60, 176–77, 178

militia, 38, 45, 47, 58, 60, 61, 70, 131, 134, 155, 172, 184, 186, 187

minkisi, 104–5, 125. *See also* religious practices in Africa

mixed race, 35–37, 65–66, 85, 147, 189

Montgomery, Sir Thomas, 140–41, 146

Montserrat, 3, 8, 39, 44, 61–64, 66, 67–68, 115, 120, 124, 153, 156, 157, 163–65, 169, 171–79, 180–83, 186, 188–89

Moryson, Fynes, 26–27, 28, 30, 35, 49, 90, 108, 124

Muslim, 6, 103–4, 214

Native Americans, 5, 33, 34, 35–36, 65, 90, 91, 175; and slavery, 34

Needham's Fort, 129, 150, 151

Nevis, 37, 44, 61, 178, 180, 186, 187

Noell, Martin, 40–41

oath taking, 39–40, 129, 136, 152, 168

Ofaye, Donat, 91, 121, 218

Old English, 17, 26, 35, 51, 108, 163

Old Pegg, 1, 9–10, 13, 42–43, 69–70, 99–100, 128, 184, 192

One Hand, 79

overseers, 71, 74, 78, 90, 94–95, 96, 97, 103–4, 119, 159

papists, 1, 9, 30, 31, 130, 140, 145, 180, 187. *See also* Catholicism/Catholic

Parke, Daniel, 167–68, 169

parliament, 18, 19, 21, 22, 23–26, 40, 41, 56

Pegg, 1, 3, 9–10, 12, 13–14, 70, 99–100, 128, 155, 184, 190–92

Pelleprat, Father Pierre, 121–22

petitions, 18–26, 40, 55, 82, 158, 175, 177

Petty, William, 47–52, 58, 66, 67; and intellectual influences, 48; and Down Survey, 45, 48–49, 58. *See also Political Anatomy of Ireland*

plantains, 87, 88, 89, 90, 100

plantation, 3, 4, 6, 7, 8, 10–12, 19, 22, 23, 39, 41, 43, 52, 54, 56, 57, 58, 63, 65, 68, 69–70, 71–82, 83, 86, 89, 90, 91, 93, 94–99, 101, 102, 104, 110, 113, 114, 115–16, 119, 121–22, 123, 124–26, 127, 129, 130, 134, 137, 138, 139, 142, 145–46, 147, 150, 151, 152, 155, 157, 163–64, 166, 173, 178, 183, 184, 185, 189, 191, 192; Bally Tree Hall, 71–72, 74, 76, 77–81, 84, 85, 88, 90, design, 84–85, 157. *See also* estate

planters: English, 3, 4, 8, 24, 36–37, 53, 55, 56, 60, 61, 63, 65, 72–73, 74, 83, 84, 87, 91, 93, 94, 95, 97, 114, 126, 129, 130, 131, 134, 140, 146, 147, 151, 152, 153, 157, 169, 171, 178, 187, 189; French, 101, 120, 189; Irish, 1–2, 3, 8, 9, 60–61, 62–63, 95–96, 115–17, 126, 127, 157, 156–63, 164, 170, 175, 177–79, 180–84, 186, 189–90; management of laborers, 65, 72, 74, 78, 79, 81, 83, 84, 87, 94–95, 97; relationship with enslaved women, 88, 170; relationship with servant women, 83–84, 156, 164–66, 167–69; Scottish, 163–64; and status, 1–4, 72, 73, 74, 82, 103, 130–34, 169, 171. *See also* landowners

Political Anatomy of Ireland, 47, 48–49, 51, 57, 66. *See also* William Petty

Political Anatomy of Montserrat, 67–68, 189

Popist Plot, 58

potatoes, 89, 90

Povey, Thomas, 53–54, 56

priests, 8, 13, 49–50, 72, 84, 101–102, 103, 104, 109, 119–23, 127, 130, 132, 141, 150, 177, 178, 200, 216. *See also* Catholicism/Catholic; Jesuits

Prince, Mary, 23

prisoners of war, 18, 21, 22, 25, 33, 40, 43, 54, 55. *See also* Barbadosed; Oxenbridge Foyle; Marcellus Rivers

property, 8, 12, 60, 71–72, 78, 113, 134, 136, 159; enslaved people defined as, 1, 3, 6, 8, 44, 45, 57, 63, 71, 76, 84, 95, 110, 153, 156–57, 158, 160, 170, 183, 191, 192; and inheritance, 1, 110, 161, 170, 184; and Irish in Ireland, 27; and status, 1, 3, 6, 58, 61–64, 95, 157, 162–63, 174, 179, 181–82, 183, 186, 191

Protectorate, 15, 19, 25, 163

Protestantism/Protestant, 17, 19, 20–21, 25, 30, 31, 33, 34, 37, 38, 39–40, 56, 61, 102, 103, 108 109–10, 111, 114, 115–16, 118, 124, 127, 152, 157, 175, 177, 180, 182, 186, 189. *See also* Quakers, Church of England

punishment, 79, 93, 94–96, 97, 151; of enslaved conspirators, 135–37, 139, 147–48; of enslaved by masters, 36, 37, 94–95, 99, 153, 185; of Irish, 1, 98, 143–44, 151, 153–54, 156, 166; of servants by masters, 35–36, 94–95, 98. *See also* torture, violence

Purgatory, 20, 108, 116, 126

Quakers, 61, 217

quantification, 10, 45–47, 58, 53. *See also* census, enumeration

race, 2, 3, 6, 11, 65, 73, 111, 152, 154, 157, 171, 186, 189, 190, 194–95. *See also* difference; enslaved; slavery

rebellion/revolt, 8, 33, 38, 50, 58, 61, 70, 129–40, 146–52, 153, 155, 172, 181, 186, 191, 192, 219–20. *See also A Brief but Most True Relation; Account of the Intended Rebellion*; conspiracy; *Great Newes from the Barbadoes*

Reformation, 6, 16, 107, 121, 137.

religious practices: in Africa, 6, 103–7, 109, 125, 126, 214, 217; in Ireland, 5, 28–32, 49–50, 109; in the Caribbean, 6, 8,

101–3, 110–26, 127, 176–77, 178. *See also* burials; funerals; *minkisi*

reproduction, 6, 50, 171; and prevention of, 113

Revell, Diana, 111

Revell, Katherine, 111

Revell, Mary, 111

Revell, Thomas, 111–12, 113, 118. *See also* Thomas, Mary

Rice, Dominick, 117, 123

Rice, George, 115–17, 188, 126, 217

Rice, Katherine, 117

Rice, Nicolas, 115–16, 118, 126

Rivers, Marcellus, 19–21, 23–26, 35, 40, 41, 82. *See also* Barbadosed; Oxenbridge Foyle; prisoners of war

rum, 71, 76, 81, 125; dangers of production, 81–82

runaways, 133–34, 138, 150–51, 153, 188–89

saltwater slaves, 131–32, 139, 140, 150, 152–53

Sambo (1692), 129–30, 131, 147–49

Sampson (1692), 129–30, 131, 147–48

savagery, 5, 13, 31, 41, 93, 98, 131, 135, 142, 143, 144, 175. *See also* barbarism; civility/civilized; heathen

Scotland and Scots, 5, 16, 19, 25, 33, 41–42, 46, 48, 53, 54–57, 62, 67, 73, 83, 85, 143, 164, 173, 187

Scott, Major John, 96–97, 172–74

Searle, Daniel, 38–39

servants, 1, 2, 4, 5, 6, 7, 10, 11, 12, 21, 34, 40–41, 45, 47, 53, 55, 61, 64, 65, 66, 67, 68, 69, 71–73, 74, 76, 78, 79, 81, 84, 88–93, 98, 100, 102–3, 130, 159–60, 186, 188, 195; English, 13, 25, 41, 42, 55, 56–57, 73, 83, 141, 145; female, 8, 63, 84, 85, 124, 156, 164–70, 171, 183, 100, hired, 3, 61, 69, 159–61; Irish, 3–4, 6, 8, 39, 41, 42, 47, 56–57, 60, 71, 73, 74, 83, 85, 86, 89–91, 93, 96–97, 98–99, 121, 122, 124, 140, 141–43, 145–46, 150–51, 153, 154, 156, 157, 159, 163, 164–70, 171, 172, 183, 186, 187, 189–90; male, 71–72, 74, 85; quarters, 84–85, 86–87; regulation of in Caribbean, 15–16, 93–96; Scottish, 25, 41, 42, 56–57, 73, 83, 187

sex and sexual: depravity of Irish, 5, 17, 18, 28, 31, 35, 50, 166, 167–69; interracial, 35–37, 46, 65–66, 85, 127, 171; violence and coercion, 31, 137, 152,

153, 166, 167–69, 171. *See also* bastardy; castration; fornication

slave trade, 21, 22, 23, 34, 65, 83, 86, 101, 106–7, 109, 125, 207; and Middle Passage, 23, 88, 106–7, 109, 125. *See also* captives, African

slavery, 5, 14, 15, 17, 19–20, 23, 24, 24–25, 40, 43, 103, 107, 112, 114, 125, 128, 130, 134, 139, 152, 155; of Native Americans, 34; racial, 2, 4, 6, 60, 152; and reproduction, 6, 64, 171

slaves. *See* enslaved

Sloane, Hans, 91, 94, 124–25, 126

Spain, 11, 33, 38–39, 40, 56, 119

Spenser, Edmund, 26–28, 30, 31, 35, 49, 51, 144

St. Christopher, 39, 44, 56, 61, 119, 121–22, 146–47, 172, 174, 178, 186

Stapleton, William, 44–45, 58–59, 61, 66, 67, 115, 157–58, 171–79, 182, 183, 186, 187

Stede, Edwyn, 140, 141, 147, 151

Stritch, Father John, 119–20, 121–22

sugar, 2, 4–5, 13–14, 16, 19, 22, 57, 58, 59, 66, 67–68, 69, 70, 84, 89, 94, 96, 98, 99, 116, 119, 125, 137, 138, 142, 145, 155, 159, 162, 181, 183, 191, 192; dangers of production, 78–81; production of, 71–73, 74–82. *See also* enslaved; labor; servants

Sullivan, Kate, 168, 169, 171, 183

Taylor, John, 124–25, 126

Teares of Ireland, 30–32

Temple, Sir John, 31

testimony, 167–68, 175, 183. *See also* depositions

Thomas, Mary, 111, 113, 118

Tony (1675), 136–37, 140

torture, 94, 131, 147–49, 213, 219. *See also* punishment; violence

transhumance, 26. *See also* land

Trouillot, Michel Rolph, 7, 195, 219

True and Exact History of the Island of Barbados. See Richard Ligon

Tryon, Thomas, 23, 79, 80, 87, 198, 210

Vane, Sir Henry, 24

Villault, Nicolas, 105–6

violence, 7, 8, 10, 11, 31, 33, 51–52, 72, 73, 74, 94–96, 97, 98, 125, 131, 134, 138, 142–43, 144, 151, 152, 153, 166, 185, 192. *See also* punishment; torture

Walrond, Sir Henry, 15

war: and Africa, 5, 21, 83; and France, 38, 39, 44, 167, 172–76, 179–81, 188; King William's, 129–30; Pequot, 34; and Spain, 33, 38–39, 44

wench, 163, 164, 168–69, 170, 171

Western Design, 38, 55, 119.

Whistler, Henry, 169

White, Father Andrew, 120

whore, 152, 156, 164–66, 168, 169, 170, 171

William and Mary of England, 122, 140, 145, 179, 182

Williamson, Joseph, 174

Willoughby, Lord William, 65–57, 174, 175, 178, 179

wills, 1, 8, 9, 12, 60, 72, 110, 111, 113, 115–18, 127, 157, 158, 161, 171, 177, 178, 184, 192, 216–17

Early American Places

On Slavery's Border: Missouri's Small Slaveholding Households, 1815–1865
by Diane Mutti Burke

Sounding America: Identity and the Music Culture of the Lower Mississippi River Valley, 1800–1860
by Ann Ostendorf

The Year of the Lash: Free People of Color in Cuba and the Nineteenth-Century Atlantic World
by Michele Reid-Vazquez

Ordinary Lives in the Early Caribbean: Religion, Colonial Competition, and the Politics Of Profit
by Kirsten Block

Creolization and Contraband: Curaçao in the Early Modern Atlantic World
by Linda M. Rupert

An Empire of Small Places: Mapping the Southeastern Anglo-Indian Trade, 1732–1795
by Robert Paulett

Everyday Life in the Early English Caribbean: Irish, Africans, and the Construction of Difference
by Jenny Shaw